Feather on the 'Wind of Change' Safaris, Surgery and Stentgrafts

To Rick Hawkins,

I hope this story holds something for you and strikes a chord.

wishing you well,

from a kindred spirit,

Michael Lawrence-Brown

Feather on the 'Wind of Change' Safaris, Surgery and Stentgrafts

Michael Lawrence-Brown

To order additional copies of this book, contact:
Xlibris
1-800-455-039
www.Xlibris.com.au
Orders@Xlibris.com.au
767571

CONTENTS

PART 3

THE ENDOVASCULAR REVOLUTION AND STENT-GRAFTS

PART 4

THE SEVENTH AGE

FOREWORD

I first met Michael Lawrence-Brown in Kenya at the British secondary school where we were both boarders. We sat in more pensive moments discussing the future and our plans to go to university in Britain. It was not to be, for either of us. Political and economic realities, and the rightful demands of a hundred nations under the Union Jack, were about to crystallise in a new policy issued by Whitehall that was to bring about an end to Britain's colonial role. As we entered our final years at the Prince of Wales School in Nairobi, the last heady waves of Empire started to recede, and we realised that with the advent of independence, if we left to study overseas, we would probably never return to live again in East Africa, the only home we had known.

The Kenya school was a transplanted version of the historic public schools of Britain with its emphasis on sports, strict hierarchy, and virtual self-government by the pupils through house prefects, with younger boys living in eight residential houses. To the outsider, the all-boys school we attended, with its acres of lawns and verdant grounds planted with jacaranda and eucalyptus, playing fields, oval cricket ground, swimming pool, tennis courts, science labs, library, and chapel, must have seemed like paradise on earth. The impressive white central building, with its Roman-numbered clock tower looking down over the large quadrangle bounded on three sides by a covered walkway with Ionian columns facing a flagpole, was used as a set in the film *Out of Africa* as a substitute for Government House.

The school itself played a pivotal part in forming our characters because it threw six hundred and fifty boys into a microcosm. Slipping through the school's fence to go out of bounds was an act of private defiance against the school and a taste of freedom from its physical and disciplinary confines. Our school was typical of the institutions Britain used to instil values of self-reliance, physical endurance, and academic achievement on growing teenage boys who were intended to keep the Union Jack flying for a thousand years, as Winston Churchill had announced, over the outposts of an Empire on which the sun never set. The hardening process, the cult of rank, and teamwork groomed the boys for futures in the colonial administration or as settlers on the land to develop the farms and plantations that supplied funds for the colony.

I remember Michael's sandy hair, wry smile, and modest manner. On the rugby and hockey field, another side of his character took over. His position as scrum-half needed physical courage and reserves of mental agility. Off the field, he was easy-going and deceptively self-deprecating. Whether at rugby, hockey, or our daily interaction, he was the person we relied on. He had an air of detachment unusual for a schoolboy, and this gave him, I realised much later, an analytic facility, allowing him to size up the situation, something that separated him from the rest of us. I think Michael's detachment had to do with his sense of purpose, coupled with a reaction to a situation at home that made him mature faster than the rest of us. Working with his father, Stan, on the safaris during school holidays also deprived him of peer group adolescence experiences. It was these characteristics, revealed from a very early age, with his determination and courage, that was to later allow him to overcome seemingly insurmountable odds to become a leading innovator in the world of vascular surgery. It was this determination that helped put the Royal Perth Hospital in the forefront of vascular surgery. But here, too, there was a twist of fate that his story will reveal.

Michael had another quality: He was also an accomplished storyteller. He owed this to spending school holidays on safari with Stan, a fabled figure in East African safari circles. He grew up listening to tales and watching traditional African dances around campfires with famous and wealthy clients who needed to be entertained at the end of the day. Under the canopy of the African sky, with its thousands of brightly shining pinprick stars, Stan Lawrence-Brown mesmerised his son and his clients with stories of the African bush. Stan rubbed shoulders with great Hollywood film stars, such as Stewart Granger, during the location shoots of *King Solomon's Mines*, and John Wayne, Clark Gable, Ava Gardner, Liza Minnelli, and other stars during the making of *Hatari* and *Mogambo*, which brought images of Africa to eager audiences in cinemas around the world. It was here that Michael acquired his storytelling skills, and it was at the Prince of Wales School that a theatrical six-foot-four-inch-tall English literature teacher with his drainpipe trousers, dandyish blazer, and Shakespearean stage manner inspired Michael to put pen to paper for his first article for the school magazine, the *Impala*.

The last time I saw Michael in Africa was when he was eighteen; we were on safari in the Kigezi Highlands, near the Impenetrable Forest in south-west Uganda. Michael had a long-wheelbase Land Rover with open sides from his father's safari company in Arusha, in the shadow of Mount Kilimanjaro, and had invited me, two other friends from school, and a teacher who was just a little older than us to go on a trip of discovery in the Great Lakes area of Central Africa along the border of Uganda with Rwanda-Urundi, as it was then known, and the Congo. One evening, we stopped the Land Rover and laid out sleeping bags on a dirt road verge cut into the side of a thickly forested mountain that was one of the last natural habitats of the mountain gorilla. Our resting spot was over eight thousand feet above sea level and was so isolated that no other vehicle came along that whole night or the next morning.

In the morning, we woke up, wearing layer upon layer of warm clothing and ex-army bush jackets, almost standard garb for Kenya European youths, to protect us from the freezing cold. While the other two boys with us, Roger Taylor and Alan Scott, packed their bags and a tarpaulin into the vehicle, Michael and I sipped strong coffee out of chipped enamel mugs, which we used to warm our hands; we stood on the rim, looking silently down at the dense cloud carpet that hid the floor of the valley with its lakes. To our left lay Rwanda's Virunga Volcanoes, while ahead of us, clouds and thick mist stood like a curtain, obscuring the view of the mountain range beyond. Michael and I stood there, in silence, for perhaps fifteen minutes, smoking Crownbird cigarettes between sips of coffee.

Suddenly, the mists ahead cleared simultaneously in two or three places, revealing the shiny white peaks of the Ruwenzori Mountains that lay directly ahead of us. Lost in our private thoughts and awed by the moment and by the location, we thought of where we belonged in all this and what the future held for us. The gleaming mountain peaks looking down on us were covered in snow and glaciers, and for me, standing almost on the equator; it was a moment of sheer awe. The Ruwenzori Mountain range, with its sixteen-thousand-foot peaks, was the fabled snow-covered Mountains of the Moon range that the Greek historian, Herodotus, and other countrymen of mine had written about more than two thousand years ago.

Michael and I, with the rest of our schoolboy party, were in a place the very existence of which had been disputed by almost everyone for millennia. Most historians and geographers in the past had virulently denied the possibility of snow in Africa, especially on the equator. But here we were now, in the very place that had been a riddle for explorers, geographers, adventurers, and writers for centuries. As we climbed into the Land Rover and started onward to our next destination, we were hushed, overwhelmed by surroundings that had not changed since the dawn of prehistory.

Political change in Africa had thrown a veil of insecurity over our futures, but simultaneously, there was something reassuring that no matter whatever happened, our roots in time, as witnessed by the ancient snows and glaciers of the Ruwenzori Mountains, were a guarantee that life would always go on, no matter what, as it had in this unique place in Africa.

Like Michael in *A Feather on the Wind of Change*, we too were about to be taken, feathers ourselves, and carried, seemingly haphazardly, to destinations that we could not imagine, uprooted from East Africa, which we had looked on as our home and country. Our numbers were not great. We were just a few thousand Europeans who were born as East Africans and believed that our families would be in Africa until the end of time. So we had been told.

The wind of change uprooted us and forced us to make the decision none of us had ever anticipated making. We were part of Africa's soil, had slept under its stars, and shared a million experiences with this most mystical of continents. Events were to prove that despite uprooting ourselves from all we had known and loved, the spirit of determination and the dream that had brought our families to Africa years before resulted in a large proportion of our old school friends making their mark in the world after leaving East Africa.

Wherever the wind of change blew the young feathers, their hearts, and mine as one of them, and surely that of Michael Lawrence-Brown, will always skip a beat when we hear the word "Africa."

One day, after losing all contact with Michael for more than forty years, I received an e-mail at my house in Greece, asking if I was Lex Mantheakis from Kenya. The email was signed simply "Michael Lawrence-Brown." We immediately caught up with each other, filling in the gaps with what we had done since that last journey in Africa. Michael had gone to Australia and qualified as a surgeon, financing his studies as a taxi driver and a truck driver. He had worked on building sites as a labourer and driven heavily loaded trucks over the Snowy Mountains. True to his modest nature, he told me very little, skipping his now world-famous medical achievements. He told me only that he had a wife and a family and lived in Perth.

I then discovered, through a Greek colleague in Athens and former surgery student of Michael's, that he had been responsible for huge advances in surgery. Michael, always modest, had not mentioned that he was one of the world's leading aorta surgeons and, together with a colleague of his in Australia, had developed and perfected a series of Stent-Grafts - internal arterial sleeves—to treat aneurysms, and that his pioneering work was recognised around the world. When I pressed him, Michael admitted as much and also confirmed that he was an adjunct university professor and an Officer of the Order of Australia.

A Feather on the Wind of Change, his autobiography, is an extraordinary and fascinating tale of how he settled in Australia and tells of his life and career in his new home. Written with humour, it recounts numerous anecdotes as one would expect of a storyteller who has learnt to spin a tale in Africa. Above all, though, *A Feather on the Wind of Change* is the story of a young doctor who never lost sight of his ambition to help others and to advance medical procedures into unknown territory in order to reduce the risks of the operating theatre.

It is also the story of his family and of the unusual circumstances he was confronted with when he fell in love with a nurse who belonged to a politically radical left-wing family, where the South African secret police and other law-enforcement agencies were always one step behind his forceful Welsh mother-in-law, who was part of the vanguard for social change.

In the manner that game trails intersect in the bush, we found that our lives had more and more in common after Michael and I sat down together when he came to visit me in Athens. It was during one of these visits that the idea of *A*

Feather on the Wind of Change took shape. I insisted that Michael go ahead and tell his life's story for the benefit of readers in Australia and around the world, and for his former colleagues, fellow academics, and medical students. His autobiography will allow readers to get to know this mischievous, inventive, decent, adventurous, and extraordinary man who has saved thousands of lives of vascular patients around the world and has affected those who have known him, for the better.

I thank him for sharing his unusual story with me and with you.

Alexis Mantheakis

PART 1

Kenya: The Formative Years

PREFACE

On the Wind of Change

In the vascular community, I am known for my work on the human aorta; some of this story is focused on that, but exhilarating as that has been for me, it can be boring for others. My real story started with a small number of British colonials who existed for a short period of time in the human history of the world. We were born in a very special place, in the land where humanity itself was born: in East Africa. For the sins of our fathers, we were uprooted and blown away like seeds and feathers on the "Wind of Change" to lands far away from home. However hard I tried, I've never been able to shed the influence of my time in East Africa; I grew up during that era of change in the British Empire.

While there is always change, there are times and events that are associated with quantum leaps of change. In a speech in Ghana in January 1960, Sir Harold McMillan, the British prime minister, announced, "The wind of change is blowing across Africa." This was the period of the collapse of the British Empire and the dispersal of its colonials. That speech was heard in other British colonies, mandates, protectorates, and dominions and repeated in South Africa later that year. It became known as the "Wind of Change" speech and signalled the shedding of the Empire by Great Britain after World War II, as one after another of Her Majesty's possessions became independent republics through the late 1950s and 1960s.

The change was heralded by the independence of India in 1947 (maybe it's no coincidence but a quirk of fate that Gandhi was born and grew up in Africa). The loss of control of the Suez Canal in 1956 opened the zip from Cape to Cairo. Independence was gained by the Gold Coast (Ghana) in 1957, and followed by Nigeria and Sierra Leone, then moving east through the Sudan, Uganda, British Somalia, Kenya, Tanganyika, and Zanzibar (Tanzania), and then southwards to Northern Rhodesia (Zambia), Nyasaland (Malawi), and Bechuanaland (Botswana). The change in Southern Rhodesia (Zimbabwe) and South Africa (Republic of South Africa) was delayed by their sizable European populations who were in control. The whites reacted with apartheid and unilateral declarations of policies; violent insurrections were required to gain independence and republic status.

From where did the wind blow? It was a global wind. From Jamaica to Malaysia, from India to South Africa, the rivers of pink described the British Empire around the world and converged in Africa. After fighting for Britain in World War II, the empire had all but evaporated by the end of the seventies. The lands of the British Empire were returned to the peoples. Only where the indigenous or first people were vastly outnumbered through immigration, decimation by diseases to which they had no immunity, or violence against which they had no weapons was there no turning back.

What's in a name? In 1950, the Empire Games changed their name to the Empire and Commonwealth Games, and in 1966, they became the British Commonwealth Games and were held in a non-European-dominated country, Jamaica; thereafter, they were called the Commonwealth Games. The force of the wind abated as attitudes changed, and the name changes tell the story.

So much has changed since I came to Australia in 1965 as a young man, seeking further education. A whole value system has been upturned. Until 1949, there were no Australian citizens;

they were British subjects, and even in the sixties, when I arrived as a British subject from another former colony, I was eligible to vote after six months, and subsequent citizenship was a formality without testing. Aboriginals were not allowed on the electoral roll until 1962 and were not counted in any census until after the 1967 referendum that produced a rare affirmative change in the constitution of Australia, testifying to the extent that the world was changing.

The question was, "Do you approve the proposed law for the alteration of the Constitution entitled 'An Act to Alter the Constitution so as to omit certain words relating to the people of the Aboriginal race in any state so that Aborigines are to be counted in reckoning the population'?" This effectively meant that Aborigines were also enrolled to vote through registration rather than application, and although voting was compulsory for all Australians, it was not made mandatory for Aboriginal people until 1982. The White Australia Policy officially ended in 1972. In recognising its indigenous and non-European people, Australia bent a little before the wind of change blowing across the Empire and from over the Indian Ocean. Australia is slowly but steadily transitioning to a republic of diverse peoples, vastly different from the country it was when I arrived.

Maybe this story speaks for the migrants who arrive with hope and for this country, Australia, that gives them the chance of a better life: for those who are driven by upheavals and rapid change, by youth, adventure, and a desire to succeed. After all, the degree of change in the twentieth century, and especially the latter half, must be unrivalled with respect to technology, politics, and human relations involving race and gender and has affected most of us in some way.

A reader might reasonably ask what global politics has to do with surgery (in particular, vascular surgery and stent-grafts for aortic aneurysms). The one is a global social upheaval, and the other seemingly just a technological advance in a new field of medical endeavour. The common factor is the driving force of people looking to find a better way and thereby make a change. This is a human and Australian story written in four distinct parts and tied together with the thread of my life. The essence is in the characters of the people and the city of Perth, said to be the most isolated city in the world. The power is in the interaction of multiple disciplines and many countries. The proceeds of the research and development have saved lives, spared thousands the pain and suffering of major operations, funded facilities to accommodate more change, and now support two academic professorial chairs in the University of Western Australia in Perth, one for vascular surgery and one for radiology. These professorial chairs hold promise to find more better ways. The wind of change on which I travelled was a fair wind.

One day in 2007, I received an important-looking letter asking me if I would accept an award of Officer of the Order of Australia (AO), which was under consideration by the panel. A reply was required by a due date, for the award was to be granted on the next Australia Day, January 26, 2008. I felt unworthy of being singled out from my colleagues for creating the Stent-Graft for the treatment of aortic aneurysms because it was the culmination of a mix of skills. It could not have been achieved without the special personalities involved and serendipitous opportunities. There had been battles with establishment; we had threatened interests that invoked passionate institutional politics and precipitated government reactions. I could not have done it on my own; it had been a team effort.

On February 14, 1975, the prime minister of Australia, Gough Whitlam, replaced the British Imperial Honours system with the Order of Australia Awards. With my history of a colonial past in another country, maybe a rebellious nature towards pomp and circumstance and authority, and just naturally wary of being exposed to publicity, I was troubled and considered to decline. Also, I wished for Australia to have an Australian head of state, and the new awards system was a step in the direction towards a republic. The letter was in confidence, but I needed some counsel, and on the last day for acceptance, I asked my oldest son, Stanley, what he thought.

His advice and view was forthright and straightforward: "It's not just for you, Dad. It's for all those who worked with you. You accept it for them without hesitation. And you must not cause any insult to those who wish you well. It's a great honour."

I accepted the award and became an Officer of the Order of Australia, but I still remain feeling uncomfortable until the story of those who journeyed with me, who sustained, encouraged, dared, and sacrificed while we researched and developed endovascular stent-grafts to treat aortic vascular disease, is told.

Struggling with the decision as to where to start this narrative, I remembered the passage in *Alice in Wonderland* when the king was asked where one should begin, and he said gravely, "Begin at the beginning, go on to the end, and then stop." This seemed to fit because I have lived in two Wonderlands, which suggested to me that I write a biography.

I had doubts about writing an autobiography because it may be viewed as arrogance and would tempt self-indulgence. Maybe this dilemma could have been avoided if I just wrote about the development of the stent-graft for abdominal aortic aneurysms (AAAs), rather than try to weave together the parts of my diverse life. However, the alternative of writing about Kenya, safaris in East Africa, migration to Australia, studying medicine, and being involved with inventive surgery was more appealing than just my life story. People with multiple skills in different settings have all contributed, and I was reassured that if I failed to interest, then some of those in the narrative would not let me down. So the story is intended to be more about them than it is about me.

Furthermore, judging by the number of TV series and films about medicine, hospitals, doctors, nurses, and allied staff, there is obviously interest in the health profession, its institutions, and its people. Recent revelations of gender bias and intimidation during the training in the Australasian College of Surgeons may have fired the curiosity of outsiders into the backgrounds of those they trust with their bodies. This story is from the inside of medical school, the making of a surgeon in the twentieth century, as well as research and development in surgery.

So I will start at the beginning.

CHAPTER 1

Home from Home

On the African plateau above five thousand feet (fifteen hundred metres), the days were often hot and the nights were cool, even though Kenya was on the equator. In the dry season, "day stars" shone through the thatched grass roof that served mainly for shade and protection from the searing, high-altitude equatorial sun. During the heavy rains, when the sun moved the trade winds meeting across the intertropical convergence zone, we had to negotiate a few buckets into strategic places on the floor until the thatch swelled to quell the leaks.

The rainy seasons were caused by the convergence of the trade winds that had played so great a part in bringing diverse groups of peoples to the East African coast. In 1498, the Europeans, paradoxically from the south via the Cape of Good Hope, were led by the Portuguese navigator Vasco da Gama. And from the north came the great Arab navigators, who traded as far east as China and sailed down the African coast for centuries as merchants and slave traders before the European arrival. Of the two rainy seasons, December (summer in the southern hemisphere) was heavier and longer. It was influenced by the sweep of the monsoon between India and Australia.

My first clear memory is of a snake moving across the middle of the bedroom floor as I lay in bed. Fear is not part of it, more a slow-motion fascination as the reptile moved over the coarse grass matting that formed a pool in the middle of the ochre-coloured, smooth mud floor. Its sheen reflected the dance of the kerosene hurricane lamp from the main room. The snake was making for the open door and the music of the African night that mixed with the reassuring rhythm of adult voices wafting in with the lamplight and the glow from the stone fireplace. Maybe it had dropped from the grass-and-wattle roof or had slipped in through an open door during the day to shelter from the heat. The doors were always open in those days, or perhaps there weren't any; the whitewashed walls between the thatched roof and the earth floor kept the rondavel cool in the sun.

The night exploded with shouts, flashing steel, and fireworks; the snake was flayed with various garden implements and thrown into the fireplace embers as a consequence of a child's word and the admixture of human care and violence. I have feared snakes, or at least admiringly disliked them, and wondered why. Is this a result of that experience, or is it innate in primates?

The snake, being the symbol of medicine, has played an important role in my life. Although some doors closed forever, other doors have opened, beckoned, and maybe, like the snake, I have slipped through. If the door of opportunity opens, go through, I was once advised, and I have (albeit sometimes hesitating, being carried like a feather on the wind).

When I was four, my mother and I took a long sea journey from England back to Africa. We travelled aboard the *Edinburgh Castle*, and I have vague memories of extreme heat and discomfort in the airless Suez Canal; it was relieved only by the magic of a white-robed peddler with a red fez and disappearing yellow chicks. There was endless seasickness, with a lasting dread of nausea.

I also dimly recall the train journey up from Mombasa and meeting a large tanned man with a moustache, who I instantly loved. He was my father, Stan. I have absolutely no recollection of him from before we went to England, or of England, for that matter. I understand that he cared for me when my mother was ill with rheumatic fever soon after I was born; it must have been then that we bonded. The trip to England was arranged after she recovered. Learning years later that my mother had intended to stay in the home country, I have a sense of tragedies at once avoided and determined. I grew up in wonderful East Africa with a father, instead of in England without one, and my mother was destined to the loneliness of a safari man's wife.

After losing her first love to a drowning accident, which had undertones of suicide (he was Roman Catholic, and she was an Anglican vicar's daughter, so they could not marry), my mother joined the British Navy at the beginning of World War II. Ronnie volunteered for Women's Royal Naval Service (WRNS, or "Wrens," as they were affectionately known) and arrived in Mombasa Harbour on a destroyer as a code-deciphering clerk. She stayed behind in my father's arms when the ship sailed out into the Indian Ocean; she was the only surviving Wren when the ship was sunk by a German submarine after sailing out of Mombasa.

Stan was a gunnery captain on leave from the Nigerian Light Battery, seconded from the Kenya Regiment, and was serving in the African Desert Campaign. He was a fourth-generation colonial, a professional safari guide, with a motorbike and a free spirit; he had enough charisma to charm Cerberus. He was like a romantic hero of British Empire storybooks. Ronnie—short for Veronica—was far from home and seeking information about a younger brother she believed was also serving in North Africa. This was an irresistible opportunity for wild colonial gallantry to display itself to the English rose. They promptly married in the standstill time of war.

After the war, my mother returned to her family in England, with the intention of never going back to Kenya. My birth in Nairobi, a bout of rheumatic fever, my father's post-war unemployment, and his inability to capitalise on a diamond-prospecting venture with John Williamson, the Canadian geologist who subsequently made a vast diamond-mining fortune in Tanganyika, made her decide that it had been all been too much. I am yet to understand what draws and holds one human being to another. Regardless, the colony called us back and gave me my first clear memory.

The rondavel had been built under my father's guidance at the end of his mother's twenty-acre block. My grandmother would come over and sit just outside the open doorway while sorting rice, Indian style, pushing unsuitable grains to the side. Sometimes, she painted scenes of the animals against a backdrop of acacia thorn trees or Mount Kilimanjaro or Kenya. I thought she was the most important person in the world and was so clever, as she painted pictures and played the piano. Her favourite tune was "Just West of Zanzibar."

Dad's younger sister, Runa, ruled a somewhat grander set of rondavels a few hundred yards away, and I often pedalled over in a toy Jeep. The Jeep was mechanically unsound, and the pedals wouldn't drive the wheels, so I would paddle with my feet on the ground or push it over to Runa's. Then I would sit in it while waiting for my big cousins, Dickie or Chris, to push me around; this was an early lesson in frustration and the uselessness of kids' toys. Runa was large but not tall, with her arms above the elbows thicker than the average man's thighs. She outlived all nine of her sibs—so much for the slim, healthy life. Dickie and Chris both grew to over six feet, six inches because of their father's genes from South Africa.

Dickie could make music with anything. He grew up as a one-man band with a combination of small instruments attached to his accordion. He cultivated a Lord Haw-Haw accent, like that of the German radio propagandist used against the British troops in the war, and entertained his army of cousins in the extended family. Chris could make models of everything from the black-cotton clay soil. He made a Disneyland arena for Dinky cars and guarded it with perfectly made clay tanks.

Dickie and Chris often squabbled, and we cousins decided that the wind must have changed on Chris while he was in one of his tearful stages; the dust also helped by reddening his eyes. He got his own back one day. Their father caught them smoking and held the older Dickie most responsible. He made them smoke one cigarette after another until they were sick. Dickie was already feeling sick from being caught, and the ensuing hours of smoking reddened his eyes; Chris enjoyed Dickie's discomfort and took the opportunity to stuff as many of the cigarettes as he could into his pockets for later. Needless to say, they both continued to smoke (Chris died prematurely of lung cancer).

This was in Dandora, where only colonials lived. It was a nice-sounding name, although it was not really the sort of area Britain would reserve for its better class of citizens: the civil servants. Later on, when things improved for colonials after the war, Uncle Geoff arranged for a grey-stone house to be built for Granny in Langata on the other side of town. Granny took my aunt Dolly with her, of course, because Dolly was the youngest of her ten children. In true Victorian tradition, Dolly stayed at home without education and adequate social intercourse. Her sole purpose in life was to look after Mum and the stepfather.

I don't think any of us knew much about Step-Granddad Allen, who was childless. All I remember of him was the day he was dying. Dickie was again encouraging Chris to cry. We younger ones were not allowed to see the dying man, despite trying to persuade everyone that our morbid curiosity was really a deep respect for the unknown. So we all wandered around aimlessly and got bored until I found Granny's Indian chilli bush and took a bite of the tempting fruit. My howls surpassed those of Chris's and were enough to wake the dead, which I am convinced occurred because we were there for a long time afterwards.

One day, Dolly's secret lover appeared from a nearby farm in Dandora. He whisked her back to Dandora and married her, and they all lived happily ever after, including Granny (they came back for her later).

I remember it also because I learned of my real grandfather, who had migrated from India to Kenya as a soldier settler in 1919, after World War I. He was an army location engineer (a route planner) and combined setting up a farm in Kakamega in Luo country near Lake Victoria with building the railway line up the Rift Valley through to Uganda. This eventually became the main line. Originally, it was a branch line from Mombasa to Kisumu on Lake Victoria, called the Lunatic Express and famous for the man-eaters of Tsavo. Those lions were hunted by Colonel John Patterson, another British Indian Army officer.

The Indian contingent and their workers contributed a significant base to both the British settlers and the Asian merchant population in East Africa. I learned that my grandfather died of malaria and blackwater fever at Soroti, near the swampy Lake Kioga, which becomes the Nile Sudd, with floating islands of vegetation and myriad mosquitoes as the Nile flows on its way between Lake Victoria and Lake Albert. He was buried in Tororo, on the border of Kenya and Uganda. The knowledge left me with a feeling of sadness for my real grandfather, whom I had never met, rather than for the one who died that day. Maybe blood is thicker than water, or maybe he was a more interesting and romantic figure to mourn.

Soon after that, we moved to Limuru, when Ronnie landed a job in Limuru Girls School. My mother had not liked Dandora. The dust from the plains, with its encores from the sideways sliding hurtling cars on the corrugated winding dirt road that tracked across the path of the wind, powdered everything. The fat venomous puff adders sat in their doorways in the gaps between the prickly pear cacti which formed the corral for Dolly's husband's cattle. My homesick mother claimed the mental asylum, Mathare, at the end of the road was beckoning her and that I needed an alternative education. She had been working in Nairobi as a secretary, and because I spent all day with the *ayah* and her friends, speaking Swahili, she started to have difficulty conversing with me.

My father was increasingly on safari. He had worked for Safariland before the war. After peace was declared, he teamed up with another safari guide, Dave Lunan, and started their own outfit: Lawrence-Brown and Lunan Safaris. As the post-war economy in America picked up and air travel from the United States via Europe became a reality with the four-engine Viscount Constellations, Americans started to seek adventures and vacations on safari in East Africa. It was the supreme destination. Americans constituted 90 percent of all clients. They no longer needed to combine a safari with a long, nauseating sea cruise.

With his long safaris, Ronnie felt the first touch of tragic loneliness that was to come. For the time being, a job as the bursar at Limuru Girls School, amongst the green hills, tea and coffee plantations, silver wattle forests, and English schoolteachers, fell as a gift from heaven; it relieved her homesickness and bestowed upon her a fair share of happiness for the next five years.

CHAPTER 2

Limuru

Limuru Girls School was a private school for the settlers' high school daughters. The teachers were from universities in England (usually Oxford or Cambridge) and spoke the King's English. Girls attended this school instead of being sent home to England for schooling, partly due to expense and partly a resistance to separation by the tyranny of distance. Although closer, South Africa was not considered an option by most British settlers. The relationship between British colonial settlers and the Afrikaaners was often strained; the settlers and the colonials in East Africa were mainly British.

It's a natural instinct to stereotype people. We classify according to the value systems instilled in us by our family and communities, and by the lessons we learn in life. It's natural to use colours and patterns of markings to identify those who are part of a group; it stems from an instinct to be with people who are safe or genetically suitable for breeding. In the wild, animals exhibit this all the time and recognise their own. We may project love towards a group we belong to and negative feelings to those perceived as rivals or enemies. It is a very strong instinct; an example in humans is the use of uniforms to identify rival sporting teams and warring armies. Comrades stand under the same flag, unashamedly, to the end.

The most wonderful instinct of all is the experience of falling in love with someone just because of the way they look. It is a survival instinct, but we can be gravely wrong. Colours and markings are also used in nature to deceive. A mamba snake is usually black but can vary from green through shades of grey. It is a lethal snake with large venom sacs, and it can be fatal to assume it's harmless if it's green.

We have erred in thinking that humans of different colour are incompatible because we breed very well together. We are merely different varieties of *Homo sapiens*. And it can be as much of an error to group humans together on the basis of colour and markings as it is to group them apart.

Into this crucible in the land where humans were born, a complex mix was poured. The antipathy between the Boers and the British matched that between the Nilotic Luo and the Bantu Kikuyu tribes, which in turn paralleled the divide between the Muslims and the Hindus. The extent to which the undercurrent could surface had only shortly before been horrifically expressed by the partition of India and the formation of Pakistan. There were many Indians of both Muslim and Hindu faith brought over to Africa by the British to help build infrastructure, and their descendants and relatives formed the merchant and skills classes extending to the furthest corners of the colonies. Way out in the bush, it wasn't unusual to find a small shop, called a *duka*, with a Coca-Cola sign and an Indian trader who could fix your vehicle. The diversity of people of East Africa with African, Arab, Persian, Indian, and European ethnic origins was such that the criterion of race was the least of our reasons for discrimination. There were other reasons for grouping; we were well aware of the importance of numbers and weapons in holding or yielding to power. The obvious and primal weapon of power was, of course, force, and that was in the hands of the British. It was ingrained in all of us, from the earliest age, that we were in Africa, and Africa is beautiful and dangerous. As the twentieth century unfurled, whatever our backgrounds, we all knew that the real power of the future was education (provided or denied).

Africa is about survival, and while grouping enables survival, it also fosters rivalries. The Boers had trekked up from the Cape as far as the equator, with the most northern reach a farm settlement called Outspan 64 by the Afrikaaners (it was later called Eldoret by the rest of us). They had moved north to get away from the British and its colonials who fought against them in the Boer War and had never recovered from the annoyance of always bumping into the British again. They never forgave the British for the terrible concentration camps set up by Lord Kitchener, where Boer women and children were held as hostages. This resulted in numerous deaths from typhoid fever, forcing the Boer men to surrender. The Boers had fought a guerrilla war and had left their families to be gathered up. Capturing and holding the undefended women and children was not a tactic anticipated by the Boers, and they seriously underestimated Lord Kitchener's ruthlessness in avoiding an ignominious return to Britain in defeat.

This war was also the birthplace of the modern war correspondent; in the beginning, everything was reported, but then Kitchener took command and silenced the war correspondents. It was the last war the British fought in their red coats, having made such good targets for the long-range hunting rifles of the Boers. At the end, through guilt for the death of so many women and children, the British made the colonies of South Africa a dominion with self-rule, setting the scene for the development of apartheid by a bitter and tough people.

In the immediate aftermath of the Boer War against Britain, many Boer families migrated north of South Africa; the remote northern Kenya town of Eldoret marks the limit. With Kenyan independence in 1963, the migration back to South Africa was the end of the Boer settlement, but the town has moved on as a regional centre, with the Wagon Wheel Hotel holding the secrets of history.

In South Africa, religion and language still separated those of British and Afrikaaner origins. It was their colour that kept them together; the language differences of Afrikaans and English was addressed by the Apartheid regime, insisting that Afrikaans be learnt by everyone. The Afrikaans word *apartheid* symbolised South Africa, a system designed to divide. The Swahili word *safari*, meaning "a journey together," symbolised East Africa. Swahili was the unifier in East Africa and became the utility language. I still speak it in my mind.

The Boers made the Great Trek north; the East Africans made safaris, and the term spread around the world. For us, the Great Trek was not an awe-inspiring adventure north to the equator through hostile lands, where deserts allied with man and beast to wait in ambush; it was the march of pubic hair up to the umbilicus in adolescence. There were many jokes, and the satirical English singer James Taylor, who was very popular among Brits, used the Dutch accent of South Africa to ridicule the Boers. The accent, however, also trekked north, and some of the inflection must have stuck with me because I've been mistaken as South African many times. In the sixties, most Australians placed me in a social context familiar to them: white men from Africa must be South African, despite Nairobi being as far from Cape Town as Perth is from Singapore.

In Limuru, the grass was always green, the little garden borders were filled with English annuals, and the manners and speech were familiar to my mother; it was just like home to Ronnie, and that was England. She was happy and eventually conceived my sister, which marked the end of her five years (in those days, pregnancy ended a job).

Stan almost ruined the English home-away-from-home scene in Limuru Girls School. First, he built a colonial-style rondavel attachment to my mother's oblong single-roomed house. Its original design had a central feature of a small English-type porch over a central front door. There was no bathroom or toilet; that was a separate small communal building. The house had originally been a garden shed and was the only wooden dwelling in the compound of picturesque grey-stone teachers' cottages. The original room was hardly adequate for Stan's frame, let alone his personality. With the colonial-style rondavel attached, it served to draw my father home.

To further contaminate the English country scene, all the weary safari trucks would roll in and park in the school grounds with increasing numbers as his business grew. He guided and organised the animal scenes for the MGM film *King Solomon's Mines*. Stan never went to the movies, never had the time, but he saw *King Solomon's Mines* ten times when it came to Nairobi. He would take me and all the cousins, and we would all stage-whisper at the appropriate moment, "Is that you?" when he or his partner, Dave Lunan, stood in for Stewart Granger or engineered a particular animal scene.

There was a long beautiful drive into the school, lined by flowering jacarandas. Stan's safari trucks rested in the shade of these majestic non-English flowers, in preparation for the next feat. Playing bridge at tea parties with schoolmarms is a picture of my father that I'm completely unable to conjure up in my mind. Instead, he played his accordion and drove them down to the Equator, a nightclub twenty miles away in Nairobi. Then the Mau-Mau rebellion started; Stan and his trusty safari crews, when they were home, were an essential night patrol force, protecting the Girls School.

For my part, life was bliss. No preschool, no local primary school, and Nairobi too far away for day school. I joined the local band of Kikuyu *totos*, the children of the school's African staff. Together, we roamed the grounds and followed the school's ox-cart. This was really Henry's ox-cart. Henry Langlois was large and florid, in the image of a Dickensian Beadle, and ruled the grounds of the school and his ever-increasing local land acquisitions. He was an earthy Frenchman from the Seychelles

Islands who married Ruby, a cultured White Russian. She had been a ballerina and was blessed with grace, a wonderful sense of humour, and exuberant energy. It was Ruby who set the example of the eventual benefits of education, an example that hounded me, an example manifested in her daughter, Geraldine.

A year or so older than me, Geraldine was the only European child close to my age in the school grounds and the only other child to play with after my mother forbade me to ride the ox-cart following the start of the Mau-Mau uprising. She went on to be head-girl at Limuru Girls School, distinguished herself in an English university, and returned as a beautiful young woman with the best Queen's English.

Proper English had changed in Kenya from the King's to the Queen's in 1953, after Elizabeth II ascended to the throne while she was up a tree—well, in Tree Tops Safari Lodge in the Kenyan Aberdare Mountains (ironically, on the way to Australia, which was a trip thereby postponed). Years later, when Geraldine returned in all her beauty from her higher education and finishing school, and I was guiding safaris for Stan, I longed to talk to her but didn't feel I had the graces. Although we had played together as small children, it didn't seem appropriate any more. Our souls drifted away, barely having contacted again. Too much water had flowed under the bridge. I had also learnt that a Black Russian was a cigarette, together with many other foul brands, and hid behind a smoke screen.

In an effort to curb my roaming, Ronnie arranged for me to learn to ride a horse. The Girls School had its own stables and riding teacher: Kitty. I liked riding. It enabled even further roaming, and Kitty was young and adventurous. We rode through wonderful hills and bracken-filled valleys, smouldering charcoal-making red earth mounds, natural forests, and planted wattle. The wattle bark was grown to tan leather hides and the wood turned into charcoal. Kitty got as far as teaching me to gallop. But one day, she fell when jumping and became a quadriplegic. I never saw her again and never became a good rider. Ronnie banned further lessons. I reacquainted with my toto friends and the ox-cart.

The ox-cart was of basic construction. A straight longitudinal post held the tray on the back end, and an iron ring at the front end attached the chains to a yoke. There was a front and sides to the tray, but no tailgate. One drizzly day, as the oxen were straining up a long, winding track from the charcoal-making valley, the iron ring came out of the end of the post, freeing the yoke. This was on the point of a bend, at the moment when the cart was facing directly uphill. Freed, it rolled back over the side of the hill, with the driver and artful dodgers abandoning ship in all directions.

I had the same slow-motion sensation as with the snake. In truth, the cart was moving too fast for me; I was too small to leap and felt mesmerised. I stayed in the cart, which sailed downhill as the post trailed behind like a rudder. A jolt, a lurch, a brief and sudden interruption by a wave of young wattle trees, from an otherwise cleared hillside, which gave a clear run into a sea of upturned, horrified charcoal burners' faces, and out I shot through the open rear. The large iron-clad wheels passed by on each side. The post was not so kind, smacking me on the back as it passed over.

I was carried tenderly, and with much weeping on my part, back to the Girls School by my friends and ceremoniously deposited on the carpet of the bursar's office, in front of the comforting fireplace. Limuru, between seven and eight thousand feet (twenty-five hundred metres), was often cold and misty or drizzling because of the altitude, and a steady fire was usual. On this day, nature also shed tears upon me, so that I was wet, blood-stained from wattle brush scratches, and streaked with charcoal. The apparition deposited so carefully on my mother's office carpet resembled a bedraggled battle flag, from which she at first recoiled.

Snashie, the matron and school nurse, took over; she cleaned me, changed my clothing, soothed me, and assessed the damage. There was just sufficient to afford me refuge and indulgence for a few days in the sanatorium, until Ronnie was completely reassured that I had survived, and then she wanted to know, "What the bloody hell were you doing on that bloody ox-cart again?" The ox-cart was banned—again.

I invariably carried a pet of some sort; Stan often brought home injured or orphaned animals. The older ones usually bit and could be unpleasant. Africa is such a dangerous place. Everything wants to bite, sting, scratch, poison, kill, or eat you. No wonder the animals developed defence mechanisms. However, sometimes a young one would turn out to be indescribably charming and provide a glimpse of what we all might be if loved early. The bushbabies and the mongoose made the best pets. Bushbabies, about the size of a small rabbit, are primitive primates with hands and feet; it's furry with very large and adoring eyes, a designer pet. They are nocturnal (hence the very large eyes). Indeed, they shun the light, hiding and sleeping during the daytime. They are very cuddly and would hold onto one's finger just like a baby does (hence its name).

In the evenings, they emerged to perform acrobatics and aerial manoeuvres that would turn circus acrobats green with envy. Like true performers, they would play to an audience and could be encouraged with a little fruit. They would perform best by candlelight or the kerosene hurricane lamp. After we moved to Limuru, we had electric lights, but power failures were common, and the bushbaby would wait until the lights went out. Unholy noises ensued, for example, when the curtains gave way in the kitchen.

Gazelles were lovely when young, but I think their heads itched as they grew older and their horns started to grow. Irritable like teething children, they would take to butting at every opportunity. They were particularly attracted to round parts of one's anatomy, which presumably resembled a lowered head, and therefore a rival. My mother was butted once too often in her roundest part when bending down to peer into a kitchen drawer, and she banned the gazelles.

Contrary to what might be expected, monkeys didn't make nice pets. If you look directly at a monkey, it takes it as an act of aggression, and if you stare at it, the stare will be returned with rhythmic widening of the eyes and raised eyebrows. Continue and return the compliment, and the monkey becomes hostile. I used to do it for sadistic fun with the little vervets but was wary of the larger baboons. Groups of baboons have been known to kill leopards in self-defence. Stan brought back a few monkeys. They were never tamed and exhibited the worst human traits— furtive, felonious, selfish, dirty, sexually and aggressively abusive, and sometimes vicious. My mother didn't need to ban monkeys.

I came to love birds, most of all the parrots. A female African grey, called Suku, was to be my best friend for years, until the wind of change blew me away. Strange, really; I feel guilty and disloyal towards her; she was so affectionate, so intelligent, so entertaining. There were no doors to her cage; she simply regarded it as her nest. Like the cage, there were no doors to the hunting cars. When travelling, she had free range of the car and would sit on my shoulder, the gun racks, or the back of the seat. When we stopped in any passing town or village, she would perform on the steering wheel for gathering crowds, especially children. She would dance up and down to the tune of "The Happy Whistler" (she knew the first few bars).

At home, she loved to call the mongoose, using the typical mongoose Morse code pips, or the dogs, mimicking their food-call whistle. Stan, being a practical joker, taught her the deceptions. She returned the favour by echoing his smoker's cough, embarrassing him so much that he tried to quit. After I left, she went into depression; she wouldn't speak, turned nasty, and pulled out her feathers. My sister's sustained efforts to console her restored her feathers but not her personality. Having been with me since a baby, maybe she saw herself as my mate and more human than bird. She had never been taught to interact with other greys. I guess it can be cruel to be kind.

Without the liberty of travelling with the ox-cart, my raison d'être as a member of its entourage was gone. I am ashamed to admit that it was not from a sense of obedience on my part, rather compliance, as a result of fearing the driver would lose his job. Therefore, I spent more time with Luca. He was from the Jalua tribe, a branch of the Luo hailing from west of the Rift Valley. He worked for Ronnie, after an introduction from Stan, and had moved with them when they moved to Limuru. Not being perceptive enough to know of Luca's relationships with the other workers, I now suspect he may have been somewhat isolated; Limuru is in the heart of Kikuyu country, east of the rift, and the Luo tribes were from west of the Rift Valley.

Traditionally, the rift had a double entendre. Luca spent time with me as part of his job (and maybe due to his relative social isolation). He taught me many things, including the F-word. It had a certain ring to it, and I tried it out on my mother that evening, asking her "to close the f'n door cuz the f'n light's keeping me awake." That was my second lesson on the violence that could be inadvertently invoked by a child's spoken word. The next day, Luca might have been very red if he hadn't been so black; we both retired hurt. No big deal, really, except we were in a girls school, and I was also the onion in a petunia patch, with no one else to understand my sense of injustice.

During the rainy season, it rained a lot in Limuru; it was misty in the mornings, and if it wasn't the rain, then certainly the dew made everything wet. The soil, a rich, fertile, volcanic red clay loam, made excellent mud. The clay component gave it a property akin to grease when wet. The red ochre content made it look like paint. After finding nice, round, unripe plums on Henry's prize plum tree, I stripped the tree and made toy chocolates by coating them in rich, red mud. They didn't taste very good, so I offered them around; Henry was most ungrateful and darkened like the pseudo-chocolate when he realised what was inside.

In the rainy season, the unpaved roads became almost impassable, especially on Banana Hill. It was twenty-one miles from Limuru Girls School to Nairobi. When it rained, Limuru was wonderfully isolated by the impassable five-mile stretch of mud that streaked Banana Hill. Four-wheel drives were rare and ex-army American jeeps very difficult to acquire; being generally uncovered, they were somewhat hostile for travellers in drenching rain, anyway. Even with chains on, an invisible hand unerringly guided two-wheel-drive vehicles into the ditch. The engineers increased the camber of the road to drain off the water and dug deeper run-off ditches. This served to deposit the cars more frequently in the ditch and raised the prices charged by the local inhabitants to lift the cars back onto the road. I eagerly helped push. Ronnie would desperately try and keep me in the car while she received a variety of steering instructions from helpful locals (while she cursed Stan for being on safari). The mud was delicious, and my favourite pushing position was immediately behind the back wheel. I loved Banana Hill in the rainy season. Progress eventually sealed it and its charms with tarmac.

About the same time that the ox-cart was banned, there were other concerns for my safety because the rebellion against the British colonial regime was growing. The rebellious movement of the Kikuyu people had turned nasty. It was led by Jomo Kenyatta and other intelligentsia, who had been schooled abroad—usually in Britain—and quite rightly had returned to Kenya with a sense of injustice that the native peoples of Kenya were being treated as second-class citizens in their own land. In the beginning, it took the form of political debate and rational opposition. In true colonial style, all the intelligentsia, who were perceived as leaders and a threat, were jailed, and precautions were taken. Strict restrictions were imposed upon the indigenous population (and on me).

Ronnie never frightened me with hypothetical scenarios concerning the Mau-Mau, although she told me later that she worried because we were in the heart of Kikuyu country; the local Kikuyu used intimidation to persuade others to join the rebellion or scare the colonials away. Most of the intimidation victims were Kikuyu who did not wish for violent rebellion; some were European children. It never crossed my mind that I was at risk from the people I played with until one day, near the beginning of the emergency, while sitting on a stone building block that Luca used for a chair, a young Kikuyu who had been discussing politics turned on me. He hauled me off the stone and then exposed the white sun-starved grass shoots beneath it. Pointing to my white skin in this sunlit Garden of Eden, he declared that I was equally unsuited to the sun and as out of place as the exposed grass. Between Luca and a mongoose that popped its head out my shirt to find out what the commotion was about, the youth was persuaded to leave further deeds for another day. I've never forgotten the moment when I first experienced real fear.

We lived surrounded by security arrangements and grew to accept them. At that age, it was all I knew. I now have two little books on my shelf. One is *The Hunt for Kimathi* by Ian Henderson, the British policeman who recruited former Mau-Maus and incorporated them into his special force of pseudo-terrorists. They infiltrated the Mau-Mau band of Kimathi and his followers in the Aberdare Forest. The other is a play written by two university students who were born after Kenyan independence; to them, Kimathi is a hero. A main street in Nairobi is named after him. History is indeed written by the victors.

The bravery of the pseudo-terrorists and the police who infiltrated the Mau-Mau is unimaginable, and so too was the brutality described by the combatants. We younger cousins listened spellbound to older cousins and their friends, who recounted episodes of their patrols. I remember being particularly taken with the edict that they were not allowed to wash with any soap or use any skin creams because these could be smelt from a considerable distance in the forest. My cousins were as wary of the British Army troops as they were of the Mau-Mau, and their description of an altercation in which the British troops broke off the ends of beer bottles and used the jagged ends to push and twist in someone's face conjured an image that has never been erased. They were reputed to be more street-fighters than forest-fighters and belonged to regiments with fearsome reputations: the Black Watch, Argyle Fusiliers, Lancashire Fusiliers, and the Cameronians.

My early feelings towards the British troops were of admiration. We stood in organised primary school groups, waving little Union Jacks during ceremonies put on for visiting royalty, complete with deafening twenty-one-gun salutes. The troops guarding the route were decorated and tanned, contrasting with the very white visiting Royal English faces, made paler by tropical gastric upsets. Later, there was direct contact with them as instructors and trainers for our high school cadet corps; we learned trench warfare, charging with fixed bayonets and yelling at a pretend enemy. It was more like WWI games than fighting the Mau-Mau. They did not seem to like colonials, and the feeling became mutual. We were introduced to military-style discipline.

One day, an instructor with a strange English accent placed his face an inch from the cadet standing next to me and yelled, "Repeat after me: 'I am a fucking idiot!'"

The terrified cadet was confused and stuttered, "Y-y-you are a fucking idiot!"

I nearly peed myself. It was lifesaving that we were schoolboys and not Mau-Mau. There were some positives for the locals, though, because the army was a boon for the trade in ex-army off-road vehicles. After the emergency, Stan sourced his trucks from army surplus vehicle auctions.

In the absence of any Limuru school for small boys, and considering the impediment of Banana Hill, I was made an honorary girl and was allowed to sit in on the most junior classes of Limuru Girls High School. Younger than the required admission age, I did not threaten the girls and was generally accepted. Girls are so organised compared with boys, and their games were fun. I enjoyed playing with them without being scorned because of the absence of any boys. We played hopscotch, kick the tin (a form of hide-and-seek), and coast guards and pirates in a wonderful new gym, with lots of ceiling ropes, vaulting horses, and wall bars. Jacks, ball tip, and murder after dark filled the hours and honed our physical and mental agility.

Being a girls school (Henry was the only male adult and was confined to the outdoors), there were no male toilets. So of course, as an honorary girl, I used the girls toilets. Wondering why and how I was different, and intensely curious like most small boys, I used my honed physical skills to climb the cubicle wall and peer over at one of the girls. She had been the friendliest and accepting of me, and I thought she would understand. She was sitting on the toilet with her head bent forwards, and her bottom, which was rounding with puberty, gleamed up at me like a reflection of the moon. In pure innocence, and as an act of honest friendship, I emitted a giggle. Seeing me staring at her like Foo over the wall, she was unnerved. The consequences were dramatic, humiliating, sad, and lasting: I was banned from the Girls School.

About a mile away, there was a small hotel with a golf course that could be reached via a track through the forest. This eventually became a beautiful, modern hotel called Brackenhurst. It was centred in the golf course and surrounded by rolling hills of wattle, pine, and bracken. At the ninth hole, set away from the hotel, was a simple cement-rendered stone structure, one room and a toilet facility. This little building was donated to be used as a school until a proper primary school could be built nearby at Tigoni. Five or six of us were installed as the inaugural students. We sang our way through the alphabet and mathematical tables until the teacher was nearly driven mad by our repetitive lilt. Not understanding her annoyance, we were initiated into the confusion which results from failed efforts to please teachers.

I knew the track to Brackenhurst well because Kitty had used it for riding. When the weather was fine, Luca would escort me to school along this very lovely track. While I didn't care for snakes, chameleons fascinated me, and they were often found on this track, if you knew where to look. So trusting, they would sit still, balanced on a branch or finger, and grip tightly with their parrot-like feet. They liked to perch on a finger; it was fun to see them change colour to match the background. Their eyes swivelled independently on each side of the head, like camera lenses. Their defence was to be motionless and change the colour of their skin to blend into the surroundings.

Camouflage served them equally well in attack. Its mouth would suddenly open, and with the speed of a rubber band, its tongue would extend at least fifteen centimetres to catch a fly. The end of the tongue was sticky, and the attached fly would be retrieved to the muncher. That was all the chameleon would hurt. As pets, they could be placed on a small tree and expected to be there from day to day. They look to be as nimble as a lizard, but locomotion was painfully slow. Balancing on one foreleg and the contralateral hind leg, the other two legs would move forward as if with an incurable stutter. With eyes swivelling and heads bedecked with horns like miniature dinosaurs, they might take a whole minute to complete one camouflaged step. I became good at spotting them; there were many on the track.

I tried to make friends with the girls again by using chameleons as gifts. The European girls liked them, but most Africans, including Luca, did not; some detested them as spiritual creatures of the devil. Yet it was an African who gave me my first one, encouraging it to move, in its fashion, from his finger to mine.

The legend goes that Man was born in the Serengeti; God lives at the top of Kilimanjaro (Kilema Kyaro, which means, in the language of the Chaga people, who live on the slopes of the mountain, "difficult to climb," but in Swahili, the closest translation is "cold mountain"), overlooking the lands of Eden, and he sent what he thought were the speediest animals to fetch humans to bathe in the cool milk that filled the crater and prepare them with a protective coating for their migrations around the world. The cheetah came, and his group bathed first. White people headed north. The various antelope then brought the second wave; the milk was somewhat muddied, and when these people left, they ended up brown-skinned in the mid-latitudes. The chameleons were chosen because they looked so fast—like racehorse goannas—but they were so slow that they were too late; the milk was gone, and all those fetched by them remained behind to care for the garden.

It was five miles to Brackenhurst by proper road, and when the rebellion turned nasty, it was considered unsafe for Luca and me to walk the track; then the proper school was completed, and we moved to a little place nearby called Tigoni and were driven to school in a car. When Stan was home, his safari car made the best school bus.

Sadly, the British had little regard for the Africans and had a lot of experience in quelling dissent. Like the Romans before, it was divide and rule. Jomo Kenyatta was jailed for years, together with the other intelligent educated Kikuyu leaders, with the rationale that removing the ringleaders would defeat the rebellion. Kenyatta was made in the mould that was then used for Mandela: education, leadership, reason, and understanding; a passion for his land and people; foresight, forgiveness, and reconciliation. Without him, the resistance resorted to superstition, violence, and intimidation. The infamous Lari massacre near Tigoni set the scene, as the Kikuyu tried to intimidate their fellow tribesmen into rebellion.

The little school at Tigoni was limited to the first two years of primary schooling; when I was seven, I had to move to Nairobi Primary School. Of course, I had to board, partly because that was the preferred British way, even if pupils lived close by, but mainly because of Banana Hill. It was the original Nairobi School for Europeans. In the main hall was an honours board for those who had served in the world wars with about fifty names, which featured my dad's name and his brother Bill; my little chest nearly burst. There was also a Victoria Cross winner from World War I, and we all knew that the Victoria Cross was the highest medal for valour; in the British Empire, that identified a hero. It was a Leakey who had been thus decorated. Richard Leakey—his grandnephew—and I were in the same class; although we played together, we were not that close. I had been sent down from the A stream to the B stream for disciplinary reasons, and I had also become an ignominious day-boy, again for disciplinary reasons. Richard was in the B stream and a day-boy, and day-boys had inferior status to boarders, and that helped put us together.

He lived close by, in Langata, where we had moved after Limuru, and we sometimes gave each other a lift to school. I considered him soft, not deserving to be a relative of someone with a V.C., besides which he played with girls; they played kiss-chase, and he persuaded me to join. One day, I passed blood in my urine and thought I had received a punishment from God. I never told my mother, and it cleared up on its own; in hindsight now, I realise I probably had glomerular nephritis from a streptococcal infection picked up at kiss-chase.

In our late teens and early twenties, he and I guided safaris, but he only guided photographic safaris while I worked on hunting safaris. I still thought he was soft. How wrong I was; later, I learnt that courage has nothing to do with physical prowess. I heard of him over the years, mainly through the newspaper. The next time I saw Richard was fifteen years later, when he was in St Thomas Hospital, London. He had renal failure and was getting dialysis; I walked into the ward, and there he was. Eventually, he got a kidney transplant from his brother, Phil. I wonder if he had had glomerular nephritis at the same time; we might have circulated the streptococcus through the kiss-chase group, with a true kiss of death. Richard's tree of courage led him to academic achievements and fame in palaeontology and anthropology. He grew taller and bore more fruit than those who blew away on the wind of change. Maybe he was rooted deeper and had resisted the wind by staying in Kenya. His early story is told in his book, *One Life*.

There are some experiences in life we must all empathise with to some degree, depending on other circumstances. The first real separation must stand out in everybody's memory. Boarding school holds it for me. I arrived for the first time at the Nairobi Primary School and was thrilled to be in a dormitory with twenty other six- and seven-year-olds. I must have appeared uncaring to Mum; she left me with our eyes dry and her upper lip stiff. I probably avoided overt affectionate contact in front of the other boys, knowing that I would have to compete and they were sizing me up for the pecking order since I was new. Suddenly, she was gone. It was getting dark. Other mothers were eventually leaving, and friends were reuniting; it was such an empty feeling, and I hid away to cry.

I guess we also derive strength from the weakness of others in similar situations. Poor Hobson, whose large green eyes would rain for days at the beginning of each term. He came to school by train from Mombasa. Bad things could happen on those school trains during the three-hundred-mile overnight trip. I don't know if anything untoward ever happened to him. He cured me of school homesickness because I felt so sorry for him. I must admit I was a little fascinated as to the whereabouts of the source of his Nile. He gave a whole new meaning to

Hobson's choice. I liked him, though, and he was always fine after the first week. I don't know what became of him.

The school fought homesickness by restricting parental access to once a week, on Thursday evenings, and leave-outs were limited to one Sunday a month. Only those few whose homes were close by ever saw their families more often than once a month. Those from afar, like Hobson, rarely. Families that did visit would bring sweets and biscuits, and their children became the targets for schoolboy beggars, who badgered more than Bali beach hawkers. Woe betided those who did not share; in a way, it was better if your family did not visit at all.

The move to Langata, when I was nine years old, like many moves, occurred because of a combination of factors. My mother's pregnancy meant the loss of her job and, with that, loss of the house and home. Langata was on the edge of Masai country. Traditional enemies and marauders of the Kikuyu, they were not considered a Mau-Mau threat, and maybe that was a safety factor for the protection of wife and children, since Stan was away on safari for such long periods. The Masai dealt with the British by completely ignoring their existence, but that's another story. Probably the main reason was that Stan was sufficiently successful to be able to have a house and garden of his own, and Wendy's conception triggered the move.

New housing estates had been set up with five-acre blocks on each side of loop roads, situated in the shadows of the folding hills of Ngong at an altitude of five and a half thousand feet. Our housing estate of Langata, just outside Nairobi, was draped over folds and little river valleys, into which washed most of the graded dirt roads in the rainy seasons. The house was at the top of a little valley and built of grey Kenya stone. It was only a couple of years old; the original homemakers had returned to England in some tragic circumstance. There was little in the way of a garden when we moved in, but Kenyan soil is fertile. My uncle Max was a self-educated civil engineer; as a sideline to fixing the roads, he used his bulldozer to make three large terraces out of the hillside. Years of growth along the terraces for the many shades of bougainvillea, jacarandas, and Australian bottlebrushes transformed the little stone house, with its colonial style peri-veranda and red tiled roof, into a sustaining picture to be carried next to my heart and into the safaris beyond East Africa.

As lovely as a picture might be, it is but sterile without the scent of life, and there is no soil that has the scent and caress as that from where you grew up. The aroma, when struck deep and forged with the electricity of tropical storms and smell of rain, lingers with a mixture of the perfume of flowers, bushes, and animals that form your fibre and make you a blood brother to the land (literally, since most plants and animals in Africa sport thorns or other sharp things to shed one's blood to mingle with the soil). That was my home. The soil cements my blood, my father's bones, and my soul.

East Africa was composed of Kenya, Tanganyika, and Uganda and the islands off the coast, with Zanzibar and her smaller sister, Pemba. I was born, raised, schooled, and cultured in Kenya. I travelled Uganda and later guided tourists through her national parks, but her soul remained distant from me. Zanzibar remained a mystery shrouded in history and Sinbad's voyages for unknown centuries. There were legends of dhow trade as far as China, clashes of culture between Arabs and Europeans, and clashes with Europeans involving the Portuguese and British. There was the awful spectre of slavery that spread its hand out from Zanzibar across East Africa, as far as the western shores of Lake Tanganyika and into Rwanda and the Congo and probably farther, to extract slaves by capture and trade in prisoners of local wars.

I never visited Zanzibar or Pemba. Their history lent depth to my being, and its teaching at school gave me the first tickle of a thirst for learning. Taught at a time when the bud of manhood was emerging, with endeavours to peer out at the world, and embarrassed with its refusal to accept any control while intruding into every thought process, the image of chained, humiliated, beaten eunuchs waiting in Zanzibar for transport to Arabia distilled in my mind countless numbers of Christs on the cross, of Portuguese priests singing the Te Deum ahead of troops who murderously rampaged at the end of the hymn, of martyrs for Allah and incarnations of Cain and Abel. If I have a religion, it swirls with images that question. Questions set to the music of hymns stirring in the uncertain changing throats of the six-hundred-strong choir of schoolboys in Adam's Eden.

CHAPTER 3

Boarding School in Nairobi

Starting boarding school at the age of seven taught me many survival skills and left an indelible scar, so much depended on peer pressure and the ability to compete. Outsiders suffered humiliation and defeat. Grouping was inevitable, and fickle loyalties underwrote affiliations. Age and strength predominated, and authorities became forever tainted with an enduring distrust of justice. Experiences of perceived injustice were familiar to all of us at some time or other in boarding school. They served to balance survival instincts, foster an ethic of never tell, respect for peer pressure, and acceptance of all dares. Fear was coupled with laughter, and one spiced the other. It is so difficult not to laugh when you also know you must not.

The rivalry between the children of colonials, British civil servants, Afrikaaners, and new migrants created an atmosphere of fun, mischief, and competition at boarding school. Yet there was always the reminder of the lurking dangers of life, especially in Africa. By the time we started high school, barbed wire surrounded the school compound to keep the Mau-Mau out (but also effectively keeping us in). After the capture of the Mau-Mau leader Kimathi and the official end of the conflict, the barbed wire persisted around the Girls School for much longer, keeping us out. We boys lived as much in fantasy as we did in reality. The essence of romance was based in the imagination and deeds performed in the land of wonder. East Africa was indeed a wondrous land that served as the crucible for a collection of youth, altitude, sunlight, biological diversity, and curiosity fuelled with testosterone. What chance did Adam ever have in this land where we were born?

Africa has a violent side, and this was expected to be dealt with rather than paralysing us. Shortly after we moved to Langata, I was looked after by neighbours during school holidays because Stan was away on safari and Ronnie worked in Nairobi. The neighbours had a petrol station and garage; they also had two sons, Ian and Barry. The petrol station was a good place to meet people, and I got to know most on the estate.

Peter was a little older, about eleven, and was also being cared for at the garage because his parental helicopter had crashed in tragic circumstances, and he had lost his father. Peter's father had been the architect and engineer for the Kenya Girls High School and had made games and go-carts for Peter that we often played with. We didn't talk about what happened; we just liked each other and started riding together on bicycles. We were free to roam, mobile and foolish and feral.

My cousin Howard sometimes joined us; we considered ourselves the three musketeers. We probably survived without further tragedy because our time together was limited by attending separate schools. One Saturday morning, we went to see a picture at the Empire Theatre. This particular film starred Errol Flynn (whom I later learned was Australian), in his famous role of the pirate Captain Blood. The audience was mixed, mainly Indian, and participated enthusiastically in the movie. It was a very noisy place with cat-calls, whistling, and cheering when heroes fought and won and heroines swooned and kissed.

Peter took a dislike to an exuberant, ear-splitting whistler sitting right behind him. The whistler was also holding onto the back of Peter's chair and steering it through the high seas along with Flynn. When the altercation spilled out onto the street after the movie, it was suggested that we have a friendly fight with knives. We were heavily outnumbered and the central attraction. We were saved by a saleswoman who hauled us off the street and into her clothing shop. She had recognised us, as she supplied school uniforms.

Pete and I formed a deep bond for reasons that might not be obvious at first glance; there was a two-year age gap, and we went to different schools. He lived close by, and we were both without fathers in the home; the only stipulation that our mothers made was that we could not leave the house before dawn and we had to be home before dark. Our bicycles provided a wonderful mode of transport; we covered vast distances during the twelve hours between dawn and dusk whatever the time of year (because we were on the equator). Fixed wheels with small rear cogs, toe clips, and strong young legs with light bodies enabled us to spin the back wheels on gravel roads.

The ultimate trip, when Peter was fifteen and I thirteen, was the three-hundred-and-twenty-mile ride from Langata to Mombasa, which was all dirt road except for about forty miles. The corrugations and sandy patches competed with the elephants crossing the road for obstacles. Our three-legged kerosene stove shed a leg from the vibrations; if we had more sense, we would have taken off the other two and embedded the stove's round bottom in sand, but we persisted with the two and an unstable prop, losing many hot fluids and dodging burns. We survived the trip and stayed in Mombasa for three weeks before catching the bus back to Nairobi. Pete left Kenya for the British Army and then Canadian paratroopers, and I finished school. After that we lost contact and over the years I heard that he died and could not trace him. Fifty years later I discovered he rose from the dead using his first name –James. The military had found it too difficult to call him by his user name of Peter, his second name, but I called him Pete when we caught up and he liked that. The reunion came about because of the story of two boys riding to Mombasa from Nairobi on bikes, it had to be us.

Graduation to high school meant taking the Kenya Primary Examination. By this time, I had been at boarding school for six years, and the move from Nairobi School (which had been built in 1902) to the Prince of Wales School (which was built in 1931) was almost seamless. On my first day at high school, we tore around in a state of excitement, and rounding a corner, I grabbed at the nearest thing to counter the centrifugal force. This was Roger's pullover. Roger came from a day-primary school where his mother was a teacher; he had never been to boarding school. He was quietly observing the antics of the reacquainting Nairobi primary boarders. My attachment to his pullover and its consequential stretch gave vent to his feelings, resulting in my first fight in high school, which I lost (he was bigger than me). I avoided him for that term, but in the first holidays, I was riding my bike to Karen Estate to see my cousin Howard when I passed Roger swinging on a gate not far up the road from my house. He hailed me, I stopped, and we became good friends and remained so.

We soon learned that high school was different. The primary school may have stayed at the original site, but the tradition went with the high school. We were gathered by Jake, the headmaster, and told that the Prince of Wales School's headmaster was on the Head Masters Board of the English Public Schools, which meant that they were a private school, if you can follow the logic, and we were therefore one of the best schools in the world.

We were told about sex in his talk without humour, innuendo, or emotion; it was a biology lesson. Homosexuality would not be tolerated, and misdemeanours on the long train trips from Kampala or Mombasa at the beginning and end of each term would be dealt with severely. He was laying down the law; we would be beaten if we dared step outside the rules. The original school had been established in 1902 as the Nairobi School under Captain Bertram Nicholson, a former British naval officer; the mainstay of punishment was corporal, with the cane across the buttocks of a student bent over a bench.

The school was divided into junior and senior high school. In junior school, boys were allocated a house faction but resided together for one or two years and then farmed to the senior school houses distant from the main school classrooms. Only the master in junior school and the headmaster, who was not aligned with a house and whose domain was the main school block and administration, were allowed to administer the cane to junior boys. All other caning was by the head boy in each senior house. The houses were named after British heroes: Clive, Scott, Rhodes, Hawke, Grigg (first governor of Kenya Colony), and Nicholson (founding headmaster). Each house had a hundred boys, six prefects, and a head boy. Prefects ran the house; they could smoke, administered noncorporal punishments, and reported those misdemeanours that drew corporal punishment.

The reports that carried the penalty of corporal punishment were taken to the resident housemaster, who would adjudicate and mete out the punishment and the number of strokes. The caning was done in the boot-room by the head boy, with a prefect witness. The maximum number of strokes allowed was six, hence the term "six of the best." Head-of-house prefects traditionally practised their caning on chalk-dusted leather chairs until they could group their strokes together. The headmaster could give eight and was well practised. The system, which was very British, was harsh.

In the houses, the policing, reporting initiative, and delivery of punishment resided in the hands of the prefects, kept at arm's length from the authority which passed the judgements. Some houses were crueller than others; cultures were a little different in each. It was advisable to avoid main school and being sent out of class to stand on the veranda in disgrace when Jake had been drinking or was in one of his moods. To stand on the veranda outside the classroom door during lesson time was a generally feared punishment because it advertised a beating if he prowled by. The feelings towards Jake were ambivalent. Many loved him and visited him in retirement when he went back to the UK. He retired a couple of years after I started; I had avoided him like the plague and was never subject to his anger. Maybe if I had known him as a senior boy, I would have felt differently.

The Prince of Wales School, being conceived in the mould of an English public school, developed a character that for the most part might best be described as a blend of *Tom Brown's Schooldays* and *The Loneliness of the Long-Distance Runner*. Rules, caning, restricted access in and out, fagging, smoking prefects, and obsession with sport were incongruities nestling in the Garden of Eden with N'gai and Adam. It was the difference that endeared it; the scent and rhythm of Africa were sensed in the nose of the wine of adventure. It was not that the masters did not try to make us into perfect English gentlemen; it was that we were different psychologically. The imported English teachers often remarked that the combination of high altitude and constant daily sun had severely restricted our brain growth. This opinion of us served to re-enforce our conviction that we may be British colonials, but we were not English. This was an important lesson to prepare us for the forthcoming storm driven by the wind of change that would scatter me and my school friends to all the corners of the world.

Psychology was coming into vogue, and my housemaster gave me a book on Jung and Adler. A team of research psychologists from the UK came and gave the senior school boys an IQ test. Two weeks later, we had to repeat the test. It was confirmed: We were all morons. The average intelligent quotient should be 100, and a score of over 120 earmarked one for university. Very few of us scored over 80. Below 80 described the mentally impaired. Our headmaster was devastated and ashamed.

The message was don't blame the individual for what is wrong; blame the system, and that held true. The problem was in the test, which derived questions on general knowledge that UK schoolboys should know, but we were not in the UK. The exercise had an effect on the English master, a tall youngish man with a hairstyle shortly to be adopted by the Beatles; he wore drain-pipe trousers. He looked like Oscar Wilde, and I think he secretly cultivated the comparison.

The following is an essay that this despairing English master set me to write. He had not got over my attempts to write on "Man the Destroyer," in which I wrote eagerly about men sailing a warship. "Forget about Charlotte Bronte and Jane Eyre," he said. "Don't worry about Gladstone and Pitt, give Gray and his graves away, let Destry ride again on his own, and don't tell me about Lady Chatterley, about whom you are meant to know nothing. Just go and write something from your heart."

He liked my essay, *a school holiday on the Tana river,* and being the editor of *The Impala,* the annual school magazine, he put it in. This is part of it as published in 1960 when I was sixteen. In that edition are a number of other articles that equally describe my peers. They depict colonial Kenyan boys of the time better than any way I can describe now.

Chapter 4

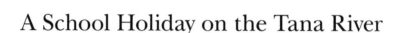

A School Holiday on the Tana River

I spent my last holiday in the Northern Province of Kenya on the Tana River, which is a green line crossing a dusty white desert. In the dry weather, as it is the only source of water, much game inhabits the bordering forests and the dry plains beyond.

One morning while I was fishing for catfish, a young Somali sheep herder told me that a large snake had just killed one of his goats. The Somalis always exaggerate, so I was not easily drawn away from the water's edge.

When I reached the spot, a clearing in the forest, I saw that the goat had been dragged into a thick bush and caught a glimpse of a disappearing python. The Somali, after much persuasion, pulled the dead goat clear and I tied it firmly to a log in the centre of the clearing.

In the afternoon I returned very quietly. I saw the largest python on the Tana, as thick as a tree trunk, draped around the goat. This monster had already swallowed the goat's head and shoulders; its mouth stretched like a large sock. At first I was too amazed to act. I simply stood and stared.

Then I quietly took a few "still" photographs. When I had taken enough, I told the Somali to throw a small piece of wood to make the python move for a cine picture. I shall never forget what happened next. The python reared its head and spat the goat out of its mouth, unwound itself and made off into the bush, its distorted head loose and sagging.

Afterwards the Somali cursed me all the way back to camp for not shooting the killer. He said this snake was a rogue as it had even killed young boys by shooting at them like an arrow and smashing the boys' skulls with its own triangular head. Pythons, however, are protected in that region so I could not have fulfilled his wish. Maybe he killed it when it returned to the dead goat.

The story continued to describe a hunt, but because so much has changed in me and in the world, I could not accept now what was part of my upbringing, such as shooting animals, without a sense of gross wrongdoing. Then, I accepted things for what they were without question. I was being taught what was considered an admired profession, glamorised by Hollywood and such eminent writers as Ernest Hemingway and Robert Ruark. Life was short in the crucible that was the colony. Comparators and politics meant nothing; life was lived or lost in the day. I recently went on a walk on a farm in New Zealand but was unable to bring myself to shoot a wild boar; this measured how much I've changed since I was a boy.

When growing up, one accepts. There is no relativity until the alternatives are encountered. We regard life as easy or hard in retrospect and by comparison. Traveling with my father on school holidays was just normal for me and had been since I was fourteen. It was natural that he would teach me his trade, and I learned how to preserve or take the lives of animals. Humans have the ability to divorce emotions from actions one minute and be governed by them the next, as if switching from one side of the brain to the other. To the English schoolmaster, my home life was very different by comparison to his childhood in England, and he was taken aback by what might be perceived as callousness. I was a little surprised by his interest and very flattered by the mark he gave me for the essay.

It was a turning point for me. I enjoyed the sense of achievement in the writing and was intrigued by the feeling of satisfaction that came from delivering something from the heart. I moved a little away from the physical and more towards the metaphysical. My thoughts and emotions have moved with time. There has been a change in me, and the world, from what might be important to me to what's more important for the animals.

On reflection, our attitudes as teenagers portrayed a basic element of human nature. Our school, the Prince of Wales, would play rugby against Van Riebeecks, an Afrikaaner school. Jan Van Riebeeck was the Dutch founder of Cape Town in the seventeenth century; the Afrikaans community named their school after him. There were some Afrikaaners in our school; I don't recall any animosity until these rugby matches against Van Riebeecks; the sideline venom was far beyond the usual, with fathers and older brothers running along beside shouting, "Kill the bastard," or "Frek 'im," according to the relative vernacular, and we learnt our lesson of tribal loyalty.

It was not the only lesson because we as humans learn to defy the negatives with mischief, love, and humour. Thomson Falls (named after Joseph Thomson, an explorer, known also for Thomson's gazelle) was nearly a hundred miles from Nairobi, and we would be transported, as per all away games, in the school bus. What it lacked in comfort, built like an army truck with a cab and side benches in the canvas-covered tray, it more than made up by serving as a theatre for song, story, and tobacco.

One year, our rugby coach Ten Cents and his son, One Cent, took a select group of us in the tray of his Peugeot pick-up truck (everyone had Peugeots because they always won the East African Safari rally). The local children and hawkers would sell fruit on the side of the road on the way down the escarpment into the Great Rift Valley, where there were parking spots to admire the wonderful view of lakes and volcanoes and mountains.

We took soft fruit with us and lobbed it over the cab onto his windscreen as we passed the hawkers, suppressing our laughter at his misdirected rage inside his cab. He never knew it was us and blamed the totos on the side of the road.

There were many accidents on the escarpment. It was tarmacked, narrow, and winding. People went too fast, and the absence of dust encouraged risky passing, despite the lack of warning for approaching traffic. It had been built by the Italian prisoners of war who also built a beautiful little chapel near the bottom of the road: symbolically and practically, a shrine for lost souls. Fortunately, we did not join them.

One year, the Afrikaaners had a real star with Hollywood matinee idol looks; he was indeed a very handsome fellow and of course played the key position of fly-half. Now, their school was coed, and ours was boys only; we were deficient in the ways of girls. The first time he received the ball, the shrieks of adoration from the girls drowned out the war cries of the bitter men; it would have shamed even the Beatles' fans. Staring open-mouthed at the sideline, we were convinced that someone had indeed been frekked and allowed him free passage to the try line, amidst the screams.

It was an introduction to the dilemma of ascribing loyalties. Van Riebeecks School was most hospitable, and we sometimes stayed overnight. There were similarities as well as clear differences. I started to see the power of language, how much and how quickly language identified someone for classification.

The first time we ate in the dining hall at Van Riebeecks School, where the language was Afrikaans, I felt how different we were because we didn't understand them. Removing the language made us the same. I paid more attention to how people spoke and the reactions of others to differences in speech. It was fascinating. It could not only be used to instantly assign an individual to a group and thereby ascribe numerous assumed valuations, but also place the individual in a social class within the group.

My mother did it all the time when people were from England; she could distinguish their British accents. Second-generation colonials spoke with the same accent, so she needed other measures to classify them. I could understand the differences and alignment of loyalty because the group factor magnified them, but I could not understand the dilemma of when it did not hold true until I worked out that it was because I loved my aunt Chris, who was an Afrikaaner from Eldoret. My relationship with Auntie Chris was personal, and that was the difference. With a strange group, I could depersonalise the members I did not know.

I've always been fascinated by the story of the end of the first year of World War I; on Christmas Day, the Germans appeared with a Christmas tree and candles, and a truce occurred between the troops in the trenches on the front line. They played soccer together. This threatened to derail hostilities, and it became a court-martial offence to fraternise with the enemy. The war-mongers cried out, "In the name of God, thou must not love thy neighbour," and "An eye for an eye." Peaceful people claimed, "Jesus said you should love thy neighbour as you love thyself," and "Do unto others as you would be done by."

Herein is the double message we teach our children (no wonder they screw up from time to time). Not everyone loves themselves, at least not all the time, and what then about loving your neighbour as yourself? When the self-dislike predominates, should we say, "Love thy neighbour as thyself"? I started to question interpretations of religious teachings; suspected religious teachings were another tool for control.

We had to attend religious instruction; most of us were from Protestant Christian families, and although mainly Church of England, it was a nondenominational chapel. The Catholics were excused and did not have to attend chapel in the mornings; they had their own services on Sundays. It was all very confusing, especially the bit about us all being "one Catholic and apostolic church," and we who had to attend, but preferred not to, thought about changing to be Catholic, except we were not sure about the disadvantages in store for Sundays. For a while, I thought they were sent outside for being heathens.

The Ten Commandments seemed a sensible guide to being a good person, except for a couple of worries. The demand for blind faith and subservience to a Supreme Being removed any right to question authority, and something seemed to have been lost in translation when it came to taking the name of God in vain. Interpreted as identifying blasphemous expletives or heretical criticism as sin, we were beaten if we swore using God's name. The alternative message behind the commandment was that it should not be used for the purposes of persuading others to do something on the grounds that it came from the higher being, who must be obeyed.

I thought the latter a better interpretation and one should not invoke a higher authority to justify one's own motive. This did not suit the establishment when they invoked God to justify an action such as declaring war or used the former interpretation to punish or intimidate. My observation was that kings such as Henry VIII and religious tyrants used this for absolute control all the time; it was a top-down rather than bottom-up tool for persuasion, and that was contrary to what we were taught about democracy.

The story of Jesus was appealing because He railed against authority, especially religious hierarchy, and excused wrongdoers, befriending many of them. I especially liked the story of how Matthew, who had climbed up a tree to get a better view, became a disciple. Survival instinct made me realise that to follow his example would lead to conflict with authority. I learned to read between the lines and avoid unnecessary trouble; I followed St Peter's example of denial.

Sport and physical prowess were simpler than politics and social debate. Sport was central to life in boarding school; certain activities were like manhood initiations. One of these was the climbing of Kilimanjaro. The African plateau is about four thousand feet high on average, rifted and divided into blocks by the Great Rift Valley. The valley runs from the Red Sea to Lake Victoria, where it divides into Eastern and Western Rift Valleys and then joins again, having encircled the great lake. Nowhere is the formation as dramatic as it is in passing through Kenya. The rift distorts the plateau, creasing and folding it into wondrous valleys and majestic hills; Ngong Hills is an example.

The earth responded to the slashes and wounds of the rift valleys by spewing forth a chain of volcanoes along the floor of the flaw and between the folds of the mountains. The most magnificent of all volcanoes is Kilimanjaro. Kibo (kiboko meaning a club in Swahili), the picturesque and famous peak, is really a side vent for the original mountain, M'wenzie. According to legend, thunder and lightning began with a contest between young and old. When Kibo grew sufficiently big and strong, he beat down M'wenzie to its lower status. Only a few really know the truth: M'wenzie is the far more dangerous and wily mountain. M'wenzie is the vestigial symbol of the powers that built this beautiful world in preparation for the original humans, who were born here with original sin.

M'wenzie mostly hides in her veil of clouds and still suffers from the terrible beating by Kibo. She is mean and nasty, and people die climbing her. In an arrogant gesture, Queen Victoria gave this mountain to her cousin, Kaiser Wilhelm, for his birthday, when the Germans had the colony of Tanganyika. If you look at the border between Kenya and Tanzania, you will see the little deviation in the otherwise straight line between Kenya and Tanzania to include the peaks of Kilimanjaro into Tanzania. To claim this as true today might precipitate a request from Kenya to have it returned.

The highest point was known as Kaiser Wilhelm Spitz until changed to Uhuru (Freedom) Peak after Tanganyika became independent from Britain. Tanganyika became a mandate of Britain after World War I, when the victors divided the spoils of the German empire. Uganda was a protectorate. Colony, mandate, protectorate; what's in a name? They were as different as taxes are from levies, and until independence, they acted as a federation, with currency and stamps common to all three. Tanganyika became Tanzania when it united with Zanzibar.

The largest crater in the world is that of Ngorongoro, a hundred miles to the west of Kilimanjaro, with its ten-mile inner diameter and game sanctuary; it is the starting point for the age-old long march of the Serengeti migration. At the northern foot of Ngorongoro is Olduvai Gorge, which in 1959 yielded to Mary Leakey "Dear Man," or Zinjanthropus, now known as Australopithecus boisei. We were taught that the name derived from the Arabic *Zinj*, for East Africa, and that the hominid was the missing link between humans and beasts. Our biology teacher was immediately nicknamed "Link."

With this find, Louis Leakey's team was launched into the world spotlight. About the same time, Michael Grzimek, at the age of twenty-two, crashed his zebra-striped research plane into the rim; he died to save the animals. His grave and the mountain look down on the annual pilgrimage of animals as they pass by Olduvai and the stone that marks the spot where Dear Man was found. Michael's father conducted the scientific study into the Serengeti migration that moves with the sun and the rain; the story is told in *The Serengeti Shall Not Die*. Later, when I was guiding safaris, these two shrines always touched my soul as we passed by.

Mount Meru, about fifteen thousand feet high and fifty miles to the south-west of Kilimanjaro, stands over the town of Arusha, which became the base for Stan and Uncle Geoff's company of Lawrence-Brown Safaris (Tanganyika) Limited. The company was set up in Tanganyika during the Mau-Mau era. It was from here that the film *Hatari* was made; soon everybody was humming the theme tune, "The Baby Elephant Walk." Mount Meru was probably the largest volcano of all. She blew her top to the east, and the rocks and boulders spread all the way across Momella Game Reserve to Amboseli Game Reserve at the foothills of Kilimanjaro. Between all the volcanoes are the deep lakes of the rift. Seen as a chain and signified by their distinctive elongated appearance, they contrast to the shallow, more rounded relief formation lakes like Lake Victoria.

At that time, there were two possible pathways to climb Kilimanjaro. The first was with the Outward Bound organisation, supported by Prince Philip with the Duke of Edinburgh Award. This route was up the north-eastern Kenyan side from Loi-Toki-Tok, in one of the Masai regions near the Amboseli Game Reserve. It was organised, supervised, and run on lines similar to mature Scouts. Of course, being averse to even more discipline, I never went this route, although I did later drive and pick up a group from their base camp, adjacent to Amboseli. Instead, I climbed three times from the south-western Tanganyika side from Marangu, home of the Kibo Hotel, named after the main volcano. Marangu was just up the mountain from the town of Moshi (meaning "smoke"). There are a number of smaller volcanoes around Moshi and Arusha.

The first time I climbed was in 1958. I was invited by my friend Roger, who was going to climb with his older brother, John. John was the leader; there were five of us. Preparation followed standard practices amongst the schoolboys. To help the Prince of Wales schoolboys climb the mountain, the hotel owner built a special hut for them in the hotel grounds. It was the POW hut. The hotel was the recognised starting point of the climb and was situated in the rain forest at the base of the mountain at six thousand, five hundred feet. It was a beautiful place with rain forest vegetation, crystal-clear mountain streams, waterfalls, bright red wineberries, parrots, singing birds, and fertile family shambas with bananas, vegetables, chickens, and goats, and with some coffee for cash flow. We gathered at the POW hut and spent a day acclimatising, as was customary. It was not really necessary for us, since our school was at nearly the same altitude. We packed our gear and then enjoyed swims and the berries.

The next morning was most exciting. We met our guide and his younger brother, who was learning his trade. We had never climbed anything before, nor trekked before, and did not think we needed porters, so we were loaded with all our gear and supplies. The equipment was mainly warm ex-army clothing, long canvas army boots, and backpacks. No rock climbing mountain gear was necessary for Kibo, but the backpack needs special mention. It was most uncomfortable and heavy, with a triangular metal frame that put all the weight on our shoulders. Our teenage appetites governed our generous supply of food tins, and our self-belief put too much skip in our start. We started thus weighed down, and all of us without exception also started with a head injury, from the low entrance door of the POW hut.

The first day, we hiked up through the rain forest. We sweated. Our enthusiasm drained, and the temperature rose. Shoulders ached, and blisters grew. It was twelve miles up a wet, muddy, slippery, insect-infested path to the first mountain hut. Bismarck Hut was built of stone and located just above the tree line at ten thousand feet. The huts up the mountain were small and had only enough room for six and needed to be booked, which we did, so we did not expect any other climbers. But when we finally staggered into the hut, we found a man of about fifty years old, accompanied by a guide and two porters, had arrived ahead of us. We were annoyed by this and felt inhibited in language and actions. We were, of course, hungry but disinclined to cook while he was in the way. After introductions, we ignored him and dropped our inhibitions as we recovered. He seemed to accept this and observed us from his corner.

There was a disturbance during night when Roger dreamt of something, called out, and then stepped off his upper bunk onto the gear-laden kitchen table below. We slept in, and by the time we got started the next morning, the man had gone. The second day was easier. It was not so steep and cooler, with open heath country and spectacular views, frequent rests, and lovely streams beside which we snacked. I still have a fondness for raisin biscuits.

The second hut at twelve thousand feet was called Peter's Hut, after a German explorer. It was built from corrugated iron, cold and draughty, and we were reminded of our physics and the lowered boiling point of water at altitude. Altitude sickness can start at this level, but again, we were used to it and felt good. The next day, we climbed onto the saddle between M'wenzie and Kibo. The track reaches the saddle just below the killer peak M'wenzie, who squinted evilly at us between her cloud veils and gave eeriness to the bare high saddle, with views for hundreds of miles north and south. Kibo stood across the saddle above the clouds in front of us, with Kibo Hut at its base at about fifteen thousand feet. The feeling was wonderful, and the joy was completed by the gentle saddle inclining slightly downward before easing up to Kibo Hut.

The guide prepared us for the next day, explaining that the final ascent started at two o'clock in the morning. We went to bed early. Getting up at four was okay, but two o'clock was associated with the fog of sleepiness of teenagers and the clinging fog on the mountain. The guide led with a small lantern, which he held backwards to light the path, and we trudged to a cave. There we rested for a brief period and ate chocolate and then attacked the scree. It was every man to himself on the steep incline of loose lava rock and gravel, two lurches up to one slide down. There was an irresistible desire to sleep at every rest, but our guide was equally persistent, warning that sleep could be death, and we struggled on.

None of us gave up, and as the dawn rose over the cloudless snow-rimmed peak, we reached the top at Gilman's Point and looked into the highest crater on earth. Ice steps to the right and a rocky rim to the left around to Kaiser Wilhelm Spitz Point. There was Lot's Wife, an ice mound at the bottom, so named as she was said to change size but never her shape, and yellow sulphur deposits staining the ground near her. It was an amazing feeling. Nearly twenty thousand feet in a pink crystal dawn, with a new moon and fading stars and a bar of chocolate.

It took three days up but only two down. After the ascent, we went on down to Peter's and then Bismarck again. At Bismarck, the guide and his brother presented us with garlands of everlasting flowers that grew in the heather, according to the custom for those who made it to the top. The man we had met at the hut was there again; he was our friend now, as we loved the whole world. We chatted on our way back to the hotel, and he invited us to dinner. We had a bath before eating; I've never enjoyed a bath like that. Dirt peeled off. The bath water was clear, not the grey water of the communal school baths, where ten boys shared one bath with the same water. Clean and clear-eyed, we dined like men; our new friend popped champagne corks, and we felt very good. We vowed to keep everlasting contact, and he gave us his address in London. We were perplexed, as it was a street address without a post box number. I had never seen a postal address without a box number and wondered if maybe he didn't want to keep in touch; he was a little secretive about what he did.

A few months later, a book was being passed around the dormitory at school, as was the custom (*Lady Chatterley's Lover* had done the same round). This book was by Ian Fleming, an author new to us. It was *Casino Royale*, the first James Bond novel. The book had started with Roger's brother.

"Look at the picture of the author on the back cover," said Roger.

It was the man from Kilimanjaro. Ian Fleming must have spent time in Africa as he wrote his factual book *The Diamond Smugglers*, published in 1957, the year before *Casino Royale* came out. I think he took the opportunity to climb Kilimanjaro. We dreamed of free books or something special from our friend and vowed to write to him. It never happened; we had lost his address, and nobody at school believed us. I've never confirmed that Ian Fleming climbed Kilimanjaro; it may be a case of mistaken identity, but I believe that we had spent time alone and drank champagne with the author who was to entertain hundreds of millions of cinemagoers and readers with his James Bond spy stories.

We really should have written as the power of a letter was vividly demonstrated a couple of years later. Lex, an extroverted and amiable member of my house, Rhodes, wrote to an American magazine, asking if anyone wanted to be his pen pal. He gave a brief story of where he lived and posted a photo. Lex was a tall, dark, and handsome Greek. I don't know what he said in the letter, but the school post room was swamped with mail of many colours and wonderful scents. Pictures of American girls adorned the walls of the common room, and rosters were drawn up to carry the mail up the hill from the main school to the house. I know that far fewer letters went the other way.

I climbed Kilimanjaro again two years later, this time with a different group of school friends and another cousin, Derek. In this group, there were two Ians. One Ian was as stocky and as strong as a bull, Ian Henderson; the other Ian was the son of a dairy farmer, Ian MeEwen. There was also Keith McAdam, the son of a professor of surgery in Makere University in Kampala and a model school pupil and sportsman. My uncle John was horrified that we were planning to hitch-hike from Nairobi to

Moshi; he got together with Ian's father from Lengeny Dairies, arranging that he would lend his Volkswagen kombi van if the dairy would supply a driver. The kombi van was left safely at Kibo Hotel while we joined with the original guide's younger brother, who had graduated to full guide status, and climbed the mountain. It was easier for me because of the previous experience, and I was older and stronger. We took a new road that had been put through the forest to Bismarck Hut, and having better gear helped. It was harder on the others because we went faster, especially the first leg, where we got a lift up the road and dispensed with the acclimatising day at the bottom. Mountain sickness took its toll.

Bull Ian insisted nobody use his ex-army pannikin, as he didn't want our germs; he knew which was his because it was the only one with numbers imprinted on the bottom. Dairy Ian was irritated by Keith's beautifully correct speech, and they clashed, in the vernacular. At Kibo Hut, nausea and headache struck Keith, who vomited, politely, into a pannikin with numbers on the bottom. His well-worded apology to the horrified Bull Ian irritated Dairy Ian to the extent that he tried to pull Keith's balaclava hood, which he had borrowed from me, off his head, stretching it beyond repair. None of this helped Derek, who was almost incapacitated by mountain sickness. The garland ceremony soothed some feathers, but it was not the same feeling as the first time.

The hotel return was indeed very different. We were greeted by the owner, a short dumpy German woman who was no longer the sweet kind lady who let the Prince of Wales School boys stay free at the POW Hut. The driver had been running an illegal bus service from Marangu to Moshi every evening, and after drinks, he had pranged the kombi van. He was in jail in Moshi. Uncle John arrived and wanted retribution. The Lengeny Dairy farmer wanted his driver back and wished Uncle John had never interfered. The proprietor accused us of bringing a Kikuyu Mau-Mau to terrorise her staff.

It was all too much for Keith, who abandoned all his correctness and laughed, in a rare moment of inappropriateness. To Dairy Ian's delight, the proprietor focused all her anger on Keith and chased after him with a broom. Uncle John drove us back to Nairobi in silence in his reshaped kombi, leaving the dairy farmer with his son to negotiate the release of his driver.

That year, the head schoolboy, Tony Levy, fell while climbing Mount Kenya and died. Mount Kenya was dangerous, like M'wenzie. I climbed Kilimanjaro once more, in my final year at school. I had a Land Rover and drove up to Bismarck Hut. We had fun and, in an act of bravado, smoked a cigarette on the top of the mountain, but it was not a remarkable time. We descended in one day, literally running down the mountain to pile into the Land Rover, waiting at the first hut. I was cured of wanting to climb mountains. There was a message waiting for me at Kibo Hotel. My father had had a heart attack in Mombasa. I drove all night from Moshi to Mombasa. He was okay, in better state than me by the time I got there, but he always had angina after that. Life became serious.

In 1961, I learned to consider others more and myself less. It was a chilling year. In 1960, King Leopold of Belgium had granted independence to the Belgian Congo. Patrice Lumumba, who led the independence movement and was the first prime minister of the Republic of Congo, was deposed by a military coup, and the Congo crisis ensued, with the subsequent assassination of Lumumba. Belgian refugees flooded across to Uganda, which they passed through en route to Kenya. Our school was closed and turned into a refugee camp. Some of us were sitting overseas exams, and Clive House was set aside for us. The stories of rape and trauma were truly awful and filtered through on the grapevine. It was the rainy season, so the skies were dark, and there was a chill in the high-altitude air. We were not allowed to mix with the refugees, but we could see some of them; they consisted mainly of young girls and nuns.

They were not British and not allowed to stay in Kenya. They were moved on.

My overseas exams that year were not as important as the following year, with the Cambridge Overseas Higher School Certificate (HSC) to come; they were overshadowed by this refugee crisis. By the start of my final year at school, all the refugees had gone. It was like they hadn't been real. Foreign-speaking shadows had passed and were forgotten like bad dreams in the night. No, it was real and could happen to us, even though we survived the Mau-Mau.

Another factor worked to turn my direction. A recurrently dislocating shoulder turned me from the man's game of rugby to tennis. My tennis coach, Alan Potter, was Scottish. He was sensitive and thoughtful and versed in finer things, such as literature and philosophy, as many Scots are. I was never very good at tennis and attributed this to my shoulder that sometimes spectacularly dislocated at the top of the serving action, crumpling me into a writhing, distorted heap. In reality, I lacked talent and regarded tennis as a girls' game. I did amuse spectators with my spectacular dislocations and made good friends with Alan. He added dimensions of mental and physical freedom.

The confines of the boarding school were hard to take at the age of seventeen turning eighteen; other friends had left for the joys of work, pay, motorbikes, cars, and girls. Such were the just rewards of doing less well in exams and leaving school. I, for my sin of passing exams, was still confined to boarding school. Alan would take me to the local sports club for practice, and over beers, we made arrangements for me to park my Land Rover in his garden within the school compound (the legal age to drive was eighteen in Kenya and seventeen in Tanganyika). Stan taught me to drive at fourteen, and a friendly policeman in Arusha had been persuaded to license me at sixteen; the licence served in Kenya until I was of age. The Land Rover meant that we could disappear on short safaris at long weekends and religious holidays, such as Easter, when we were granted leave by the school to go home. There were three of us who would inform the school of a fictitious family destination and then head for the bush, with Alan in tow. I knew much of the country well, having spent most school holidays with Stan. Alan considered this a fair exchange; the group would meet at his place on Friday evenings to cook curries and plan the next adventure.

CHAPTER 5

Leaving School and Time in the UK

In our final year at school, apart from one more memorable trip to the Mara River, where Stan had lived with the Masai for a while as a young man and blazed trails in the Marijo Hills, Roger and I curtailed our adventures to study for the Cambridge Overseas Higher School Certificate. After the exams were over, we took a special trip into Uganda.

We took Alan and Lex and crossed to the western Kigezi Highlands; we went back through Queen Elizabeth and Murchison Falls parks, and then across Lake Kioga and back to Kenya via Tororo, where my grandfather was buried. I knew Uganda reasonably well. It was different from Tanganyika and Kenya. It was wetter, more tropical, and in the north, along the Nile, uncomfortably hot and humid. In the Kigezi Highlands, overlooking the Virunga volcanoes and the Ruwenzori mountains (which Herodotus called the Mountains of the Moon), it poured with rain.

Our custom was to string a tarpaulin from the Land Rover to the ground or a convenient tree and sleep under the awning. Near the Queen Elizabeth National Game Park, Lex worried about the lions that could be heard calling in the night: "Whooooose country's this … Whooooose country's this? Mine! Mine! Mine!" The lions had been clearly visible during the day, as they climb trees in that area. The five of us were sleeping in line, with our heads towards the vehicle. The rain was heavy, and the awning sagged. As it sagged, it filled more, but the ropes were strong. When about forty gallons had accumulated, the canvas split straight down the middle over the sleeping Lex in the centre, who had wanted to be as far away as possible from the first lion that might make a call.

At Murchison Falls, we stayed in the campground near Paara Lodge; we watched crocodiles and hippos in the river below the falls before wandering up to the top to feel the thunder of the White Nile as it roared through the narrow gap. A dead hippo floated below. It had gone over the falls, and its legs were pushed into its body so it looked like a sausage. That night Lex, not trusting any awning, slept under the vehicle. It rained so hard that a river formed in the wheel tracks and broke its banks over Lex. He woke with a start and smashed his head on the underside of the vehicle.

We spent the next night by the road as it passed through Lake Kioga. The mosquitoes were as thick as a sand storm, but the only one of us with a mosquito net was Alan. The rest of us slept buried under blankets, known as a Dutch oven. In Lake Kioga, it was almost unbearable in the heated fart-filled atmosphere, and when briefly emerging to gasp for cooler air, we filled our mouths with mosquitoes. Lake Kioga was treeless, with an earthen causeway built across it. Alas for Alan, he could not hang his net and taunt our jealous natures with mosquito net comfort. Unperturbed, he wrapped himself in his net and slept while the mosquitoes feasted through the holes. The following morning, he looked like he had measles; he must have been on anti-malarial meds because he survived without getting a fever.

Lex, who lived near Lake Victoria, had had enough and called for alternative transport to take him home from Soroti. My grandfather had died in Soroti, and it was a poignant parting, as we knew we may never see each other again. I was expecting to go to England and St Thomas, and Lex to Greece.

I left school at the end of 1962 and was called up for national service, which was due to start in July 1963 with the Kenya Regiment, if I was not successful with medical school. Four years as a cadet and army camps had prepared us well for the army, although I had already developed a dislike as I tended to fall foul of the blind discipline. I was spared national service in that year of independence; the Kenya Regiment was to be disbanded, and I looked forward to going to England and studying medicine.

There are days in our lives that stick in our memories, with vivid recall for a particular moment; time stands still. Some events are common to us all and evoke a mass expression of emotion, like the bombing of the World Trade Centre in New York, the death of Princess Diana, and the assassination of John Kennedy. Some events are shared amongst a close-knit few, like the loss of a parent, and some are only for us. Not all are tragic, but each is unique. For males, the first production of sperm is such a moment, and for girls, maybe it's menarche, heralding the first egg, and for both, it is the loss of virginity.

We are changed by that moment, and it sets off a chain of events we negotiate and call life experiences. That moment affects our lives and alters how we react to circumstance and other people. We may empathise and harmonise with others as a result or fall into misunderstanding and disarray when there is a void disconnect. Sex is but one such current in the river; education is another, and each indelible event is rooted in a base emotion. Failure can be emotionally taxing in memorable ways; the standstill moment for me was the news of failure.

I had never failed an examination at school, and despite not being a very good student, I had surprised everyone (including myself) with exam results along the way. I was set to go to St Thomas Medical School in London, provided I passed the Cambridge Overseas Higher School Certificate A levels in physics, mathematics, chemistry, and biology. No credits or distinctions were required for acceptance, a concession for the colony, perhaps. We sat in December. In January, a close friend and classmate drove up to the house and slowly told me that he had seen the posted results: I had failed to qualify for entrance to university. It was one of those moments; I remember exactly where I was standing when he broke the news to me.

I reflected on my school days. I had not always been a good student, more interested in sport and adventure, but it was a good time. I had liked to sit at the back of the class, where there was more fun, schoolboy humour, and alternative interests. A degree of undiagnosed astigmatism made it harder to read the blackboard from that distance, and in the beginning, there was little expectation of me academically. Movement to the front row, for disciplinary reasons, improved my marks because I could see better; it also gave me opportunity to pass red herrings across the master's radar screen. Hooked on the red-herring bait, they would engage in stories and anecdotes of real-life topics instead of Latin, French, date-ridden English history, or the detailed geography of the Cotswolds and Rhine Valley. The Latin master, Teddy Boase, could be drawn into describing Caesar's battle strategies and would animatedly arrange the classroom into a battlefield to illustrate, only to discover at the end of the lesson that we had learnt no vocabulary, and the only thing declined was the discipline. Local matters about dhows, the slave trade, explorers, the building of the railway, and the diversity of the fauna of our wonderful birthplace held us fascinated.

One tall maths teacher was so prone to charging off into anecdotes of adventure that he was nicknamed the Galloping Tapeworm. The stories and topics we craved were not the priority for the curriculum organisers in Cambridge, who set the exams for the colonies. Ours was a single-sex school; female teachers were rare, and male teachers were probably as prone to distraction as their students. The girls from the Kenya Girls High School always did much better at the overseas high school examinations; I am sure it was the same then as it is now, with boys and girls at school.

The saving grace had been the rapport derived from sport, and it continued to keep my faith in education alive. I had taken it all for granted and never learnt to deal with failure. Now with East Africa gaining independence from Britain, we were no longer favoured sons. Should I make my life in tourism and continue training with Stan to be a professional safari guide? That's what he wanted. Ronnie, however, pushed for the security and opportunities of education and encouraged me to try again.

Very soon after learning of our failures, Roger decided to try his luck in the UK and joined his brother John in a flat in London, where he applied to join the Royal Air Force. A year later, he was ensconced in London. Keith McAdam, another school friend and classmate in biology, with whom I had climbed Kilimanjaro, had also wanted to be a doctor and follow in his father's footsteps. He was a brilliant student and enrolled in an elite school in the UK, pushed through with a good High School A Level Certificate in six months, and was admitted to Cambridge to study medicine. He eventually became an immunologist and professor in the London School of Tropical Medicine.

Like them, I had to try again, and so for me, it was back to my alma mater: the Limuru Girls School and the biology mistress who had never had a student fail A level biology. She was sure she could coach me through and redeem my chances of becoming a doctor. After all, nobody had passed A level biology in the previous three years at the Prince of Wales, and so the failure could not have been my fault. Ah, alas, sweet lady, real biology took over, and I fell for Fiona, who lived on the neighbouring tea estate. My heart was in the wrong place, and I failed on both accounts.

To everyone's surprise, I had performed as well as Keith in our Higher School Certificate, but it was not good enough for St Thomas. I thought if Keith could do it, then so could I. Armed with my special tuition from Limuru Girls School, I applied to re-sit biology in the UK and duly arranged a flight with East African Airways in the new Comet jet aircraft (before the wings started to fall off). Roger had agreed to let me stay with him in London while I sat the exam, waited for the results, and applied for higher education. Therefore, off to England to try the direct approach.

On the flight over, I sat next to Liz, an airline hostess who worked for BOAC and was returning home after a holiday in Kenya. She was good company; we smoked and chatted for some time (imagine smoking on a plane today). She quickly ascertained that I was new to London and offered to help me find Roger's flat when we got to the city. Our elderly white bus driver tried to lift my suitcase into the luggage-well of the airport bus, and Liz smiled when I tried to help him. She understood that seeing a white bus driver would have been unusual for me. The bus driver was annoyed that I got in his way, and I was introduced to a world that was very different.

More surprises were in store for an early riser. It was a Sunday, and we arrived at the flat in Bayswater mid-morning. The English apparently slept until midday on Sundays; the doorbell of the basement flat was answered by an irritated, bleary-eyed, pyjama-suited stranger, who turned on his heel and yelled for Roger. There were three bedrooms, a lounge, kitchen, and bathroom and at least ten people of both genders. If I had been embarrassed by the bus driver, I was even more so now with Liz accompanying me, in that I should have brought her to such a den of iniquity. Liz was completely unfazed, and after a cup of tea, she left me, comfortable in her knowledge that I was in safe and normal hands.

The flat in Bayswater was just around from Lancaster Gate Underground station, Hyde Park, and Kensington Gardens. It was spring, with flowers in the park and people lying on the grass petting, spruiking from a soapbox in Hyde Park corner, and boating on the Serpentine. I was wide-eyed and fascinated by historical monuments and the reality of being immersed in what I had learned in school about the home country.

I was like Dick Whittington and soon, like him, learnt that the streets were not lined with gold. I could not get over the cold and damp, the rubbish, the underground dwellings, and the trains. The air was filled with soot, and the buildings were mostly black. The air was so soot-laden that no one bought shirts with collars. They bought one shirt and many collars that could be attached. That way, blackened collars could be washed out and changed every day without changing the shirt. Bathing was infrequent and at a premium, and this added to the pervasion of grime. The girls wore so much make-up that they looked like clowns, and the dresses were so short, I didn't know where to look. It was, however, the sixties, and music was everywhere, especially in Soho. Roger proudly showed me around Soho; with his arm around his girlfriend, he bantered with the girls on the sidewalk with remarks such as, "I'm okay, I have my own."

Basement flats, underground railways, sooty collars, being called a poofter because I wore shorts in the pub after going to the park, the call girls in Soho, and the crowded flat made it impossible to contemplate study. After sightseeing and introductions, it was decided that Roger and I would move into a flat of our own. John, Roger's older brother, was one of the legitimate flat dwellers and thought it was a good idea too because his girlfriend had been spending too much time showing me the sights of London; in the cramped setting, that could have led to trouble.

We found a flat in Earls Court near the Overseas Club and around from Exhibition Hall. Another school friend, Guy Riegels, joined us. School friends popped up in many unexpected places, seeking and seeing the home of the Empire. I approached a policeman in Trafalgar Square to ask for directions and was surprised when he turned around to reveal another school friend. In reality, there were not that many East Africans compared with the number of Australians and South Africans. Earls Court was home to the Overseas Club of Australians and South Africans. They filled every available space and spawned a culture depicted by *The Adventures of Barry Mackenzie* and sustained by his compatriots, Dame Edna and Sir Les Patterson.

While I settled down to study, Roger and Guy set off each day in their false starched collars to work as clerks somewhere in the city for ten pounds a week. I became domesticated and started to cook and go to the local laundromat. That prompted the other two to get me to do their washing; I didn't mind sitting in the warm laundromat, reading biology amongst a group of women.

It was customary for Kenyan schoolboys to sleep in a kikoi, a cloth like a sarong that wraps around the waist and hangs down to the feet. First, one had to overcome the challenge of keeping them on, but after that, they are comfortable and convenient. They can also be very attractive, with blended colours and patterns. I had a lovely mauve one. One day, I put too many clothes in a machine because of limited finances and oversupply of washing. They came out tie-dyed in streaky mauve with beautiful variegated patterns, especially Guy's and Roger's long-sleeved cotton business shirts. Their reaction was ungrateful, and I learned that it's just not worth trying to help some people.

Then I met Ginny at Habari, a club formed by a group of ex-East Africans (*Habari* is Swahili for "How are you?"). Like the Overseas Club, I did not really take to it. Yes, the culture was familiar, but people one knew vaguely (or did not even like you before) in Nairobi would greet you as long-lost friends.

Ginny was English and had come with a friend. We liked each other; she liked rugby, and her brother was a member of the Richmond Ruby Club. We went to matches at Twickenham, walks in Richmond Park, and dances at the Richmond Club. Ginny was good for me, had access to a car (an Austin Princess, no less; her father was important in the Royal Automobile Club), and brought out the best that London could give. I'm not sure I was good enough for Ginny, but I could have stayed for her. As it turned out, I failed the exams—again—and ran out of money.

Should I stay in a poverty trap in London or take up my dad's offer to go back and work with him, as before? There was no real choice, and I flew back to be greeted by Stan at the airport with "My God! You look as white as a sheet; are you all right?"

CHAPTER 6

Safari Life

Returning to work for Stan was like sliding a cartridge into the breach, and this time, it was for real, unlike school holidays that were more like work-experience. The prospects for the future rose like the morning sun, and warmth flowed back into my body and soul after the cold and damp of England. The chore of trying further studies evaporated like the dew. The company was based in Arusha, in the foothills of Mount Meru and the shadow of Kilimanjaro. Stan had moved the business from Kenya during the Mau-Mau years and teamed with his brother Geoff, Jacky Hammond, and George Six. Geoff eventually gave up hunting to head the wildlife and conservation efforts of the Tanzania government.

Jacky lost his life to a shotgun accident; the antique gun fell out of his Land Rover, and the hammers cocked on the running board and discharged as he caught it and lifted it back into the vehicle, with the barrels pointing at his head. George Six emigrated from Tanzania, and Stan was left with the company. Stan had a number of professional guides based in Kenya, but only Royce, who married Jacky's widow and had grown up near Arusha, lived in Tanzania. Royce and I were closer in age and temperament, and it was natural for us to become good friends. My time with Stan while growing up counted for something towards my training, and I was granted a restricted professional safari guide's licence in Tanzania. Stan was happy and saw a succession line to his business. After returning from England, I guided safaris from this picturesque town for two wonderful years.

Having grown up in emergency times, I ignored the politics and changes around me, which seemed irrelevant in a world seen from inside the bubble of biodiversity; that was life on safari.

Our day started at four in the morning and turned off to the howls of the hyenas and grunts of the lions at nine in the evening, as the signature tune for the news started. News time was traditionally bedtime on safari. It dated back to before two-way safari radio, when urgent communications were relayed by the Kenya Broadcasting Corporation, which would announce safari messages after *The Nine O'Clock News:* "A message to Stan Lawrence-Brown on safari ..."

After that, there was no need to stay awake, and the outside world eddied by unnoticed. Maybe the internal hormonal turmoil and the intensity of life in the bush left no room for external affairs, maybe I didn't want to hear or understand the firelight discussions with the Africans, or maybe I had learned to just accept that colonials lived beyond the halls of power.

United economically under British rule with the same currency, postage, laws, and freedom of movement between each state, it had been easy to travel and work in the three countries of Kenya, Uganda, and Tanganyika. Uganda was granted independence from Britain in 1961 and Tanganyika in 1962, but the freedom to travel between the three continued. Tanganyika was not a colony. It was a mandate of the League of Nations incorporated after World War I into East Africa under the British, together with the colony of Kenya, formerly British East Africa, and the Protectorate of Uganda.

Although sparsely populated by Europeans, the architecture in Tanzania (Tanganyika) had a lasting German quality. Swahili, the utility language derived from Arabic and the coastal Swahili people, reached into this land, marking the trade routes with the stain of the slave trade. Mango trees lined the routes as far inland as Lake Tanganyika, and we bought fresh local dates in Mpanda, western Tanzania. The elephants ate the mangos and spread the seeds in fertilised packages. Livingston haunts the shores of Lake Tanganyika, the land of hope and horror. Is humour a refuge? Are poverty and desperation a piety? Is that why the Tanzanians have such a wonderful sense of humour, a sense of dignity, a pride of spirit? They formed the backbone of the King's African Rifles, as the story was told to me by the British recruiting officer, who spoke Swahili to me forty years later in my consulting room in Perth. The songs of the safari crews conveyed it, and the liberation of Uganda after Idi Amin proved it. Their ethic is exhibited in the quality of their Swahili, and we probably owe them most for this utility language. For me, it is special and meaningful because I lived there in a formative time, and I vividly recall the day it turned from Tanganyika to Tanzania.

In the lead-up to the change to Tanzania, there was an interval between safaris, and I arranged to do a job that had been pending and had a distasteful element. Baboons were classified as vermin on farms because they loved to raid the maize plantations, and they were often culled as a form of game control. Having been offered a contract to supply baboon brains to a Texas university, I set out with Kip, an old school friend, who had been working with Carr Hartley, a famous game trapper, and was good value in the bush. The task was to clear the maize farm and supply baboon brains to the university in jars of formalin for the purpose of comparing them with human brains. I had been spared the personal experience of war so far in my life, and this experience was void of the fear and anger that soldiers presumably feel, but it was awful. We encountered a troop of baboons in a ravine, feeding on the maize.

To escape us, they had to climb out the other side and were clearly visible at about two hundred meters. You know when you've hit a target because the bang of the rifle is followed by the thud of the bullet. Professionals use accurate single-shot rifles with magazines, making every bullet count. I had only ever killed for food or necessity when guiding and had never shot in quantity for game clearance or at primates; most primates were protected in the wild, and being of the same family, it felt inherently wrong. The experience drove home a profound sense of wrongdoing and thoughts about the extremes of human behaviour, with constructive compassion at one end and destructive annihilation at the other. How effortlessly we descend from one to the other, and how readily we send the young of one country to kill the young of another.

It was this experience more than any other that influenced me to continue my ambition to be a doctor. The desire was necessarily incentive but insufficient in means, and for the time being, there was no practical alternative to a safari guide.

If the killing had been repeated, I am sure that my human brain would have found a rationalised defence, and I guess I would have hardened and killed thereafter, ruthlessly, with lessening qualms. Fortunately, the trend to desensitisation was broken during the retrieval. While driving into the ravine, we needed the brakes from time to time, despite the low-range four-wheel-drive of the Land Rover. The master cylinder in the brake system failed, and we were unable to repair it, so we turned back to Arusha. Around dusk, we hit the tarmac thirty miles from town and sped up on the smooth surface, with thoughts of home comforts. There was little traffic on those roads, and usually lots of warning came from any approaching vehicle because of dust by day and headlights glare at night. We had tightened the hand brake cable before leaving, and the habitual notion that the road was ours dispelled any concern about having no brakes. But on rounding a corner in the twilight, we faced a roadblock of military and police. Kip was driving and smashed his way down through the gears as I hauled on the hand brake, which twanged like a guitar string. We stopped inches from the raised rifles.

Tanganyika had just become Tanzania. The army in Zanzibar had mutinied, and an estimated ten thousand Arabs had been driven into the sea by Africans fired by a desire to seek vengeance for their ancestors being sold into slavery through the slave market of the East African island capital. The Tanganyika government in Dar es Salaam had set up roadblocks across the country for fear of the army mutiny spreading and precipitating a military coup. They never knew we had no brakes, and we, being of European descent, were not seen as a threat. We were allowed to pass, with our racing pulses (and lack of brakes) unnoticed by the police.

In southern Tanzania, the rainy seasons converge into one long wet season, like the top end of Australia. Professional safaris didn't travel there in the wet, and it was a good time to explore the country in preparation for the next season, but there was a risk of being rained in for days. When I was twenty years old I spent such a rainy season in the miombo-treed savannah and bamboo forests near Lake Tanganyika. It bucketed for three weeks, and Royce and I were confined to the tent. An interesting experience; we would sleep for hours, only moving to pass water of our own. Even eating seemed too much trouble, as we hibernated to the siren call of Radio Lorenzo Marques, which was the only obtainable radio station. It played popular English songs all day; we never heard a word of Portuguese.

Then one day, the sun came out briefly, and we emerged like weak kittens to go hunting in search of food. The rain brought everything with it. The strong smell of rain in the air and the wind moving the leaves heralded the coming of another downpour. Animals skipped in anticipation and then turned their backs to its pelting force. Fertility lustily thrust itself forward with a multitude of reproductive forms. The locusts swarmed, and the flying ants and sausage ants zigzagged across every space, filling every hollow and recess. Collected and fried, they served as hors d'oeuvres to the African gourmets but were a nuisance to the unfamiliar, as their conglomerated egg- and sperm-laden bodies blocked pipes and choked the kerosene lamps.

Ephemerals and new grasses transformed dust bowls to gardens overnight, and plagues of army worm caterpillars marched across the land to the beat of the rain. The black-red safari ants emerged from swarming crater-like nests, replicating the Serengeti migration out of Ngorongoro Crater in miniature, to form their never-ending, tightly packed columns of bearer worker ants and slave ants streaming between sentinel soldiers. The soldiers had powerful nippers and were ready to swarm over any creature daring to disrupt their convoys and inject intruders with stinging formic acid. My first impression of a mature woman's pubic hair was that it looked like a nest of safari ants (and it stirred within me an excitement akin to the coming of the rains).

Southern Tanzania between Mpanda and Lake Tanganyika must have been part of the Garden of Eden. There was an abundance of wild fruit, like none other I've ever tasted, some with a flavour suggestive of the filling in a cream biscuit and another like stewed plums, but all a little astringent, like a fresh date. Honey was to be found in most hollow trees; many of the trees dangled honey-collectors' hives that hung like small drums. The lure of honey was irresistible.

This particular trip was an off-season personal safari to explore the area in preparation for a professional safari and to get away from the towns that would swallow our savings. That was a gamble because a vehicle breakdown or injury could be expensive, but we never seemed to consider those possibilities.

The elephants in this area had the reputation for having the heaviest and largest tusks, and we hoped to see some. It was customary to avoid all rifle fire if possible, even for the pot, for fear of scaring the elephant from the area, and therefore the honey had an added attraction.

There were five of us altogether. Royce, a fellow European, worked for Stan. N'Dwai, a gun-bearer and Royce's soulmate, was Wa N'drobo, an outcast band derived from the Masai because they had adopted hunting and eating game meat. Saidi was a safari truck driver; he could rev the ex-British Army seven-tonne Bedford RL 4X4 trucks higher than anyone else could without driving the pistons through the head; he ploughed through impassable sand and mud trails with imperial style. And Makou, an older safari statesman and gun-bearer with a sad soulful face whose failing eyes and legs were compensated for by a wealth of knowledge and experience. Makou was of the Kenyan Kamba people and had served with the King's African Rifles in Burma. He loved to sing and taught us all the lyrical, mournfully stirring Swahili songs of the homesick African troops.

World War II continued against Japan after Germany surrendered. Just before Germany gave up, Prime Minister John Curtin withdrew Australian troops from Europe to justifiably focus on national defence. Churchill, even with the history of Singapore, still asked the Australians to call into Burma and was so intent on defeating Germany, he seemed oblivious of the strength of the Japanese.

In any case, Churchill failed to persuade the Australians to enter Burma, and so there was another recruitment drive for troops from East Africa. The Burma campaign was brutal, as you can imagine from the stories of prisoners on the railway. That campaign was won by African and Indian troops with British officers, before the atom bomb was dropped, and Japan was essentially defeated in Asia by the colonial empire.

If you haven't heard that story, I'm not surprised. It was fought by what is now known as the Forgotten Army, composed of mainly Indian divisions from before the partition of India and so includes Pakistanis, Nepalese Gurkhas, West Africans from Ghana and Nigeria, and the 11th East African Division. The 11th East African Division was specially formed by recruitment drives through Kenya, Uganda, Tanganyika, Somalia, and remnants of those who went through North Africa to Palestine, which included my dad, who was a gunner and fought with the Nigerian Light Battery. It is said that there were almost a million men in that army.

I knew many veterans of the King's African Rifles in Kenya and Tanzania; I loved their working pull-together chants of "Harambe ... Heh! Harambe ... Heh." They would sing their mournful war songs with the descant in the evenings around the campfire. "Harambe" became President Kenyatta's catchphrase for Kenya's independence and "Funga Safari" the song of the King's African Rifles and safari crews.

While we all had a taste for the honey, Makou had a passion for wild honey scented with woodsmoke. The wooded scent lingered from the smoke used to quieten the aggressive African honeybees before raiding the wild hives. On this occasion, led by the call of the little honey-guide bird and N'Dwai, we found a wild hive in an old hollow tree. Bees could be seen entering and leaving via two main entrances: one a few feet from the bottom and the second from the chimney at the top. For some reason, the smoke introduced through the lower hole would not flow out properly through the top, probably because of a side hole halfway up. Hence, the bees at the top were irritated and active.

It's amazing how quickly smoke affects the bees, but it must be adequate in concentration, and this was inadequate at the top. We were aware of this, and so the plan was to smoke the bottom as much as possible without setting fire to the old chimney tree, which was dripping with honey inside, chop the tree down, race around to the top, stuff the smoking grass into the top hole, and then harvest the honey. We could stand the odd sting. Saidi was in charge of the smoke, while N'Dwai chopped the tree down. It broke and splintered into many pieces as it hit the ground, confusing Saidi, who had raced to be first to the top end of the toppled tree, ahead of the rest of us smoke bearers. The rattled, disturbed, ousted, and alert bees were turbulently angry. Then they amassed into a storm swarm and descended upon Saidi and N'Dwai, who took off racing downhill in single file: where N'Dwai went, Saidi followed in faith. It was blind faith, faith born of habit of single file through the African bush, and faith because N'Dwai was a true bushman and must know an escape. N'Dwai found his escape. He suddenly dropped flat, leaving Saidi amidst a cloud of angry bees as the sole decoy heading for the sanctity of the river. The momentum carried the swarm straight over N'Dwai, who then took a different path to the river. He, and eventually Saidi, joined the rest of us hiding underwater until it was safe. None of us escaped unscathed.

Knowing what I know now, it's a wonder we all survived, especially Saidi. Thank God no one was allergic to bee stings. Saidi had a huge dense black beard, befitting his imperial nature, and it turned white with the stings; that may be what saved him. Only our hands and faces were ever exposed to the full ravages of sun and insects; the rest of the body was protected by clothes. Although we were still hungry, none of us could eat for the swelling of our hands, faces, and tongues, and the pain of jaw movement was excruciating.

Our diet was supplemented by mushrooms, which were huge and abundant. The largest we found would have been sixty centimetres across. It was as tough as meat and made a good stew. That's not a fishing story, but the catfish in the area were also the largest I've ever seen.

There are a number of species of catfish. The catfish is especially adapted to this part of Africa and is able to survive the dry seasons by burying itself in the mud and hibernating. Like the American catfish, some species were fun to catch and good to eat. They were also an addition to the smorgasbord provided by the African bush. After the rainy seasons, the professional safaris, as opposed to the personal, would roll in and visit sites known from previous trips and knowledge passed on by others, or discovered during the exploratory off-season reconnaissance, like the one just described. The camps were usually close to a water source. The rivers would dry up into a series of waterholes, where the fish would concentrate.

On one such safari on the Ugala River, in the same area, I noticed that local honey hunters and gatherers often passed the camp with their catch. A typical catch would be two or three fish strung through the gills on a stout stick, carried on the shoulders of two men walking in single file along the game trails or vehicle wheel tracks. The tails of these huge catfish would often trail in the dust between the men while the stick bowed under their combined weight. Try as we might, we could not catch these fish in the large pool near our camp. We observed the local method, which was to use a gaff hook on a short stick. The men would wade through the drying waterhole, sweeping the water with a scything action to foul hook the fish. Once engaged, the hook would detach from the end of the rod, and a short rope maintained the connection and provided flexibility. We thought it might work to just sweep the pool with a net and devised a plan to do this.

The typical camp layout would be as follows: Sleeping tents were typically strong, double fly, and A-shaped, and they would be pitched on either side of the mess tent, which was square and more like a small marquee; all the tents would be in a line facing the most attractive view. On this occasion, they viewed the waterhole. In the mess tent, the viewing side was unimpeded; food boxes were always arranged along the other three sides of the tent, with the kerosene fridge standing in the least windy corner (so the pilot light didn't blow out). The sides of the mess tent could be rolled up or down, depending on the weather. In hot drier climes, dictated more by altitude than latitude, a net was rolled down to keep out all those dudus that want to bite, infect, or poison, especially tsetse flies during the day and mosquitos at night. This net was attached by press-studs to the eaves of the tent. It could therefore be removed and was made of apparently durable shade cloth. Taken down and opened out, it made an appealing fishing net to drag the waterhole.

This pool in the Ugala River was about half the size of an Olympic swimming pool, so muddy that it was like chocolate milk and the fish were invisible. It was set in the heart of the miombo, a bright green savannah with new growth of leaves and grass after the annual burn-off that was practised in the area; the pool was watched over by the black trunks of the singed trees. These trees stood silent and majestic, as if representing the jet-black sable antelope, so suitably camouflaged for the area. The sable would stand motionless until they knew they'd been spotted. It is nice to think of them as possible spectators to the scene amongst the trees.

The waterhole was deeper in the middle than anticipated. It never occurred to me that men could not swim, but only three of the nine of us participating from the safari crew could do so; after rescuing the first nonswimmer, we three took the middle of the net, while the others dragged the net from the sides of the waterhole. Only those who've lived in Africa can really appreciate the enthusiasm and rising joyous excitement, complete with rhythmic chants, that fuelled this endeavour. When we passed the middle of the pool, the water ahead began to move, like the stirring of a river approaching a rapid. The odd snag briefly interrupted progress, and as we closed in towards the end of the pool, the turbulent water swirled to the rising chant.

Catfish are not renowned for jumping, and we never saw them. They simply turned and stampeded back to the middle of the pool between us, terrifyingly because of their poisonous spines, through our legs and the net. If it had not been for the unexpected return of buckets of small butter fish, like short fat sardines, from the sides of the pool, where the netting had not been battered, I would have had a lot of explaining to do about the huge holes in the mess tent netting. The ensuing welts from multiple insect bites as a result of the loss of the fly net and a very swollen hand from one of the poisonous spines of a catfish were our only punishment. African resourcefulness prepared the catch and fed the safari for days, softening the response of the camp manager.

CHAPTER 7

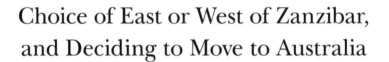

Choice of East or West of Zanzibar, and Deciding to Move to Australia

The Wind of Change speech was the death-knell of an empire which encircled the globe in British pink and carved a pink corridor through the middle of Africa from Cape Town to Cairo, an empire that Sir Winston Churchill said would last for another thousand years. The collapse of the British Empire left widespread turmoil. The extent and influence of this once-great nation is marked by the use of Greenwich Mean Time (which evolved into Universal Time Coordinated), the point from which all longitude is measured, and the widespread use of English, now a global utility language and the enduring legacy of the greatest empire the world has ever seen, with all its glories and disasters.

Kenya, despite the struggle for independence (or because of it), seemed to slide away from British rule; life changes were more subtle than dramatic, with a feeling for the inevitable, someday. Uganda was always different; Idi Amin was still rising through the ranks of the Ugandan army at that time, and thinking of the future did not stir any feelings of necessity. Life was obliviously Edenic in Tanganyika, and I heeded the Sirens' call. And then, Tanganyika changing to Tanzania was the starter's gun for me. We had for now survived another gust of the wind, "Just West of Zanzibar," but it was clearly time to start thinking seriously about our futures.

"Just West of Zanzibar" was the tune my grandmother often played sweetly for me on the piano when I was little. Later, on safari, Stan taught me the bawdy version in Swahili, which he played on the accordion. The reference to where I lived escaped me for years, until one day, the tune and the lyrics mingled with the names of Aladdin, Sinbad, and Saladin and echoed from the walls of Fort Jesus in Mombasa as we strolled below. I had learned in history class that the original name was Bombasa: the Portuguese island of war. That was west of Zanzibar.

As a young boy, I was fascinated by the fish in the market at the Old Dhow Harbour of Mombasa, especially the sharks. The harbour was set in the shadow of Fort Jesus, into which the dhows would sail like ghosts from the past. My father told me not to get onto a dhow if invited, unless I wanted to end up in Arabia without my balls. I reminded him that it was the islands of Pemba and Zanzibar that were reputed to have been the holding points for the Arab slaves, where men were castrated before being shipped north, and not Mombasa. He didn't register a difference because in the slave-trade days, the sultan of Zanzibar owned the ten-mile coastal strip of Kenya as a result of an early treaty with Britain. Yet that day, his words echoed like a dare to leave. We had been lifted by the gusts of wind and were airborne. Kip left first; with farm experience, he went to a job on a wheat and sheep farm near Geraldton in Western Australia and then to big money drilling for oil on Barrow Island, off the Western Australian coast. He called me after a near-death experience in a fall off the rig as a derrick-man, saying, "Come over and we can farm together."

I was forced to make a decision as to whether to take Kenyan citizenship, to which I was entitled, and thus renounce any claim to being British, or give up my right to Kenya citizenship by keeping my British passport of the colony of Kenya. It turned out that my passport was in effect worthless because although my mother was born in the United Kingdom, as a female, she could not pass on her citizenship to me. My father was born in India and had the same passport as me. While he chose to become a Kenyan citizen, I was worried that I'd be trapped without further education or vocational prospects if I did the same. I was concerned that independent Kenya's policy of affirmative action would not apply to white Kenyan citizens. The overall picture indicated that my options were to take Kenya citizenship, stay, and work with Stan or seek British citizenship somehow and migrate to another country, following my earlier dream of becoming a doctor.

I was now faced with a serious dilemma. My heart belonged to Kenya, but my head suggested that maybe I should fly on the wind and follow Kip.

Although I had seriously considered taking Kenyan citizenship along with Stan and my cousins, the decision to retain British citizenship or become a Kenyan citizen was taken out my hands by two factors. The first was that it would be difficult for me to go to another country as a Kenyan for further education without government sanction. I would have to return afterwards, and there would not be any support because with my school results, I wasn't eligible for any scholarship. That would put me in an impossible financial situation and remove all options for migration in the future, should I wish to emigrate for economic, career, or political reasons. The second factor was that Ronnie, being staunchly British, was adamant that I not renounce my right to UK citizenship.

When my mother learned that British citizenship was not possible for me because she was female (my father's family had left several generations before), she was most indignant. Ronnie presented herself at the British High Commission in Nairobi and, as a British subject, demanded an audience. Ronnie in her heyday was as fiercesome as any colonial trooper there ever was. She asked the high commissioner to explain why her son could not be a British subject via her lineage, since the British government had sent her overseas, and she had fought for her country in the navy. I'm sure she was, in her way, a significant contributor to the eventual change of the British law, removing gender discrimination. She had accepted loss of employment because of pregnancy and overcame financial discrimination in banks by threatening to transfer the company overdraft, but to have her son denied a British passport was unacceptable for her.

Of course, the British high commissioner could not change the law, but nor could he change my mother, or evict her, and she was making life very uncomfortable for him. He was at a loss as to how to explain why a naval officer should be so discriminated against. Knowing my father was not born in the UK, but that my grandfather had been a major in the British Army in India, he asked where he was born, on the grounds that he could use that as an excuse to grant me citizenship.

"In India" was the response.

"Well, where was his father born? Was he in the British Army?"

"In India, and no, he was a seaman with the BI line."

"Oh, well, where was his father born?"

"In India."

"Well, someone must have gone to India in the first place; who was that?"

"That was George Brown, who served with the British Army in 1820."

"Where does Lawrence fit in?"

It was my mother's turn to hesitate, knowing that this was controversial because it implied mixed marriages or liaisons in the early British Raj, when unmarried mothers attached the soldier father's name to their own to claim sustenance payments from the British. At that point, she became as vague as that part of the family history was obscure but assured the commissioner that the lineage had been traced by Stan's older brother through Somerset House in London; the double-barrel name had been approved when my grandfather moved from India in the Soldier Settlement scheme after World War I.

"That will do," the high commissioner said.

It always puzzled me why I obtained British citizenship but my cousin Howard, who obviously had the same lineage, was not granted the same privilege. That his mother was Afrikaans should not have affected them, by the same reasoning that UK citizenship was patriarchal, and this led me to the conclusion that it was the "Ronnie factor."

Why Australia? The brief sojourn to London to sit an exam and try again for A levels in biology had left me miserable with failure. A sense of distrust of the establishment bubbled as I contemplated the difference between what knowledge was sought by the examiners and what I had studied. When I had been in the UK, I did not particularly like Australians. An encounter with a group of intrusive, intoxicated Australians wearing pyjamas near Earl's Court at midnight had not endeared them to me. There were, however, a couple of Australians who worked in the safari business, and two travelling Aussie girls, a little older than me, treated me as an equal despite my age, and they changed my mind. The Australians I got to know displayed a kindred attitude to life, and their sense of humour appealed to me. Emigration to other parts of Africa did not appear wise. America was offered up to me as an option by a safari client, but the Americans we associated with were those wealthy enough to afford guided safaris. They gleamed with soap and body oils, they used scents and toilet paper to dispel or wipe away all things unpleasant, and their scent could be detected in the bush for some considerable distance. I came to understand why the troops fighting the Mau-Mau had been ordered not to wash. Some Americans, although always genial, well-mannered, and knowledgeable, seemed to live by unwritten codes, and some were overtly racist, and that raised alarm bells and distanced them from me. Britain had no draw left for a banished colonial with a worthless British passport of the colony of Kenya, which meant I was excluded anyway. Britain decided to keep her colonials at bay, and a sense of being unwanted prevailed in my psyche.

My London experience of small basement flats, grimy Underground stations, girls with make-up-caked faces hiding acne spots, warm beer, poverty, sooty disposable collars, and a different-but-the-same language drove me in the opposite direction. Canada, an alternative, was a little known frozen waste, and in those days, I could not distinguish between Canadians and Americans. The decision not to go to North America had already been made, anyway. Australia, on the other hand, wanted those who were white and British; more importantly, it offered opportunity and a place in a university.

Songs can have a strange and disproportionate influence in our lives. Music weaves its spell, binding our emotions with our actions in response to love and war, marriage and parting, and especially our farewells. "We'll Meet Again" by Vera Lynn and, contemplating Australia, I also associate Slim Dusty's "Pub with No Beer" with this time. I heard the song repeatedly towards the end of my time in Kenya, while helping to build the Safari Lodge for Stan in the Meru Game Reserve in northern Kenya during time off between safaris. Now that I was deciding to leave Kenya, I thought of the times Stan and I had spent together; he had taught me a lot, and I had taken a lot for granted.

By this time, Stan had placed me as the second guide, or off-sider, in the Australian idiom, to Michael Hissey; my time off did not always coincide with his. Farewells are accompanied by reflections, and I had time to reflect on this beautiful part of Kenya and the nascent national park. I had often wondered whether Stan started to take me on safaris with him because I was getting into more serious trouble as I entered my teens, or whether he just wanted me to be with him and be his apprentice. I preferred the latter motive, although it did also achieve redressing my growing-up problems.

Stan had patiently taught me to drive the trucks in the bush, on and off the difficult gravel roads. He taught me how to shoot and handle the heavy double-barrelled rifles. He taught me to respect all animals and never kill unless it was for a purpose and then to do it with respect and as humanely as possible. He instilled the importance of the sensible game laws of never shooting within five hundred yards of a watering place, never shooting from a vehicle or at night with a blinding spotlight, and only shooting adult males, leaving the young and breeding stocks alone.

Automatic weapons were banned in East Africa then, and he taught me to make every shot count. I found he intensely disliked wanton killing and disregard for animal psyche. He taught me people-skills as a guide and how to handle some difficult people without causing offence. Stan was a superb safari guide because he thought the way an animal would and instilled the belief that animals felt the same emotions as people. It was his job and provided him with a living. The challenge was to be the best, and his advice was always the same to me: endeavour to do the best at whatever you try, according to our school motto, his and mine: "To the Uttermost."

Good guides understand the importance of reputation, and he was certainly regarded that way, especially in Tanganyika. Stan's abhorrence of wasteful killing posed a dilemma; most clients wished to fill the annual licence quota in the time they had allocated for their holiday. A year's licence involved a lot of animals if a visitor was only there for two weeks. As a consequence, he refused to guide short safaris and accepted none less than one-month duration (this extended progressively to three months, then six months, and ultimately to his longest continuous safari of eleven months). In this way, he distanced himself from the madness of killing for the sake of killing.

He was not religious, despite his early schooling with Quaker missionaries, who he called "God-botherers." He decried bureaucrats who advocated mass exterminations in the name of science. He saw both as misusing the power of a higher authority, be it a foreign God or a foreign country. Examples of hare-brained schemes are numerous in the colonies; the mass extermination of all game animals in tsetse fly areas, to rid the country of the reservoir of trypanosomes that caused death in cattle and sleeping-sickness in humans, is one. When this failed and the parasites became endemic in the cattle, the British government baulked at the political fall-out should they advocate killing all the Masai cattle and instead ordered the clearing of all vegetation in the tsetse areas to eliminate the shelter for the tsetse fly during the heat of the day.

This turned parts of the country into a dust bowl and gave credence to the line "Only mad dogs and Englishmen go out in the midday sun." Stan had often expressed his wish that the foreign Gods would send the missionaries to the bureaucrats. Instead, they would visit Stan's camp, drink his whiskey, and explain that he was the way he was because he had left his first missionary school in Kijabe in the Rift Valley too early. Stan's relationship with the game wardens in the field was invariably a good one, but his view of the game department was ambivalent, to say the least. He despised the practice of game control, whereby shooters were sent to kill en masse to reduce the number of animals to clear the land for farming, or to save the environment from overpopulation or for disease control. These culls were aimed at the females, young, and breeding reservoirs. They were contrary to all nature's laws and usually an excuse for some secondary motive. When these practices were proven wrong, they were difficult to reverse for fear of undermining authority with admission of error; maintenance of authority was the keystone of the British Empire.

I asked Stan why he didn't switch exclusively to photographic safaris after hunting was banned in Kenya; he had been successful with guiding for Hollywood films, the World Wildlife Safaris with Sir Julian Huxley, the Lincoln Park Zoo, and many others. I pointed out that Sid Downey and Donald Kerr, who started

Kerr and Downey Safaris (which competed with the original famous Safariland), had moved to exclusively photographic expeditions.

Stan replied that he didn't want to become another package tour national park circuit guide; he had taught me to do that, and it could be my business. Most of all, and typical of his adventurous nature, he said he treasured the remote and secret places he had explored and were outside the worn trails of the national parks. So apart from the occasional special purpose photographic safaris in Kenya, Stan had continued to guide those safaris to remote places in Tanzania where trophy hunting was still part of the fare.

Stan's exit strategy was to build and run a game lodge of his own and give up guiding. Kenmare Game Lodge was his purpose, and the idea grew from the example of one of his early mentors, J A Hunter from Safariland. J A opened a lodge about one hundred miles south of Nairobi on the Mombasa Road and called it Hunter's Lodge. The reception table proudly displayed his book, *Hunter*. Stan took me to meet his old mentor, and I could feel the regard he held for J A. To me, he was a shrivelled, unkempt old man with little blackheads on his face and a fading memory.

Stan may have been disappointed by my lack of admiration, but he didn't show it. I gave no hint that I wasn't impressed. However, Stan could read me like he could any other animal, and I am sure he knew. The visit served the purpose to gel the idea of a lodge in Stan's mind and take up the author Stuart Cloete's suggestion of writing a book.

He approached the government for permission to build a lodge in his beloved Marijo Hills in the Masai Mara district, where he spent his unemployed youth living with the Masai. He was too late; the government already decided to build one there. Stan opted for his second most favourite place, which was northern Kenya; he was granted permission to build in a new park that was being created behind Mount Kenya and Meru

Township; it would be called the Meru Game Reserve. That is how I came to be there away from my kindred, listening to Slim Dusty, and wondering what an Australian pub was like.

On a special photographic safari, Stan had met Lady Kenmare, who was a daughter of the Australian wine Barron Lindeman family, and her daughter, Pat Cavendish O'Neill. Lady Kenmare was a widow and socialite who had survived three wealthy husbands. She had been teased by her friend, the playwright Somerset Maugham, that she should be called Lady Killmore. Lady Kenmare had a house and extensive garden at the foot of the Ngong Hills, a few miles outside Nairobi and not far from our home. It was agreed that she would back the building of the lodge, and in return it would be called Kenmare Lodge.

It was exciting in the beginning, and between safaris, I spent time there and helped with the building and ferrying supplies. One trip was in a little Thames truck that had been used in the film *Mogambo;* Stan had come across it stored in Nairobi. He bought it for sentimental reasons and to spare his safari trucks from providing transport for the lodge. I was given the honour of making the first trip, and the truck was loaded with supplies. Leaving very early in the morning while it was still dark, I discovered the headlights had been altered for the sake of the film so that the beam was reduced to a bare slit; they emitted only sufficient light for the special effects on the film. It was a difficult drive until dawn and required watching the edge of the road for guidance, but it was a symbol of the fun of the endeavour that was fraught with unexpected problems.

The lodge became embroiled in the conflicts between Kenya and Somalia and was eventually destroyed by a fire. Stan spent so much time there that his business suffered. Subcontracting safari guides progressively abandoned him for the sake of their own survival. The larger safari trucks were still used to carry things to the lodge, and the equipment deteriorated. The gleam of the professional safari outfit dimmed. My mentors, Michael

Hissey and Royce Buckle, left the company. Royce, who had learned as an apprentice to Stan and ran the Tanzania part of the company, moved to South Africa to work on the Durban wharfs. It was during this period, when building the lodge and listening to Slim Dusty, that I started to think seriously about migrating to Australia. The fact that Pat's surname was Cavendish O'Neill escaped me because she dropped the O'Neill after separating from the Australian Olympic swimmer, and I was unaware of any family connections with Australia or the Lindemans.

Ronnie supported my seeking a future away from safaris and persuaded me to approach Australian universities with the hope that my school qualifications might get me into some course, even if not medicine; to my surprise, the University of New South Wales offered me a position to study science, with the prospect of changing to medicine after one year. The assisted migration scheme did not apply to colonials outside Britain, so I cashed in the insurance policy that my mother had paid into for over twenty-one years, and the money was just enough for a one-way ticket to Sydney.

Stan, Ronnie, and my sister Wendy took me to the airport. I knew Ronnie would miss me and at the same time was clearly pleased that I was heading for an education, away from Africa and safari life and towards a promise for the future. Stan's face haunts me still. We had become close after spending so much time together in a lifestyle overwhelmingly rich in experience and steeped in nature. His vision had been to pass the business to me. He found the pain of the reality hard to conceal. All those years of building and striving and passing on bush lore to his son was being blown away. The wind twisted the strained smile of goodwill. I have drawn psychologically upon the memories of him and that period when faced with failure, adversity, and difficult decisions. It was fifteen years on before he fully accepted my leaving Africa, and that was when he was dying, and I could offer something as a doctor.

With the wind blowing, my friend calling, my mother a prophet of doom, and my spirit free, I turned and left my dad's sad face behind me. His wish for a business to be passed on dying in the weathered lines that were burnt into his skin, with the colonial trails of India and Africa, his dream disappearing like the fading images in the celluloid that held *King Solomon's mines*, *Mogambo*, and *Hatari*.

I flew out to Australia, way, way east of Zanzibar.

PART 2

Australia and Becoming a Surgeon

CHAPTER 8

On the Wind of Change:
Australia and University

Unable to cross the Indian Ocean directly, the plane hopped around the edge: Aden, Bombay, Madras, Singapore, Perth, and finally Sydney. I spent five hours in Bombay, observing a group of long-haired, differently dressed Englishmen and a young woman, all about my age. Their extrovert behaviour attracted the attention of some earnest note-taking Indians, who were obviously journalists. The Indians were attracting as much of my curiosity as the preening young English group. One journalist was persistently seeking their views on classical music. At that point, I lost interest because the only classical music I had ever heard was late at night at school through the earphones of my crystal set, tuned to the only local Nairobi radio station available. The only opera I had ever seen was *Aida* at the drive-in cinema from an open Land Rover in the rain, the arias coming from a speaker that looked like a parking meter. It was not a good introduction to opera.

The pop group attracted more attention at the airport transit lounge in Madras (Chennai), but I was deprived of sleep and too weary to understand the attraction. We arrived in a hot Perth at midnight in mid-January 1965, where a crowd of hundreds of blond, tanned, lightly dressed young people thronged the airport, with benign police lined up along the runway to hold them back. For me, fresh out from an African setting, it was an amazing scene, especially since all this activity was taking place at midnight. It was quite an introduction to Australia. Then it was on to Sydney.

In Sydney, newspaper headlines informed me that the group were the popular entertainers Manfred Mann, Herman's Hermits, and the Honeycombs. They were on tour in Australia, giving combined concerts around the country. Their popular acclaim and my ignorance of them marked the cultural gap between me and Australia, a gap I needed to cross if I was to succeed as a migrant in the country I had chosen for my new home.

It was hot and airless that mid-January day. Customs raised a curious eye to my memorabilia: a hunting knife, odd clothes, photos, and boxes of slides. The customs man looked disappointed when he found they were only slides of animals as opposed to something racier and more titillating. Just as London's taxis were distinct from other vehicles on the streets, so Sydney's taxis were unique to the Australian setting. Their uniqueness was in the colour schemes and the lighted "Vacant" signs on the roof and passenger side of the windscreen. My driver kindly stopped for me to buy a toothbrush, and the scents of the city rose strangely from the hot tar and cement and mingled with a mixture of Italian delicatessen aromas, the balm of salty air, suntan oil, and Woolworths. Absent was the pungent richness of Indian incense, mud in the dust of open drains, and the scents of the earth and flowers of home.

I had arrived in Australia—a surviving dominion—from Kenya in January 1965. Not as a "Ten-Pound Pom," as the Australians referred to new assisted arrivals from the UK, but as someone whose English family had been in the colonies of India and Africa for five generations, dating back to 1820 with the British colonial army in India. Ostensibly seeking education in Australia, I was really seeking a future in the British Commonwealth and arrived from a Black country in the middle of the White Australia Policy, bolstering the white population by one. In this crucible of anachronism, Aborigines were excluded from the vote, but I was required to vote after six months, since I was considered British. I would have been eligible to be conscripted for the Vietnam War if I had been a year younger (and if my marble was selected in the conscription lottery).

Interestingly, Vietnam had the same nationalistic dynamic towards independence from a colonial past, and it's ironic that the Vietnam War was justified by the West on the domino theory that Asian states would progressively fall to the march of Communism from the north: instead, it was the wind of change from the west blowing over the dominoes, and Australia, as a dominion in the British Empire, was a standing domino, resisting indigenous restoration and republic status.

The University of New South Wales was fledgling and modern, many times removed from the architecture and historical atmosphere of Oxford and Cambridge. It had just been upgraded to the status of a university from its former title of the New South Wales Institute of Technology. I had written to Basser Residential College for accommodation, and the taxi now dropped me there with my total possessions in one suitcase. The residential college was closed to students for the summer vacation and was being used as a conference centre when I arrived. Compassion, I suspect, prompted an offer to let me stay—at least for a few days—subject to an interview by the master of the college, who was to see if I was worthy of a place in the university residential college. I was bemused because I had been expecting a simple cash-based entry qualification. I was duly seated across from his desk and surrounded by the intimidating academic atmosphere.

"There is no apartheid in Australia, you know," he said after a few minutes.

I thought nothing of the remark. Only after he said it a pointed third time did I realise that he assumed I was a South African. I respectfully informed him of my multiracial upbringing, said that Kenya had an independent African government, and enquired politely as to whether the White Australia Policy persisted. This was two years before the 1967 referendum to change the constitution to have Aboriginal people counted as Australian, widely interpreted as practically giving Aborigines the vote because they would then appear on the electoral roll. The White Australia Policy was in force until formally ended in 1973 under the Whitlam government. Compulsory voting for Aborigines in line with non-Aboriginal descendants on the electoral roll was enacted under the Fraser government in 1983. The federal government retains the power to enact laws specifically for indigenous people, which allows for affirmative action but also a loophole for discrimination.

We were both embarrassed. The master of the college because he was a campaigner for abolition of the White Australia Policy, and me because I had not intended to offend him. Exhausted, I declined an invitation to tea, but being young and always hungry, I accepted the offer for supper.

I thought five thirty a little late for tea, as that to me meant afternoon tea in the English sense of tea with biscuits or cake. Ten o'clock at night seemed very late for supper, a term with which I was familiar for the main evening meal, usually just after dark, at about seven. After a few hours of sleep, I was ravenous by the appointed time of ten. I was accustomed to rising at four in the morning on safari and being asleep soon after the news at nine in the evening, following the broadcast of the safari messages. Ten o'clock was indeed a late time to have the main meal of the day; it seemed extraordinary to me. I had heard of the Spanish custom of eating at midnight in the summer, so I greedily imagined a sort of feast. I was chastened to learn that tea was the main meal and supper a cup of coffee and a biscuit.

John O'Grady's description, "They're a weird mob," relates the migrant's dilemma of the language gaps of the times. Nino Culotta understandably had problems with the Australian vernacular because he was Italian, but so did I.

After enrolling in the university for a science degree, with a plan to change to medicine later, I found a job as a builder's labourer to fill in the time and pay for my board until university started in March. Finding a job involved merely walking up the hill from Basser Residential College to the Prince of Wales Hospital, walking onto the building site, and asking the foreman. Foundations were being laid for a building next to the Nurses Home. I prided myself with a shovel, having learnt the art digging out safari trucks from sand and mud. I could pitch the earth accurately and rapidly. The Aussie ethic of "Give 'im a fair go" prevailed.

After a while, the carpenter's apprentice chided me that I wouldn't last until lunchtime at that rate and advised me to pace myself. I was grateful for his kindness and good sense. Although younger than me, he was life-wise, in a Sydney sort of way, and I paid attention.

It was the sixties, and music was everywhere. He per cerebrated with the tune "Gee it's great after staying out late, walking my baby back home", but he had changed the words to "Gee it's great when you are rooting your mate ..." He was a classic bronzed Aussie of the times, blond and tanned with shoulder-length hair. He never wore a shirt, sported a hammer and nail pouch on his belt, and was rippled with muscles built by surfing and the hammer, and at the end of the day, he piled into a panel-van with his brother and mates. His name escapes me, but his singing and wolf-whistle lingers between the shaking memories of the jackhammer in my hands.

There were distractions. We were building next to the Nurses Home. The gentle sway of hips beneath upturned breasts and noses was a positively dangerous distraction on a building site. It was a time with a unique culture. There may be few things that are better than sliced bread, but the invention of pallets is one of them. This was the age before Brambles invented pallets, and the truckie would turn up with the bricks stacked on the tray-top and lift them off manually by holding a number of them horizontally between his hands. It was part of my job to help him. A silent competition of strength ensued to display the number of bricks that could be held this way. Three is easy, four a little more difficult, and eight a feat.

Needless to say, the truckie's stack was always much larger than mine; the leading hand (second-in-charge to the foreman) wondered whether he should find a stronger labourer, and the reason for wearing heavy steel-capped boots became obvious. Then, already exhausted from competing with the truckie, I had to run the wheelbarrow along an obstacle course of planks and paths to the chatting brickies, who effortlessly raised walls with a voracious appetite for even more bricks. As the walls got higher and the obstacle course steeper and my legs more wobbly, the reason for the legends surrounding Brickies' Labourers became apparent.

Overall, it was a pleasant time. The nurses looked gorgeous as they minced in their crisp military-styled uniforms, dating back to the Crimean War era. There was a little more wiggle to the whistle as they went past the carpenter's apprentice. The sun blazed, music blared "Under the Boardwalk," brickies demanded bricks, jackhammers provided a techno beat, and the carpenter's apprentice was still "rooting his mate." There was milk at lunchtime, beer and play after work, and fun at the weekend.

Mondays were mournful, with recounts of blissful Sundays. Sydney was a chauvinistic society at that time. Public bars were for men only, with the exception of a much-ogled barmaid. Women sat in the lounge bar, if they came at all. The carpenter's apprentice had a simple practical attitude to girls and sex, which threatened my romantic notions of candlelight dinners and safari vistas.

For him, the weekends were a hunt. A girl would be attracted by his friendly demeanour, wholesome appearance, and an invitation to go to a beach in the panel-van. If the beach was some distance away, then sex was traded for the lift home. I have often reflected on the law that states that ignorance is no excuse. When I suggested that what he was being led into at the weekends by his brother and older friends amounted to rape, he was most indignant. Also intelligent, he immediately asked the foreman, who told him it was. Rape was rewarded by seven years in jail at that time, and newspaper reports of gang-bang rapes were not uncommon. I suspected that ignorance and culture rather than malice was the root-cause of the problem and innocence its main victim. The young are so vulnerable. The law is not made to be fair; it is for control, and trouble better avoided than confronted. Nowadays, I ponder why if ignorance is no excuse in the eyes of the law, and so many young people get punished, why is ignorance of the complications of surgery or potential civil injury ever an excuse, and so many rewarded. After all, both are written, and legalese is much less comprehensible than medical terminology to most of us who just sign on the dotted line. I wonder also if the community should be liable in the same way when a prisoner is injured in jail by others, while essentially defenceless. My philosophy to my sons has always been to avoid the law enforcers and steer clear of the press. Perhaps my attitude is a product of a colonial past and its inherent distrust of authority. "If you sup with the devil, you will dance with the devil" has always been an axiom for me.

University started. I don't know if the carpenter's apprentice learnt from the foreman or ended up in jail, singing his song. The contrast of a free spirit and a sordid captive was too painful for me to contemplate.

There were two sides to university, and I had to adjust to both. On the main campus, I shuffled into impersonal lectures on physics, mathematics, chemistry and biology. No one cared if I attended or not, passed or not, or indeed lived or not. With a percentage of less than 20 in each of maths, physics, and chemistry, I lived to fail the first term. With the bar set at credits for all subjects in order to qualify for the crossover to medicine at the end of the year, the task ahead of me appeared impossible.

The residential college was a stark and intrusive contrast to the impersonal university campus. The average age of the intake of freshmen and -women was seventeen, and most courses were designed for three or four years. Medicine took six years, and in 1965, this was a fledging medical school in only its third year. The residential colleges practised humiliating initiation rites, and for me at twenty-one, and a graduate of colonial British boarding schools and initiations, freshman initiation was unacceptable to me. I had been through too many. I threatened violence in return and was rewarded with ostracism as a result of my stand. It did not last long, and as it often is with life's irony, my stand won me friends. There were two special friends: Harry, a surfer from Byron Bay, and Charlie from Canberra. We developed a lasting friendship.

Hockey helped me win friends. Hockey was a prominent Kenyan sport because of the Indian and British population mix, and my family's India connection had made it a natural pastime. I played for the university and looked forward to the National Intervarsity Tournament. My first semester exam results extinguished any further involvement, and I was led by fear of further failure to the library and the books. Fortunately, my previous multiple attempts to pass biology finally paid a dividend, and at least I did well in that subject.

One is unaware of the magnitude of a difficulty while living through it, if there's no comparator. For most migrants, there may be none, and it is all new. Life is not necessarily seen as hard or easy. The parameters of novelty, friendship, achievement, and physical and mental pleasure act to displace self-indulgence, self-pity, and despondency. Failure became a stimulant because it was unacceptable and unthinkable, like the alternative to growing older, and the only real alternative was to keep trying again when making a new life. The measures of survival are made against the relative equivalents in the stream. I was used to that from the years in boarding school and had a degree of self-reliance gained from my safari work. My strategy was to select a student who was predicted to succeed academically and compete directly, albeit silently, with that student. Achievement was the lotus.

My experience as a builder's labourer helped me get weekend work in gardens, and advertising was by word of mouth. Sydney was growing. Houses were usually built on large blocks with substantial gardens requiring soil for filling or soil to be removed by wheelbarrow, mostly from the back to the front or vice versa. The dean of the medical school, Francis Rundle, learned of my prowess with the wheelbarrow. He had a very large garden on a hillside at Darling Point, near the family house of the author Patrick White. He whispered darkly to me about White, complaining that he was unfriendly and had suspicious leanings, and I nodded knowingly, even though at the time, I had no idea who he was talking about.

I was learning some of the arts of medicine early and being discreet about knowledge gaps. Garden lunches with the dean were pleasant, and I worked for him that way for a few years. He was a good man, a thyroid surgeon of renown. He was proud of the fact that he could lay bricks as proficiently as Winston Churchill, who was apparently a master at the trade. The dean made harsh decisions when he had to. He was kind to me but kept me at a distance because I was a student and might fail, and he was strictly impartial. I never saw inside his house, and he worked as hard as I did in the garden. He did, however, improve my African method of bricklaying, which was to apply the best-fit principle. Apart from tips in medicine and surgery, which I exchanged for information from the student side of the medical school, we spoke little.

In retrospect, the first year was hard. I'm not sure whether I softened over the six-year course, but they all seemed hard in retrospect, although wonderful at the time. I guess it is when you are sick that the underbelly is exposed. I only experienced it once, as I was rarely sick, but on this occasion, I had the flu and was hard up for cash. Darling Point, where the dean lived, was about twelve kilometres from the university residential college in Randwick as the crow flies. The bus would take me diagonally to the city centre, from where another would take me back on another diagonal out to Darling Point. A long way round plus waits for buses, which I still hate. So I used to run over to save time; it felt good in the cool of the morning and evening. On this day, there was a lot of soil to move, as the dean had purchased the property next door and was reshaping the hillside.

I would not let him know that I was struggling, as I needed the money, but knew I was because we were discussing heart rates and how astronauts were training to go to the moon. The heart rate should not be allowed to go over 180, he said. My heart rate was over 180, and I had a fever. I suddenly had an overwhelming desire to ring home, for the first time. My pay for the day was good—for the times—ten dollars, one dollar an hour. The basic wage was about forty dollars a week. For the day's pay, I could buy a six-minute phone call to Nairobi. I rang my mum from a call box on the way back. The phone worked. She was surprised and pleased to hear my voice and, like all mums, immediately thought something must be wrong if I rang long distance out of the blue; she burst into tears, and the six minutes were soon over.

Eventually, I passed the exams sufficiently well to jump across to medicine and went on holiday to Byron Bay with Harry.

CHAPTER 9

Byron Bay and Beyond the University

We drove in Harry's Mini. I found the area strangely disturbing, and it puzzled me until I realised that the grass and woodlands that looked so much like Tanzania was devoid of any visible wildlife. No giraffe to look down on us. No plains game to dart across the road or turn tail for distant hills. Just the same blue and eucalyptus. It is what you expect to see that contents the soul. Now I see so much more when I look on the Australian landscape. It was always there, the exquisite fauna and flora, rather than the show. That is a measure of the change in me, but as a new migrant, it was an empty feeling.

The drab woodlands gave way to fields and then sugar cane. The contacts with the coast were thrilling for an inlander (or prairie oyster) like me, and the beaches of the Northern Rivers District of New South Wales were truly beautiful. Harry stopped on the hills just south of Byron Bay, and we looked down on the beaches, the little town with its pub, the abandoned whaling station, and the Norco milk processing plant. The houses were half holiday-type dwellings and half homes, giving an appearance of complete happiness, and the atmosphere was scented with passing exams. Harry was welcomed home by his faithful girlfriend and close-knit country family. They were not sure of me, but that was dispelled when they all heard that my upbringing was one of similar dwellings and country outhouse long-drop toilets.

Harry was made in the mould of the archtypical Aussie of the era that had shaped the bronze Anzacs. He lived for the surf and could hang ten on a longboard. He showed me how to fish and caught beach worms for bait with his toes. At night, we caught yabbies in the streams with a torch and forked stick. His circle of friends was of similar ilk, and we roamed the hills in search of rabbits in the afternoons and wandered the pubs looking for girls in the evenings. The Saturday night barn dances were a country institution that has faded away, but the memory shines bright. The town hall or church hall or pub floor was polished, and the circles of couples wheeled to the fiddlers and brass instruments played by a mixture of retired soldiers, amateur enthusiasts, and church organists. The venue would do the rounds of the country towns. It was a uniquely Australian country culture of the Northern Rivers of NSW and worthy of special historical record.

Harry arranged a day trip up to Surfers Paradise to see the Dolphin Aquarium, the wooden-floor roller skating rink, and the pictures. The dolphins and seals were magical, and roller skating was an opportunity to at last show some balance, considering the exhibitions on the surfboards that I had watched from the shore. No smoking in the picture theatre was a surprise, but Australia has often been ahead of its time. Not all was perfect, though. Harry had arranged a blind date to make up the four. We did not click and spent a lot of time looking in opposite directions in the back seat of the Holden borrowed for the day. Thank God, it wasn't the Mini.

We toured the country towns and then made a special trip to a university acquaintance's farm in western New South Wales, near Glen Innes and just south of the border (and Texas: that is, Texas the small town just north of the Queensland border). This was a countryside more familiar to my eye, with golden grasslands, savannah-type woodlands, dry river beds, and chains of waterholes—and wild animals—albeit mainly feral, such as the wild brumby horses and rabbits. There were some kangaroos at night, but we saw very few during the day. The wildness was made complete by the screeching sulphur-crested cockatoos.

Although I was more in my element in this sort of country, the hunting aspect did not appeal to me. Harry expected more of me as a shooter, and the shift in balance of our friendship sat a little uncomfortably between us. Shifts in relationships are likely to occur in a changed environment; they can be a trap for a migrant. Dominance in a relationship is often based on practical or local knowledge and particularly by a sense of belonging, and when the parameters change, the ties may slip apart. For example, many migrant marriages break up as a result of the shift in the balance between dependence and dominance. A common observation is to see restrictions imposed on a partner to avoid this (usually upon the woman).

In particular, dependency is assured by restricting language and thereby blocking equal exposure to the new culture and way of life, with secondary limitation on mobility. This use of restrictions on a language has often been used for control; the English did it to the Scots, and Australia similarly did it to the Aboriginal. Years later I learnt, during psychiatry and from reading John Pilger's book *A Secret Country*, why I saw Aboriginal markings on the ground and heard the unfamiliar Aboriginal names for places and yet saw no Aborigines among the second-hand British street signs and honour roll calls of war memorials. Like the savannah being devoid of animals, the country was eerie for lack of black people. I seldom saw an Aboriginal and rarely one without European genes. Smallpox, like the virus in H G Wells's *War of the Worlds*, had almost wiped them out.

The student who had invited us to visit was a typical country farming lad who studied agriculture; he drove a Holden ute fast on corrugated dirt roads, rose early on cold mornings, rode a horse, and cracked a stockwhip, reflecting the hard nature of the land. An unexpected tender rapport developed between me and the farmer's wife, the lad's mother. She was a tall, dignified, and beautiful woman who had trained as a nurse in Sydney in the days when nurses paid to train, and work in the hospital was unpaid "work experience." Her father had been a doctor, and she had wanted to do the same. Why she never did, I cannot remember; maybe because she became one of those women who married a farmer and shaped the outback. She had a clever illustrated atlas of human anatomy that she had always treasured. On the first page were all the bones. Each page after that was translucent, and as one turned the pages, the muscles appeared and then the vessels and finally the nerves were laid down to complete the picture for every part of the human body. We studied it together in bittersweet sadness, with her in nostalgia and me in anticipation. Thereafter, I felt I carried the flag for her, and she gave me to understand the Australian relationship of culture to resilience born of settling the hinterland.

My comfortable relationship with Harry was restored on return to the coast by the magic of Byron Bay; Harry was back in charge in his own land, and I left to contemplate the depth of meaning in the vast land beyond.

The observation of ethnic population disappearances since the fifteenth century is more than coincidental. The South American Incas and other indigenous groups such as the North American Indians suffered like the Australian Aborigine in the southern half of the Australian continent. Most disappeared, with few exceptions. War and violent killings never succeed in doing this, Europe and Asia and Africa being good example of the attempts. The shores of the Mediterranean Sea must have been washed with almost as much blood as sea water, yet the populations are still at it. Without a global near-extinction of life, as has occurred nine other times (probably due to celestial collision), only disease will do this.

The Europeans exchanged smallpox for syphilis in the Americas: a pox for a pox. They brought both to Australia. It is cruel to be kind: the blanket was the instrument for demise, with disease conveyed by it or under it. The gift of a blanket was passed on from one to another as each died, and the children being the most vulnerable meant that the population was wiped out in one or two generations. Smallpox is quickly lethal and quickly takes the children. H G Wells in his classic novel *War of the Worlds* had it in reverse, when the invading aliens died after contracting a virus from the Earthlings. The lost world of El Dorado in the Orinoco Valley that the Spanish could never find again (it's now been tentatively identified by pattern recognition from satellite) may have really existed before the pox.

I attended a speech given to the Australian College of Surgeons by Judge Pat O'Shane of the Stolen Generation called "Turn Back the Blanket," which is the story of the well-intended but condemned policy to remove part-European Aboriginal children from their families and educate them; the image she conveyed has stayed with me. She told of a sailor from Captain Cook's ship giving a blanket to an Aborigine as an introductory gift and gesture of friendship. European genes imparted some inherent resistance to smallpox. Most of the sailors would have been immune to smallpox, but some arrived with the disease, and the virus was carried with them. In their close quarters, there was no possibility of isolation, and immunity was the only reasonable explanation for resistance.

Purposeful acquisition of smallpox was actually used as vaccination in England at that time, and Edward Jenner himself was intentionally inoculated with the virus when aged thirteen, as was the custom, and isolated to live or die (a violent form of vaccination). Thank God, he lived. The Japanese restored his house and created the Jenner Museum in appreciation of saving Japan. The Canadian Indians have also formally expressed gratitude. The English debated his worth, built a statue to him in Trafalgar Square, and then replaced it with a monument to Nelson. Jenner now gazes into a murky pond in Kensington gardens. Maybe he contemplates his achievements as a student of the pioneer surgeon John Hunter. Hunter, so well-remembered as a great surgeon, never forgave Jenner for returning to practice as a GP in the country. Maybe Jenner, as he gazes stone-faced into the pond, does not think of his medical achievement at all. Instead, having been exhausted by the political arguments against his theories and condemnations of his vaccination practice, he ponders his wonderful nature study of the cuckoo bird or the youthful innocence of the lovely complexioned milk-maids with cowpox sores on their hands.

Does he know that he made the greatest contribution ever by a man to living creatures? Jenner is the father of immunology, but too late for many, and nations have been lost, too late for the wonderful Incas and many Aborigines. No one has ever asked whether the Inca rituals of child sacrifice were a form of quarantine or euthanasia. In the light of the post-colonial era, should we discount the Spanish versions that demonised the Incas on grounds of misinterpretation or conflict of interest, since the Spaniards introduced the disease—on purpose, it is said—but that may be reverse demonisation. Fortunately, some groups of Australian Aborigines far out in the central deserts or northern tropics remained isolated and were spared from the European spread of feral diseases. Then compulsory vaccination eradicated smallpox so they could emerge intact.

My circle of friends at Basser College widened. Among these was Jim Kirumba. Just before Kenya acquired independence, the Hon. Tom Mboya, who was the leader of the Luo peoples in Kenya and the architect for Jomo Kenyatta's release from British detention, visited Australia during his worldwide lobbying for education opportunities and spoke to the Students' Union of the University of NSW. (The Luo people of Kenya are also the root for President Barack Obama; Tom Mboya may well have known Obama's father in his capacity of generating scholarships overseas.) The students were moved by Mboya's oratory and raised money for a scholarship for a Kenyan to study medicine at UNSW. Jim was the recipient. He started medicine a year before me. I had not known him in Kenya because I would have been two years ahead at school, and we went to different schools. Our rapport developed rapidly, and he helped me adapt to the Australian ways. He introduced me to Michele to further my education.

Jim was astute. He was clever, was intelligent, and passed his exams with relative ease. He was comfortable in college and mixed well with the other students. He was far worldlier than me and had a much better understanding of politics. I was so naïve and colonial, politically an ostrich, and struggled to pass exams. My fierce resistance to freshman initiation isolated me in the beginning, and my general education was needed. So Jim thought it was a good idea if I met Michele.

Michele was a nurse training at Royal Prince Alfred Hospital, attached to Sydney University on the other side of town. She organised nurses to go to the African Students' Association social functions. Michele had schooled in Kenya and lived in Uganda, where her mother had worked at Makerere University, running a residential college. They had to leave Uganda when Idi Amin started to rise to power, and she had migrated to New South Wales in 1964. After working at the Sheep Station Haddon Rig, Michele started nursing.

I was wary of meeting other colonials; I didn't want to live in the past and resisted Jim's urgings, on the grounds that he was misguided in trying to match me with other colonials. I eventually rang her after the final first-year exams and arranged to meet outside her hospital. Having given a false description of myself, I waited on a bench beneath the big Morton Bay fig tree on Missenden Road and watched. We had agreed to wear our bracelets of elephant or giraffe hair, which were commonly worn in East Africa in those days, so that we could find each other. It would have been easy for me to avoid this blind date if she was ugly, since I had given the false description of myself, but I was taken aback by a petite, honey blonde, bouncing bundle of smiles and freckles. We had a lovely time that evening in Sydney, and all I had to do was listen. We went out a few times, and then I kissed her good night, and she said sweetly, "Good night, Ron."

Good night Ron?

About six months later, Michele rang me and asked if I would accompany her to an African social dance. That evening, she kissed me good night and called me Michael. I took her to the Sydney show and gave her a great time on the Wild Mouse, which frightened the life out her so that she clung tightly to me, and then on to the Ferris wheel to see the lights of Sydney from high in the night sky. We climbed in, and because the wheel was taking on people, it revolved slowly and stopped. It stopped when we were at the height of its circle, offering a wonderful view of Sydney and its bridge. That was when Michele lost it. She had had enough. The Wild Mouse had terrified her, and she hated heights; believing the machine had broken down with us stranded high in the air, she started to scream so loudly that the showground crowd turned to look. Nobody wanted anything to do with this Ferris wheel. The driver brought us down and sympathetically told us to "bugger off."

My real education was just starting. I agreed to meet Michele's mother, Enid. We planned to meet her at the pictures in George Street, just down from the town hall. We were waiting demurely in a crowd at the theatre entrance when from about a hundred metres away came a blood-curdling, ear-splitting cry of "Yoo-hoo" from a stout, strong-featured woman with peroxided short hair and arms akimbo as she strode towards us and bayed loudly to all and sundry that I looked much younger than she expected. It is said that if you want to know what the girl will look like in time, look at the mother. I didn't want to look. Enid, who passed away after her reward of being presented to President Nelson Mandela for her contribution to his struggles, was like no other person I had ever met: a Welsh miner's daughter, communist, teacher, adventurer, a vocal pugilistic feminist, and a divorcee who had the courage to migrate on her own to South Africa with two little girls. She had been on the South African Secret Police list for being a member of a multiracial teachers club and forced to flee Durban for East Africa. She was on ASIO's black list for being a member of the Communist Party of Australia after migrating from Uganda to escape Idi Amin.

"Dear God," I said. "I've fallen for her daughter."

"Would you like to come to a party at Mummy's place on Sunday?" she asked me. "We are planning a rally against the Vietnam War because conscription was based on a date on a marble, and if that was your twentieth birthday, then you would be in the army."

"Fuck'n hell, what am I getting into?"

Michele immediately told me, "Mummy doesn't like swearing and says it shows a paucity of intellect."

I was speechless and not ready to add politics to my list, but went to an enjoyable party; met a lot of Communists who ate, drank, and were merry like everyone else I had met in Australia; and gazed at Michele.

I passed the first-year exams and obtained the credits to enter second-year medicine (first-year science having the same subjects as first-year medicine). I also received a Commonwealth Scholarship that would pay for the fees. Elated, I looked for a job to finance myself for the next year's living expenses. A fellow student who came from Canberra, near the Snowy Mountains, suggested I try the Snowy Mountains Hydroelectric Scheme and gave me a lift to Canberra. From there, I went to Cooma and the Administration Centre for the scheme. Since I had a truck driver licence, I was offered a job subject to a test.

"What sort of truck do you drive?" asked a busy Italian migrant who was in charge of transport.

I replied, "A Bedford," thinking of the simple 4X4 Bedford ex- British army safari trucks.

I was tested in a civilian forward control Bedford with a lottery stick gearbox and taken on a dirt track up a steep little hill. Things were going fine, and I recalled my truck driver test in Africa; the examiner had two tricks. One was to suggest you do something illegal, and the other was to ask you to do something overtly stupid. He failed you if you did either. Another was to see if you put all the parking brakes on the truck at the end when finished. Halfway down the other side of the hill, which I was comfortably negotiating in low gear, as is correct on such a decline, he instructed me to change up.

Ah, it's a trick, I said to myself.

It wasn't a trick; he wanted to see if I had the skills to change down from the higher gear when we inevitably picked up speed. I refused. Good thing Enid wasn't in the cabin, or she would definitely have pronounced him devoid of intellect. He revealed an Italian emotional side, and what he couldn't articulate verbally in vernacular English, he communicated explicitly with his hands and body. Migrants in work camps learn a lot of English swear words, which they add to their own. When we arrived at the bottom of the hill in the same gear and then played Lotto with the gears, he went very quiet, while I contemplated hitch-hiking back to Sydney. I sadly applied all the parking brakes and switched off the engine. He must have liked that bit and gave me a job, albeit as far away as possible, on the other side of the mountains in Khancoban.

A small group of us were flown over the Snowy Mountains that afternoon. I was given a single three- by three-metre cabin in a block of four in the row. A set of steps at each end led onto a communal veranda (a structure known in Australia as a donga). There was no air conditioning and only a single-bar electric heater. It was bloody hot some days and freezing cold on others, but I was happy and independent at work and grew to like the big old Leyland Hippo trucks. The engine between the driver and any passenger roared; it was exhilarating and drowned out conversation. With courage and practice, the crash gearbox could be snap-changed to sound like an accelerating sports car with a racing gear box.

Snap-change means that the driver keeps his foot flat to the floor on the accelerator until the roar of the engine just reaches the right harmonic to engage with the cogs of the next gear up; he then stands on the clutch while hauling as fast as possible on the gear lever, which was a huge grey stick. The idea is that the gearbox and everything else is so taken by the element of surprise that the gear cogs don't have time to make all those dreadful grinding noises, and the cogs of the lower gear being at just the right place speed mesh with those of the next one up. If one misses, the truck joins the gearbox union and refuses to work or puts it in the wrong gear and stands the truck up on its nose with the load over the cab and in front on the road (the latter more likely when having to cross the diagonal with the gear lever while also pushing it forwards).

More than fun, it was a necessity in the mountains because allowing the revs to die down before slipping into the next gear meant that one would never get out of first gear on hills when loaded, and that spelt lose the job with that truck. To snap-change was absolutely necessary in the mountains, especially when being escorted carrying wide loads such as housing barracks. If the truck could not keep up with the escort going uphill, then trying to catch up once over the hill was dangerous because impatient tourists and busy delivery vans would creep along to be invariably met on a sharp bend. I am absolutely sure that the veranda of a house went over the top of one small car that had dived for the ditch near Dead Horse Gap on the way to Jindabyne. It presumably missed, as the name did not change to Dead Tourist Gap. There's no such fun in a modern truck, and they're no longer a male domain.

The safari experience with the 4X4 ex-army Bedford truck proved to be valuable; the Snowy Mountains Authority had one in Khancoban that was used to service hilltop and remote installations, communication towers, and fire control sites, and I was allocated these trips, which widened my exposure to this beautiful region.

Many of the camp occupants worked for contractors to the Snowy Mountains Authority, such as Thiess and Peconet. No single women were allowed to stay in the camp, and female tourists were only allowed one night in the camping and caravan grounds. No wonder men were chauvinists. There were immigrant men from many European countries: Yugoslavia (as it was then), Italy, Greece, Hungary, Czechoslovakia, Germany, Poland, Holland, Ireland, and Great Britain. The White Australia Policy still existed.

In general, behaviour was courteous and orderly. Alcohol was limited, and in those days, the pubs in NSW closed at six o'clock. Corryong was the next nearest town, thirty kilometres away, just over the border in Victoria, and its pub stayed open later. I still like Victorian bitter. Saturday afternoons were more Bacchanalian in Khancoban.

Some of the work was dangerous in the construction tunnels built to divert the water from the east-flowing Snowy River to the west-flowing Murray, and the Snowy Mountain Authority was very safety conscious. However, in the relatively short time I was there, I recall at least two fatal work accidents, which always quietened the mood. A man a mile of tunnel was the accepted fatality rate, and the Snowy Mountain Authority boasted a good safety record of a man every mile and a half. I asked once why people worked in the tunnels if they knew they had a 1 percent chance of being killed every year.

"Well," they said, "if you told us at the beginning of the year which one of us it would be, he wouldn't work there."

You take your chances, like going into a surgical operation.

Despite keeping single women out of the work camp, there were some fights, especially in the pub, and there was a stabbing following a game of Monopoly. For me so desperate to have some money for the following year, I couldn't believe they played Monopoly for real money.

A wonderful opportunity to see more of the Snowy Mountains Scheme befell me when given the job of driving the pay-car every two weeks. Men were paid on the job in cash. Every workplace had Snowy Mountains employees, even if the construction work had been subcontracted. Concrete testers, inspectors, surveyors, engineers, supervisors, and administration were all represented. I got to see every worksite on the western side and travelled every construction tunnel. 1966 was the year the Aussie dollar was introduced, and we went metric overnight. There was much discussion on what to call the new currency.

"How about calling it an Elizabeth?" suggested Prime Minister Robert Menzies.

"A Lizzie," said a pom.

What would we do with names like a "zac," which was a sixpence, or a "dina," which was a shilling? A shilling was also known by its English nickname of "bob"; what would we call a two-bob watch? There would be no more quids, and we wouldn't be able to call some people a "nine-bob note." Whatever we were to call the new currency, we were determined it should not be called a dollar, but we called it a dollar and lost our vernacular.

Occasionally, I would transport over to the eastern side and stay overnight in Jindabyne or Tumut; I traveled as far as Wagga-Wagga and Cooma. I enjoyed the longer trips and solitude in the strange work camps. After all, truck drivers have a mystique and are a sort of higher being—some literally, especially in those days of Benzedrine and Dexedrine to keep them awake on long distances. One truck driver reported that he was taking it wide to avoid the ship coming the other way.

A local lad called Graeme worked in transport and befriended me. He was very big and very strong, an excellent swimmer, who had been considered for competitive swimming but couldn't be bothered with all that training stuff. Graeme showed me swimming holes, remote campsites, and trout streams. He was the strongest man I've ever known. He walked into the Snowy Mountains Weight Lifting Club one night when we had nothing to do and just picked up the weights that their strongest was struggling with and held them above his head. At

the fair that visited each Christmastime, there was a stall with a
sledgehammer to hit a point at the base of a pole, which would
drive a weight up the pole to ring a bell at the top for a prize.
The proprietor was doing quite well until Graeme showed up
and demonstrated to everyone's delight how it could be done
with just one hand. After distributing some of the crappy prizes
to all and sundry, Graeme got bored and wandered off. The stall
closed for a while until Graeme was way out of sight.

Graeme's nanna's home was halfway between Khancoban
and Corryong. There were a couple of horses he kept there,
and one was a captured wild horse, a little fat chestnut brumby.
Graeme was too big for her, and she was more like a pet. He let
me ride her bareback while he rode a bigger hack. The little
brumby was a joy to ride because she never stumbled and moved
to the slightest pull on her mane. We had a lot of fun.

Although Graeme was young, he was the lead driver and
in charge of the Scammell heavy haulers, converted tank
transporters used to haul the huge turbines to be installed in
the dams. I escorted sometimes and marvelled at how the prime
mover would buck and jump as it crawled up the mountain with
the enormous weight. On some hills, they would use another
prime mover with a huge cement block over the axles to give
traction and push, as well. The pace was slow as a slow march,
and the gear ratio and power of the huge truck engines would
spin the wheels of the pusher, making better skid marks than
any hoon could ever make.

When I went back to college, I invited Graeme to the college
ball, and he was a great hit. For some reason, he ended up with
the smallest partner. After the ball, we headed for King's Cross,
and Graeme carried his partner up the rise of William Street
on one shoulder. He was the symbol of the Snowy Mountain
Scheme and the epitome of an Aussie to so many migrants.

The Snowy Mountain Scheme essentially closed down over
the Christmas and New Year period, and I had a ten-day holiday.
The thought of the honey blonde in Sydney drove me to walk

and hitch-hike to Albury, about one hundred miles away (which officially changed with the decimalisation of the currency to one hundred and fifty kilometres), to catch the train to Sydney. I organised to stay in a flat with a friend and meet up with Michele.

"Charlie," I said to my close university friend, forgetting the Tennessee Waltz, "you must meet this fantastic honey blonde bundle of freckles. I am meeting her at Bondi Beach; come with me."

We stood on the boardwalk and scanned the bodies on the beach, slowly. No honey blondes could be seen anywhere. I was sure I had been stood up, and we discussed introducing ourselves to some of the sun-bathing beauties instead. We debated the method of handling the inevitable rejections and were recalling the words of wisdom of our Nambucca surfing university colleague who made a practice of receiving such rejections with the philosophy, one yes is worth a thousand nos when a strawberry blonde came bouncing along. Michele had dyed her hair. The freckles still looked nice, the dye washed out, Charlie went home to Canberra for Christmas, Michele and I cemented our friendship, and then I went back to the Snowy Mountains to make enough money for the next year's expenses. Things were certainly looking up at university.

CHAPTER 10

White Coats and a New Medical School

It was most exciting starting second-year med. This was the real thing; my first year was a repeat of the last year of school, but now this was university and medicine.

The very first class was anatomy, which is considered a foundation stone for medicine. One hundred and twenty of us gathered in the lecture hall. A film of a postmortem examination started with instructions about how to respect the human body and especially cadavers which had been generously donated by the souls before they left their mortal shells. The mortician was then shown taking a scalpel and cutting the cadaver from the supra-sternal notch, at the top of the chest, all the way down to the symphysis pubis at the base of the penis. We lost half the class in a dead faint.

When the film was over, we were different people, changed forever. We had witnessed the removal of the abdominal and thoracic organs and seen the top of the skull excised to reveal the brain, which was also removed for examination. I had seen countless animals harvested and prepared, but the clinical postmortem examination of this cadaver, a human being, in the hush and swoon of the darkened lecture theatre during the already emotionally charged first morning, had a profound effect on me. I am sure it did on all of us; in some way, it paradoxically imparted a sense of honour and respect for the human body that has never left me.

From the lecture theatre, we were taken upstairs to the dissecting room and given white coats, shown how to sharpen a scalpel, and led into the cool cadaver dissecting room. There were thirty cadavers on metal tables, and we nearly lost the second half of the class. Students were paired according to their place in the alphabet and each pair assigned to one side of a body. Dissection was commenced on the arm. If there was any asymmetry, then each pair had to notify the other two on the opposite side. The room had an overpowering smell of formaldehyde and an atmosphere like no other: different from a morgue that's always cold and where there's usually little or no odour. The preserved old people were greyer than grey. Livida gravida mortis, the result of pooled disintegrated blood cells, stained the tissues along the lowest level of the stored bodies and made them appear ghostly and bruised, as if their end had been violent. Examples of professionally dissected (prosected) specimens were on display in glass cabinets around the room. Trailing nerves, muscles, blood vessels, exposed bones, and joints added to the unnatural and eerie Dr Frankenstein atmosphere. It was a form of total immersion in the human body. At the end of the day, we each purchased a real skeleton in a long cardboard box imported from India and carried it home to study.

My dissection partner, Peter, was handsome, well dressed, and studying medicine because he was very bright. Whether it was his burning passion could be in dispute. Our white coats became stained with preserved human fat and imbibed with the smell of formalin. Peter's strong and sensitive nose clashed fiercely with the formaldehyde; after leading him into the depths of intimacy with the body, it would leave, hooting, snorting, angry, wounded, and bleeding.

To protect his nose, Pete decided more could be learnt from the books in his room than in the body proper. However, it was necessary for him to put in a minimum appearance to pass, and he made a point of being seen to be seen. Whenever an opportunity presented, he would describe in a loud voice all his findings to the studious and conscientious Chinese pair on the other side. I don't know what they thought of Pete.

Nerves and blood vessels often run together in a neurovascular bundle like a multifibre cable. We were required to carefully dissect and display all the branches. Pete and I, dissecting on one side, displayed the nerves, and the pair on the other side displayed the vessels because it was expedient for us to separate the tasks and demonstrate to each other later. One day, Peter went to great lengths to show what we had done on our side to the other two, making sure that he did this when the tutor was close and would notice. Finishing with aplomb after punctuations with sniffs, snuffles, and snorts, he asked for the other two to take him through what they had done.

"Ah, we are very sorry, but this is not our side of the body; we are from another body and just looking," was the reply.

"Jeez," said Pete. "Bugger off. Why do you guys all look the same?"

He was certainly noticed by the tutor and 35 percent of the class who were Chinese and thought we "long-noses" looked the same (although they must have recognised Pete's nose as something special).

Every two weeks, we would have an oral examination (known as a viva voce in respect for the Latin origins of modern medicine). The viva would be on a particular body part that had been assigned for dissection. The examiners had complete licence in this oral exam to pursue any anatomic structures they wished within the prescribed area, whether it was visible in the dissection or not, whether it should be or not, and branches of branches that supplied parts of parts of organs. We had to know every curve, hollow, line, and ridge on every bone. What structure was attached, originated, inserted, or merely passed by had to be known and identified. These fearsome exams were a core medical training exercise. The detective examiner pursued the crevices and crannies in the knowledge gaps and exposed speech impediments and latent stutters, together with any deficiencies in knowledge and dissection.

Dennis Kerr set the standard. Immaculately dressed in either suit and tie or fashion-row sports coat and bow tie, he would present on the day in his laundered white coat complete with perfect dissections and fountains of anatomic knowledge, delivered in a measured voice that would be the envy of Sir Laurence Olivier in *Hamlet*.

Dennis and the dissecting room must have been one of the inspirations for another student, George Miller. George gave up medicine for the theatre as soon as he graduated and made films like *Happy Feet*, *Babe*, and *Mad Max* (which launched Mel Gibson into stardom).

I think Pete enjoyed the dressing up but not the demonstrating and describing of the dissections; he avoided poking his nose into the deeper anatomical mysteries of the body. He was excellent at maths and became an anaesthetist.

We did nothing but anatomy for a while. In addition to the fortnightly vivas, I sat four formal examinations in anatomy to become a surgeon. The body is like a huge city; one will never know all of its wonders at the same time, and it is almost impossible to remember all the streets. Surgeons live in this intricate city, and surgery is based in anatomy. Doctors with a good basis in anatomy may be ghouls, but doctors without are fools. Beware before you are fooled.

Biochemistry and microbiology followed. These were straightforward, clean subjects. Both seemed to always be going in circles and cycles, like Krebs's cycle, the life cycles of hydatids and flukes and mosquitoes, and rows of circles that were red or blue according to whether each was a Gram-positive or Gram-negative bacterium. Sometimes, the circles were in chains like streptococci or clumps like staphylococci. Microbiology always smelled funny. However, I don't remember any failures or dramas. But then came physiology.

I don't recall anatomy, for all its intricacies, being a stumbling block to progression through medicine. Anatomy was a benign problem. That is, it was difficult, but it was taught very well, and there was a solution in straight, hard study. Not so physiology: The solution to any problem spawned two others. It was like the dragon's teeth that Jason sowed. Many of our classmates failed, and we were, in one fell swoop, reduced from one hundred and twenty to less than eighty original starters in our year.

The dean and the professor of physiology had a disagreement. The dean wanted to know why so many intelligent students had failed. His view was that the problem was in the teaching of the subject. The professor of physiology was German and renowned for his work on hypertension and blood pressure. His standards were very high and so too became his blood pressure; he resigned.

There were more lessons than just medicine in this third year, and the most important life lesson was to never underestimate the power of an institution. The possibility of failing and losing my scholarship gave me nightmares; it would have been a disaster for me to fail that year, losing the Commonwealth Scholarship, without any financial reserves to fall back on. I have often been reminded of the importance of that year and how essential physiology is to understanding surgery and the responses to sickness, injuries, and shock.

Physiology is fundamental to surgery. I only really came to understand it when I had to study it again in depth six years later for the primary surgical examinations. I was fortunate enough to join the training anaesthetists through a friend. The teacher had a passion for physics and revealed a secret with this statement: "The key to circulation physiology is to equate it to electrical circuit theory."

The reason for learning all that physics in school and first-year medicine became clear, as physiology suddenly made sense. The world makes so much more sense when described in terms of maths and physics; so few seem to study these subjects nowadays, which explains why there is so little sense in the world. How many politicians do you know who have a science background, particularly in physics? There should be a quota of scientists in parliament.

The second event occurred even later when, as a young surgeon, I made a special visit to Bob Lusby, a highly reputed expert in carotid disease in Sydney. Bob had just returned from San Francisco, where he had been studying with Professor Jack Wylie; he brought duplex ultrasound technology back to Australia. The physics and application of ultrasound was becoming a fundamental tool for vascular surgery. Bob had taken up a position in Sydney University, and I went to see his lab. After a most enjoyable afternoon, during which I greatly admired the courage, fortitude, and expertise with which he had set up his lab with the new technology (it's not easy to introduce new technology), I had a strong sense of déjà vu that I could not shake.

Eventually, I said that I was sure we had met before somewhere.

"Yes," he said, "we were in the same physiology year."

The most powerful teaching aid is emotion—be it with pleasure, pain, aggression, or fear—and associated emotional highs and lows indelibly imprint the memory and trigger recall. Biochemistry and microbiology were devoid of such emotions, and while recognising how important both have been, I don't recall either with emotion.

The preclinical year hurdles of anatomy and physiology were cleared, and we moved out of the university campus, jeans, and tee shirts and into the clinical years of medical school. We shifted into the teaching hospitals and changed into trousers, shirts, and ties. Years later, when teaching medical students, I was repeatedly asked the familiar question as to why we had to change our outward appearance if the inner soul was pure.

I returned the same answer that I had received: "We do it not for ourselves but in respect for those patients we hope to serve."

The rank of medical personnel was signified by their white coats. They were very short for medical students and lengthened progressively with rise in the ranks. The higher the rank, the longer the coat; a professor's coat almost brushed the floors. Filthy things, they were. The lower the rank, the less they were washed. Smeared with body fluids, spots of blood, beads of pus, and bits of hasty meals that rotted in the recesses of the whitish coats, they would hang on shoulders by day and side-by-side on racks at night.

Here's a powerful story about the difficulty in introducing something new: After Ignaz Semmelweis introduced hand-washing for doctors (a simple measure that's surely been one of the greatest advances in combating infections), he was driven to madness by the derision from his peers. Semmelweis was beaten to death in a mental asylum in Austria by his carers.

After persuading doctors to wash their hands between patients, the next improvement might be getting rid of the white coats. This should be followed by prohibiting the wearing of stethoscopes and used face masks around the neck, and ties which had accompanied fingers and instruments into various orifices should also not be worn.

At the time, I was very proud of my white coat. It signified that I was a clinical medical student and going to be a doctor. Brimming with expectation and enthusiasm, I attended the ward at the appointed hour, dressed in my new white coat and stethoscope and tie around my neck. I opened my mind and soul to pollination.

CHAPTER 11

The Clinical Years in Medical School

The teaching in the clinical years is like a lucky dip, but one in the family of a rich household. You don't know what present you'll receive but expect it to be expensive and good. So it is with your appointed clinical teacher. There had been no formal teaching of the teacher. It was an apprenticeship rather than a class. You were most likely to be taught the way they were taught. Medicine, despite the appearance, is a sometimes humbling reminder of the nearness of failure. I was very fortunate; the enthusiasm in the new medical school of New South Wales was tangible, and the clinical tutors seemed to enjoy teaching as much as we did learning. I remember them all vividly.

There were some really colourful characters. Professor Billington of gastroenterology was short, rotund, and bald; only his tongue had a sharp edge. He is one of the most memorable and loved doctors of an era no longer. At Christmastime it seemed to me that he would fill every available bed with the downtrodden, winos, and homeless of the streets of eastern Sydney so that they would be loved and have a good feed at least once a year. After Christmas dinner, they were given all the leftover chocolates, biscuits, and goodies from the surplus of holiday gifts to nurses. Then on discharge, they would be cleaner for the next year's street minding.

Professor Jim Lance of neurology was handsome, lithe, energetic, and encyclopaedic. He acquired a huge number of patients; each seemed to have a different syndrome, and each syndrome had two or three names linked together in recognition of the doctors who described the condition or the places they were first found. His ward round encompassed nearly the whole hospital; the entourage of white coats of every length swept through like a strange army where the drill was to extend the neck with the head turned slightly to right or left, depending on which was the better ear.

Hard to believe that in a relatively small population such as Sydney, there would be so many of these syndromes. Maybe the seemingly endless number of neurological diagnoses in Sydney was the result of biodiversity bestowed by migration from so many different parts of the world. For most, it didn't really matter what you called the collection of symptoms and signs because it didn't seem to warrant a different management. It did, however, generate a lot of learning and admiration. While a stethoscope was taken for granted as essential equipment for a doctor, I was somewhat financially disadvantaged by the insistence that we should also acquire an auroscope and an ophthalmoscope if we expected teaching from Professor Jim.

"The eyes and ears are the windows to the brain and the body; look through them," he would declare, and off we would go around the ward.

His colleague was quiet and thoughtful and of Greek family origins with mythical airs. He would trail behind the group, staying to chat with the odd patient. After the chat, he'd offer them a chocolate. It was the time when migraine researchers believed in the myth that chocolate was a precipitator of migraine. I use the term *myth* in its literal sense of a belief in an unproven fact. As a renowned specialist and expert in the field, he was going to prove it. Beware of Greeks bearing gifts.

So where did the humiliation fit in with the teaching? Well, it was at the next level. Whether a student knows something or not, it doesn't really matter, but if a doctor doesn't know, it can be a matter of life or death. Doctors need to be taught humility. The rationale of teaching by humiliation is that the teacher who humiliates is human, if not humane.

The next teacher is nature. Mother Nature is the least tolerant of inadequacy. She is the final auditor and respects no social standing or reputation. If she is ignored by a lack of humility, she is not forgiving, and the result may be irreversible. My first lesson in the use of humiliation was in the infectious diseases block at Prince Henry Hospital, which was located on the North Head to Botany Bay, near the Aboriginal community at La Perouse. It was set far enough away to be an isolation facility, and it still had a special block for infectious diseases, including leprosy. Jaundice was a common presentation associated with infectious disease, such as hepatitis A, B, and C. Fevers were another; a fever pending diagnosis was known as a PUO (pyrexia of unknown origin).

So this block was fertile ground for teaching signs and examination techniques. I would try hard to feel or see what the tutors wanted me to find. I was never quite sure whose imagination was better, theirs or mine. During this particular tutorial, the teaching clinician was called away, and we were left to examine the patient on our own. Clinicians were always uncertain about when they would return; sometimes, they didn't come back at all, and that's why doctors' wives are such especially tolerant people (if they stay).

Our group of four students was left to chat to a very jaundiced patient in his mid-fifties. The bright orange-yellow gaunt man with a large round abdomen graciously allowed us to examine him. This we duly did in solemn fashion and tentatively palpated his rotund abdomen, a veritable Californian navel orange. There is a prescribed sequence to examining an abdomen that follows a general pattern, looking into the patient's face for any reaction and conducting inspection, palpation, percussion, and auscultation (in other words, look, feel, tap for resonance, and listen with the stethoscope for sounds). A principle of palpation is to either keep the body part still or keep the examining hand still while the other moves. In the abdomen, patients can move the viscera when they take a big breath because the diaphragm, working like a piston, descends and pushes the organs down (especially good for examining an enlarged liver or spleen). Many of the jaundiced patients in the infectious diseases block had liver failure due to alcoholism, to the extent that the block had lost the infectious tag and was known as the jaundice block. Alcoholism leads to a large scarred liver that is good for teaching students because it's easy to feel, and there are many associated signs that test the powers of observation. It's also often associated with ascites, a large amount of free fluid in the peritoneal cavity.

When the tutor returned from his call, he expected us to have found an enlarged liver with ascites in a patient in liver failure from alcoholism. It was not his patient, and he had not seen him before. The young ward doctor had recommended the patient as a good teaching case and given him the presumed diagnosis. We related our findings: a history of painless development of jaundice with the signs of a low-grade fever, an enlarged liver, a palpable gall bladder, and ascites. The tutor said nothing. He moved us aside, sat on a chair on the right side of the patient, which is the correct position to perform a proper abdominal examination, placed his hand gently over the liver area just below the ribcage on the right side, and asked the patient to take a large slow breath.

He felt the liver move down to touch his hand and felt the smooth round tennis ball of the distended gall bladder on the margin of the liver: signs and symptoms of someone with cancer of the head of the pancreas. The low-grade fever that can occur with cancer for one reason or another had prompted the admitting young doctor to place the patient in the jaundice ward with PUO for investigation, and the history of excessive alcohol had prompted the overworked ward doctor, in an attempt to be helpful, to suggest to the tutor that this patient with jaundice would be a good teaching case.

The tutor rose and went to find the young doctor, and they both soon returned. In front of us, he made the doctor examine the patient until he felt the gall bladder; he concurred that he had been inadequate in his admitting examination. The patient (and hospital) would have been greatly inconvenienced and put to much unnecessary cost if the lowly students had not, unlike him, done the correct examination. The humiliation was palpable.

The lesson for him, and us, was that mistakes are unacceptable. I guess, as a medico, if you aren't taught this, then society and the law will do so at some time. It's a harsh tool that has sometimes been overused; there is a line between teaching and bullying. The line may have been crossed that day. I vowed I would try not to teach by humiliation because most medicos are so self-critical that it's merely necessary to point out an inadequacy, but I have seen many a junior painfully humiliated.

Maybe the humiliation was cruelty to be kind. Like a predator learning to kill through play, humiliation was part of learning, teaching, and practising medicine. There were other emotions, as there always are with winners and losers. The thrill of being right stimulates the pursuit of excellence, buoyed on by its partner, competition. I don't think I felt sorry for the young doctor but maybe a bit embarrassed. Mostly, I felt satisfaction and elation for being right.

Diagnostic medicine is like a thriller story, and you are the detective. Observations, sequencing of coincidences, hunches, experience, persistence, and deduction are the elements driving a good detective doctor to that eureka moment. For a surgeon, the thrill of diagnosis is tinged with the senses of danger and reward. Many diagnoses imply a treatment that must be carried out, like a mandatory sentence. If you diagnose appendicitis, you take the appendix out. That's why people often hear relatives say, "He is ill, but the doctors don't know what it is." Maybe the doctors don't, but alternatively they won't say until they're ready to face the consequences of the diagnostic label.

The rewards of making someone better by performing a life-saving procedure are very special. The look in the eyes, however brief, of the knowing patient or their loved ones is the special touch of souls. Then there are the dark feelings of inadequacy and failure when wrong, however long the odds of being right might have been, that also touch deep inside, and there they lurk for the next time. Another cliché that shadows a surgeon, who might be deemed arrogant or uncaring, is that pride goes before destruction and a haughty spirit before a fall, but how does a surgeon deal with a mistake, handle a death, and console others amidst his failure? They then need the strength to bear the wrath of society on bowed shoulders and still carry on. That was what I knew I had to learn if I wanted to be a surgeon: how to deal with perception as much as with reality. The words from around the campfire echoed back: it is the man who never worked who never made a mistake.

After two years in the Basser Residential College, Harry, Charlie, and I moved out and shared a flat in Coogee, up the hill to the south of the beach, on the east side of Sydney. We learnt to cook and made a one-in-three roster. If you didn't cook when it was your turn, you bought dinner. We cooked badly, and Harry was the first to relent and bought Chinese take-away from an array of warm metal trays in Coogee Bay Road, thereafter known as the "Chew and Spew." It was coupled with the Coogee Bay Hotel, which we affectionately called the "House of the Rainbow Yawn."

We developed our own brand of flat culture. This was the sixties: the pill, women's liberation, the Vietnam War, demolition of censorship, waves of migration of New Australians, recognition that Aborigines were citizens in their own land and given the vote, and abandonment of the White Australia Policy. Rightly or wrongly, we made only one house rule: no girls were to live in the flat, probably because we were unaware that platonic or commercial cost-sharing relationships could exist.

Our observations of the flat across the hallway suggested coed flats and houses were unbalanced, financially and space wise. The girls seemed to pay in kind, took advantage of the non-partnered members, and were just as untidy or disinclined to washing and cleaning. Anyway, Harry's Joan was seven hundred kilometres up north in Mullumbimby. She worked on the telephone exchange and had a method of ringing cost-free, so Harry lived as much in the telephone booth across the road as he did in the flat (he was the original Dr Who). Michele lived in the Nurses Home of Royal Prince Alfred Hospital on the other side of town, and Charlie didn't have a sweetheart (that we knew of); maybe the flat was all male by circumstance rather than by design.

There were six two-bedroom flats in the two-story block. Each floor had three flats, with the rest of the floor taken up by the stairwell, incinerator, and communal laundry, with a large copper washtub and a mangle. "I haven't laughed so much since Aunt Nellie caught her tits in the mangle" always popped into my head whenever I washed my clothes. The flat was a happy place, close to the beach and pub. Harry was in the main room, and Charlie and I took the other two rooms. We ate and lived in the kitchen. Harry was studying industrial chemistry and Charlie chemical engineering. Both started university a year before me and were in their fourth and final year, so study was quite a strong ethic.

Harry, being in the main room, was more aware of the other tenants in the block and relayed his suspicions that a couple of girls in the flat above were taking hard drugs. One day, there was a noise like a fall on the stairs, and we heard someone scream. Harry was first on scene and found one of the girls collapsed in the stairwell, with her friend in panic mode. Harry was a lifeguard from Byron Bay, so he applied mouth-to-mouth, and Charlie went for a doctor he knew up the street.

I can't remember how the police came to be there, but after the ambulance came and took the girl away, the police began searching the flats. The chemical textbooks and diagrams in our flat naturally caught their attention, and the medical obstetrics and gynaecology books strewn amongst artefacts and skeletal bones fixed it. The top of the skull, or calvarium, was removable, having been sawn off to allow study of the inside of the skull. This convinced the police that they were really on to something; at the very least, a backroom abortion clinic (and abortion was illegal in New South Wales).

It took some time to allay all their suspicions with respect to our flat. Fortunately for us, the police accepted our explanations, but the taxi driver was not so lucky. He had waited patiently for his money after dropping off the girls and eventually came in to see what all the activity was about. The police latched on to a new suspect and inspected his cab. Poor bugger. The girls had not paid him, he had lost time waiting, and now the police wanted to book him because he had alcohol in the cab; after all their efforts, the police were "bloody well going to find someone to arrest." Harry was rewarded for his life-saving efforts with the flu, which he caught from the mouth-to-mouth resuscitation.

I had worked on the Snowy Mountain Scheme for two summer vacations and assumed that I would do so again at the end of the year. I had bought an old four-cylinder Wolseley, with the lovely feature of a little light in the badge on the grill. It was a fitting car for a gestating doctor, and like me, it smoked. During the midyear vacation, Michele and I smoked it up to the mountains, past Canberra, Cooma, Thredbo, and Dead Horse Gap to Khancoban. It was beautiful in the summer when I worked there; it was even more beautiful in the snow and when one was in love. The greeting in the transport administration office at Khancoban was warm but the job prospect for the next summer vacation icy cold. The Snowy Mountain Scheme was winding up, and my vacation would be too short. We slept in the car (we were used to that) and then made our way back to

Sydney the next day, wondering how to make enough money to survive the next year. We crept into the flat about midnight so as not to wake Charlie and had a shower and went to bed (Harry was away visiting Joan).

At dawn, we were woken by the most God-awful noise. There on the tiny lawn between the flats and the road was a portly, half-naked man; he looked like a hermit crab without its shell. He was beating a large saucepan with a metal spoon just outside Charlie's window, through which Charlie was demanding to know what the hell he was doing.

"Well," said the man, "if you take a fucking shower in the middle of the fucking night and wake me, then I am going to fucking wake you up when you're asleep."

Charlie was more bewildered than ever and was informing the man that he was mad and should consult a psychiatrist. Apparently, our water pipes, which passed through the walls of the upstairs man's bedroom, vibrated. He had taken the girls' flat, and they had never complained (but they probably never heard nor cared while stoned). Michele and I kept very quiet for a while until the naked hermit crab sidled back upstairs.

Towards the end of third year, flat life was drawing to a close; Charlie and Harry were to graduate and set forth into the industrial world. I searched for cheaper single accommodation until Michele could move out of the nursing home when she finished training. Val, an elderly woman who lived down the street, had a medical student lodging with her. He was in the year above me and was moving out at the end of the year, and she said I could have his room.

She seemed nice, and she was. She let me use her garage to work on the Wolseley, as she no longer had a car. I could move in at the end of the year after Harry and Charlie finished their courses; it would be good. In the meantime, the Wolseley took up residence in her garage. The old car needed repairs and something other than the light in the badge to function properly. My friend Pete was most encouraging and explained that because his father had a vehicle rust-proofing business, he could get auto parts at trade rates. Armed with this discount, we arranged to recondition the car. The plan was to remove the engine, rebore the block, get some new and slightly larger rings, and grind the valves. The end result would be the smoothest, smokeless Wolseley in Sydney. Pete was keen to get his nose into something that didn't smell of formaldehyde and would be more interesting to him than studying medicine.

We laid part of a telegraph pole on the flat roof of Val's garage, with the end just protruding over the edge, so that a Westin pulley could be attached and used to lift the engine out. It worked; the engine was to be dismantled, the pots rebored, and new rings and bearings put in. The old girl was going to give up smoking.

At the crucial moment when the engine was in the air and being swung out of the car, Val came out and wanted to know why there was a large pole on her garage roof. She declared an immediate (if not sooner) halt to the proceedings on the grounds that we would destroy her garage. She was probably right, but we had a problem because the engine was halfway out. We had the presence of mind to put it on the garage floor rather than back in the car. The pole was removed, Val was soothed, and the new rings and bearings made ready.

Now the problem was how to get the engine back into the car. Well, Charlie had not woken up in the middle of the night when we came back from the snowy mountains, so maybe Val wouldn't either. We went at midnight and put the pole back on; the engine went back in the car in the pitch-dark, broken only by the thin shielded beam of a small torch. It didn't seem to puzzle Val as to how we had been able to lift the engine back in. When it was ready, there was a grand collection of friends to witness the smokeless wonderful Wolseley. It was indeed smokeless, but it wasn't wonderful. In fact, the engine had seized.

After much consultation and examination, we realised that the bearing cases were numbered according to the firing order and not in sequence from one end to the other, as we had put them in. Installed in the wrong order, they did not fit perfectly and acted as a brake on the crankshaft. So at midnight, the pole was placed on the roof again and the engine lifted out in the dark. The next night, at midnight, the engine went back in for the second time, in the dark, and the Wolseley started to cheers.

Poor old girl; she had been so stressed by the whole ordeal that she took up smoking again and smoked furiously to catch up on the lost time. When the smoke cleared, my friends, using the smoke screen, had vanished. They had got as far away from the pole and the car as they could; before I could turn the engine off, they were all gone.

I taught Michele how to drive, and left her with the car at Christmastime. We had had our first terse words while I was teaching her the basic principles of driving. After the lurching phase, which was in a paddock until she mastered the clutch, we took to the open road. At that time, New South Wales had a road rule that you always had to give way to vehicles on the right. Even vehicles on six-lane highways had to give way to cars entering from the smallest of streets on the right.

Consequently, everyone in NSW developed torticollis, driving with a twist of the neck to the right. With respect to what might be happening on the left, people completely ignored that side. If someone hit you from the left, it was always their fault, but if you failed to give way to the right, then it was going to cost. It was a rule made by someone with only half a brain that had been screwed onto the wrong end of their body; thankfully, it was finally abandoned when the insurance companies began going broke. Funny that things change when the insurance companies start hurting.

Michele concentrated firmly on the road ahead while I, in the passenger seat with no dual control, watched fearfully to the right and uttered repeated and increasingly louder warnings.

After a few near misses, I lost my urbane courting manners and yelled, "Look to your bloody right!"

"Don't you speak to me like that," she snapped as the most expensive car in Sydney passed in front with the horn blaring.

Another coat (or the even the original coat) of paint, and we would have swapped colours. I saw love and marriage disappearing like a runaway horse and carriage.

As pride goes before destruction, I accepted the shame of failing her expectations of me teaching her how to drive. The plan was for her to have a couple of driving lessons before sitting the test, while I went back to Kenya during the vacation to help Stan guide a safari, make some money to pay for the fare, and help finance the next year. There were no problems with the second part of the plan, but the first part was a disaster.

The driving instructor arranged to teach in his vehicle and called at Michele's little flat in Newtown to collect her. History does not record the first lesson, but on the second occasion, the instructor knocked on her door, walked in when she opened it, and went over and sat on the bed. Michele prepared for fight-or-flight and was going to resist forced entry, but the instructor started to weep and informed Michele that he could not face teaching her that day.

I nodded with a sense of sympathy for the instructor (which she did not appreciate as she continued to relate the story). It turned out that it was not due to her failures to look to the right. The young man had recently been in Callan Park, the nearby psychiatric hospital, and was distraught that they were going to make him prime minister (Harold Holt, the Australian prime minister, has just drowned at Cheviot Beach near Melbourne). Michele slipped into her nursing role and successfully consoled the young man, reassuring him that he was not to worry; it would all take a long time before an election would be held, and Callan Park could get him into a stronger state of mind.

As he was in danger of self-harm, she also persuaded him to let her call for an ambulance. She then decided with this revelation of her nursing skills that psychiatric nursing was to be her true calling; she also decided to try the driving test on her own in the Wolseley. She didn't like Callan Park when she visited it, and the police impounded the Wolseley for smoking and declared the vehicle terminal. Michele was psychologically deflated, put the psych nursing on hold, hired a new instructor, and planned to take the test in his car. (Coincidentally, a major inquiry into Callan Park exposed it as a cruel and terrible place, which led to an overhaul of psychiatric services in New South Wales.)

Fourth-year med started out as the happiest year. Michele passed her driving test. I came back from Nairobi with a family ring in my pocket, and Michele and I became engaged. She had passed her nursing exams and only had to serve out time to graduation. She had a job at Royal Prince Alfred Hospital and was living in a little one-bedroom flat in Newtown, near the hospital. She shared this with her friend Robyne; they had different shifts, which suited us all.

Problems only arose when she was on night duty and had to walk the narrow streets up to her flat. Newtown was a fringe city suburb on the railway line, and its station was the one before Redfern. These were the roughest suburbs in Sydney. Getting off at Newtown was no better than getting off at Redfern, the station before Central Sydney. For a Sydneysider, "Getting off at Redfern" was the colloquial expression for coitus interruptus; these suburbs gave one feelings of dissatisfaction. Good thing she could run fast and kept her eyes open. After she escaped a chase one night, we decided that I would buy a small motorbike (since I no longer had the Wolseley) and ride over the twelve kilometres from Coogee to take her the one kilometre to her flat when she was on evening duty. Now that's love (and the power of lust).

It became increasingly difficult to live at Val's. With her Jewish family ethic, she wanted to love me to death and be my Australian mother. I was being asphyxiated and had to move out. Enid sold her house in Balmain and, in true socialist style, bought two others with the profit. One was in the suburb of Annandale, which she rented out, and the other was in Camperdown, close to the hospital and opposite a park; not fancy, but cheap and convenient. In Balmain, Camperdown, Annandale, Newtown, and Redfern, where we were, one did not look at the surroundings as one might in leafier suburbs.

Instead, we saw warmth and intimacy, hope and refuge and only a way up, as there was no further way down. Enid provided the compensations. She knew how to survive and did it with spirit. She was far more liberal in her views than most mothers in the sixties and offered Michele and me the large front room overlooking the park. It worked well. I studied when Michele was on duty or late at night when she was asleep. Tom, my budgie, lived on the curtain rail or sat on my shoulder and kept me company when on my own studying. I would listen to the Ashes test cricket on the radio with one ear and to Tom with the other. Enid was out most evenings, socialising with the Australian Socialist party (it had changed from the Communist party after the unacceptable events in Hungary and Czechoslovakia). Stanley was conceived amongst the bliss.

We planned to get married in October that year after Michele graduated; our goal was for Michele to support me through the rest of medical school, and then we'd have kids and live happily ever after. Now we lived happily before and were having a kid, and then we were going to get married; she wouldn't be able to support me for some time.

The professor of obstetrics was responsible for the change in plan. He supplied free contraception to all wives and girlfriends who agreed to participate in his research. This was to develop a low-dose contraceptive pill. A vaginal temperature chart was kept, and if the contraception worked, then there was no rise in temperature during the menstrual cycle. He would then lower the dose each time for those women until they ovulated. His plan was to find the threshold at which ovulation would occur and then lift the dose slightly.

The problem was that he effectively found the threshold for pregnancy; some of the women fell pregnant when the temperature rose, and others had a variable threshold. Michele was one of many. There were more babies in the class of our year than there had ever been before. Two of my friends had two each. When we finally graduated, there were almost as many babies present as there were graduates. So my son Stanley was at our wedding, listening to the music in the womb, and also at my graduation; that could be the basis of our lasting bond. My mother, being a dyed-in-the-wool Tory and daughter of a village vicar, disapproved of everything from afar but didn't ask for the ring back, and so we married as planned in October, with Stanley listening to our heartbeats from inside.

All marriages may be special and each different in its own way. Mine was certainly different, and Enid made it special. She was a confirmed atheist but went to church regularly. Her Welsh miner family history imparted a great love for music and the stirring Welsh hymns, so she loved the church for her choir singing and probably, in parts at least, nostalgia for Wales. We were married in the little Welsh Chapel in Chalmers Street, to the strains of the Welsh Choir and a soloist Welsh tenor. Then we retired to Enid's house for the reception. With little money, the reception was a backyard affair, with a sheet draped over the Hills Hoist clothesline for a garden umbrella. The little garden and small two-storey house were packed with medical students, nurses, socialists, diehard communists, a few cousins from both sides, African students, and friends, and then it poured. It was chaos with everyone packed in the house, and an African student beamed at me through the gloom with large white teeth and exclaimed how wonderfully lucky I was because it was raining on my wedding day. That meant we would be fertile (well, I already knew that), and we would have many children. And that made me happy.

That night, we moved into a tiny one-room flat with a veranda kitchen in a house converted to a number of small self-contained rooms with a communal bathroom. It was newly converted and freshly painted. We were the first tenants on the upper level, with a view from our veranda kitchen overlooking the Randwick rugby field. Although small, we thought it beautiful, and I'll never forget the first morning of married life on the veranda, with the sun coming up over Coogee Beach.

The problem was not love but money and time. I needed a job that I could do when I could find the time, and so it had to be casual and at my call. That was a tall order. I recalled that the master of Basser College's son had driven a taxi part-time and decided this was the solution. There were some hurdles, though. First, I had to pass the locality test. It was in two parts: a written test and an oral test. It was like med school. I had no idea about the streets and important buildings in Sydney, but I knew how to pass exams, and the streets of a city are like the vessels in the body. They all have names, and they are all going somewhere. The police sergeant told me after the oral test that he was sure I had no idea where anything was, despite getting the answers right, and wished me luck. I thanked the God of all things (including atheists) for the land of a fair go. This meant that I had a taxi licence and could now find a taxi to drive. In the meantime, I was poorer for the investment in the tests and licence.

Taxi shifts went from 4:00 a.m. to 3:00 p.m. for the morning shift and 3:00 p.m. to 3:00 a.m. for the night shift. Taxis were on the road for twenty-three hours (the spare hour was for cleaning). It was for the night driver to wash and clean the cab out for the day driver; there were two practical reasons for this. First, the customers were more likely to mess up the cab during the evenings and late at night. They would drop things out of hamburgers, sit on bits of pizza, rainbow-yawn after drinking, and so on. Second, the day driver was usually the owner (or more senior, if it were a depot-managed cab). This was the custom with Yellow Cabs, anyway. Some owners who did not want to drive or had more than one cab and did not want to manage them would lease to a depot. It cost ten times as much to own the taxi plates as it did to buy the vehicle. The number of licensed cabs was limited. Owning a cab plate was a significant investment and much sought-after as a cash cow. That's why it had to be on the road continually.

To get to drive, if you did not know an owner, you registered with the company and stood in line at the depot at three in the afternoon. The manager then picked out those he knew (if he didn't recognise anybody, he'd pick out the most likely, by age or beauty). Once the managed cabs had all been allocated, the rest of us left in hope for another day. After repeated disappointments and almost ready to give up trying, I was allocated a cab. It was grand-final day for the rugby league, and I guess a lot of drivers either wanted to watch or knew better than to drive on such a day. I was just thrilled to get a cab.

South Sydney won, and the inner city was packed. I picked up a fare at the end of the match and took them down O'Riordan Street to Central Station, where they could catch a train home to the outer suburbs. There were four passengers (that was the limit), and they were in high spirits. When we got down to the junction with Elizabeth Street just outside Central Station, there was a cop directing traffic, as was the custom on very busy days and the traffic lights were switched out.

While I was neatly waiting with the cab at his feet, the customers became impatient, and they all got out right in the middle of the busiest intersection in Sydney, on the busiest day of the year, and right next to the cop with traffic going everywhere. Well, I couldn't let them go without paying the fare, could I? The cop became apoplectic; he told me to drive across to the other side and wait because he was going to fine me heavily and cancel my licence.

I was mortified; it was my first fare, and I was going to lose my licence. After some considerable time, he was too busy to get across to me and dismissed me with an impatient wave and shouted warning. The rest of the shift involved many trips to

and fro from South Sydney Ruby Leagues club; much later that
night, a young woman was so happy she tipped me with a kiss
and informed me that it was all too much excitement; she was
giving up football.

"Do you really play football?" I asked.

"No, you bloody nong. I am a fan," and then I remembered
Van Riebeeck's rugby game and how passionate girls could be
about rugby.

I started to get chosen regularly from the line-up by the
manager. Whenever picking up a fare, I always asked which way
the customer wanted to go (knowing the route on paper didn't
help with recognition of the street). After a while, when I knew
the streets and best route, I still asked the way because many
people wanted to go their way, and by doing that, I erased any
suspicion of fare cheating.

The Vietnam War was on, and fellow taxi drivers described
cashed-up American soldiers on rest and recreation (R&R)
leave in Sydney getting in the cab and booking it for the whole
day or wanting a trip with hundreds of miles of sightseeing, but
it never happened to me. I mainly drove them the short distance
from the R&R centre in Woolloomooloo to the night spots in
Kings Cross via Liverpool Street, where all the doorways where
lit and filled by the shapes and shadows of call girls.

"How come you know all the flesh pots in Sydney?" my
friends would ask suspiciously.

"Oh, yeeah," they would respond to my answer.

"Why are they called call girls instead of prostitutes or
whores?" I asked the cab manager.

"Well," he said, "you have to show some respect for social
workers, and anyway, most of them have a day job on the Sydney
telephone exchange."

By contrast, my greatest pleasure was boring. I liked to call in
at home for meals whenever I could get there at an appropriate
time, but I often had to accept a late warmed-up plate. I didn't
know that I was inadvertently setting the trend for years to come.

I learnt a lesson about not engaging the public with familiarity. One evening, finding myself close to home on the stretch between Bondi and Coogee, I did not raise my flag after the fare got out and remained not for hire. It was a busy night, and patrons from the nearby Bronte Charles Hotel thronged the streets. It was early evening, and being in the eastern suburbs, I was looking for an opportunity to call in at home for a meal; you never knew where the next fare might take you.

A young fellow and two girls said they only wanted to go to Clovelly, which was next to Coogee; as it was on my way, I agreed to take them (they appeared in good honest spirits). We all entered into some repartee, and the young fellow came off second best. They wanted to be dropped off at a house near the end of a cul-de-sac and I pulled into the driveway The two girls got out of the cab and left the young fellow to pay, as was the way of many girls. The fare was small, and he suggested we flip a coin for double or quits. Because I was in a happy mood close to home, I agreed. He flipped a coin onto the back of his left hand, covered it with his right, and declared himself the winner.

Impulsively, I blurted that I had not seen the coin.

He calmly put the coin in his pocket, walked around to the open driver's side window, and punched me in the mouth.

As he drew his fist back to hit me again, I opened the door as hard as I could and pushed it against him with my legs, and he fell back over the low brick wall that delineated the street verge from the front garden of the house, landing in a rose bush. He picked up a large lump of wood, ran around the wall, back along the drive way and charged at the cab. In my haste to reverse out of the driveway and the cul-de-sac, I pulled the gear shift past reverse into drive and planted my foot to exit at speed. The cab leapt at him in a counter charge, to which he gave way and disappeared back over the wall again.

Whether he was without cash, generally annoyed by the discourse, or just feral, I didn't wait to find out. On finding the correct gears, I left skid marks on the road on exiting. I didn't get much food past my bruised mouth, but Michele kissed it better, and I vowed always to be strictly business with all forms of public intercourse from then on.

We had married in October, and by that time, I was well into the clinical years and constantly interested in the hospital, to the extent that study was not a chore to be done to learn but a fascinating research pastime. I knew that I would pass the fourth and fifth years; there were no guillotining exams until the final hurdle at the end of the sixth year. I only had to survive and keep my family alive. The scholarship paid my tuition, and because I had demonstrated more than three years independence, I was paid a living allowance (fourteen dollars a week) as an independent student (with an extra four dollars for our child). This I supplemented with the taxi driving one night a week, weekends, and public holidays. Michele worked as a nurse in a nearby nursing home until she began to show. These were still the days when women were sacked when they became pregnant, but for a while, we were okay and even made some money. We bought an old VW, and with my motorbike, we were both mobile.

This was a hard but very special year. The little flat with the veranda overlooking green rugby fields, sandy Coogee Beach, and white-maned seahorses on the sunny blue ocean lost its charm. The night parties at the rugby club next door and the disgusting communal lavatory combined to make this an unsuitable place for Stanley. So we moved. We were very lucky and found a little wooden house on the hillside at the upper end of Dolphin Street, number 21: a number with meaning. It symbolised the coming of age. I've always liked the number 21. My mother never gave her age and always said she was twenty-one when asked (this had caused endless confusion with the Kenya bureaucracy). The taxi radio-controller had little quips when giving out street numbers and addresses; 21 was always "your age" (and he didn't know my mother).

21 Dolphin Street, Randwick was dilapidated, to say the least, but that suited us well because that made it affordable; we fixed it up with paint, paper, and a few tools. It was on a slope with stairs down to a garden and an under-croft that we turned into another flat for Bill and Margaret Ward, who also had a child under the "Low-Dose Pill, Have a Baby" project. It was very close to Prince of Wales Hospital, and friends and colleagues called in all the time. Charlie's younger brother took the spare room and boarded. I built a Heron sailing boat in the garden from a plan; the inside of the little house took on a carpenter's shop appearance. Michele made the sails. It was not built to race. It was too heavy because I made a stronger transom than suggested, in case I never learnt to sail and needed an outboard motor. I built it for the occupational therapy of the woodwork, and we sailed Sydney Harbour, discovering picnic spots. It turned out to sail beautifully; we could direct it and sail happily without even using the rudder, just the mainsail. We were very happy in Dolphin Street and lived there until we moved to Western Australia after my hospital residency.

In the mess and tangle of intense times, there are certain aspects that burn and etch the memory deeper. Although not always momentous, they are most often associated with an emotion. Hand-washing was one of these. We studied paediatrics in Michele's third trimester. The instructor was Professor Beveridge, and he was the ultimate protector of children. He demanded more of the medical students than the other disciplines in medical school and quickly terminated career intentions if we did not comply. He absolutely insisted on washing hands between every child that was touched; to do this, the sleeves had to be rolled up and watches or bracelets removed. If not done properly, he would suspend ward privileges. One might think that there would be no problems getting students and doctors to wash their hands between patients—not so. It can still be difficult; watch what your doctor does next time after touching another person.

Although I have some stories about the lack of hand-washing, I can't tell one better than the original story of Ignaz Semmelweis, who introduced routine hand-washing before touching a patient. Semmelweis was an Austrian obstetrician who noticed that women would avoid the hospital's doctors and instead seek the midwives in another building. On researching why, he found that women attended by the doctors were dying after delivery at a higher rate.

Semmelweis deduced that the doctors were spreading death from one woman to another. Puerperal sepsis was the killer (this was before the discoveries by Louis Pasteur that bacteria were the cause of infections). We now know this to be due to a streptococcus that infects the birth-canal, spreading an internal infection called cellulitis and causing death by septicaemia. Semmelweis observed that after a woman died in childbirth, the docs would rush to the morgue to examine why and then return to do more deliveries. Semmelweis correctly assumed the doctors were carrying something lethal from the dead woman's body in the morgue to the next woman giving birth. He introduced bowls for hand-washing before and after delivery. This simple practice reduced the mortality down to a level that competed with the midwives.

However, the senior doctors were offended by the label of unclean and fought the hand-washing protocols; they ridiculed and ostracised Semmelweis. They had him dismissed and eventually committed to a mental asylum, where he continued to rail against them. There are some versions of his death there suggesting the establishment was innocent, ranging from suicide to septicaemia from an infected scalpel wound on his hand. The accepted version now is that he was beaten to death by the staff.

This story rivals that of Servetus, who defied the church's teachings (and the pope) when he correctly described how blood circulated around the body. He was burnt at the stake. These stories lent some meaning to the advice not to buck the system. Fearful of a forced career change during paediatrics through upsetting the professor, I always washed my hands.

We had to reside in the hospital during certain nights of the week, on a roster system, like junior doctors. This caused a problem for me, especially at weekends, as there was no pay for this, and I would have to forgo the taxi driving. I also had to leave Michele on her own while she was nearing the term of the pregnancy. I started to dislike Professor Beveridge but feared him for what he could do to my aspirations.

To make matters worse, the ward I was assigned to dealt with childhood malignancy, birth defects from obstetric mishaps, and congenital malformations or diseases. One child who had been mistreated just rocked back and forth all the time; I could not stop thinking about it. Medical students often believe they suffer with the diseases and illness they study and internalise them. I started to imagine what could happen with our unborn Stanley, and I just didn't know how I would cope. I lived with growing poverty, fear for the unborn, and trepidation for the professor.

It came to a head one Saturday morning. Professor Beveridge ran a Saturday morning clinic and insisted that those students rostered on for the weekend attend his clinic. Michele's waters had broken at five o'clock Friday morning, and I had taken her to the hospital. Now I was in his clinic on Saturday morning, trying to concentrate and answer questions while worrying about Michele and wondering how to tell him I couldn't stay in the hospital that weekend. I was more wary of him than of a wounded lion or bull elephant.

After a while, he asked me tersely what the matter was with me; I'm am sure he attributed my poor performance to an indulgent good Friday night out. When I told him that Michele was in hospital having a baby, he reacted by chastising me for being in the clinic and demanded that I immediately go to be with her in hospital.

My heart went out to him because I had so misjudged him. He was really a passionate and worthy pioneer in the clinical teaching staff of New South Wales' fledgling medical school. I owed it to him thereafter to be a diligent teacher of hand-washing after touching any patient during ward rounds. Hospital-acquired infections (called nosocomial infections) are an increasing problem with antibiotic resistance. Semmelweis's story is therefore fused with my emotions of the birth of my first son and remains a special story for me. It turned the spotlight on other sources of cross-infection such as white coats, ties, stethoscopes, and used face masks hanging around the neck.

Although I was relieved to find Michele comfortable and okay, and felt much better being with her, I need not have rushed to the Royal Hospital for Women in Paddington. The professor was being very good to Michele and had taken a personal responsibility to manage her delivery; this was, after all, his first low-dose baby.

He was experimenting with an oral form of contraction stimulant and was not sure of the dose. Too much and her contractions were too painful and frequent, too little and they stopped. So Michele was going in and out of labour and getting tired. Once the membranes have broken and the waters drain away, it's advisable for the birth to proceed with gentle haste, but she was getting nowhere. Just after midnight, a senior registrar came on duty; declaring that Michele had already been in labour far too long, he put up an oxytocin drip, regulated the contractions, and delivered Stanley (with the help of forceps) at seven o'clock on Sunday morning, forty-eight hours after the breaking of her waters. As he was born, I ran my eyes along his body; Stanley was perfect. The professor called in to check on all his good work and appeared as proud and pleased as we were. I felt elation and joy and wide awake. I left Stanley with the professor and Michele, all clean and sleepy, and went off to pick up my taxi.

By this stage, I had been introduced to a private taxi owner who wanted a Sunday driver, and he let me use his cab on a fifty-fifty basis for as long as I wanted on Sundays and holidays. He lived at North Bondi. I readied the cab and my cash-change pouch that hung from the steering column and drove down along Bondi Beach, looking for my first fare. It was a beautiful day; Bondi was not only at its best but also bathed in a rosy glow.

By the time I got to the end of the beach, though, sleep started to take over. I stayed awake long enough to drive the taxi back, went home, and settled down to sweet dreams. Having a baby was exhausting.

There were no dramas in the sixth year, just a steady workload of study and taxi driving, punctuated by the joys of a baby's development. As the final exams were predominantly oral, I practised my answers to hypothetical questions while driving the streets of Sydney and then on a tape recorder when at home. How awful I sounded to myself as I listened to "... umm" and "... er" and "... You know." Funny how one's voice sounds so different outside your head; I have never liked mine very much. I spent as much time practising lines as I did acquiring facts and then self-criticised both delivery and content. Then I learnt a rude lesson when I tried what I thought was a good answer on a friend; he kept interrupting and diverting the line of thought. He responded to my objection with the blunt truth that it was what the examiners would do.

When Stanley was a year old, Michele got a job with the Sydney Home Nursing Service, and the job supplied a car. She arranged care for Stanley and could deliver and pick him up in the car. We were back to plan, and I could give up the taxi while she supported me before I became a doctor. Very few medical students fail their final exams; the filtering process over six years ensures this. Some succumbed to tragic or difficult social circumstances, and in our final year, one was lost to a road accident and one to alcohol.

The challenge was not so much to pass; it was to pass well. Medicine was taught entirely by specialists in their fields. The perception was that the pinnacle of success was to be a prominent specialist, and if one was to succeed in medicine, it was necessary to land a job in a teaching hospital. Only teaching hospitals had pathways to specialisation. All graduates had to serve at least one year in a hospital under supervision before getting a licence to practise independently. Junior hospital appointments were applied for based on the choice of the applicant, but the selection by the hospital was subject to merit based on the final exams result. A non-teaching hospital appointment effectively restricted one to general practice.

There was no specialty of general practice then; that only came about later when general practitioners, objecting to an implied label of being second-tier doctors, formed the specialty of general practice with their own college. I wanted to be a surgeon from the moment I decided to study medicine, and I was desperate to get a teaching hospital position. There were about twice as many graduates as there were teaching hospital positions, and final year was competitive for that reason. The study and practice for the examinations was focused on this purpose.

The final exams were a blur, except for one strange memory carrying yet another lesson. The major clinical exam was viva voce, with an array of volunteer patients with any number of signs and diseases that the examiners could choose to test on. The examiners worked in teams of two. The time allocated to the examiners for each student was twenty minutes. While one pair of students was being examined, there was always another waiting pair. Some students tried to glean information from each other that may have leaked out about the test patients, and others wanted to check on something that they thought they might be asked.

My colleague was from South East Asia and carried the extra burden of taking the examination in his second language. We were both nervous, but he was clearly extremely nervous, to the extent it threatened his performance (maybe I was that bad too). We spent the time calming each other down with rational thoughts and the reality that we were destined to pass. The lesson for me was that thinking about him gave me the benefit of clearer thought. He greatly helped my state of mind, and the exam was actually enjoyable, with a feeling similar to playing sport and winning. The sense of winning gave me more confidence and further improved my performance.

There were multiple examinations, at least two in each subject (except paediatrics, which had been examined at the end of the term). There was an oral and a written test for each; the whole examination process took five days, and then there was the wait for the result, which would be posted on a notice board the following week.

It was a very long week. On Friday afternoon, a member of my class, Gordon Pullin, also known a s Pull-Pull, burst into 21 Dolphin Street and said, "You sneaky bastard; you passed in the top ten." The top ten were offered what were called professorial posts in a university teaching hospital, which meant that as a junior resident (first of two years in the hospital; known as an intern in the United States and also now in Australia and equivalent to a houseman in the UK), I would work only for the professors in each discipline through which I would rotate. My chances of specialising and becoming a surgeon were greatly enhanced.

I was walking on air, an amazing feeling. I guess it was really one of relief and disbelief. If I was so high with a pass, how low would I have been if I had failed? I wondered how different I was going to be as a doctor from the safari guide that I had been.

After graduating from an arduous, intense, and absorbing course such as medicine, it takes some time to wind down. Conditioning for exams leaves an irresistible trigger to speak about the studied topics, and consequently, there is a risk of boring everyone to tears when in conversation (except possibly your colleagues who suffer from the same conditioning). Parties and social gatherings thrive on small talk, and impromptu lectures on the details of a disease kills conversation. People drift away as if from a bad smell.

During my years of medical school, I had kept in touch with a Texan clinical psychologist, Gayle Rettig, with whom I had developed a closer relationship than usual between guides and clients. One of the reasons was that he had given me a lot of moral support and encouraged me to embark on the unlikely path to medicine. On hearing of my graduation, he and Chris, his wife, planned a visit to Australia. I planned an itinerary up the coast of New South Wales through the beautiful Northern Rivers region and into southern Queensland. He hired a car and paid most of the expenses, in exchange for my guidance and local knowledge.

I was not a very good as a guide in Australia. My economic circumstances had governed my experiences, and because we had always camped in Africa, I assumed he and Chris would be happy to do this in Australia. So the trip was planned as a camping trip. For Michele's and my benefit, we stayed mainly in caravan parks or cheap motels. This was no luxury safari; the rough camping in caravan parks is very different to campsites way out in the bush, be it Africa or Australia, because of the close quarters and lack of privacy.

Our topics of conversation, social circles, and interests had changed so much that however hard Gayle and Chris tried, it was difficult to rekindle the rapport; the only remaining intersect was medical. Gayle, like many Americans, had a passion for guns and especially rifles. His favourite had been a double-barrel Browning over-and-under, a masterpiece with special carving and silver ornamental work around the breech; it had been custom-made for him by Browning. Over-and-under shotguns by Browning were common, but not heavy rifles, and this rifle was a measure of his calibre, as well as that of the rifle. Most of us avoided firing heavy weapons, unless absolutely necessary to sight them in, for fear of developing a flinch, which is as devastating to a rifleman as a shank is to a golfer and goal-fever is to a footballer. Gayle had loved his 0.458 to the extent he would self-load his ammunition and practise whenever he could. He never flinched, but he did have a slightly high-pitched giggle.

We could no longer talk guns because of Michele. We couldn't talk politics because of Gayle's Texan views and my education by Enid. Michele was vehemently opposed to the Vietnam War and a veteran of anti-war marches; she kept quiet for my sake whenever that subject came up. The intersection between clinical psychology and medicine is limited, and I sounded like a know-it-all medic, although I had no real experience in medicine yet. I pontificated with a hint of anti-Americanism in a way unbecoming to a friend. I cringe at the thought and should have sacked myself as a guide; in retrospect, I'm ashamed as a friend. Our age differences and economic circumstances came more to the fore, and I realised how much I had really changed and how different Michele was from the girls I had grown up with; they would have had much more in common with Gayle and Chris than she did.

The excitement of passing and enthusiasm for becoming a doctor, the beautiful countryside, the perfect weather, and their American good manners combined to save the trip, although they were not sufficient to maintain contact afterwards. It was like the final ties with Kenya and Tanzania had been cut. I realised that I was indeed, for better or worse, a new man; I wasn't sure whether I preferred the older man with the new ideas over the younger one with the colonial values. Shakespeare might merely have observed that three stages of my life had passed. Now I was to enter the fourth.

Chapter 12

The Young Doctor

The year was divided into quarters, and my rotation as a junior resident was surgery, medicine, casualty, and psychiatry. Junior residents wore all-white uniforms, including shoes, which looked like golfing shoes. The white coats were a little longer than those of the medical students and worn with long white trousers (in the winter months) and shorts and white knee-high socks on hot summer days. There was an orientation introduction week, and then I started on the university department of surgery ward.

As I walked into the ward in full white regalia, a nurse called out, "Quick, Doctor, Mr. Jones has gone into a coma."

"What do I do?" I blurted.

She turned her eyes briefly towards heaven and then said, "He is a diabetic and had his usual insulin this morning; he's fasting for surgery, so put in a drip, take some blood for analysis, and give him some IV glucose."

The nurse produced a small trolley with the necessary bits and pieces. I felt inadequate and almost paralysed by the realisation that theory was of little use without experience, and putting a drip in on my own was something I had never done. I fumbled, missed the vein, and a haematoma started to develop. The nurse had seen it before, and rather than being sympathetic to my plight, she was impatient with worry and exasperation. I tried again and failed again. I feared for the patient's life as he lay silently dying before me; all the elation and pride of being a doctor was evaporating in the real test. The sounds of the ward faded into the mist of the surroundings, and I heard only the beating of my own heart and felt the condemnation of the nurse beside me.

Jackie, a second-year senior resident, was hurrying along the aisle of beds; she sized the situation in a glance and almost on the run had the drip running and the glucose waking the patient before my eyes. It was like a miracle; would I be as good as Jackie after one year?

"Don't worry," she said. "That's why you start in a hospital; the nurse would have found someone else if you couldn't do it. Remember to take the time to get it right the first time."

At lunchtime, a dining room was set aside for hospital doctors only; the room was ablaze with the recounts of the morning's experiences of the initiates, with a background cackle of mature interaction and casual consultation of the more experienced. It was reassuring, and the acute anxieties of the brand-new medicos settled down during the week. The reality took hold when the surgeons came back from Christmas and New Year breaks and started to work again. Theatre operating began at eight o'clock, and before that was a ward round to check on the patients and make sure all plans for the day were in place for each. Blood samples had to be taken and put on a small table, ready for collection by nine o'clock. There were four surgeons on the unit, and each expected the resident to assist at every operation, leaving little or no time to work in the ward during the day. Admissions and the next day's plans were dealt with whenever a spare moment or delay allowed, and the rest of the chores (which means the most) were handled after the theatre finished and post-op ward rounds were completed.

There was no overtime; we were on fixed salaries and told that we were lucky to be paid at all, in view of how much we were learning and for the privileges afforded to us as doctors (in the past, people would have paid to get the experience), and that was true. The real world was changing; those outside the hospital did not see it that way and wanted to be paid for services, and therefore we did too. The public were not sympathetic, believing that doctors were overpaid and did not distinguish between junior hospital doctors and those in practice. There was neither sympathy nor charity for junior doctors.

Every third day, we were rostered on, which meant that we stayed overnight in the hospital (hence the derivation of the term *resident*, dating back to when the junior doctors lived in all the time and were not allowed to be married). To cope with the load, we would take the opportunity to catch up between emergencies when on and start at five in the mornings when not. On off days, we would finish and go home at about nine or ten in the evening. Every third weekend, we lived in. A one-in-three roster was considered very modern and light compared with twenty-four-hour duty or one-in-two rosters. The workload depended on the type of medicine, the productivity of the unit, and the efficiency of getting through the work.

The hospital chose not to employ staff for blood collection and ward work, instead directing junior resident to perform the tasks (as part of the salary they were so lucky to get at all). Blood sample collection was the prime example. Twenty patients needing blood tests meant twenty times five minutes: an hour and a half, if they were all straightforward, had visible veins, and didn't chat. Add the ward round and half an hour to fix immediate problems, and two hours or more were needed prior to theatre in a busy surgical unit. That is a start time of half-past five. This was a time of exponential expansion in medical knowledge and available therapies. For example, antibiotics other than penicillin and different types of penicillin were being discovered and made available, and steroids were introduced as the panacea for everything. This meant a concomitant burgeoning of tests and tasks. The mark of a specialist, and specialist in training, was the number of tests and possibilities they knew for each condition. Their seniority was measured in the number of tests and tasks they could delegate.

Prince Henry Hospital was spread out with long, single-story wards like army barracks, with two three-storey blocks added after the war and the separate infectious diseases ward described before. The beauty of the hospital was in the golf course along the cliffs of Little Bay; on fine days, fisherman on the rocks caught black bream on hospital grounds. The specimen collector travelled between wards with a three-wheel motor scooter that had a carrier tray with canopy on the back. He would limp, scowling and hunched, into the foyers, sidle up to the tables with the waiting blood samples, and with a majestic sweep send them all into his bucket. He would then throw the bucket into the scooter canopy. We could gauge his mood and anger at the world by the force of his throw. Damaged blood samples had to be collected again, and there were no second collections. Second samples had to be hand-delivered to the labs, situated some distance from the wards. One dreaded the frequent call from lab or ward using the words, "Sorry, Doc, the blood sample for Mrs. Smith was haemolysed." It was probably this call that immortalised the Australian vernacular adjective of "bloody hell."

There were often samples other than blood waiting for collection: twenty-four-hour urine samples for phaeochromocytomas or twenty-four-hour faeces for fat assay for malabsorption syndrome. The worst term for a junior resident doctor was that for all the so-called minor surgical specialties. They were lumped together with only one junior resident medical officer (JRMO) because from an administrative perspective, there were few things that went wrong; consequently, it was regarded by administration as a lighter workload, but the ward work of full admission, blood collection, and discharge summary was the same for every patient in the hospital, and whoever had that job was severely overworked looking after eyes, ENT, and gynaecology.

The administration threatened to withhold pay from residents who had not completed their discharge summaries. When doctors are stretched, they work to priorities, and those matters that do not immediately threaten life or limb—such as discharge summaries—take low priority. The inevitable happened: blood samples from one of two patients with the same name were damaged and had to be recollected. Rushed out of theatre, the sample was taken from the wrong patient with the same name, and subsequently, the other patient was given a transfusion of the wrong type blood, with adverse consequences.

To make matters worse, the lid of a twenty-four-hour faecal collection was not secured properly, and the lid came off when all the samples were thrown into the back of the courier's scooter. The lab refused to take the samples, the courier refused to either clean or drive his scooter, and the residents refused to collect all the samples again. The administration accused the doctors of doing it on purpose; on the back of the lawsuit for the mismatched blood transfusion, they called for an inquiry, with the view to terminating someone's career. They say, "It's an ill wind that blows no good"; the job was revised and much improved. It was the first in a series of events that led to major changes in working conditions for junior doctors.

At about that time, there were few newsworthy items in Sydney (it had been a long time since a shark attack). Consequently, the press turned to one of their old favourite fallbacks, which was to criticise doctors' earnings, stirring the public into calling for an Industrial Court Arbitration hearing in New South Wales. We thought this a wonderful idea; led by a registrar and a politically savvy senior resident medical officer (SRMO), the junior hospital doctors requested a hearing. The commission asked how many junior doctors were members of the Public Service Association (PSA). This was equivalent to a union. Only 5 percent of the total workforce had membership in the PSA, and the rest of us had never heard of it.

We had never considered being members of a union and looked to the Australian Medical Association, but at that time, the AMA disallowed membership for junior doctors. "Go away, sonny," was the retort from the arbitration commissioner to our representative. That really got him going.

The junior doctors in the hospital had a social organisation that was well supported; the RMO Association arranged fun things like the hospital variety concert, which made fun of the idiosyncrasies of prominent members of the consultant staff and hospital circumstances. In those times, some of the skits were becoming political, and the RMO Association was popular, with almost 100 percent membership. At the beginning of the following year, those who joined the RMO Association also became members of the PSA, with an option to decline if they wished, and we called again for arbitration.

"How many of you are members?" was the smug reply.

"Ninety-five percent," we answered, and it was backed by a survey showing a working week of between one hundred and one hundred and twenty hours a week.

The tone changed dramatically. "How about we give you an across-the-board rise of five thousand dollars a year?"

This was effectively double our salary, but we were irked by the standard clause on our pay slips that said "for forty hours work," when we worked in excess of one hundred. We wanted recognition and an hours clause. In 1972, doctors in NSW went to arbitration.

The judge said, "I didn't know that such conditions existed in the Western world, let alone in Australia." He ruled that a recognition of the actual hours worked was required.

In the negotiations that followed, we accepted that a working week would be fifty-four hours. We would be paid half the hourly rate for every hour over fifty-four worked during the week and the full hourly rate at weekends. It might seem amazing that we would accept less than the hourly rate for overtime, but we recognised that we were gaining experience and needed to put time in to gain it. We also had achieved a principle that could be renegotiated in the future. The immediate consequence in Australia was the progressive introduction of blood-collecting services and ward clerks.

The need for experience always dominated the thinking of those seeking specialist careers, especially surgical ones. Aspiring surgeons invariably headed abroad to gain experience and further overseas qualifications. The English custom of calling surgeons "Mister" instead of "Doctor" prevailed in Australia. This dates back to when surgeons in England were part of the Barber-Surgeons Guild, which is why barbershops traditionally display a red and white pole, as a symbol of blood-soaked bandages. Barbers were more like military surgeons, and surgeons were an inferior type of doctor who cut people open and were considered beneath the dignity of a physician. Physicians were often called "leeches" because of the practice of bloodletting using the parasite. By the way, leeches were liked because they draw blood painlessly and are not associated with infection (they inject anaesthetic and disinfectant when they attach and then seal the hole when they detach); they are really quite wonderful, but I don't like them.

Anyway, Henry VIII merged the barbers and surgeons, as depicted in the historical painting by Hans Holbein. The surgeons were later separated from the Company of Barber-Surgeons to form the Company of Surgeons; in 1800, this progressed to the Royal College of Surgeons of England by Royal Charter. In British circles, the title of "Mister" has been maintained for historical reasons; this serves to distinguish them from other nonsurgical specialists. To be called Mister in Australia was justifiable, on the grounds that nearly all surgeons in Australia had also acquired a British college fellowship by examination while overseas.

In the latter half of the twentieth century, Australia was perceived as having an inferiority complex towards the British; young doctors would go back to get a BTE (Been to England) or even better still, a BTUSA. With my background, I seriously looked to work in Africa, where the amount of experience and pathology was unlimited. I was dissuaded in this by David Starr. David was the brightest in our year; in fact, he's the brightest person I've ever met, and I've met many very clever people. During his medical course, he achieved first class honours, top of the year, every year; he became a TV technician and repaired televisions for people in nursing homes as a community service, studied the history of Australian law, and acquired a second degree in medical science; when asked by the professor of surgery what he intended to do with his career, he replied, "I am going to travel and then return one day to take up your chair."

He caught trout in the Snowy Mountains at weekends or surfed when the waves were up at Maroubra. I had trouble holding a conversation with him for more than a few seconds, as I felt intimidated by his intellect, but Michele was friends with his beautiful albino girlfriend, Jill. David said, "Learn once how to do it properly with good instruction rather than learning on hundreds by trial and error."

I decided to train in Australia. David, on the other hand, went to Houston, worked with the famous pioneers Denton Cooley and Michael DeBakey, and became a cardiothoracic surgeon. He then studied American law and passed the bar. We still see Jillo but have not seen David since. He travelled but did not return to become the professor of surgery at the University of New South Wales. I never took an overseas degree and believed in my Australian training. When I eventually became a surgeon, I called myself "Doctor" and only used "Mister" on travel bookings and other occasions when I didn't wish to advertise my medical background.

My second term was medicine. Most health professionals and many laypeople understand what that means. For those who are not sure, the explanation is that not all medicine is medicine. Medicine is when you do not perform surgery; in British terminology, a doctor is called a physician. Not all doctors are medical. Proper doctors have a doctorate (e.g., a PhD) that may or may not have anything to do with medicine. A surgeon is not a doctor; he is a "Mister," unless he's a female, which historically was not possible (and now would be an oxymoron). In America, a surgeon is also a physician because all doctors are physicians, but a physician is called an internist. Australians have a right to be confused at times.

To add to the confusion, because of different training in different countries and differences between the states, Australian specialist medicos have not been consistent across the country about what they wanted to be called (except they want to be called to eat on time). If in doubt, address a medico as "Doctor" because calling a physician "Mister" would cause offence.

The professor of medicine was a cardiologist whose research was in the risks of heart disease from the fat in the diet. He championed nonsaturated vegetable fats over saturated animal fats, and we converted from butter to margarine. Coronary artery surgery in Australia was in its infancy; the routine treatment was still strict bed rest for six weeks after a heart attack. Heart attacks were therefore usually followed by severe constipation and deep venous thrombosis. On being released from the enforced bed rest, there were a number of inevitable fatal pulmonary embolisms during straining in the bathroom. The clots from the venous thrombosis were dislodged by the straining at stool and flowed up through the heart to block the blood supply to the lungs.

The ward would have been full of bed-restricted patients and would have been boring if it were not for the haematologist on the ward. His name was Maurie Rosenberg, and he made life very interesting for me. He of course had many deep venous thromboses to deal with and used much anticoagulant because of all the heart-attack patients. One of his research interests was streptokinase (secreted by the streptococcus bacteria, it spreads infections instead of abscesses because it does not allow the blood components to seal off the infected area). Such bright red spreading skin infections were called blood poisoning when red streaks were apparent along the lymphs of the arm or leg because that was the pathway to septicaemia.

Streptococci were also responsible for after-birth infections (puerperal sepsis) that killed so many women with internally spreading infection; this led to Semmelweis's work and the practice of hand-washing.

Maurie's hypothesis was that a little streptokinase would dissolve clots. The risk was the danger of precipitating iatrogenic bleeding: a doctor-caused problem. George Bernard Shaw wrote in *Major Barbara,* "The sins of commission are worse than the sins of omission," which fits with the Hippocratic oath: "First do no harm." To add to the difficulties, the dose was unknown and critical. What was unclear at the time was that the dose varied from person to person and also with each person after a dose. To administer too much was like giving someone a snakebite, and that was an act of commission.

Maurie was Belgian, and with his French accent, he coloured the ward with French-speaking patients from New Caledonia and Noumea. The human collection was white, brown, black, and purple (turning yellow through green from the ecchymoses, or bruises; these bruises were either from the diseases he treated or the streptokinase he treated them with, which caused bleeding under the skin). My school French was stretched to the limit and added stimulation to the already absorbing work. Maurie was also the expert in chemotherapy because of its growing use in blood cancers. He was a strong character with a face to match. It was more the face of a boxer with a broken nose than that of a kindly physician.

Therein lay the next lesson for me as a doctor. A young man in his early twenties was dying. He was thin with the deep yellow (almost orange) tinge of jaundice and covered in lumps of various sizes all over his body. His illness was polyposis coli; he had developed hundreds of separate malignant tumours in the large bowel. The visible lumps were all secondaries, and those in the bones caused pain; the jaundice was from packed secondaries in his liver. He had been married about two years, and his wife, as you can imagine, was grief-stricken. Single rooms were rare in public hospitals in NSW; the long Nightingale wards, with beds parked on each side, were the norm. Maurie converted an office to a single room, inserted a double bed, and arranged for the wife to stay. The matron was most indignant; it was like a scandal was being perpetrated. Maurie then arranged for morphine to be given second hourly, and the young man went to sleep forever in his wife's arms.

There were two other notable features about that ward. A section was reserved for the police force. They were a jovial and grateful bunch and mostly young. There was a large open envelope near the main desk where a sergeant was on duty; we'd put our traffic citations into it, never to be seen again. The risks the police take for us every day continue, but this practice ceased before I left the hospital and was booked for riding my motorbike to work without a helmet.

In the other section were two gastroenterologists, who also worked the ward. They managed liver failure, most of which was alcohol-related; that meant that the police and the drunks were neighbours. This was the ward that admitted the homeless drunks at Christmastime so they would get a Christmas dinner and then be cleaned up by New Year's Day in preparation for another hazardous year on the streets. This was another fine medical practice that has long since demised, along with the policeman's envelope. The police and the drunks should be friends. Maybe they were.

The final term in the first year out of medical school was psychiatry. Our job as resident junior doctors on the psychiatry unit was to look after general health and ensure there were no underlying nonpsychiatric problems. Of course, we were included in the psychiatric management as part of a team. In my final medical examinations, psychiatry had been my highest mark. I found the psychology and mental changes associated with migration most interesting and explained so much of the Australian psyche to me. I was also interested in the research on development of indigenous children and how they diverged from migrant children in education and development. I found myself looking again at Enid, Charles Perkins, the legacy of Robert Menzies and Arthur Caldwell, and my family history. To say I had a clear understanding of race, religion, and nationalism would be akin to believing I could read the future in tea leaves. Reality taunted with flashes of understanding across my mind that were just beyond my grasp, like a would-be lover illuminated by flashes of light in a discotheque.

As for considering a life as a psychiatrist, I decided I lacked the patience and the mental fortitude to share such torments. Convict origins, a factor so much the butt for jokes about Australia and substance for Australian history, did not feature as an aetiological contributor to mental illness in the psych unit, and genetics did not feature in psychiatric analysis, perhaps because of a national sensitivity over Australia's penal history.

At that time, psychiatry differentiated between the mentally ill and the criminal. The Prince Henry Hospital was close to Long Bay Jail; there was also a prison ward in the hospital that was run by the department of medicine. One of the psychiatrists had a special interest in criminology and ran a clinic in the jail. I was given the opportunity to go with him. He seemed to listen understandingly to the attendees, but when I expressed sorrow for a prisoner, my concerns were gently brushed aside with the irrefutable argument that it was lies and manipulation by the criminal mind, and I was the victim. The psychiatrist knew best and explained that the prisoners had personality disorders and were essentially untreatable.

Again, it was like being in a discotheque. I remained vaguely disturbed by injustice and felt helpless and hopeless, like watching someone drown in a whirlpool I could not enter to save them, despite the beseeching cries for help. Like most of us,

I walked away and accepted that as a member of the community, it was my responsibility to support the punishment. Where did my duty of care begin and end? What if the conviction was in error? What if the crime was not malicious and relatively minor, and the man got raped in jail? I walked away from my duty of care on the grounds that I was gullible and could be subject to manipulation. I should be consoled by the argument they were convicted criminals and deserved whatever happened to them. Was this the way we were spared the responsibility should a prisoner be raped while in jail? It seemed so easy to kill a mockingbird.

I saw the results of the worst kind of surgery, as there was a neurosurgeon who performed frontal lobotomies and was fed patients by the psych unit. No, not the grey dawn for me. I still wanted the bright lights of real surgery, and my path was set.

The prison ward is worthy of description, and I admit to a soft spot for the inmates. Maybe because "there, but for the grace of God, go I." During my medical term with Maurie, I had a number of patients in there. There were bars and a guard at the door into the ward that was otherwise typically Nightingale in style (albeit a smaller ward, with only ten beds: six against the far wall and two on either side of the guard). There was humour, often black, and there was manipulation.

Two prisoner patients were memorable. A young boy with a polio-affected leg was in for rape. He was slender, poorly educated, and inadequate in personality (to give him a label). It was a case of a gang bang, which sadly were not that uncommon up and down the coast of New South Wales at the time.

Ask a silly question and you get a silly answer, and I asked him why he was in jail.

"Well," he said, "because of my leg, I was at the end of the line and never got my turn before the party was broken up, and then I was too slow getting away."

He was in the ward for investigation of blood in his urine. Eventually, he was caught peeing over his finger into the specimen bottle, after having made a small prick in his finger for the blood. He was desperate to stay in the hospital ward, where he was safe, and was terrified of going back to jail, where he was in real danger of being raped (if it had not happened already). I thought of the carpenter apprentice I had worked with on the building site, who had a poor understanding of what constituted rape. Sad, really, although some might say it would be his due deserts; others probably feel that two wrongs don't make a right and we definitely don't have the right to supervise the eye for an eye. Surely, each of us as members responsible for the community punishment have a duty of care for those who are essentially defenceless in jail. But then, as a realist, I put my head in the sand (by the way, I never saw an ostrich with its head in the sand).

The other case made me laugh. A burly man of thirty, who looked like Burt Reynolds in his prime in the movie *Deliverance*, had episodes of severe high blood pressure. This is a sign of phaeochromocytoma, a tumour in the adrenal gland that, if found, provided the surgeon and anaesthetist with an irresistible challenge to remove. Removal would cure the patient, but it was a difficult challenge. This was before computed tomography (CT) and ultrasound scans, which provide easy diagnosis now; diagnosis was made by measuring the noradrenalin levels in the blood during a hypertensive attack. They never found a high level of noradrenalin and concluded that he somehow induced his high blood pressure.

There was a German biochemist at the hospital doing research into phaeochromocytoma, and she would rush over to his side from the lab (or from her bed if in the middle of the night), with trays of sample bottles and paraphernalia to take the blood sample while his pressure was high. To her disbelief, the noradrenalin level was always normal, and she blamed the guard and the gate for delays in getting the blood sample. The prisoner was delighted by the special attention and developed increasing expertise in periodically raising his blood pressure at most awkward times, such as at mealtimes or during long holiday weekends (I think the sight of her put his blood pressure up). He was given a special diet that was the envy of the others to provoke the tumour and was able to enjoy the prison ward and relief from Long Bay for some considerable time. I don't know the final outcome, but one day, both he and the biochemist were gone. Maybe he was freed, and they married and lived happily ever afterwards.

The year ended with hospital Christmas parties and a dinner for the junior hospital staff. I nearly became unfaithful. It would have been so easy and so tempting, but my little son and his trusting mother won over, and I rode the bike home, with the wind blowing the alcohol out of my system.

For the first time in years, we went on a real holiday, and we chose a campervan trip around New Zealand. There was really nothing more special personally than this time together, but nothing particularly different to other people's good holidays that would warrant description.

There was, however, an incident on the plane back that invoked an adrenalin rush. This announcement came over the loudspeaker: "If there is a doctor on the plane, please press your call button." I was in old jeans with two weeks' growth of beard and more than somewhat dishevelled, so I sat still. Again the call came, and Michele said I should answer.

I couldn't.

Again the request came, sounding more desperate.

I pressed the call button and waited.

"Not now," the hostess said, obviously believing I wanted to get a beverage, not offer my medical services. "We're busy."

Just then, a neatly dressed middle-aged gentleman with a black bag hurried up the aisle past us. They had a real doctor, and I obviously had some way to go.

Staying on in the teaching hospital for a second resident year (intern in today's terminology) invoked a declaration of intent to be a specialist; one was encouraged to indicate one's chosen discipline. All my terms in the second year were surgical. Urology was my first term in the year. I looked forward to it because I owed much to the young and upcoming urologist, who had been a very good tutor in med school. It left me wet and cold. The hours in the darkened cystoscopy room caged up with a grumpy professor and a virulent, equally bored anaesthetist (whose main amusement was to swat the errand-running resident with the bat-wing theatre doors) led to feelings of discontent and suppressed anger, serving only to obscure the skill set.

The bladders either wouldn't empty or constantly leaked, and the smell of stale urine pervaded everything. Although kidney transplants had just started and were one of the most exciting developments in surgery of the time (we were involved in celebrating the hundredth case), they carried little excitement for the residents. They were always done deep in the night, when theatres were quiet and staff available. Tired and of secondary importance, hanging on to a Deaver wound retractor for hours just outside the field of view of the operation did nothing to restore any desire to be a urologist. A fellow resident was unwell one night and requested leave to abandon his post, pleading an irresistible urge to vomit. The surgeon, fearing for the open wound, dismissed him. That was a lesson on how to make a request with a reason too good to refuse.

I then moved to neurosurgery, which I enjoyed very much. The registrar finished his training during the term and was sent to Vietnam; his marble had come up during conscription, and he could no longer defer service. He also wanted the experience in war. So I was given more responsibility and also closer interaction with the consultants. They were skilled and gentle men who fostered and tolerated the aspirants. Why did I not pursue a career in neurosurgery? In balance, I found brain damage depressing, the back surgery insufficient to hold my passion, and an anecdotal tragedy lastingly influential. When making medical policy, anecdotes carry little weight as evidence because, like expert opinions, they are false arguments in logic; they have led to too many errors. Anecdotes are still strong indicators and certainly influence perception if not reality. My perception of neurosurgery was marred.

A young, athletic, and vital young man about my age was struck down with a cerebral haemorrhage due to a cerebral aneurysm. The damage to the brain was too extensive to recover, and yet his body on life support was healthy. He was the ideal donor for transplant surgery. The task of informing the family of the diagnosis, that there was no hope for their son to recover, and then ask them for permission to harvest their son's body for organs to transplant fell to me.

I could see in the parents' faces the horror of the sudden loss of their beautiful son, conflicting with the guilt of selfishness to refuse the request to help another. It was tearing them further apart. They clearly resented any distortion and violation of their son's now immortal body, because it was their abiding memory, but they were good people. Internally, I was struggling with my own feelings and my ebbing fortitude to meet their demands of me. Was I the lions' jackal or the saints' messenger? First-time experiences impact heavily, and this was my first real test of the strength I would need to continue. I realised then that there would be many tough times to deal with when life and death flirt with each other and others can only watch on. I did it as best I could and suffered with the family. I grieved for the boy in an emotional, involved way, helped harvest the organs, and dealt with the paperwork in automatic pilot mode. The experience coloured my view of transplant surgery and darkened any desire to be a neurosurgeon.

Maybe this field of surgery reminded one of the frailty and vulnerability of human life that is so brain-dependent and strips the neurosurgeon of the dangers of arrogance with reminders of inadequacy to the tasks. Except for the one who did lobotomies for the psychiatrist who was the least skilled, I liked and admired them all, but Boris had a special place for me. He was of Polish origin and spoke with a discernible accent. Handsome and suave, he would walk with his dove-grey suit jacket casually draped over his shoulder in the hot Sydney summer. He was courageous in his surgery and introduced cerebral carotid angiography via direct carotid artery needle puncture. These procedures were accompanied with considerable stress and anxiety. The tension would show on occasions in theatre, and he could be interpreted as brusque if not rude when moments taxed him in his second language. As a consequence, some of the theatre staff nurses disapproved of the terse interactions and perceived him as short tempered and rude. On one occasion, he was desterilised by a circulating nonscrubbed theatre nurse (the "go-for," if you like) when she brushed against him during an operation. The timing was awkward, at an important point in a brain operation, and the usual procedure of rescrubbing carried dangers because of the time that would be involved to do so. Boris could not afford to leave the operation at that moment, so he asked the nurse to put a drape on him and cover the area that she had contaminated (not an uncommon practice). The drapes in an operation are held together by instruments known as towel clips. The commonest type has two sharp points on jaws that clip together. The risk, and well known by surgeons, is that the clips will go through the drapes and easily through the skin beneath. Some surgeons even used this to fix the drapes to the anaesthetised patient.

"Please be careful," Boris said, "and don't put the clips into me."

But she did, and Boris howled and hopped and swore with his favourite relatively mild expletive: "To hell! To hell!" Then, in releasing the tension from the operation and pain in his shoulder, he lost all sympathy when he hissed, "You did that on purpose."

It is really very hard not to laugh sometimes and even harder when you know you should not. I was exploding inside. Thank goodness I had a mask on to hide my facial contortions, but I could see the veins standing out on the anaesthetist's head; so much pressure built up inside him that something had to give, and he snorted and farted at the same time. The rest of the operation was completed with strict composure and silence, except for necessary requests or polite instruction. Any amount of suave shoulder-wearing jackets, smiles, and genialities afterwards could not really assuage the nurse for loss of dignity or convince Boris that she hadn't done it on purpose. What did happen was that any future requests for towel clips, for any reason, were accompanied by hints of a smile.

I realised that becoming a surgeon would involve much more than bright lights. I would have to choose a discipline in surgery, and each was special; each branch required something special in the character and nature of the surgeon, and the fit of these qualities was the keystone.

More is demanded of a surgeon than just technical expertise while operating. Traditionally, they must diagnose, prognosticate, advocate, operate, and provide aftercare. The modern trend is for increasing specialisation to the extent that diagnosis will be separate from therapy and aftercare. Maybe in the future, a surgeon will be required only to perform the therapeutic procedure determined by the diagnosis made by another and hand the aftercare over immediately to a third. Therapies change with technology, and the highly trained surgical technician is becoming too expensive to perform other tasks as well.

The pathway becomes complete with a team, and that brings strengths and weaknesses. The lead person, still the surgeon, is ultimately responsible and has to understand, and perform if necessary, each component of a quality cycle. Trust is at the core of a good team, and the ability to strengthen a weak link in the chain is the mark of a good leader. The person performing a therapeutic procedure is assaulting under licence granted by the patient, in the true meaning of patient, which is someone on whom a procedure is being performed. The surgeon is responsible, and to be able to assess the risk/benefit analysis of any action, a surgeon needs to understand the process, even if parts of the process are delegated. This is a long-winded way of saying that the next term in intensive care was also a foundation stone in building a surgical career. I had decided that the most complete surgeon was the general surgeon, and that is what I wanted to be.

The new specialty of intensive care was gestating. In the fifties, a special ward had been built at Prince Henry Hospital to cater for the epidemic of infantile paralysis (better known as poliomyelitis, or polio). In severe cases, the breathing muscles were affected, and assisted breathing was needed to sustain life. The iron lung was developed for that purpose, and a respiratory unit was built at Prince Henry Hospital to deal with New South Wales polio victims. Vaccination rendered the respiratory unit redundant for polio but ready-made for intensive care. It was here that I learned of tetanus, gas gangrene, and septicaemia, the rare, sudden, and catastrophically severe events that befall humans.

In ICU, the stark contrasts of almost instantaneous succumbing to death and sustained resistance, ending in miraculous saving of life, are like a Pro Hart narrative, and the kaleidoscope of varying human emotions and character was like a Jackson Pollock painted all over the floor. The defining lessons for surgery were to be wary of human frailty, to be ill at ease when everything looks good, and to think laterally. "If you think everything is perfect, it means you don't know what's going wrong." To meet the emotional and physical demands of working in intensive care, there seemed to be a wry, dry sense of humour mixed with perseverance. The sustained effort towards preserving life more often brought hope and success, but sometimes, it was necessary to switch off the emotions, submit like a bitch to the dog of failure, and switch off the machines.

There were no ICU specialists as such. There were pioneers with that interest, and they came from different backgrounds: anaesthetists, physicians, surgeons, and even general practice. The common factors were dedication and special interest. Tom Torda (or Tom Terrific) was head of ICU. Tom's other job was cardiac anaesthetics; he was famous for his ability to put tubes into the difficult trachea. Intubation is often needed to save a patient's life, and it must be done in the space of their oxygen reserve. Can you hold your breath for a minute? Some skin divers can hold their breath for five minutes. However long it is, that's the time available in which to get a tube into the lungs to ventilate. Tom would be called urgently when others failed. Witnesses describe Tom flying out of the nearby theatre with theatre garb billowing and mask trailing in the slipstream as he tore down the ICU aisle. Left arm out straight to grab the jaw, fingers curled ready to open the mouth, while holding the jaw forward with neck extended. All the while the right arm was drawn back like an archer's, with the fingers gripping the endotracheal tube aimed and ready to shoot through the larynx. Done!

I saw it once. A teenage boy had been fishing with his family in Nowra, about two hundred kilometres south of Sydney. There is a common fish in the area that's good to eat called a leatherjacket. It's a funny-looking fish and is similar to some puffer fish. The boy had caught a puffer fish that was not recognised as such and proudly ate the fish. Paraesthesia started in his hands, the pins-and-needles spread to his feet, and he started to get weak. Even the Japanese die sometimes when they eat *fugu*, a delicacy made with puffer fish.

The boy was brought straight to ICU by helicopter and ambulance for life support. He had stopped breathing and was difficult to intubate. Tom intubated as if from a distance. Stepping back with aplomb to the palpable but silent applause that proceduralists live for, he promptly tripped over the cables leading to the defibrillator machine that had been wheeled in behind him. The wry dry humour was like static electricity in the air after a crash of thunder. The applause was silent while he sat in the tangle on the floor; nobody laughed. The boy survived. Tom tested every muscle relaxant reversing agent and wrote up a research report that appeared in *The Medical Journal of Australia*.

The next term was a country term (or maybe better described as a term in a satellite secondary hospital). For me, it was the surgical teams of Port Kembla Hospital. Port Kembla is a conurbation with Wollongong, about one hundred kilometres south of Sydney. I had to live in the hospital except for every second weekend. It was like going back in time, back to true hospital residency. For me, it was very useful learning. Out of necessity, I learnt to do things at the limit of my experience and beyond what I could have done in the parent teaching hospital, where more experienced people were available. I could practice things I learnt in ICU. Sending young doctors out to satellite hospitals may provide for a need in the more rural communities, and it may encourage some to return to practice there later, but giving them experience was the main motive.

I learnt a lot, including a little Croatian-Serbian and a lot about myself. The hours were long because the Port Kembla steel works never stopped; injuries and illnesses were not divided into night and day but distributed across all shifts. Elective surgery filled the days and urgent surgery the nights. After a particularly long day and heavy evening, a worker presented to casualty about midnight following his evening meal and drinks with his mates. He had a superficial cut across the nose that had been sustained in a minor accident earlier in the day, but he was not particularly worried about the injury. He was reporting because it was required of him to report for a medical check of any injury sustained at work. The nose wound was cleaned and dressed, and I arranged for him to come back in the morning for review because it was a facial wound; he needed an X-ray in case there was a break in a thin nasal bone.

The next morning, however, I was in trouble because the plastic surgeon noted the injury in the casualty book and that it was classified as workers' compensation. He was annoyed because he had not been notified. A fuss was made; the plastic surgeon took the man to theatre, scrubbed the small wound, and stitched it with fine stitches, explaining that it was necessary to do this to avoid dirt pigmentation and scarring on the face and adding that it should have been done at midnight, however tired I was. He reported me to the medical superintendent.

I was full of the self-pity of one condemned unjustly. The lesson for me was that in medicine and institutions where rank was involved, justice follows rank, and it is brave and foolhardy to contradict your senior, as authorities will support the higher rank. If money is involved, righteous indignation is manifested. If the injury in this case was not workers' compensation, attracting a fee, my handling of it would have been appropriate, according to the time, the nature, and the action. Whether I was right or wrong, my sense of proportion was disturbed.

The superintendent's face told a story, and the contrast of ICU dramas with this episode played on my perspective. The birth of modern plastic and reconstructive surgery during World War II, with the work of the New Zealander Harold Gillies and the American Archibald McIndoe in the Victoria Hospital in East Grinsted, is one of the most inspiring stories in surgery, but I believe I set cosmetic surgery too low in the list of priorities to pursue that line.

I missed Michele and Stanley during that time and was pleased to return to Sydney for the final term in the year, which was cardiothoracic surgery. This was surgery as I dreamed it should be. There was high morale with a crisp, organised staff and high-tech theatres sporting whirring machines, pipes carrying blood, and stacked electrical equipment on mobile racks, distributed like fans around a boxing ring, with the bright lights shining on the operating table at centre stage. The open chests gleamed like the stainless steel retractors as the light played on the pericardium and pleural membranes, contrasted with the dark red of the muscle and bright red of the sternal marrow and spilt blood. The theatre garb of dark green completed the scene, and background music added to the atmosphere.

There were few malignancies because patients with lung cancer, despite being the commonest cancer of the time, seldom came to surgery. The dominant operation load was vascular, with the new coronary artery bypass surgery that had been developed at the Cleveland Clinic. Heart valve surgery was still the most fascinating to watch as a technical exercise in surgery. The twirl of the hands doing knots danced with the strings of the ties that were held up like parachute cords, ready to run the new valve down to its place at the root of the aorta when all the sutures were in place. And all the time, the heart was stopped as machines moved the blood around. The anaesthetists ran the theatres like the engineers on a ship. They also ran the parties afterwards and built them into shows as Christmas approached. This type of surgery had a high success rate; there were very few losses. It made for a happy unit in a time of change for cardiovascular medicine. It was changing from prognosticating life and diagnosing heart problems with stethoscopes, also known as guessing tubes, to relieving symptoms and prolonging life with angiograms for diagnosis and operations for treatment. People were grateful, and to receive gratitude is a blessing.

Children with heart defects were brought across to Prince Henry Hospital at Little Bay from the sister hospital of the Prince of Wales in Randwick. Children in an adult hospital pose their own set of problems. Surgery in children is usually straightforward except for neonates, congenital abnormalities, and malignancies. For children with heart disease, congenital abnormalities make up the bulk of those needing surgery, and this was fraught with difficulties. There was a desire to postpone heart surgery as long as possible in very small children because the surgery would be technically easier and the benefit expected to last longer. Pure scar tissue will grow with growth of the child; this is seen clearly if you look at a scar in an adult from a wound made in childhood; when adult, it will be much longer. A scar all the way down an infant's chest is about five to eight centimetres long. When adult, that same scar will be about twenty centimetres. While the natural tissues grow, synthetic tissues do not, and placement of synthetic prostheses and permanent suture material in small children poses long-term problems.

Blood loss is also proportionate rather than absolute and is a delicate management problem in young patients. Loss of half a litre in an adult is usually of no consequence (unless it's very sudden or unexpected or in a person already compromised). In a child of four, this amount is nearly all the blood they have, so the loss of one hundred or even fifty millilitres has an effect. The heart-lung machines of those days took many litres to prime, and there were difficulties when trying to balance replacement and loss while accounting for amounts in transit through the machines. Some of the children were already at the limit of their endurance, without a margin of reserve to be relied on by either surgeon or anaesthetist. Too much replacement drowned them, and too little shocked their little bodies. Heart surgery in children was both essential for life and lethal. Heart surgery in adults was a surgical frontier, but in children, it was behind enemy lines.

Is it appropriate to call a surgeon brave? Surely it is only being brave with others' lives. Brave people die, and the realms of bravery pass quickly into the realm of the foolhardy. Again, the sins of commission are worse than the sins of omission. What if a surgeon loses the person, especially a child; should they ever try again? Is to try again callous or criminal? Was there ever a surgeon who never made a mistake? Should they resign for a mishap or for the wrong decision made in a split second? And if they try again, how do they cope with repeat failures and tragedies?

Yes, there is a kind of bravery taking on high-risk, demanding surgery. I wondered what tests lay in wait for me. The great pioneer thyroid and gastric surgeon of the nineteenth century, Christian Bilroth, many of whose techniques have survived, had to have the courage to continue in the face of unforeseen hypothyroid complications, loss of patients, and accusations of heartlessness. William Halsted, arguably the greatest surgeon ever, struggled with his cocaine and morphine addiction, acquired through contamination while using cocaine as a local anaesthetic agent. After being confined in a sanatorium, he emerged to be one of the founders of the prestigious Johns Hopkins Medical School, despite his personality change from extravert to introvert. Are these the qualities needed for pioneer surgery or the scars of psychological trauma and defence mechanisms for the anxiety of failure and the shame brought on by criticism? At the time, the head of unit, John Wright, whom I greatly admired, was a role model and the function of the cardiothoracic unit admirable, but the inclusion of children led to his demise some time later when the repeated loss of children proved too much for the professor of paediatrics. I think my involvement with Jason, a four-year-old who had surgery for Fallot's tetralogy, was the test of me as a doctor and omen for my career.

The heart is two pumps set in series. One of the pumps, the right, intakes blue blood from the veins and sends it to the oxygen chambers of the lungs. The second pump, the left, receives the red blood back from the lungs and sends it via the aorta to the arteries throughout the body. In Fallot's tetralogy, four things happen: The primary abnormality is the root of the aorta sits astride the outflow of both pumps, making them pump in parallel. The right usually pumps against much less resistance in the lungs than the left to the body, even though the volumes must be the same because they are designed to be in series. The left is therefore stronger than the right. It has bigger muscles and more thrust and why, even though the heart is a central organ, one feels it to be on the left.

In Fallot's, with the aorta sitting astride both pumps, the force into the lungs is too high, and the right heart must strengthen, and the pressure rises in the lungs. The usual outlet from the right to the lungs is called the pulmonary artery; it is squeezed by the aorta encroaching on its space, making it narrower and less able to carry the equal amount of blood to the lungs. This is a highly inefficient, exhausting arrangement that soon destroys the lungs and the right heart. The surgery is demanding. An analogy might be the task for a spoke wheel-maker who has to replace the hub of a wheel while under water in a river.

Jason came through the operation, which took all day, and was transferred to a special post-operative room close to ICU. I was on duty for the night. I had backup with a phone to the surgeon and could call on colleagues in ICU. By today's standards, I don't think I really had the expertise to care for Jason, and those on at night in ICU were without any more experience than me. I monitored Jason's blood oxygen levels and the haemoglobin levels in his blood as I dripped in fluids and blood transfusions in small quantities, trying to balance the amounts in against the amounts out in the urine and drains from the chest. Such measures are crude and assessed by monitoring the pressures in the arteries and veins. After such surgery, there can be distortions in pressure. All is dependent of the fluid lines into and out of the body being open and working.

There is a dangerous space that lies hidden in the recesses of the chest and abdomen. It is the third space. It is the space that could not be seen in the days before scans were available and the space that hides bleeding and fluid. It is like having an equation with a hidden factor so the answer is always wrong. Jason was bleeding slowly into a third space inside the chest. I struggled to keep his blood pressure and oxygen levels normal and his urine output in an acceptable range. The hidden third space hid the vital information that I needed to communicate to the surgeon; Jason bled quietly and steadily through the night.

Herein was the dilemma: Was there enough evidence to open the complex theatre and mobilise all the special staff, still tired from the day before and scheduled to face a load again in the morning? Should the whole team be called in the middle of the night? Would unnecessary further surgery stress Jason beyond his reserve to withstand the trauma and surgical assault a second time? At my instigation, I could upset the whole unit and further risk Jason's life if I was wrong. How sure was I that he was bleeding? I wasn't. Jason's numbers were okay. I judged we could hold on for the sureness of the day. Was my judgement sufficiently experienced and was it good at four in the morning, considering I had not slept twenty-two hours? I was truly in the dog watch.

In the light of day, with clear heads and a wealth of experience, it was not a difficult decision to take Jason back to theatre with the full team to stop the bleeding and clean out the third space. Of course, the real question was not whether Jason should go back to theatre but was it better the next morning in optimum operating conditions or, in the context of slow and steady bleeding, would he have had a safer chance earlier at three or four in the morning with an emergency team. This is a common surgical dilemma, and if surgeons lose, they are always responsible for the decision. Surgery, I was learning, is as much about risk/benefit analysis as it is about technical prowess. Surgery is about having everyone pulling together; the patient is only one, albeit the most important, of a surrounding family and a medical team that is involved inextricably, to the chagrin of those who ignore the circle. Surgery is about scheduling for availability and logistics. I should have also communicated with Jason's parents, but I don't remember ever meeting with them because their dealings were with the paediatricians. A surgeon should not be alone; for a brief period, he must think like a member of the family.

Mother Nature smiled on us that night, sparing Jason and saving me from a test too much to bear. Mother Nature is beautiful when she smiles. I learnt that it is better to work in optimum conditions, that worry is good if it is productive, and that a sixth sense of knowing when someone is okay or needs intervention is real. That sense is inexplicable, like the contents of a dream that come together for no apparent rhyme or reason from different seemingly unrelated stores in the brain. Experience teaches one to accept the sixth sense, use it, and trust it like Mother Nature. While the sixth sense calls for action, it does not give the direction and can be overwhelmed by overconfidence. Some surgeons are called lucky because they get out of difficult situations. They have mishaps like all surgeons, but the difference is that they prepare for them and recognise them when they happen; they have an acute sixth sense that works for them subconsciously. I had to develop mine.

The trial period was over. I made the final commitment to be a surgeon, and now I had to plan and determine the next steps. The first decision to make was where to study, train, and sit exams. Did I go to the UK to train and sit for the English and Scottish exams and then come back to Australia with my BA (Been Away) degree and then sit the Australian exams, or did I stay in Australia and travel later? A change made that decision for me. Until 1973, the Australian and English primary examinations to enter surgery were reciprocal, but now each would be necessary to its own country. I decided to study and sit for the primary in Australia.

The exam was in May. I applied for a part-time research job with the university department of surgery at Prince Henry. The pay was minimal, but I would have time to study, spend more with Stanley, and make some income doing radio call locums after hours.

CHAPTER 13

A Taste of Research and Radio Locums

The research world was very different from the clinical world. The building lacked the bustle of the hospital, the support staff had other interests, and the underlying pressure of clinical judgement was absent. Instead, there was personal pride and a sense of responsibility to perform each experiment diligently. I did not expect to encounter a loneliness that delved into the depths of despair. True poverty of equipment and finance became desperate when accompanied by poverty of ideas. The ranks of researchers included full-time scientists, medicos who were full-time researchers, and medical practitioners acquiring further degrees such as masters of surgery or PhDs for career purposes. There was also a squad of university staff who had to research in order to publish or perish, research assistants like me, and an odd-bod or two who were just around to help. Then there was an infrastructure of a vet, animal carers, a veterinarian nurse, and an administrator.

Newton's Third Law is that each action has an equal and opposite reaction, and the principle applies universally beyond just physics. The depths of poverty and despair in research are dispelled by the ecstasy of realisation of an answer or a success: eureka, no less. This was my lesson for the future, but in the meantime, I experienced working with a poor idea with poor support and little scientific method, with long hours research from which I wrote no papers.

"It's an ill wind that blows no good," and I learned two valuable things to take with me into future practice: Landrace pigs have a recessive genetic predisposition to malignant hyperthermia in response to halothane, an anaesthetic gas. Although not common, humans can suffer with this, and so learning on the pig to recognise the signs early can save lives. It can be quite difficult to insert a tube into a pig's trachea for ventilation. Humans can also be difficult, and the experience in endotracheal intubation in the pig has proved most valuable for the occasional times it has been necessary for me to do this in emergency situations with humans.

Most of all, no pigs suffered, as they never woke from the anaesthetic. It was a job that allowed me to study for the primary examinations in surgery, and the anaesthetic connection introduced me to the best physiology tutorials in the city. I passed the Surgical Primary in May and was free to plan for my surgical training. I decided on Perth, for a variety of reasons (teasing Michele that it was because Perth was farthest away from Sydney and Enid).

The most persuasive factor was Charlie, who was working for Western Mining and said, "Come over. The West is booming," and I followed the call to go west, young man. We decided to leave Sydney at the beginning of August, drive around the top of Australia to Perth, and then backpack through South East Asia, India, and Kenya to visit my family for the rest of the year.

In the time between the exams and travel, I took on working for the Sydney Radio Locum Service.

Radio Locums supplied doctors to cover general practices after hours, nights, and weekends. It was mainly staffed by off-duty junior doctors in their third year after graduation. Most were studying to become specialists or filling in time before travelling overseas. This group of medicos had a rich vein of knowledge. They had been well trained in teaching hospitals, with extensive experience in many disciplines. The service was popular with patients and practices alike. It was well run with the supply of a car, similar to a taxi fitted with a two-way radio to base. A list of about hundred emergency and most commonly used medicines and drugs was available in all pharmacies and supplied free to registered doctors on request to stock their emergency bags. I converted my imitation leather lunchbox from my labouring days into a doctor's bag. The shape of the lunchbox and its much-used appearance gave me an immediate experienced look, and I sallied forth under radio instruction with the expectation that I would have no trouble with finding addresses because of my taxi experience.

It turned out to be harder than the taxi. One couldn't drive away with a shrug of the shoulders if no client was found, with the justification that they must have found another ride. They were not waiting in the street or waiting to respond to a toot of the horn, nor were they sitting in the back seat, giving last-minute directions when I was unsure of which way to turn. The target address could be at the top of a high-rise apartment block in the poorest suburb, without a working lift and dark stairwells late at night. It was not always urgent; some people would only use the emergency doctor as they could not, or would not, sacrifice working time to take their children to a regular doctor during daylight hours.

I have vivid memories and gained insights into a type of general practice that left me with a special admiration for doctors on the front line. There were no special boundaries of expertise; there were no immediate colleagues to lend a hand or take over. It was difficult to get overloaded hospitals to accept a sick patient; great powers of persuasion were needed. It became easier to understand how a doctor's personality can assume a demanding characteristic and why sometimes they will not accept the answer no. The lighting in some of the homes could be so bad, or yellow, that it was almost impossible to see if a patient was anaemic, flushed, or jaundiced.

I was called one evening to a small house in Malabar, not far from the Prince Henry Hospital, to see a man who lived on his own. Over the radio, I was told he had symptoms of nausea and fever. Probably a touch of gastro, I mused, a good call because not too far from home, and I could drop in for dinner after the call. It was one of those calls that leave an emergency doctor uneasy and dissatisfied. There was nothing to support gastro; the patient looked unwell but obviously was not going to die soon. He did have a fever and even in the yellow light looked sallow and jaundiced. The jaundice was clearly seen in the sclera of the eye, which almost gleamed like the eyes of a cat.

"It's okay, Doc," he said. "I don't expect you to know what's wrong with me because I have been in the jaundice ward at Prince Henry, and they couldn't find out, either. Please just give me something to make me feel a bit better."

I gave him something for nausea and some soluble aspirin to bring the fever down and then prepared to let myself out of the dark, depressing little house.

As I reached the door, he asked, "What causes a fever, Doc?"

On instinct, I replied, "The commonest cause of fever is malaria, but there is no malaria in Australia."

"I was in New Guinea last year," he said.

I rang the hospital, gave his name, and told them that he had malaria and I was sending him back. The on-duty registrar thought I was arrogant and wasn't convinced; the man had been in hospital for six weeks under investigation without a diagnosis, and of course, he said there were no beds. After checking that they had never looked for malaria while he was in hospital, I pointed out how embarrassing it would be if he was confirmed to have malaria by another hospital (I was learning the art of persuasion).

He did turn out to have malaria, and the admitting registrar took the unusual step of ringing me up later to tell me the results. Most times, the Radio Locum emergency doctor got little or no feedback. I admit I did bask in the compliment, but I didn't feel that clever because having had malaria a number of times in Kenya, Tanganyika, and Uganda, I should have recognised it. I learned two invaluable lessons. A doctor does not need to be very intelligent, but he needs to be well trained, and more is missed by not looking than not knowing.

There were many rewards working for the locum service, and I enjoyed the experience very much. I treasured the looks of gratitude in a mother's eyes when I could really do something, and no amount of money compares with that form of payment.

I am disturbed by the memories of two particular calls. A mother of four children called about a sick one with asthma. This was not an uncommon call in Sydney; the severity ranged from mild concern to desperate need. For the former, an inhalant, a prescription, and some advice would suffice. The latter might require more; some needed a subcutaneous injection of adrenalin or intravenous hydrocortisone as an emergency, with hospital admission to follow. Injections formed a large part of the emergency armament, and we carried a lot of them. However, just like overprescribing antibiotics, we tried to avoid overuse of injections and save them for when essential, especially with children. The mother was worried about the sick child and having trouble controlling the others, especially her four-year-old.

"Be quiet," she yelled, "or I'll get the doctor to give you a needle."

I should have whispered gently in her ear that it would be better not to make the children frightened of the doctor, but I admonished her for the transgression, and she disliked me so that we lost rapport. She probably disliked doctors as much as her children did. Although the child responded to treatment, and the four-year-old was very quiet, there was no gratitude in the mother's eyes; I was paid in money. I had missed a great opportunity.

A single mother put a call through late one night because her baby would not stop crying. "Not urgent but please call in when close by" was the radio directive. The baby was about seven months old and crying incessantly. I could not find any physical reason. It was well nourished, clean, and well clothed. It just kept crying.

"She cries all the time," the mother said after I stopped by, "and I don't know what's wrong; the doctors don't seem to know, and I am exhausted. I am so frustrated and worried; I want to make it stop."

The professor had advised against sedatives, and she had a row of bottles for the baby prescribed by others that she deemed useless. The prof had taught us to distribute the load amongst the family and make some respite for the mother to allow her to get some sleep. Good idea, but hard for a single migrant mother. The stress of motherhood, poverty, and loneliness in an alien culture stared out of her eyes. I tried to comfort the baby but only succeeded in making her yell louder.

I was essentially ineffectual and had no way of coping with the social causes. I worried about missed cancers in the brain and kidney that might be causing pain but could not justify a hospital admission, even to give the mother respite. I received no feedback and still wonder about what happened to that baby. I learned that in the real world, there are some things that medical school just does not teach.

The mother looked competent (though sleep deprived), but I'm still haunted by the memory. I start to reassure myself with the knowledge that all infants have to cry to teach the mother to recognise her baby's call, and to exercise the lungs, and that the infant probably turned out fine. Then doubt comes back when I see a baby who won't stop crying; I know that everyone has a sleep-line limit somewhere in the sands of time. Is an overtired mother as dangerous as an overtired surgeon?

Chapter 14

Around the Top End

When Stanley turned four years old, I passed the Australian and New Zealand Primary Examinations in Surgery, allowing me to formally enter surgical training. He was good fun to have around. He noticed things, things I had started to take for granted. Stanley reintroduced me to stick insects, butterflies, coloured pebbles, things to walk on for balance, ball games, and other people. It was an opportunity to spend time with family. Michele and I had been working long hours, and although we shared the childminding when we could, Stanley needed childcare. Michele eventually found a woman who was going to have a late surprise child and wanted to get back into practice.

She was a very good mother, but it had not always been the best care, as it was governed by what was available. We felt a little guilty and wanted to spend more time with him. Michele had always wanted to travel but had married me instead. Having passed the exams early in the year meant that we could make amends and spend the rest of the year travelling. After ensuring a job in Perth for the following year, we planned a trip around the top end of Australia, followed by a circle around South East Asia and the Indian Ocean to end up in Kenya for Christmas to introduce my new family to my old one.

Luck came our way in the form of the death of the VW engine. A mechanic bought it for spares and pointed us in the direction of a fairly new Ford Falcon XT station wagon that had been repossessed and was going cheap. It was perfect. A mattress in the back for Michele and me, bench front seat at night for Stanley, and luggage and supplies on a modified roof rack. With fond goodbyes to Enid and friends, and chicken wire across the windscreen to protect the glass from flying stones, we pointed north.

Just like forgetting about malaria, I had forgotten how to set up for the open road, and Michele's idea of packing was, and remains, different from mine. The first night's camp on the side of the road was strewn with every bit of luggage opened to find the essentials. The phrase "Where's the ..." has been forever banned in our family. After that, there was a box of utensils and food for two days and a similar bag of clothes that we kept in the back, and the rest went on the roof. At night, we would pull off the road and drive out of sight, make a hole in the ground for the cooking fire, and camp for the night. There was never a hint of need, but I had bought a .22 calibre rifle to take with us. Strange thoughts of protection lingered from my upbringing (and maybe something for the pot). Michele would not contemplate a rabbit being shot, let alone a kangaroo, for the pot, and the rifle was only fired when I thought it a good idea to teach Stanley (an idea that was soon ended by Michele's abhorrence of guns, especially guns and sons).

It was good to get out of Sydney and into the north. Sydney had always strived to rid itself of Australia and be London in Australia. In those days, the streets of Sydney had English names, and terraced houses were built from plans brought straight out of London. Mother Nature's daughter in Australia forced her way through the cracks, using the climate and vegetation, creating a necessity to adapt. The British pushed back by killing the natives, clearing the trees, shooting the koalas and kangaroos, and turning surfboard riders into feral animals. However, the beaches were invincible and would not be changed, so the Australian way became a compromise with natural beaches and British seaside towns; they introduced European animals and weeds and the back and beyond, back of Burke and beyond the black stump.

We were heading into the back and beyond with dirt roads, dust, dry river beds, endless plains and deserts with low blue hills in the distance, more equal days and nights, real black people, and boab trees (*Adansonia gregorii*), related to the African baobab (*Adansonia digitata*). It touched a chord. We bathed in the cool of Katherine Gorge and the warmth of Mataranka and Howard springs; we watched buffalo wallow and brolgas dance as we passed through the Northern Territory the year before Cyclone Tracey hit Darwin for Christmas.

We entered Western Australia via Kununurra. The Ord River had just been dammed, and the huge artificial Lake Argyle was filling rapidly. This was going to be a vast, irrigated food bowl. The dam was new; the roads to the dam gleamed with black asphalt stark against the new and sun-reflecting glaring wall, and everywhere there were signs in red and black demanding licences for boats, warning of crocodiles, forbidding entrance, and threatening fines. In contrast to the government infrastructure and signage, the town looked tired and depressed; we were the only ones in the park near the water.

The incongruity between the two spelt out the nature of the West. So much hope, water, and government, and so little return for the country people. Countless birds and insects appreciated the food bowl and overwhelmed the locals with migrants that came down from the rice paddies of Indonesia. Wyndam sounded exciting with the port for the cattle industry, and we imagined crocs lying on the mud banks. We didn't see a croc, and the town was even less stimulating than Kununurra, so we headed down the hot, sandy gravel road to Hall's Creek. Here there was no semblance of massive expenditure, such as we had seen at Lake Argyle. Just a collection of corrugated iron buildings, and we passed through.

On the way to Fitzroy Crossing, it rained, and then it became interesting, with water quickly starting to flood the road due to the flat country with slow run-off. The two-wheel-drive Falcon appeared out of place with the sparse but uniformly four-wheel-drive traffic. As we drove through the wetter areas, the four-wheel drives would wait like angels and demons. We were not sure whether they waited to help with care and concern for our welfare or for the fun to start with the bogged vehicle. The Falcon flew across the water without help, and we took time out on the banks of the Fitzroy River at Geikie Gorge before heading for Broome. The road was all dirt and corrugated, with little traffic. The names like Sandfire Flats were more interesting than the places, and a sense of wilderness and desolation accompanied us all the way. Broome was small, with an interesting history of pearling, Japanese migrants, and Japanese warplanes; we stayed a little while in a caravan park by the beautiful Cable Beach.

Port Hedland again projected a massive infrastructure; it was if Western Australia lay like a blanket on some huge monster that surfaced from time to time. It rivalled Lake Argyle in human effort with huge structures to load the iron ore; everything was red. The red dust from the iron ore and unsealed roads infiltrated to the extent that even the air and salt piles were tinged. We headed out to the source of the redness and made for Tom Price via Wittenoom. The road was pleasing to the eye as it ran along the side of the newly built railway; the iron ore trains were huge and there were all sorts of rocks and patches of broken lava eggs filled with purple crystals. It was very hard on the Falcon. We started to limp as the vibrations from the corrugations fractured the roof rack, and the back brake line was ripped out by a rock-impregnated ridge between two wheel ruts caused by a truck in the recent rain. Then punctures started, and Wittenoom seemed to be getting farther away rather than nearer. Fortunately, the Falcon had two brake systems, and so we at least had front brakes.

About halfway between Port Hedland and Wittenoom, we were passed by a Holden station wagon travelling at a great speed for this dirt road; we were showered with dust and small stones. We were becoming very dubious about the hospitality of Western Australia. A little farther along, and we came across the Holden, stopped on the side of the road, steaming from the radiator; a wild-eyed Celt waved us down. Should we stop? After all, he had nearly smashed our windscreen with the stone shower. Bush etiquette demanded we did.

"So sorry for passing you like that," he said. "The radiator has a hole, and I was trying to get back to Wittenoom before it drained out again. Do you have any water? I've run out and had to use all my beer in the radiator."

We had water and filled Jock's radiator; his eyes filled with tears while he insisted that we stay at his place in Wittenoom.

Jock explained that he was a chef by trade but found it easier to make a living installing coin-operated pool tables around the pubs and Pilbara Iron ore mining camps. His wife Sylvia had the most serene face I've ever seen, and her children played happily in the grey silky asbestos dust that slipped enchantingly through their fingers in the substitute sand-pit surrounded by the dry red baked earth that was the backyard. Following introductions to the family, we were allocated a room. Jock asked for a lift to the pub to meet his friends before dinner, and Sylvia smiled.

In the Wittenoom Hotel, we met the publican (whose name escapes me), Wilkie the phantom pilot of the north-west, the doctor, and a man with Korsakoff's syndrome. Wilkie's history is one of the legends of the area, a sheep station manager who was an excellent flier by reputation; folklore attributes him with thousands of hours of flying time. The DCA apparently recorded none because Wilkie was a diabetic and not allowed to fly. Legend has it that he dodged the flying police for years; the Wild West shielded him while he worked the stations and flew the prospectors and station owners around the Pilbara. One story has him leaving the landing carriage of his Cessna in the back of a Holden Ute that he was buzzing; according to another, he buried the plane with a bulldozer to hide it from the DCA.

Some said that the DCA actually did not want to catch him because it would then have to be explained why he had accumulated so many flying hours. The gentleman with Korsakoff's (a syndrome which causes loss of short-term memory because of extended alcohol abuse; the person compensates for his condition by confabulating and making up stories to hide it) could remember all the adventures but forgot how he had got to the pub. An irate denizen walked in and demanded to know why he had been left holding something in the shed as a neighbourly gesture, only to find from a passer-by that Korsakoff had walked away to the pub. The gathering raised knowing eyes to the ceiling.

The doctor was quite interesting; he was an amateur botanist and a complete authority on Western Australia's unique wildflowers (WA is known as the Wildflower State). It also explained why he was always so hard to find.

I learned an invaluable lesson from him: "When confronted with a procedure, such as setting a fracture, inform the patient of the worst possible outcome and that you have done your very best to save the patient from this worst scenario. Since the worst is not likely to happen, but the patient invariably thinks it will, the chances are the patient will believe that you have done a really good job."

This, he said, was very important in the remoter areas, where the best outcomes have the odds stacked against them, and any improvement on the worst possible outcome a bonus. I can't remember if we got back from the pub for dinner and suspect I was started on the road to Korsakoff's syndrome. The next day, we were guided through the beautiful gorges, experiencing the microclimates of their depths, and then toured the Pilbara attractions. We watched jewellery being made from asbestos and ran our hands through the fine, silky dust. Asbestos was the lifeblood of the town.

A few years later, the doctor's message was reinforced when I worked as a surgical registrar in Royal Perth Hospital. I saw a man with non-union of a tibial fracture as a result of a poorly applied plaster; this simple fracture should have healed strongly. Instead of being upset with the outcome, the man was very grateful to the doctor in the Pilbara who had saved his leg.

I met up with Jock and Sylvia again later in Perth, after the town of Wittenoom was closed down (asbestos had been condemned as a carcinogen, and the mine had been closed down, with the evacuation of all the inhabitants). I was working as a surgical registrar on rotation to Princess Margaret Hospital for Children when Sylvia came into casualty with her daughter, who had received a nasty gash to her leg. When it was healed, Sylvia invited us out to lunch. After leaving the Pilbara, Jock had gone back to being a chef and was working at the Wooroloo Detention Centre outside Perth. The facility for low-risk offenders was next to El Cabala Blanco, which was famous for its show of Andalusia dancing horses. It was a popular weekend outing for Perth families. Michele, Stanley, and I arrived at the duly appointed time of ten in the morning. Jock suggested that Michele catch up with Sylvia while he and I went to the bar in El Cabala Blanco for one prelunch drink.

Three things happened to multiply the number of drinks: First, the bartender turned out to have worked the Wittenoom pub, and recognising Jock, she gave us each a beer on the house. Second, Wilkie turned up in his American-style Ford Fairlane (I suspected Jock had secretly arranged this). Wilkie was very short and could just see over the dashboard of his car; he had very small eyes and looked just like Mr. Magoo. His likable visage lightened everybody's mood. Then the manager appeared in an agitated state because the projector wouldn't work, and he had twenty kids turning up for a special film on the dancing horses. So Wilkie screwed up his eyes even tighter and scrutinised the offending machine while gently tapping various parts with a screwdriver. The machine worked, and the manager expressed eternal gratitude and an afternoon of free beer on the house.

Sylvia just smiled serenely when she served up a burnt cold roast for tea. I was pissed, Michele was pissed off, and Stanley wanted to know where the dancing horses were. We lost touch with Jock and Sylvia, but they have always been part of why I love WA.

The mechanic at Wittenoom lacked the parts and the expertise to fix the Falcon's back brake lines, so he blocked the lines to prevent fluid leaks, and we set off to Carnarvon. We had to stay a while for the parts to arrive from Perth and got to know the woman in the caravan park site next to ours. A great fishing enthusiast, she introduced me to the long Carnarvon jetty, where we caught king fish. Even more informative was her story: Her husband was a pilot for a French firm. They were from New South Wales, and he flew a plane carrying geologists and a Geiger counter. They were mapping the outback of Australia for radiation, looking for uranium; Australia is now known to have approximately 30 percent of the world's resource. Her son was being schooled by correspondence, which made it a small world since Enid worked in the correspondence school in Sydney. All the communications were by post; the system a precursor to online education.

From Carnarvon, we meandered down through the wildflowers of the Wildflower State in full bloom, and all doubts about where our home was to be were dispelled. We arrived in Perth in September; Charlie put us up in a rented house in Cottesloe near the beach. After a short rest, we headed up through South East Asia via Bali and Kuta Beach (before any hotels were built), to Singapore, where street food and markets thrilled, to Malaysia and Kuala Lumpur, where we witnessed a large man suffer a heart attack and cascade all the way down the long steps leading to the Batu Caves, to a fishing village in Penang at Batu Ferringhi Beach during the ethnic Malay and

Chinese conflict, to cruise the Water Market in Bangkok, and to ride a motorbike through Nepal, with Stanley on the petrol tank and Michele on the pillion seat. We spent time in Pokra, with its sensuous statuettes of loving couples, and drove along the road to China for as far as we could go with the exposed Himalayas hemming the skyline.

Our utopian expectations for Nepal were scarred by a visit to the shrine of the Living Goddess; Stanley sat in the evidence of her life that she had deposited on a low wall. We visited a pitiful zoo where we witnessed stones being thrown at the tigers in their cages. Reality can be very different from perception, and the Nepal of Han Su Yin's *The Mountain Is Young* was somehow different in fact than in fiction. We left Nepal with ambiguous feelings for its beauty and its squalor. I prefer to think of it as the home of the Yeti, incomparable mountaineers, and the supreme Ghurkha warriors.

We were considered foolhardy to travel with a four-year-old in such fashion, but Stanley never got sick. Rather, he was a travel aid and an asset. Our flights included a number of bonus stops in India as tourist promotions. Unfortunately, the generosity of Indian Airlines had not extended to their staff, which went on rolling strikes for better pay. With our limited budget, prolonged accommodation posed a financial burden in the bigger cities, and in Delhi, we resorted to camping in the airline office. The Indians are a kind people, especially when it comes to children, and Stanley was showered with attention; people wanted to touch his very blond head. He was invited off the street to a birthday party in Bombay and loved by everyone except the airlines office, where he was a major distraction for the overworked booking clerk, dealing with extensive demands for rescheduling. For his peace of mind and for his own sake, rather than ours, the booking clerk put us on the first available flight out.

Maybe we were just lucky, or maybe the experience of growing up in Kenya led to in-built rules of preservation and preventative health. We only ate fruit that could be peeled and recently cooked food that was still hot. There were no raw salads or roadside juices or tepid tea; it was a vegetarian diet for us. We carried a gas stove and always boiled the water for our own tea, and drinks were bottled. Amazingly, considering today's world, we carried a little gas stove, complete with cylinder, on the airplanes. Michele was the only one of us that got sick. She had an out-of-bowel experience on the way out of Bombay after eating prawns on the plane. The message was, eat what the local healthy people eat because if they are well, so also should we be, and common foods have less storage time with rapid turnover. After all, the Hindus are vegetarian curry eaters, and so therefore we were too.

After visiting Stan and Ronnie in Nairobi, we headed back to Perth. The flight path took us back via Bombay, where we changed to a Qantas flight. Hearing an Australian voice over the intercom on a Qantas flight was a revelation for me. Going back to Australia was like going back to my rightful home. No longer was I a Kenyan. Leaving Kenya on this occasion was like leaving a left home, but we had had some fun times, and it was good to introduce Stan and Ronnie to Michele and Stanley. Stan very much enjoyed teaching his grandson, whom he called "Copy Cat" for having the same name, how to catch bass in Lake Naivasha. It was not so much that Kenya had changed since independence from Britain, although it obviously had; it was that the visit made me realise how much I had changed. My mother, being from a Victorian family, had difficulty accepting that Michele, Stanley, and I would all get in the bath together, that we made our own beds, and that we generally lived independently of the servants. Stan struggled with the temptation of calling us hippies, for whom he had little time and every justification, since I had grown a full beard while travelling, Stanley's hair was down to his shoulders in Beatle style, and Michele wore Indian costume jewellery. We all wore coloured garb gathered throughout South East Asia. Michele struggled with the temptation to take Stan to task over hunting animals. It was a measure of how much each loved me in their own way that they got along with each other, and that has been important to me in keeping a fond memory of old and new families and a lesson in the strength of family ties born of tolerance.

Chapter 15

Start of My Surgical Career

I expected to start as a general surgical registrar in Royal Perth Hospital on the first working day of the New Year, which was Monday, January 3, and was surprised when rung early on New Year's Day by a caller aggressively asking me why I was not in the Orthopaedic Theatre with the trauma case that came in through casualty.

"Well," I replied, "I have not yet started at the hospital, and my appointment is as a general surgical registrar."

I was asked to please come in to the hospital anyway, and the rest could be sorted out later. And that's pretty much how my surgical life has been ever since.

It turned out that there was no correlation at all between what the hospital had offered and what it had allocated. I was assigned to Orthopaedics as a registrar. A registrar is like a non-commissioned officer in the army. They give orders but are not in charge. I knew almost nothing about orthopaedics except that the professor at the University of New South Wales was George Huckstepth, a recent British migrant who had invented the Kampala nail while working at Makerere University in Uganda. He invented a metal rod with knobs at one end that was driven down the marrow cavity of a fractured femur. This enabled immediate mobilisation instead of twelve weeks in bed with traction. His work in Uganda with trauma and lack of beds with traction equipment had prompted him to invent the nail, which was adopted as a forerunner to modern fixation. People with fractured femurs could then go home walking in four or five days. I only really appreciated the significance of this when attending a military history lecture on World War I, and the speaker described how a fractured femur was a death sentence. It was a heart-rending story of how young men would take days to die in no-man's land, with their moans heard in the lines, being unable to be rescued or make it back. I was proud of the connection to East Africa.

Although we had a famous professor at UNSW, we did not learn much orthopaedics, and I was put to shame by my ignorance, especially compared to the most junior doctor of the unit.

"Don't worry," said the boss, who was affectionately called the Pink Panther because of the way he walked and held his scrubbed hands out to dry. "We can teach you how to do it our way."

I worked for him for a year instead of the six months and was offered a training post in orthopaedics. I declined on the grounds that I came to the West to train in general surgery; that upset the Professor of orthopaedics very much. Sir George Bedbrook was unfamiliar with the word no. I was in the wilderness for two years after that without a mentor, and a mentor is an important factor in surgical training. I wandered through plastic surgery, paediatrics, and two difficult terms of general surgery. Again, "It's an ill wind that blows no good," and the plastic surgery experience has proved invaluable throughout my career. I found a talent in skin grafting. Maybe it was based in my lessons on how to skin animals. I almost became a dedicated burns surgeon and introduced pressure garments to Western Australia, but I came to the West to do general surgery. I loved paediatric surgery, and after my term at the Children's Hospital, I stayed on the emergency roster for two years for after-hours relief for the paediatric surgical trainee. The joys of rapid recovery and healing in children are plumbed by the depths of sadness for those who don't survive. I could see myself as a paediatric surgeon, but I came to the West to do general surgery.

My first term in general surgery exposed weaknesses in my surgical technique; the atmosphere was also tense because two senior consultants did not see eye-to-eye. Coupled with my inexperience, I was becoming disillusioned. Fortunately, a dedicated junior consultant noticed this and took me under his wing, saving me from my first near-failure in general surgery.

I moved on to the second general surgical term with confidence, but it was shattered by the head of the unit, who was the most senior surgeon in the hospital; he had a position on the council of the Australian College of Surgeons and carried much influence. The four surgical registrars on his unit before me had been so traumatised that one switched to orthopaedics, one to urology, and one to plastics; the fourth was informed that he could no longer be employed in the hospital and what's more, any doctor who had the same referees would be guaranteed not to get a job at Royal Perth Hospital. He moved interstate.

The first two weeks of the term were enjoyable with the other consultant surgeon on the unit, as the boss was overseas in South Africa at a conference. I was unprepared for the ambush on the first ward round with the boss when he returned. He believed in the traditional technique of teaching by humiliation, and he did his best. His conference had been in Cape Town, and again I was labelled a white South African (he was fiercely anti-apartheid).

Prejudice severely affects performance (this has been clearly shown during ethnic comparisons of performance); my performance was in decline and accompanied with disillusionment. However hard I tried, I could not please, and the boss seemed determined to terminate my career. He did not tolerate errors, and I made one that led to an unnecessary operation. These were the days before CT and ultrasound scans, and a young woman came to casualty with severe abdominal pain, what is termed an acute abdomen. When the muscles of the belly are tight like a board, it implies peritonitis. When the white cells are raised in the blood, it implies infection and bacterial invasion, and when the pulse rate is high, it indicates general stress. All these factors were present, but at operation, there was nothing I could find in the abdomen to explain it all; I called the boss and asked him to check, as I feared I had missed something serious. He also found nothing wrong, and the young lady got better without further treatment (it must have been a viral illness). She had to carry the scar and I the responsibility.

I was miserable in the job, and it was difficult to function when lacking confidence and under hostile assessment. My operating privileges were curtailed, and when called to operate, which the boss signalled without warning by standing in the assistant's position, I was unprepared, out of practice, and intimidated by silent or terse monosyllabic criticism. I operated less and less.

Another young woman was admitted with a twenty-four-hour history of symptoms and signs similar to the one who had the unnecessary operation. This was on Tuesday. The boss, not trusting me, examined her and advised not to operate and to observe her progress. She continued to complain of severe pain; a gynaecology opinion was sought. The gynaecologist's opinion was that while she was ill, it was not gynaecological. By Thursday morning, her pain was difficult to control, and X-rays of her abdomen were not conclusive. I placed her on the operating list for Thursday afternoon. The boss said to take her off. He was angry that I should take the liberty after the previous experience.

This girl was clearly very ill and in a lot of pain, and I refused, saying that I wouldn't take her off, but I would put her second so he could reassess her. The boss was very, very angry with me for my defiance. The operation revealed a twisted loop of small bowel about twenty centimetres long that was strangled of its blood supply; it was purple-black, dead, and smelt gangrenous. There was only fluid in the loop, and its site just beyond the duodenum accounted for the absence of X-ray detection. Another few hours, and it would have fallen apart and killed her.

Our relationship mellowed a little after that, and the boss, who was an excellent technical surgeon, started to teach me more, until one day there was almost a disaster. Although more tolerant of my performance, he was no less impatient, and one day, he was assisting me with a gall bladder removal (called a cholecystectomy). This was for cholecystitis: multiple gallstones and recurrent bouts of inflammation. There is a duct that goes from the gall bladder, which hangs from the underside of the right lobe of the liver, to the main bile duct that connects the liver to the gut. The gall bladder stores bile and concentrates it, releasing it in response to a meal so that fat can be digested.

The operation was difficult because of a previous inflammation. I was slow to reveal all the ducts, and the dictum is that the confluence of cystic duct from the gall bladder with main bile duct from the liver must be seen before cutting and tying any bile duct. There was a famous case of an incorrect cutting and tying of a main bile duct of Sir Anthony Eden when he was British prime minister. As a result, he became extremely ill and nearly died. His bile ducts were repaired with difficulty by doctors at the Lahey Clinic in Boston; Britain lost the Suez Canal during his absence due to illness.

I exposed a relatively small bile duct but was not sure where the main duct was or whether the exposed duct was certainly the cystic duct. The boss lost patience and said, "Cut it." I cut it. Then we realised when taking out the gall bladder that it was not the cystic duct but the main duct from the liver. I had visions of Sir Anthony Eden's ghost. Repairing such a bile duct was beyond my capabilities at that time, and the boss took over.

"Take out the gall bladder while I do this," he said.

Easier said than done because the recurrent bouts of inflammation with subsequent scarring made it like unravelling wool impregnated with glue, and the gall bladder was breached, depositing, much to my horror, lots of small gall stones in the wound. The operation was completed in silence, all the stones painfully retrieved, and the bile ducts repaired.

The next morning, neither of us said anything on the ward round. I then sat down at the desk and wrote out my resignation for the hospital and was preparing for my last day in surgery.

The boss sat down next to me and said, "Don't worry about yesterday, it was my fault, and the patient is going to be fine because we recognised the mistake and fixed it."

I didn't submit my resignation and remembered the lesson that to err is surgery, but to miss the mistake and fail to fix it is lethal.

A few years later, I was given a job with the university through this boss. The Don, as he was known, had taught me humility, how to handle mistakes, technique, and to stand strong when convinced of being right. Many years later, he paid me the greatest compliment that one surgeon can pay to another when he came to me about a surgical problem.

There are many trials in training to be a surgeon, and each of us must face them at some time. There is often an imperative for a procedure or therapy to be advised and performed just because a particular diagnosis is made. Appendicitis implying appendicectomy is a common example. If a surgeon makes a diagnosis of acute appendicitis, he is committed to taking out the appendix. Sometimes, there is cause for hesitation, such as doubt or lack of evidence, despite clinical intuition, and because the consequences of error may be dire, this hesitation carries through at every step. In many instances, the risk of a procedure may be greater than the disease; this depends on the other circumstances involving the patient.

For example, a history of heart disease or diabetes and the presence of obesity affect the risk/benefit analysis; assessing risks is like working out an insurance premium. A selfish motive that stays the hand is the fear of litigation. More often, it is genuine trepidation for causing more harm than good. This may also be selfishly motivated if one asks who is being harmed if something goes wrong. Is it primarily concern for the patient or concern for the surgeon's reputation and peace of mind? Richard Dawkins, who was also born in Kenya, writes in his first book, *The Selfish Gene,* to the effect that there is no true altruism without secondary gain. If this is accurate, then it casts a shadow on the cry, "We must do such-and-such for the patient's sake."

Although it is said that the patient must come first, there may well be an undeclared secondary agenda that is more important for the surgeon. The secondary gain, which may be subconscious, slips through under the patient's banner, since harm to the patient is also harm to the surgeon.

If there is a selfish motive for surgeons to avoid harm to themselves, it also protects patients, and that's a good thing. Surgeons who tend to hesitate or retreat from a prescribed act of intervention are known as conservative or safe, and those who move quickly to intervene with an invasive surgical procedure are called aggressive. Too conservative, and all may be too late and lost; too aggressive, and they go where angels fear to tread. So if pure altruism cannot be the only (or even the prime) motive, what is it that drives a surgeon to exhaustion? Sometimes, surgeons will operate for hours beyond the expectations of the stomach, the bladder, the brain, and the simulator.

Simplistically, some of the motives may be seen as money, pride, status amongst peers, esteem in the community, power over people, personal satisfaction in achievement (as in climbing a mountain), just plain stubbornness, or maybe a desire for a peculiar type of gratification. Undoubtedly, receiving gratitude is a very powerful and forceful motive. Beyond the satisfaction of a job well done is the gratitude peculiar to lifesaving. It is not always expressed, and there are few medals of recognition. More often, it is taken for granted as part of expectation of professional expertise. Sometimes, however, it is the gratitude expressed by the patient with sincerity in a look more meaningful than words could ever do.

Money is a motive for some, but it is a limited motive, and the limit varies. While he was training to be a surgeon, a very left-wing friend of mine from Malaysia would expand on the virtues of public service and the attendant evils of consumer medicine. On my first visit to his private clinic some years later, I discovered an exclusive and busy facility geared to delivering medical services at premium market rates. When I asked him what had happened to his socialist ethic, he calmly replied, "Michael, my heart is on the left but my wallet is on the right."

Apropos of this, there is the old story of where to hide a hundred dollar note from a doctor: with an orthopaedic surgeon, slip it into their textbook; with a radiologist, just put it with the patient; and with a cosmetic surgeon, it's a trick question. You cannot hide money from a cosmetic surgeon. Obviously, there is a tinge of professional jealousy here, but there again, many a true word spoken in jest.

After medical school and basic training as a junior doctor in a hospital, there is competition to train formally in surgery. The successful aspirant undertakes a number of years of advanced surgical training to emerge as qualified with the passing of the college examination. This takes thirteen to fifteen years from entering medical school. Persistence is the mark of a surgeon. When you really need that person, you need them to commit to stay with you until the end, whatever the end may be.

We view the commitment of a surgeon as professionalism. Responsibility and dedication to task are assumed qualities demanded of a professional. Excuses for shortfalls and errors are seldom adequate and especially viewed askance should they be in the nature of personal problems and home-related issues. Consequently, there is little tolerance for a surgeon who puts his own problems or his family before his duty and his patient. Continuity of care and responsibility were core teachings. This aspect steered surgery towards male dominance and the expectation that it was the wives and partners who kept the home fires burning and the kids' noses and school records clean and trouble-free.

The twentieth century changed so much for women; the world wars were not only an epidemic of trauma and innovation to deal with that epidemic but also an opportunity for female expression of roles beyond the home. The Battle of the Somme gave blood and bone to fields of poppies and a need for women to step into the breach. The strength of the women who emerged in the first half of the century was powered in the latter half with the freedom to choose whether to become pregnant or not. Based on the law that every action has an equal and opposite reaction, the change for women had to lead to a change for men. Stresses and strains were being felt on the two fronts by surgical trainees. One was duty and the other family expectations. Women were intruding into the sanctity of the surgical precinct, directly and indirectly.

Although Michele and I had a partnership, with her background and mettle, it was inevitable that she would define a path of her own to be weaved with mine. Like me, she wanted children and a career. She was determined not to stagnate at home and become boring while I soared into the operating theatre. In our first year in Perth, she enrolled in an arts degree course in the University of Western Australia, with a view to becoming a teacher. She stopped taking the pill and announced that there was no hurry for another child, but if it happened, we would cope.

It happened.

It was spontaneous combustion. Gone were the days when pregnancy thwarted a woman's career; she proudly walked the campus with the ripening fruit of our loins and was given the favoured seats in lectures. Trevor, like all boys, was reluctant to leave the womb and had to be sucked out with the aid of a vacuum cleaner. He looked like a Jewish rabbi with a purple skull cap, but after six weeks, he grew a smile as wide as his mother's at his birth.

Michele soon returned to university part-time, and Trevor started his academic career early, as she took him with her to the university. The university judged the times well and had the foresight to provide preschool care. It may have been set up primarily for single mothers, but the effect of this was felt far beyond the university because it allowed us both to pursue our careers.

In my second year of advanced training, I was pleased to be working for the university's surgical department, which had the reputation of being progressive, up to date, reasonably aggressive, and yet judiciously safe. Most of all, they trained their young doctors conscientiously and with good support. The days of the week were divided between the surgical units in the hospital for emergencies. The degree of supervision and support of the young surgical aspirants varied, as does human nature, between and within units. As I was new to this unit, one of the professors stipulated that he wanted to discuss every case that was admitted. He would then decide if my decisions were correct, according to the information I had given him, and whether he would come into the hospital to check, assist, or take over. This was a sensible, reasonable, and fairly standard approach. He made one restriction absolutely clear: I was not to take anybody to theatre without his knowledge, and he would not tolerate any breach of this rule.

On a Saturday afternoon shortly after I started, a young man was brought into casualty with a stab wound to the abdomen. He was obviously bleeding, and we were just managing to keep him stable. There was a clear indication to operate because of continuous bleeding, and the emergency staff pushed for me to get on with it. Try as hard I might, I could not raise the professor. I was in a dilemma. The certainty was that my career and whole life was at stake and on the other hand, the young man's life was possibly at stake because of the ongoing bleeding (and blood transfusions can cause bleeding problems of their own). Eventually, with one sword in my hand and the other held by Damocles over my head, we went to theatre in the professor's ignorance. The bleeding point was secured, and all was well for the patient, while I waited in trepidation for my fate.

Perth was a small city, and it turned out that the junior doctor working with me was a family friend of the professor and a member of the same yacht club. He learned from the grapevine that the professor had decided to move his boat in the marina at the Royal Perth Yacht Club that afternoon, and a minor accident deposited him in the water, rendering him incommunicado. The inevitable presentation of the stabbed young man on the next ward round was met with a fleeting expression of gratitude that made my heart sing. It was a good lesson in that the community is kind if one is right, and the law holds the sword in trust should you be wrong. It also put a dent in the concept of zero tolerance when it also affects the lawmakers.

Chapter 16

Examination and Licence to Cut

Brian Vivian, a university professor of surgery, became my mentor, and my training entered green pastures until I approached the gate to the Fellowship of the College of Surgeons of Australia and New Zealand. These exams were like no other. They were held over the course of a week with written papers, short-answer questions, and oral exams in pathology, anatomy, operating surgery, and clinical cases. The grading system was based on nine points; nine was excellent and almost impossible to achieve. Six was a failure, and seven was doubtful. Eight was a pass. It was not necessary for an examiner to fail a candidate; a mark of doubt sufficed, and if two doubts occurred during the week, they amounted to a failure. If only one doubt was registered, then discussion and reasoning in the court of examiners was required. Oral examinations were overseen by two examiners, who had to agree with their mark.

Consequently, the failure rate was high, at about 70 percent. Failure was so common that first-timers were usually consoled by past candidates before they even took the exam. I felt a special bond with one of my close friends, who later became president of the college, because we climbed that mountain together—twice.

Imagine the stress of these exams. Every diagnosis potentially committed the candidate to an invasive act, and indecision about an action pathway for a surgical problem was death to the candidate. Theoretical death to the patient, or a hypothetical action that would lead to complications, led the candidate to a similar end. These examinations were as much a test of mental strength as a test of knowledge. No wonder stories abound, such as the following:

Examiner to candidate: "Mr. Brown, can you see leaves on the trees outside the window?"

"No, sir, being winter, they are bare."

"Indeed, may I suggest you return and try again when the leaves are on the trees?"

Or as one more kindly examiner is known to have remarked, "You look nervous. Relax. By the way, haven't I examined you before?"

"Yes, sir."

"Ah well, what was the first question I asked you last time?"

"Sir, you asked 'Haven't I examined you before?'"

The first time I sat was in Melbourne, and to ensure I passed, I attended a six-week pre-examination course. I started the course full of confidence and ended extremely doubtful about my ability to pass. As a stranger to Melbourne, I felt uneasy amongst the best in the country; these men were the elite of Australian culture (there were no women surgeons). One of the course candidates, Tony Noonan, was also from Western Australia (he schooled in Melbourne), and one Saturday afternoon, he suggested that we have a break in a pub.

"Okay," I replied.

"It's a really rough but interesting pub in Fitzroy," he explained. "Reckon you can handle it?"

"Sure."

"Okay then," he said, and off we went.

Tony was tall and laconic, with a quick wry smile; he always wore a blue blazer, open shirt, and trousers. He was a good

Catholic boy, schooled by the brothers in Melbourne. The pub was dark and dingy, and the floor beer-soaked and pot-holed. The football was playing on the silent TV, and the drinkers loomed and lurched in the shadows and flickers of light. Tony smiled at me to see if I was impressed and sufficiently distracted from study. He then sauntered over to the bar and duly headed back with a frothy beer in each hand. Halfway across the floor, a somewhat dishevelled middle-aged woman crossed his path and neatly grabbed his balls, one in each hand.

"May I have one of those, please?" she asked sweetly.

On his return to our table with only one beer, he announced that there was a lesson to be learned from that experience for the upcoming examinations: to never answer a question with a question, but respond in a positive manner. He said it with such aplomb that one would be forgiven for thinking he had planned the whole thing. Never one to lose his cool, he headed back to the bar for another glass, keeping one hand free at all times.

My operative surgery viva was the first of my oral examinations, and I was coiled more like a spring than the snake that is the symbol of my profession. I was asked to describe how I would remove a spleen. This is a straight-forward operation for normal-sized spleens; in those days, it was most often for trauma, and I had done my share. However, research was shifting the management of splenic trauma towards preservation of the organ for immune response reasons, and the indications for splenectomy were shifting towards larger pathological spleens. According to a recent flurry of journal articles, the operation for large pathological spleens might have to be modified and could be difficult or much more extensive. Large spleens could be stuck on the diaphragm and theoretically even necessitate opening the chest as well as the abdomen.

"How big is the spleen?" I sprung back at the examiner.

I saw the glint in his eye and felt the stab of the point in his steely pupil as he replied, "It is as big as a football." (He omitted to say, "Now deal with that, you smart bastard!")

All I could see in my mind was Tony in the pub under the football on the flickering TV and realised I had answered the question with a question. My hopes flickered and died, and I knew the examiner had me by the balls.

Melbourne held no joy for me in those six weeks, except for the pub experience. To commiserate or celebrate (as the case might be), the three of us from Western Australia indulged in some of the finer Melbourne culture and went to the public bar at Young and Jackson's, opposite Flinders Station. There at the bar, demurely luring through the drifting blue smoke across the head and sunburnt shoulders bulging through blue singlets, was Chloe, a life-sized nude painting. If her life had been so hard and she was so beautiful, what right did I have to be dejected? I replaced Florence Nightingale with Chloe for comfort and planned for the next attempt.

Tony passed. Kingsley and I tried again in Sydney at the next round of examinations, when the leaves were back on the trees and the sun shining more brightly. I was determined to pass the second time and set my mind to abandon all that was new in research. I changed from football to cricket and refused to play the hook shot. I responded to questions with textbook answers, gave no opinions, and asked no questions. My philosophy was that if they failed me again, they would fail the textbook. In the interim, I had to study and returned to Western Australia a much wiser man.

Shortly after my return, there was a medical and political crisis in the Kimberley, in the north-west of the state. There had recently been a state government election, and the member for the Kimberley had been disallowed because of election fraud. A by-election was to be held, and coincidently, the surgeon there resigned. The state government could not afford to lose the seat and could not go to the election without a surgeon for the vast area. The Royal Perth Hospital medical superintendent approached me and said the hospital had to send a young surgeon; there were only two of us who were sufficiently trained, and the other one, who was more senior than me, had refused to go. I informed him that Michele and I were expecting our third child. He retorted that it was therefore even more important for me to have a job, and if I wanted to continue in the hospital, it would be wise of me to accept. I started to wonder if the examiners and the superintendent had taken lessons from the woman in the pub.

The next six months were spent as the surgeon to the Kimberley. This is where Australia departed from any semblance of Europe. It was populated by black people with white administrators, government officials, pastoralists, and itinerants. The hospital was the main industry and demonstrated an Australian presence to countries to the north, namely Indonesia, which had only shortly before driven out the Dutch colonials. Like a research base in Antarctica, it was isolated. The roads were dusty, the land harsh, and boabs and anthills dominated the landscape. Crocodiles were in the rivers, and I felt at home. Those of European descent were known as the mad, the bad, and the sad. There was no television or cinema or sporting club. In Derby, there was a jetty in King Sound, where the tides would rush in at over twenty kilometres per hour and rise over seven meters so that the State Ships, which were flat bottomed and supplied the region during the cattle industry days, would sit in the mud at low tide.

The Spinifex Hotel was rough and ready, with a special area for Aborigines shielded from the main lounge by a cyclone fence. The Spinny provided the main entertainment at changeover time for the New Year, when the band played at the cockroach and frog races. Most of the Europeans were nurses from the hospital, and the main recreation was barbecue and alcohol. It was a dangerous place for a young man, and I sent for Michele as soon as she finished her studies for the year. She arrived, pregnant with Gareth, and stayed long enough to tide me over the Christmas period.

The women in the region were remarkable. Koolan Island, situated in the Buccaneer Archipelago at the mouth of King Sound, was one of the richest Iron ore mines owned by BHP in Western Australia. One evening, the doctor on Koolan Island had to deal with a patient with a severe workplace head injury. The patient needed transfer to Perth for specialised neurosurgery and transfer would be through me in Derby. Arriving with the *Flying Doctor* She worked the ventilation air bag with one hand and held her breastfeeding baby in the other.

When I asked how she came to be on Koolan Island, she replied, "My husband applied for a job as an engineer and asked if there was anything for me. They wrote back and said there was a job for me, and he could come too."

The matron of Derby Hospital was a young bone cancer survivor whose leg had been amputated just below the hip. She walked stiffly, swinging her prosthesis with a rotating rhythm in her pelvis. Her passion, after nursing, was flying planes. Having grown up with the inspiring story of Douglas Bader, who had lost both legs and became a World War II fighter pilot ace in the Battle of Britain, I did admire her. There was lots of opportunity because this was flying doctor country to clinics and emergencies all across the Kimberley. One of these clinics was in Hall's Creek

The Halls Creek Hospital was a collection of corrugated iron dwellings, and on my first visit, a welcome lunch was organised. Amongst the mad, the bad, and the sad in the December heat was a pale young woman who glowed red and sweaty beneath her ginger hair. She responded to my greeting in a broad Scottish accent. She looked so out of place that I politely enquired how she came to be there. She had been recruited in Inverness by the Australian Inland Mission and flown from the dead of the northern Scottish winter to the one of the hottest places in Australia, at the height of summer. She had been transported without a break from Scotland via Sydney and Alice Springs to Halls Creek and was close to tears. I had no remedy, only understanding that she was indeed with the mad, the bad, and the sad.

The flying doctor service to the Kimberley was the Victorian Branch. Sadly, Victoria was too small for a flying doctor, so WA kindly let them have the Kimberley region, should they be mad enough. The flying doctor organisation was set up by Dr John Flynn of Outback Queensland and worked essentially as an ambulance service, with the best outback pilots in the world. Doctors who flew with the service did so as volunteers, without recourse to compensation or insurance for any injury sustained. I only know of one doctor who has ever refused to fly with the service, and that was for medical reasons. The Royal Flying Doctor Service continues to be treasured throughout the Kimberley.

My time in the Kimberley was special for the clinical and social experience. The fireflies kept me company at night while I studied for the fellowship again. I returned to work at Royal Perth; Tony Noonan took up the position as the permanent surgeon for the Kimberley area. Tony had been a general practitioner in the Kimberley and had been persuaded to train in surgery by the College of Surgeons. He served the area for a number of years after obtaining his fellowship but then left when the Department of Health rejected his request for time to refresh his training in Perth. He was lost to Darwin where, amongst other things, he fought for Lindy Chamberlin to be freed following her wrongful conviction for infanticide (a dingo took her daughter near Ayres Rock).

The world was indeed changing for women. When Gareth was born, Michele determined to resist all attempts to interfere with her birthing this time. Back at Royal Perth Hospital, I was on duty with many emergencies that night and rang her between cases, while she stayed at home until we thought the delivery was close, and then she went into the hospital. Michele, for all her fire, was never going to be quick. A friend, another senior registrar called Terry Jenkins, was on duty that night at King

Edward, and she was delivered naturally and gently. Gareth was our largest baby, and Michele was ecstatic to have done it on her own. It was not long before she was back at the university, complete with her sleeping breastfeeding bub in a sling during lectures and tutorials. When he woke and cried, disturbing a lecture in anthropology, she rose to take him outside for a feed. The lecturer invited her to stay and breastfeed in class. How much had changed in just a few years.

I sat the College Fellowship examination again in Sydney, where I felt much more comfortable in place and mind. This time, I passed, which was one of the greatest reliefs I have experienced. The depth of feeling approached the silent sadness I felt for the killing of animals on safari. One part of me was finally gone forever, and another about to start.

Chloe was rewarded by being encased in glass and moved to a higher place, upstairs in more salubrious surroundings in the hotel, to be honoured as a national treasure. I visit her whenever in Melbourne and drink to the health that she lost but I might have given to others.

CHAPTER 17

The Young Surgeon and St Thomas at Last

Up to this point, any patient I cared for or operation I performed was as an apprentice; the ultimate responsibility for good or bad outcomes belonged to the boss. Now I had a licence to receive patients in my own name and assume direct responsibility. My reputation, not that of the boss, was on the line. This would rapidly determine whether I would attract or discourage patients; I would be directly responsible for the outcomes. I would no longer have to pass on the gratitude or have the luxury to deflect the problems. There were changes in how I was perceived and how I perceived myself.

This presented a whole new set of problems that I now know, having observed my own trainees mature, to be common to all younger surgeons. I started to resent always having the most junior support nursing staff in theatre, the most inconvenient operating times, the wastepaper basket of surgical chores, and the questioning of my ability in the eyes of patients and staff. There were often questions as to whether I was really capable of handling difficult situations and body language that suggested the problem should be passed on to an older surgeon.

The quality of confidence was strained and fragile. Confidence had to be exuded in sufficient quantity to disseminate amongst all those I worked with and who needed confidence in me. Where did confidence cross the line into brashness or, worse still, arrogance? Too many Catch-22s and double binds to handle. Too many in the hospital had seen me in my surgical nappies. I could no longer deal with challenging patients and operations in the name of a boss, and as time passed, I became impatient, more assertive, and competitive. There are many ways to describe younger surgeons in their "old bull–young bull" conflicts. As with grown teenagers, there comes a time to leave for a while, gain other experiences, and dim the images held of the junior doctor. I needed to acquire some mystery; I needed to go and work somewhere else.

Tony House, the professor of surgery and head of the department of surgery, had a special interest in transplants. He rang one afternoon and offered to arrange a job swap for me at St Thomas Hospital in London. A young surgeon there, Kevin Burnand, who also with a special interest in transplant surgery, wanted to come to Perth and work with Tony. Kevin and I were the same age, but he was a little more experienced than me because his career had progressed from school, whereas I had spent those years working for Stan. I was offered his position as senior surgical registrar at St Thomas, working for Sir Hugh Lockhart-Mummery, the colorectal surgeon to the Royal Family. I had serious doubts about my ability to fill Kevin's shoes. However, I had introduced a new procedure to Royal Perth Hospital, using staple guns for bowel anastomoses, and this was the ideal opportunity to further that expertise. There was the added lure of a BTE degree (Been to England).

Tony House tackled problems in life like he tackled problems in the operating theatre: quickly, deftly, and with complete confidence. It was arranged, and a prized position, to which I felt inadequate, was mine for a year. The wheel had turned all the way around; I was going to St Thomas after all.

It turned out that there was quite a strong connection between Royal Perth and St Thomas; there had been a number of exchanges, including the medical superintendents. It was some comfort to know that I was not unique. Kevin and I exchanged jobs, houses, cars, and status (but we kept our wives). I was broke because we had just built an extension on the house, but I considered myself very fortunate. Without hesitation, I packed up Michele and our three sons and headed to England with just my last pay-packet. It was June; the buildings that had been so dirty looking in the sixties were cleaned of the soot, the sun was bright, the sky blue, and the flowers splashed colour between the green of the leafy horse chestnut trees. How England had changed in less than twenty years. We found Kevin's little white house in Worcester Park in Surrey and saw the London sights.

I guess it's good to be pushed a little beyond our expectations; a guess because the line is in a minefield: too far and too fast courts disaster and defeat, from which there is no recovery; too short and too easy fails to test the limits and bring out the best of ability. The job at St Thomas set the bar higher than I had ever jumped in surgery. To be pushed beyond expectations also expends pent-up energy and emotions, rather like a radio transmitter needing to work against the resistance of its aerial, or it will heat up inside and burn out.

The question was, how far should a young surgeon be pushed? I was reminded of an experiment that was done to measure how fast a cheetah could run before speed could be measured accurately with a radar gun. An experiment was set up to test the speed of a cheetah against a greyhound on a track. The greyhound was given a start and the cheetah released at increasing time intervals. The cheetah's top speed remained elusive because it easily caught the dog, until the dog got a start that the cheetah thought was too good, and then the cheetah simply would not run. There was a lesson in that experiment that can be carried over to testing a surgeon's skill: Surgeons cannot afford to fail. Choosing when to refuse to run is called judgement.

On arrival at St Thomas Hospital, I met Barry Jackson, the second surgeon on Sir Hugh Lockhart-Mummery's unit. This was a team of eminent surgeons in a prestigious hospital. Surgeons appointed to the Royal Family worked up through three ranks. At the beginning, a surgeon is appointed to the Royal household, then the extended family, and finally to the monarch and immediate family. Sir Hugh was the surgeon to the Queen, and Barry already the surgeon for the Royal household. St Thomas is one of the oldest hospitals in the UK and situated on the River Thames, opposite the Houses of Parliament. The Germans attempted to destroy the Houses of Parliament during the war. The bombs fell short, landing on St Thomas Hospital. They succeeded in demolishing one of the buildings and irreparably damaging another. The two damaged buildings were replaced with a large square white building in modern Chicago skyscraper style, contrasting starkly with the harmony of the original sandstone masterpieces of the eighteenth century.

Contrasts can be beautiful or disturbing. Contrasts convey feelings and emotions, maybe a sense of peace or war, of happiness or despair, of love or hate. For example, most of us feel something when seeing a beautiful sunset or sunrise. For me, it is a sense of life as the colours blend, tinting the clouds, or peace at the end of the day, as contrast spreads and fades into black, as each colour falls out of the spectrum and the sun sinks behind a hill, behind the veil of a thorn tree, or into the sea. In Bali, the colours at the edges of the clouds had been enhanced by the forest fires in Indonesia and the grass inside the cigarette paper. On the Dampier Peninsula, the red Pindan cliffs glowed, reflecting the sentiments of the sun magnified by the red dust hanging in the air. Sunsets are a dance of the ages by the elements of earth, fire, and water and contrast at its best because of a paradoxical harmony.

The new block at St Thomas was contrast at its worst. It was so bad that there were moves to demolish the row of Cartwright's historical buildings in order to build new ones to match the square new building across from the Houses of Parliament. It was too stark and uncomfortably out of place, as though a skyscraper had been moved out of its birthplace in Chicago and dropped in by helicopter after the fire (the fire was the war). The architects were blinded to the past. The past of St Thomas extends back to the fourteenth century. It is a past of charity, faith, and kind human endeavour, of Cheselden, barber-surgeons, Lambeth Palace, Queen Victoria, and Florence Nightingale, the Lady of the Lamp.

Few characters I learnt about at school have etched themselves more into my mind than Florence Nightingale. At fourteen and knowing that I was due for a caning for some forgotten misdemeanour (maybe being late for a meal or speaking during silent study period), I lay awake after lights-out, night after night, expecting to be called to the boot-room. Usually, the punishment was meted out quickly, but in this case, there was an inexplicable delay, and I hoped against hope that it had been forgotten.

The inevitable harsh sound of steps reverberated on the wooden floor and grew in volume as they approached down the dormitory. They were followed by the dreaded tap on the shoulder before the steps receded, and a strip of light appeared under the boot-room door across the narrow passage at the end of our dormitory. Pyjamas were thin, and kikois, the East African sarongs some of us wore, were not much better; a cry was weakness, a gasp involuntary, and often only the whack of the standard UK Department of Education specification cane could be heard to intimidate the listeners. The uncertainty of whether it would be tonight was as stressful as the physical punishment was painful. There was a sort of pride in not showing the mental hurt while proudly showing off the cuts on the arse afterwards, in all their glory of red, blue, and green combinations. The pain was alleviated by mental freeing of completed punishment. Tears were hidden. The Lady of the Lamp would visit me in my mind during the wait, and I kept a soft spot for her. It was character building. At St Thomas, I needed that character to meet the challenges here in her domain.

Florence Nightingale gave the nurses dignity and lifted their image; before her time, they were considered sluts and harlots, and nursing was work only for the desperate, widowed soldier's wives, and abandoned women. The uniforms signified all that was, and is, noble in the nursing profession. The nurses' uniform at the Prince of Wales Hospital and Michele's uniform at the Royal Prince Alfred Hospital were costumes from the Crimean War, replete with blue or red capes. The hospital colours were like colours of a regiment; they sported a pinafore with cross straps at the back over a drab grey or blue dress, with or without pinstripes. The rig was crowned with a starched white headdress and carried on heavy dark stockings and strong black shoes. The nurses needed only a musket over the shoulder and the march of the toy soldier to complete the picture. It became ridiculous in the sixties, when flower power took over, and the nurses marched with folded arms.

Florence Nightingale is remarkable for not only reforming nursing, improving the British Army conditions, and comforting the imagination of small boys, but also for doing more for the standing of women than anyone in history. In a list of respected and trusted occupations, nursing consistently tops the list (at last survey, doctors were fourth). Florence Nightingale lifted the status of nursing to such a height that women paid the hospitals for the privilege to train, and men were attracted to the profession, as well. In the sixties, it was rare to encounter a male nurse, except in mental hospitals, where physical strength might be required (before the days of tranquillisers); the mentally ill could be strong ("with the strength of a madman"). The inmates, as they were called in mental asylums, were like prisoners; most were physically able to perform basic needs and not need toilet care. This meant that the men nurses did not have to deal with bodily messes, which historically has always been a problem for males.

General and maternity nursing was essentially a female occupation, and they were treated as the handmaidens of doctors, particularly surgeons, who were males. As a junior doctor in Sydney, nurses were addressed as "Sister" (or "Sis," when trying to be more familiar); most doctors were too busy, wouldn't bother, or just did not know their proper names. The term "Sister" had a basis in the Sisters of the Catholic church because so many nuns became nurses. The church was associated with hospitals and nuns dedicated to service. Male nurses caused a dilemma. They were not church-based monks, they did not wear toy-soldier uniforms, they could not be called "Sister" (although some were called "Mister Sister"), and they expected reasonable pay. Flower power and the wind of change in the sixties started to drive out the army-style uniforms and discrimination and bring in equal pay for equal work for women. Nurse training was elevated to university degree status, and nurses began being called by their title and proper name. It is likely that doctors in primary care will eventually be replaced by nurse practitioners.

The nurses at St Thomas were rightfully proud and were called Nightingales. Their modern uniform was practical and smart, and it conveyed dignity with authority. It was a dark blue dress with tiny white dots. I don't mean to be demeaning and drag them back to the past, but they did look like guinea fowls when they streamed off-duty. Guinea fowl always look busy; they can fly but seldom do, and only as a last resort to escape; they hurry and they run, in their dark blue with tiny white dots.

Barry Jackson eventually became Sir Barry Jackson and president of the College of Surgeons of England. He had started as a surgical instrument maker with Downs and had a passion for medical history. Surgical instruments often bear the name of an inventive surgeon who had been driven by necessity, and each tells a story that Barry knew. Barry was most knowledgeable about Florence Nightingale. Later, after returning to Perth, I was able to arrange for Barry to be a visiting professor for the medical school of the UWA. There has never been a surgeon who drew more people to his lectures or more listeners to the radio. There were requests for him to speak to other schools of medicine and lay groups, such as the Historical Society. His drawing card was Florence Nightingale.

At St Thomas, I learnt beyond the traditional school teaching of Florence Nightingale's work in the Crimea. After the Crimea War, she retired to her bedroom, expecting to die at a young age. She may have suffered with what we now recognise as post-traumatic stress disorder. Anyway, she did not die for another fifty years. It is said she never left her bedroom, but that is not true. Such was the power of her pen and personality that the powers that be visited her, and she reformed the British Army conditions and nursing in parallel from her home office. I learnt that simple public health measures save lives on a logarithmic scale, compared with individual patient doctoring.

For example, by insisting through the home secretary that each soldier should have his own bed and defined space, she halted the ravages of contagious infections like streptococci and staphylococci. Golden staph caused abscesses, and streptococci caused blood poisoning, scarlet fever, nephritis, kidney failure, rheumatic fever, and heart valve disease. Its allies, pneumococcus and meningococcus, killed many in confined spaces with pneumonia and meningitis. With hygiene and good water, Florence Nightingale dispelled diarrhoea and septic infections. And she proved you don't need to exercise to live a long, productive life.

There were the usual attractions and wishes for home that all who travel for work experience. But where was my home? The Brits detected an Australian inflection in my voice, and I was Australian trained. The Brits in the hospital reminded me of the Brits in the colonies with traditions, hierarchy, and unspoken rules of etiquette that one is meant to know. I seemed to be excused for social ignorance when regarded as an Australian but was expected to know if from another colony, such as Kenya. My origins were eventually exposed; my family name was recognised by a medical student who was the son of the surgeon who had removed my appendix in Nairobi. Then Richard and Philip Leakey were admitted so Philip could donate one of his kidneys to Richard. I had known for some time that this was going to happen, as I had visited the Leakeys during my farewells to Stan earlier in East Africa when he was diagnosed with inoperable cancer of the lung. I expected Richard's fame to create a stir, but it was Philip who was more conspicuous in the hospital. Philip was a member of the independent Kenyan parliament and had an official Kenyan bodyguard assigned to him. There was always a bodyguard at Philip's door. Assassinations were close to the heart of Kenyans after the killing of Tom Mboya, who engineered the release of Kenyatta from prison and independence from Britain.

When Stan died in November, my Kenyan roots were fully exposed. While it was expected, the end was sudden, and I was thankful that we had said our goodbyes in April. I did not have time to make the journey before he died after collapsing with haemoptysis.

It was a busy time at the hospital. The registrars had changed; an excellent but inexperienced junior female registrar had replaced the experienced registrar. A registrar is like a sergeant in the army and a senior registrar akin to a sergeant major. We had battled together to meet the demands, with me as an outsider in a prominent position of senior registrar and she as the first female surgeon ever to be accepted at St Thomas. We had been very fortunate that the support from Sir Hugh and Barry had been so good, to the extent that Kevin, with whom I had swapped jobs, remarked that they were too gentlemanly to be real surgeons (Kevin believed that Sir James Robinson Justice portrayed the epitome of a real surgeon in the film *Doctor in the House*).

We were broke, and the airfare to Nairobi for the funeral was prohibitively expensive, but what daunted me most was how to ask permission to leave at short notice. I admit that I hesitated before asking Sir Hugh if I could have leave for the funeral. On the one hand was the sense of duty and on the other was family. My little sister Wendy, nine years younger than me, had had a very tough time as a border in high school. The relationship between Mum and Dad was even more poisonous after the affair Stan had with Pat Cavendish. Wendy had lived through the demise of Lawrence-Brown Safaris, which Ronnie and Stan had worked so hard to build, the failure of Kenmare Lodge and the changing times. Wendy escaped to a family up the road and eventually married their son, Adrian. I was needed to help Wendy and Ronnie tidy up family matters.

Wendy was settled in a happy marriage with Adrian and two children, but funerals were reminders to Wendy of her miscarriages, a stillborn child and the death of her five-day-old Brenda. My mother had borne the brunt of loneliness of the safari man's wife, the shame of the family affair, the sorrows of her children, and the loss of her children (physically, in my case, and psychologically in Wendy's). She had had to bear Wendy's obstetric history and loss of grandchildren to go with her own experience of a stillborn child. I had to go for their sake and realised I had to go for mine. Blood is thickest when it's your own.

I never expected the hole into which I dropped. If my dad was mortal, then so was I. My Horatio on the bridge to death had fallen. I plumbed the source of my Nile, and tears flowed between gasping sobs. Where was that strength of character now? I could not stop the tears that threatened to dehydrate me, and my mouth was bitter with salt.

Sir Hugh reacted reflexively to my request for leave, which I made to him in the change-room after surgery (he was a gentle and loving man).

He said, "Of course you must go; we will manage."

This was 1979, the year leading up to the Moscow Olympics. Ironically, the United States led a boycott of the games over Russia's involvement in Afghanistan, and the British, who would have never learned of Sherlock Holmes if Dr Watson (alias Sir Arthur Conan Doyle) had not been a recuperating traumatised army doctor back from Afghanistan, supported the boycott. Consequently, Aeroflot was almost giving away tickets to Moscow. The Soviet Union was busy educating African students, as were the United States and Western Europe, and combined, they were making Africa the chequerboard of capitalism and communism. Flights from Moscow to Africa were also cheap. Michele, bless her, organised a return flight for me at about a fifth of the price of British Airways.

Whatever you do, said my friends and family, don't fly Aeroflot, but I arrived from Russia with love in time for the funeral.

Stan was buried in Langata cemetery, opposite Nairobi National Game Park, close to the animals. We planted a thorn tree on his grave. In his prime, he had been six feet tall and about a hundred kilos. As they lowered the coffin, it was so light that it swayed in the wind; the rollers stuck, and it needed a push to send it down. He ended the era of the great white hunters. It was all so still.

After that, I never wanted to visit Kenya again, and yet so much of me was still there. It is said that home is not where you were born, but where you go to die. I am not so sure of where I want to die, and when I drive past fields and forests in other lands, I still look for the animals: I realise that there is something missing inside me, as well.

The flight over had been pleasant and the plane new and sound. Although the seats were comfortable, they were practical rather than attractive. We landed in what I presumed to be Moscow; I had never seen so much snow and ice. Because of the weather, we didn't land at Moscow's main airport; it was a military facility, I suspected, from the appearance of officials and the number of soldiers on guard. The buildings were low and appeared prefabricated. The officials wore fur hats and spoke little or no English. There was something wrong with the screening machine, and I had to go through it many times and was searched repeatedly until they were embarrassed and resorted to declaring nasty things about the security machine (at that moment, I wished I could speak Russian). Screening for weapons had started because of the growing global trend for hijacking, especially after the Entebbe and Ethiopian hijackings.

The trip back was completely different. The rear half of the plane was screened off and loaded with something in Egypt that we were not allowed to see. We were kept on the plane with orders to keep the window shutters down. So of course, we imagined various conspiracy theories. I was seated amongst a band of Brits who were members of a variety show that had played the nightclub in Nairobi's New Stanley Hotel. An American girl whose husband was with the Peace Corps joined us with her child. She needed help carrying huge bundles of hand luggage, and the Brits gallantly obliged.

It was an American, Henry Morton Stanley, who found the missionary David Livingston on the shores of Lake Tanganyika. Stanley confirmed the ancient Greek legend of the existence of the Mountains of the Moon (and also inspired the naming of my father). He worked as a journalist and was funded by the *New York Herald*, but Americans were relatively uncommon in British African colonies, other than as tourists and missionaries (or God-botherers, as Stan called them). Henry Stanley was born and raised in an orphanage in Wales and was nationalised later as an American, taking on his adopted father's name and country. He always had a passion for Africa and travel, and was one of East Africa's most prominent explorers, ironically benefiting his country of birth more than the one that gave him a life.

President John Kennedy's Peace Corps introduced many young educated Americans to the treasures of Africa. This girl was loaded to the gunnels with hand luggage because of the weight restriction for baggage, and she became part of our little group because we all took a piece of her hand luggage while she carried the child. The vodka flowed on the way back to London, and the troubadours put on a superb performance, entertaining everybody on the plane; even the Russian crew joined in. We were given Misha dolls intended for the Olympics and other goodies to distribute amongst our families and friends, as they had a surplus of Olympic souvenirs owing to the boycott.

Moscow Airport was the real thing on the way back, with bright lights, duty-free shops, and everything that was new and working. How silly of me, influenced by Cold War stories and movie images that had coerced me into preconceptions, to have thought the airport on the flight over had been Moscow (the explanations had been lost in translation). I vowed that I would go back someday and see Russia properly. The plane landed smoothly in London, and the winter cold restored sobriety and reality.

Life became bleak at St Thomas; the train journey into Waterloo Station in lamplight was followed by a short cold walk to the hospital through a tunnel under the road leading up to Westminster Bridge. I often thought of my uncle Peter, whom I had met only once when travelling through Uganda; I had visited him at the Kilembe copper mines at the foot of the Mountains of the Moon, as the Ruwenzori Mountains were called by Herodotus, the ancient Greek historian who spoke of a snow-covered mountain range in Africa. Family legend has it that Uncle Peter disappeared one day (that part is true) and fled to Britain, where he became a London wino tramp (that part may not be true). I studied the faces of the tramps sheltering from the cold in the tunnel and half-expected to see him.

I had never experienced a European winter and anticipated clean white snow with pyramid-shaped fir trees standing next to little red-roofed, gaily decorated houses with lighted lamps inside and red-breasted robins outside, sitting on snowmen surrounded by dancing children. Well, it was dark and grey with windblown papers in railway tracks and station corners. The horse chestnut trees were bare and witch-like, and there were no birds. The children were inside creating havoc with unspent energy, and the walls were damp. The winter seemed endless.

To make matters worse, the workload in the hospital was heavy, and I precipitated two serious surgical complications that wore constantly on my mind and made it hard to steel myself to go to work and face these problems. As a surgeon, I had to fight to separate these problems from the daily work that required concentration. However taxing, I could not afford to allow them to distract me from the other work. The danger in surgery is that an ongoing distraction will lead to more problems with other patients. To explain my despair and sense of guilt and inadequacy, I will describe the cases.

One night, an elderly woman in her seventies who had schizophrenia was admitted very ill, with abdominal pain. A diagnosis of a perforated duodenal ulcer was made from X-rays, which showed free air in the belly with large pockets of air under the diaphragm. This sign could only mean a perforated bowel. The alternatives were to let nature take its course, after alleviating her pain and making her comfortable, or operate and try and save her life. It was a dilemma that family members usually resolved when given the alternatives. She had not spoken for years and had no family; my experience was youthful, without a fully developed sixth sense, and an air of "Your call, Doctor" prevailed amongst the hospital staff. Who was I to judge her life? I took what I thought was the right way and operated for the problem, not the person. The operation for a perforated duodenal ulcer is usually quick and straightforward, involving plugging the hole with omentum (fatty tissue inside the peritoneal cavity), a good washout of debris, and closure of the wound.

She must have perforated her ulcer days before and suffered in silence until her extreme sickness was obvious. The gut was rotten, the hole enormous, and the tissues so affected by infection, digestive juices, and time that no stitch would hold. I plugged the hole in the gut of the duodenum with all the tissue that could be found and drained the wound. No stiches held. Not for the plug, nor for the wound, and this poor silent woman lay in bed with a hole in her abdomen that would not heal. Eventually, support was withdrawn, and she passed away. It took several days. I was probably the only one who remembered her.

I've always found death after surgery quite difficult to bear and struggle to be fatalistic about it. A second woman was dying in the ward after surgery for cancer of the pancreas. Her demise was due to surgical failure of one of the multiple joins of her pieces of gut and ducts from the liver and the pancreas. This operation is like taking the hub out of a wagon wheel and then joining the freed spokes together. Leaking digestive juices mixed with bile were digesting her insides, and there was nothing more we could do.

Modern medicine increasingly gains in the ability to prolong life but it sometimes prolongs suffering. I continually suffered along with each failure or shortcoming in surgery and worried on how it could have been managed better. It's made me wary of advocating treatments known to be associated with potential complications. It's never helped for colleagues to reassure me that all was done that could be done and that it had to be done. It didn't help that it was inevitable. It didn't help that it was not my fault; I always felt it was.

The sins of commission are worse than the sins of omission, and yet, for the sake of the rewards of life, limb, and gratitude, it's sometimes necessary to make a commitment. To know when to and when not to is called clinical judgement. It takes time, and it's the man who never worked who never made a mistake.

If we sacked every surgeon who made a mistake, we would have none left. To reduce the number of surgical errors caused by mistakes of clinical judgement, modern medical wisdom says that decisions should be evidence-based. Problems occur when there is no evidence or when what is available is not relevant.

An example of this lack of evidence was related to me by a colleague who established protocols for managing lethal illnesses, where sometimes the treatment was worse than the disease. He achieved great things and became world-famous in the field of stroke prevention and determining when surgery could help. The dictum followed was that if a treatment is intended, then show the evidence that the benefits outweigh the risks: a noble sentiment. Then it became very personal for him. A routine chest X-ray revealed that his aorta was expanding into an aneurysm that could burst or stretch the valve in the heart, in which case his heart would fail.

His surgeon advised replacing it because it would continue to expand, with anticipated fatal consequences, if left alone. That it needed to be replaced at some time was self-evident. That's like saying one does not need statistical evidence to say you are better off with a parachute if you jump out of a plane. The question was when to operate, and the analogy is when to pull the rip cord. Too soon, and the balance of problems from the surgery outweigh the risks posed by the expanding aorta. Too late, and it's too late. There was no evidence to guide him or the surgeon, only intuition and surgical judgement; he had to rely on trust. Evidence is accumulating in modern medicine, but the values are sometimes unknown, and a multiplicity of parameters makes factoring in all the variables impossible. Sometimes, the numbers are too small to have any evidence beyond the anecdote. He resorted to intuition and anecdote, where experience was the X factor. This was the era of the X factors. There will always be an element of trust. He is alive and well as I write, so many years later.

The lead-up to Christmas should be a happy time, but I was miserable. Sir Hugh sensed it and invited me to accompany him to a special memorial lecture. It was a social event in the College of Surgeons on wound closure, but that's all I recall because I fell asleep and woke intermittently, feeling silly with my head lolling from side to side or resting on his shoulder. I felt I disgraced him, but he said nothing and invited Michele and me to dinner, which was very pleasant.

The ward started to run smoothly again; it was festooned with colour and punctuated by chocolates and gifts from patients to staff. There was a bar in the hospital, and the atmosphere did brighten up as parties started and mulled wine dulled all that was negative.

Sir Hugh gave me a bottle of VSOP Champagne brandy for Christmas, and I took it home to share with Michele and a taste for the boys for Christmas dinner. I only registered the word Champagne, VSOP meant nothing to me, and the word *brandy* was in small print, which I missed. Don't try drinking neat Champagne brandy like it's wine. It put the boys off alcohol for some time, and Michele was very disappointed until she started laughing. We should not have thought of encouraging the boys to drink alcohol; serves us right. We toasted with apple juice because it looked like wine.

When spring emerged, then so did we. We caught up with old friends and the odd relative. We visited Roger and met his wife, Zillah, and his two boys. We talked about how the Royal Air Force had changed him and studying medicine had changed me. At the same age as me, he was confident, self-assured, seemingly in charge of his life and family, and a reasonably well-off officer in the RAF. Where he had gone forwards, I felt I had reversed.

I also met with Derek, my cousin from Kilimanjaro, who had been to Sandhurst and was a major in the King's Own Regiment; he had served in Ireland and commanded his own regiment. We had dinner with Lynn, who had led the way for

Derek at Sandhurst and had been in the Tank Corps. Lynn had changed his name to Tim and had a job in the Middle East, training troops in Dubai for the sultan. Uncle John came, and we remembered Uncle Max and received sympathy for Stan. They all fitted easily together in the family history of soldiers and adventurers. They were not sure why I was doing medicine and thought a doctor should be better off financially. I told them it took longer than planned.

I had caught up with my family, and then a really big moment came for Michele. She had been in touch by letters with her father, David Howard, and arranged to meet him. To her, he was a stranger, as she had been eighteen months old when taken away from him. All her notions were derived from descriptions (mainly adverse) from Enid, but Michele's sister Lenore remembered him from before she was stolen away and tracked him down after she got married in England. Lenore reassured Michele that he was a nice person, although a little eccentric. He had been jailed during the war for being a pacifist. Michele had mixed emotions and was churning like an urn, but it was a wonderful experience for her.

David was gentle and wiry with a tweed sports coat, long white hair to his shoulders, and a curved pipe in his hand. He looked like a cross between Doctor Who and an English country gentleman. He lived with his second wife, Eileen, who looked like a gypsy, in a sixteenth-century Elizabethan house in Norfolk. They lived surrounded by artwork and antiques; he made his living as an art dealer. The majestic Tudor-heritage house was flanked on one side by spring flowers tended by Eileen and growing vegetables and fruit trees on the other, tilled by David.

The boys and I sensed that this was not our moment. They watched, wide-eyed, as their mother met her father in quivers of anticipation and outpouring of thirty years in waiting. We stood back, quietly hushed by the moment. The weekend was theirs, and they clearly savoured the time to catch up on lost years. Michele was never mechanically minded. I realised that even if she had had the opportunity to grow up with her father as a role model, she would have been no more mechanically minded.

Many of David's views were similar to Enid's; the arts, literature, and politics were to the fore. Their commitment to social justice and the ideology of communism were what had forged their relationship. It was their levels of action that separated them. Enid was an activist, and David was passive. It explained why Enid took off around the world, joining the multiracial club in South Africa, defying the apartheid doctrine, and David stayed at home, conscientiously objecting to war and accepting the humiliation of prison. He had not fought legal battles to have his daughter returned to Britain. Even Enid's brother was on David's side and professed he would give evidence to bring the children back to the UK, but David would not pursue legal action. Both were defiantly brave in their own way, and their moral, stubborn strengths mixed and lived on in Michele, with more balance and astute awareness of weaknesses. I wondered if her natural recoil from acrimony was genetic from David or a phenotypic reaction to Enid.

It wasn't long before David wanted to know about Enid. "And how is the Welsh dragon?" he asked. "Ooooowha, she could be angry."

He recounted the story of when Enid and he had arranged to visit Russia in the 1930s. They crossed the channel, and on landing in Calais, David was immediately detained because his passport was out of date. Enid railed against the world as the days of her holidays slipped away. Her Russia and Utopia would have to wait for another day. She made the necessary arrangements for David to get a passport; it took some days, during which David had to wait in detention. The day arrived when David was released, and the French police, in a way only the French can do, informed him that Enid had arrived to pick him up and enquired as to whether he really wanted to go home, extending an invitation for him to stay if he wished. At least Enid's dreams of Utopia were intact as they sailed back to Britain.

He was strangely without vehemence, and the old house, full of antiques, imparted a rich sense of peace. David's trade had been of a printer and typesetter in the old method of printing, with a piece for each letter. That particular trade required attention to detail and patience approaching perfection. It served him well as an antique collector and dealer. Where the hobby ended and the business started was blurred into a wide line. His special interest, again in tune with his trade, was fine old prints and postcards. They adorned the walls and peered out of ancient oak cabinets. David quietly made a good living from his antiques and was very knowledgeable but did not wear this on his sleeve. He treasured his garden and balanced the things of the dead with the fruits of the living. He had little time for flowers, which puzzled me, as he had an eye for beauty and was dedicated to vegetables and fruit trees. Maybe it was his way of giving Eileen her own domain, or maybe because he grew up on a fruit farm. He was in earnest competition for the ripe strawberries with the creatures of his garden, and the contest was conducted with the intensity of a cricket test match between England and Australia. He objected to war, and especially chemical warfare, so he plucked the creatures from the leaves and rushed them to the rubbish bin. He never merely walked; he would flash past the window with white hair streaming out behind him and bug-laden hands stretched out in front of him as he ran.

David had a daughter with Eileen; Michele's half-sister was called Amanda. Slim, red-haired, and adorned with large earrings and heavy necklaces, she lived in Brixton in London and danced the calypso with the West Indians. She was everything a carefree girl could be and a child of the next generation after me. Britain was no longer a colonial power, and she did not have to travel to the colonies; they were coming back to her. She wasn't there that weekend; we met her later in London.

I had the feeling that Michele wished I was black. I was white and boring and from Africa. Amanda's partner was black and exciting and from England. We were the sons of slaves, soldiers, sailors, and slave-masters. We did not meet as strangers but more like cousins, knowing the dark and lighter sides of families on both sides. I felt an understanding between us.

Some years later, after Amanda had children (who were Afro-Brits or Euro-Africans, depending on the classification and degree of American influence and implied racial distinctions), they all came to live with David and Eileen. The children were beautiful, with hybrid vigour, and Eileen serene as a grandmother, but David was showing uncharacteristic signs of resentment and clearly wished for a better lot for his daughter and grandchildren. His peace was shattered by the noise that only children can make; it was not his nature to gambol with balls and toys and goalposts in fields. He seemed unable to discern their games from their squabbles and complained that the children were undisciplined, the partner unhelpful, and Amanda trapped in disarray. Amanda's mix of zest for life and passive acceptance of her lot prevailed in the old house, amongst the treasured antiques.

Yet, the vein of living is irrepressible in West Indians, and Amanda's partner was great fun to be with. It was never boring in his company. His trade was French polishing and furniture. His job range was wide and varied and held interest for me. One job was beating new pine furniture with chains and then French polishing them so that they looked like oak antiques; you can imagine what that did for David's purist sensitivities. He also worked as a model, with his beautiful body. The modelling was a little different from modelling clothes, because there weren't any, and the photographer strived to be artistic and creative. He put an ice pack on the gluteal region until it developed goose-bumps and then took a close-up pictures in black and white. The result was a smooth, round, black hillock on a pale grey background, with a perfect symmetrical pattern of raised bumps and the odd glistening drop of water. It took quite some time to realise what it was.

We didn't divulge to David what is was and enjoyed the joke when we asked his professional opinion of its beauty. David seriously considered the print for some time until he worked it out from the rise and curve of the natal cleft. Pent-up laughter was released in a West Indian peal, and David's expression was unique. He retired to a little glass alcove that he called his conservatorium and in which he could enjoy the sun and watch over his garden. In effect, he sulked and fumed and was heard muttering.

To make it up to David and do something nice for him, Amanda arranged to have the little garden shed outside the conservatorium painted, knowing that would please David very much (it was dilapidated and spoiled the garden's neat appearance). By lunchtime the next day, the painting was halfway around. David literally beamed out over his lunch and garden and waited with anticipation for it to be completed. If he were alive now, he would still be waiting. The unfinished garden shed served as a constant reminder and irritated him beyond words. I wondered why he never finished it himself; maybe he derived some perverse pleasure in witnessing the veracity of his character judgement. Anyway, it stayed half-painted.

CHAPTER 18

St Helier Hospital and the Lure of Vascular Surgery

St Thomas Hospital was the mothership for a number of regional hospitals around London. It provided an academic contact and supply of well-regarded registrars and senior registrars. In return, St Thomas acquired training centres and a larger pool of trainees. As I was taking Kevin's job, I also took his rotation at St Helier Hospital in Sutton, south London. Sutton was near Cheam, and I knew that name well. In the headphones of the crystal set after lights-out at school in Nairobi, I had listened to *Hancock's Half-Hour*, which was set in East Cheam. There was no recognised East to Cheam, but there was a Cheam, and it was a nice surprise for me to see the imagined materialise. St Helier Hospital was also closer to Kevin's house at Worcester Park. My mentor, Brian Vivian, who had pulled me from the wastebasket for surgical aspirants and done so much for my ambitions, had trained at St Helier and married one of the operating theatre nurses. I had a good feeling about going to work in St Helier.

There were a number of subsidiary hospitals that were similarly attached to St Helier's, and so the patient drainage and training exposure of St Thomas was a vast network. St Helier was named after a Belgian monk who had healing powers; he was adopted by England because he is said to have brought Christianity and healing to the island of Jersey. Some believed he did it with miracles and made him a saint; others believed it was magic, and some believed he was mad. He is said to have literally lost his head.

The hospital was large and busy, and had a history of employing Australians and New Zealanders who were seeking further training in surgery in the UK as a matter of course, so much so that ANZ surgeons before 1973 invariably had both an ANZ and a British degree in surgery and could legitimately claim the right to be one of Henry VIII's "Misters."

I followed in a long line of Antipodeans who worked as surgical aspirants in St Helier Hospital. Aubrey York-Mason (a surgeon who became known for an anorectal operation that bears his name) was said to have had only Australian and New Zealand registrars work for him. As York-Mason's reputation for favouring Antipodeans grapevined across the Indian Ocean, my compatriots competed ardently to work at St Helier during his time. York-Mason fostered this competition and provided the attention and training they sought; he was rewarded by a loyal, reliable, hard-working cohort that discounted money for experience and left without demand for debt or favour.

He had retired by the time I worked there, and St Thomas had enfolded St Helier to herself. It was mere coincidence that I worked there as a senior registrar and that one of the registrars in the contingent of two senior registrars and two registrars was Digby, another Australian, and the other a New Zealander. Digby did justice to Barry Mackenzie and did his best to sustain the ANZ image of a larrikin, hard-working, and hard-playing son of the sun. Digby left for home via a stint as the ship's doctor on the *Queen Elizabeth* passenger liner; he started home via the United States in grand style.

Digby was symbolic of the young of Australia (and her little sister, New Zealand) who were unknowingly caught in eddies of the wind of change. Subtle, inevitable changes were occurring, like the separation of mother and child. With gentle but definite resolve, Britain was pushing her children out and trying to shut the doors behind them. The Australian people could not recognise, let alone accept, the reality of forces way beyond Australian and New Zealand shores that were changing the mother country. To be fair, why should they? How could they see these changes coming from their side when the upbringing had rendered them amblyopic? It was almost as if Africa between South Africa and Egypt did not exist for Australians, and the Indian Ocean connected Australia to the UK. The UK was divorcing its colonies and remarrying a European Union bride. Its children from the first marriage were in denial and, like youngsters on the threshold of independence, kept returning home to live.

Australia is an urbanised population based in cities and towns transposed on blueprints from England. Nowhere on earth was there a population and culture so insularly British and so vociferous in wanting to be loved by its parent than Australia. The names of the cities, towns, streets, and people roll-called the culture, and the English language pushed all else from the nest, like Jenner's description of the cuckoo bird. It was entirely natural that her people fought the British wars; upheld the traditions and monoculture of beer, pies, sports, and education; and at least one road, street, lane, park, or building in every suburb was called Victoria. They still stood for the national anthem of "God Save the Queen" at the beginning of each picture show, long after those in Britain had ceased to do so.

Britain, in siring Australia, had coddled and disciplined her child and suppressed all that threatened. She had succeeded to Europeanise the land with feral animals, plants, architecture, infrastructure, and rolling fields of wheat and sheep. The suntan, accents, and bastardisation of soccer and rugby with Irish football served only to provide a veil. No wonder the Brits

sought to conscript the anglophiles. This verse from *Australia,*
a poem by A D Hope, says it all:

> And her five cities, like five teeming sores
> Each drains her: a vast robber state
> Where second hand Europeans pullulate
> Timidly on the edge of alien shores.

The changing surgical training in Australia was a symptom
of the severing of the umbilical cord and rejection, however
gentle, by the mother. After 1973, it was no longer automatic
that the ANZ surgical examinations were reciprocal with those
of the UK. I was in the initial group to sit the new age ANZ
surgical primary, and my full surgical training was Australian.
This change was not in isolation. It was part of the trend with
the young turning away from Europe and more to South East
Asia; this was evident in their travels, just like the trail we had
followed through Indonesia, Singapore, Malaysia, Thailand,
Nepal, and India.

It was by good fortune that I was in the UK to gather
experience and not to gain a British degree. The Australian and
New Zealand College of Surgeons degree sufficed. In fact, I had
every incentive not to sit any UK surgical exams. I could work
with the ANZ fellowship degree and risked loss of face (and
valuable family time) by sitting an examination I might fail.
Also, the thought of another exam-driven study was absolutely
abhorrent to me.

I did enjoy St Helier's and met another mentor: Tony
Chilvers, a technically proficient surgeon with a mind like a
scalpel. He was different, which is probably why I liked him.
He was artistic, musical, had made films, was part of a radio
program, and lived and loved life to the full. I learnt a lot of
surgery from him; his special interest was vascular surgery. He
opened my eyes to Surgical Camelot and the Knights of the
Operating Table, where the Sir Galahads of Surgery strode into

crises to save life from ruptured aortas and spare limbs from death by torture. He guided me through the fields of blood and sweat, of rewards and death, of fine margins for error and no forgiveness for mistakes.

When I started with Tony, my knowledge of vascular surgery was minimal and theoretical, at best. Of all the surgical disciplines born of general surgery, I had the least knowledge in this one. All of the vascular surgery units around the world were part of general surgery units except at Royal Perth. Vascular surgery in Royal Perth Hospital had separated from general surgery acrimoniously in the late sixties because the founder of the vascular unit, Bob Paton, strongly believed that standards improved in dedicated units. When he rejected general surgeons, they rejected him. Consequently, as a general surgery trainee without a special interest in vascular surgery, I had a paucity of knowledge in the area. I knew only the minimum required to get my fellowship with a little luck and had relied on my depth of knowledge in colorectal work.

In fact, I had effectively swapped a vascular year at Royal Perth for a colorectal year at St Thomas. The exchange was primarily because of Kevin's desire to work in Perth with Tony House in the vascular and transplant surgery unit, but it suited my special interest, which was colorectal work and the use of the new technology of stapled joins in the bowel instead of hand-sewn sutured anastomoses. The opportunity for me to work for Sir Hugh was irresistible and most valuable. Now at St Helier's, I was introduced to vascular work in earnest by Tony Chilvers, and a serious challenge was posed to my hitherto special interest of colorectal work.

It is possible that my fascination with the workings of the anus was waning, or maybe a change is a good as a rest. Either way, the vascular surgery appealed to me. Certainly, the rectal clinic at St Thomas had nearly wrecked a special interest in the rectum. The rectal clinic was the most important and busy clinic for the senior registrar. It was the bread and butter of the colorectal unit and investigated any hint of rectal and anal bleeding. It was a blend of piles, fissures, fistulas, abscesses, cancers, and many rarer diseases of inflammation such as Crohn's disease and ulcerative colitis, infection, and infestation. The setup of the St Thomas rectal clinic was a room with three doors and two alcoves. The middle door was for entry into the main consulting room and the other two from the alcoves were for exit. The patients danced through like a Scottish reel. For new patients, it was into the middle and out through the side after a do-si-do. For routine check-ups of the anorectal condition and post-operative care, the nurses dispensed with the middle and set the patient up in the alcove via the exit doors. From their point of view, it got through the work in some semblance of allotted time. I learned that a *lot* is short for allotted. By the end of the morning clinic, I moved robotically from one alcove to the other to be greeted by a loose sheet-veiled anus and an upside-down face peering at me expectantly, as I approached with examining instruments in hand.

Mumbled greetings and answers were exchanged between puffs of wind in by me to expand the lumen and puffs of wind out for relief of bloat. There was no sense of smell. The nurses used some sort of spray that affected the nerves and fogged the atmosphere and numbed the senses and the mind. There was never time for lunch, not that it would have appealed anyway, if there had been time. Following the clinic, there was an operating session in the afternoon for minor anal and rectal conditions. The endless array of ani continued into the afternoon. The winking brown eyes spared the mind of strenuous thought and the body of hunger and bore witness to feats of stamina. It was a full, brutal, and shitty day, and it was every Monday. Mondayitis took on meaning.

The advent of acquired immune deficiency syndrome (AIDS), the legal and social controversies surrounding it, and the focus on the rectum affected my interest and took the path away from the technical and towards the abstract. Vascular surgery was different. It was defined and clean. It was technical and unhurried. It was red and white and shades of pink. The rewards and punishments were usually instant, and the shows were complete stories in one episode rather than serials. The number of conditions and their treatment options were defined more by physics than moral, social, and legal argument.

Vascular surgery was changing from seek-and-remove to see-and-repair. The new era of contrast X-rays and intra-arterial injections made angiograms possible, computed tomography (CT) scans revealed the aorta in all its layers, and ultrasound technology echoed from the walls of the vessels and listened to the rhythms of blood flow in harmony (or the roar of turbulence when the flow was disturbed). It was the new age of repair and prostheses. It was born of the war in Korea, where surgeons started to replace traumatised arteries in order to save limbs. It was swaddled in synthetic textiles, originally produced for shirts, especially Dacron, from which the first aortic and limb artery prosthetic grafts were handcrafted by surgeons and their wives, who turned sheets of Dacron into tubes. Arterial vascular surgery was the surgical child of the latter half of the twentieth century.

In 1518, Machiavelli wrote in *The Prince*, "There is nothing more difficult to plan, more doubtful of success, nor more dangerous to manage, than the creation of a new system. For, the initiator has the enmity of all who would profit by preservation of the old institutions and merely lukewarm defenders in those who would gain by the new ones."

The new technology emerging in vascular surgery threatened administrators with cost blow-outs and traditional general surgeons with redundancy. I joined the ranks of the lukewarm but knew, even then, that this was to be my real story. This would be the field of challenge.

I met the challenge of the ruptured aorta head-on. The aorta is the arterial pipe that carries the blood from the heart to the pelvis, passing down through the chest and belly. Its branches irrigate every nook and cranny of the garden that is your body. In an adult chest, it's a pipe about twenty-five millimetres in diameter and narrows to an average of twenty millimetres at the level of the umbilicus, where it divides into the iliac arteries that lead to the lower limbs. It is an irrigation pipe that is big enough to irrigate a large suburban garden. At idle speed, when you are resting or sedentary, the heart puts out about four or five litres of blood a minute. An athlete in a sprint has a heart pumping about thirty litres a minute. Next time you or someone fills the car with fuel, look to see how fast your fuel bowser is pumping; it's about thirty litres a minute. The aorta is built to last seventy years, and some last over one hundred. The physics of this pipe is as alive as the living it provides; when torn, it can empty your body of blood in seconds. If you are adult, you only have about five litres of blood. It does not take long to empty your life blood through an inch pipe. A leaking aorta is an urgent surgical challenge of the greatest magnitude.

The constant throbbing of the heart and the surges of blood during stress or activity puts great strain on the aorta. Imagine the garden hose on a hot day at 37 degrees Celsius (that's the normal body temperature); in Fahrenheit, it's 98 degrees. On a hot day, the garden hose can weaken and bulge; like a balloon, as it weakens further, it expands and then finally leaks or bursts. When this happens, most people, at least 80 percent, die suddenly, but for some, the leak is minor or temporarily self-sealing, with nature's anti-bleeding mechanisms. This is the window of opportunity that allows a few people to get to the surgeon, and about 50 percent who do will survive; that is less than 10 percent of all those who burst their mains. The part most likely to burst is at the end of the aorta, which is about the level of the navel. Like dancing, the steps of the operation are defined but the end uncertain, and for the surgeon, this becomes a navel encounter of a different kind, although the battle is likely to be equally bloody. Because of my colorectal background and the quarantining of vascular surgery in my alma mater, I knew the steps but not the dance.

In preparing to operate for a ruptured aorta, resuscitation and anaesthetics served to further strain the aorta and the failing heart, often delivering the coup de grâce. So preparation for operation was often done while the patient was awake. The operation was like handling a broken egg. Gentleness and judicious moves prepared the fading life vessel for the start of the operation that was a rapid anaesthetic, with most people losing consciousness as a slash with the scalpel from breastbone to genitals exposed the paling flesh. The bowel was pulled out of the belly and the aorta grabbed under the end of the breastbone, just where the arteries to the kidneys take root. The site of rupture with the leak from the aorta is usually below that level, but not necessarily so, and in the days before scans, it was a chance taken blindly. Thereafter, the operation could be straightforward if all was controlled, or it could be a bloodbath with litres of blood being poured in at one end by the anaesthetist and leaking out below. A stage was reached when everyone knew the cause was lost, but the battle went on until the end.

There were many ruptured aortas at St Helier's. When the call came, and I was home or sightseeing with the children at weekends, all family life stopped in an instant. If the pager went off, like Superman, Dad appeared out of the telephone booth and flew away. But unlike Superman, Dad more often than not returned, dispirited and weakened with "Sceptonite." My children grew up expecting me to leave before the evening meal was over and never expected me to fulfil my promises to take them out or be somewhere.

One day, when another eagerly anticipated outing had been spoiled for her and the kids, only to have me return tired and dispirited, Michele said in exasperation, "There has to be a better way."

I tried but did not save many lives operating on ruptured aneurysms at St Helier's. I was not as good at the surgery as I became a few years later. Most of the patients had been transferred from smaller feeding hospitals and were too far gone when they arrived, and there was a general lack of conviction in the hospital that it was really worth the effort to keep trying in the face of poor outcomes. People who survived the insult and surgical assault had a fifty-fifty chance. If they survived the operation, then they only had a fifty-fifty chance of getting out of the intensive care ward. They were not really welcome in the ICU because they were elderly, too old to be useful in society, too sick, and rarely rewarding if they required any prolonged treatment. In short, it was dispiriting to treat the ruptured aorta. So why did we all persist and not just accept an inevitable death and make it as kind and comfortable as possible? Well, this option was invariably offered and usually declined by the desperate individuals and their loved ones. There is no doubt that the odd win was uplifting, and like one yes being worth a thousand no, one life was worth a thousand deaths.

A steady march against abdominal aortic aneurysms received a triple A rating; AAA means only one thing in surgery. Progress was made and pathways emerged from the debris of ideas and failed attempts. Tony Chilvers's idea was to clip the aorta just below the arteries to the kidneys with the clips used to close the umbilical cord of newborn babies, put the same clips on the arteries that went to the legs at the end of the aorta (the common iliac arteries), and thereby isolate the tear, then make a bypass to the legs from the arteries to the arms (axillary arteries). It might have worked for Tony, but not for the rest of us, and the idea joined the Library for Lost Ideas.

Albert Einstein died of a ruptured aortic aneurysm. His aneurysm started leaking on April 17, 1955. He had been treated with a protective operation in 1948, when the aneurysm was wrapped with a material to prevent its further expansion, and that worked for a while, but it was an operation that also did not last and another idea that went to the library. He was offered the new operation of aortic replacement with a Dacron graft but politely declined and retired to his hospital bed with the words "I prefer to die elegantly."

It is said that Einstein was not only clever but also wise. In that story are three important messages. It is worth taking protective measures against rupture for an AAA, be wary of new operations, and choose, when you have a choice, to take an elegant pathway.

The first of these messages was heeded with the aid of imaging technology and the advent of ultrasound and CT X-ray scans. The scans were able to clearly show the existence and extent of aortic aneurysms. Most importantly, the scans could measure the size of the AAA; doctors learned to tell when it had reached a size that heralded rupture. Preventative operations to repair the aorta in the cold light of day could be planned when the aneurysm was large, and the aneurysm could be monitored for growth while smaller. The results of planned elective surgery were rewarding, with fewer deaths from the once-feared operation. The durable prosthetic textile grafts and nylon sutures instead of silk, greatly improved surgical techniques, and structured teaching of new surgeons combined to lift the expectations. The techniques that were developed and the experience gained operating electively to prevent rupture gradually transferred to better results for ruptured aortas, even at two o'clock in the morning. Although the operation was effective, it was not elegant.

Some years after returning to Western Australia, I was called upon to operate on my next-door neighbour. I was working for the university in the Veteran's Hospital at the time; our home was in the area where homes had been built after the war for returned servicemen. My neighbour, who had been in the navy, was a large man with slim legs and arms and a rotund belly (what the surfing fraternity call a fat skinny-bastard). It signifies a once-fit man who has ceased to exercise in the surf but continued to eat and drink like a young man. On warm summer days, he would proudly parade up the street with a long livid scar vertically displayed on the convex parchment of his belly, announcing that this is what Michael had done to him.

Michele's comment was that "there has to be a better way."

Some of the experiences with the aorta were truly horrific, and some were simply awful. The Americans have a way of countering British understatement with explicit statement, and the aorta provides a fertile ground for both. Sometimes, the aorta is filled with old clot and cholesterol plaques that hang from the walls like water plants in a stream. The Americans descriptively call this a shaggy aorta, and if the wall-hangings break off, the British call it multiple emboli (Americans just call it trash). It is a most-feared event, and when it occurs, it's usually human-caused. If it happens, and thankfully it is rare, it can happen when the aorta is manipulated or squeezed during surgery. When it happens, the arteries beyond are filled with debris, and the flesh, deprived of blood, dies. To see a person dying with buttocks that are already dead and have no remedy is horrific. To operate on an aorta that tears beyond reach or disintegrates to touch while pouring blood is awful. To see people suffer and then die after being dragged through an operation of such magnitude with desperate measures blurs the purposes of saving patients with saving the surgeon from his critics and himself for his failures. It calls for some inner strength from the surgeon to try again and fight the doubts. Persistence is a good quality in a surgeon, but where does persistence end and the cross over to blindness to exacerbation begin? The failures and sufferings fuelled the cry for a better way.

The experiences of my time in England stay in my mind like a picture through a telescopic lens, with the periphery blurred and only one or two objects in focus. The aorta was at the focal point. The visits to museums, palaces, towers, castles, and dungeons spawned imaginings of horrendous tortures in medieval times, decorating the periphery. St Thomas Hospital's history was steeped in surgery without anaesthetics, in dungeon-like operating theatres. The imagery fused with reality one day, when Michele lost Trevor for about twenty minutes in the Hall of Horrors in Madame Tussaud's Waxworks. The relief of finding him was like waking from a bad dream to realise it wasn't true. I wished the challenges of the aorta and the emotions evoked were all a bad dream, and I could wake to find there was a better way. The experiences with the aorta stayed in focus in my memory and overwhelmed the larger volume of general surgery that formed the surrounding blur.

At the end of my time in the UK, we acquired a small Fiat Amigo campervan and sardined it on a tour of Western Europe, but that joins the blur of memories. I returned to Western Australia wiser and poorer, but much richer with my BTE and qualification to join the ranks of the general surgeons, with a special interest in vascular surgery.

CHAPTER 19

Back to Australia and Metamorphosis to a Vascular Surgeon

The journey back to Australia could be dismissed as just another long jet flight with kids, and one need say no more, except for a few things that stick vividly. First, I still have no idea what happened to my degrees; they were lost in travel. I had to take them with me to prove to the UK that I was indeed qualified, and after that kerfuffle, they evaporated. I have a replacement, but it is smaller in size because it is only a certified duplicate. My stature as a surgeon was thereby symbolically reduced by my trip to England.

I comforted myself with the lesson that I learned as a taxi driver when I once complained to the radio controller that the fare did not show and what should I do about it.

"Just put it down to experience," he said, ever practical.

We broke the journey in Kuala Lumpur, as we were travelling best rates with Malaysian Airlines, to give the kids a rest, but that's a misnomer. It was less than ten years since we visited there on our hippy travels, and KL had become a beacon of Asian development. The hotel was huge and utopian. The kids discovered a device that with the press of a button projected out to the centre of the toilet bowl and then squirted a jet of water at their bums to clean them, and their hysterics put an end to any rest period. The hotel bus driver was cross because we delayed departure from the hotel by a few minutes and was worried that four hours in the traffic in the early-morning was insufficient to make it to the airport in time. Indeed, the traffic was interminable, crawled with congestion, and was woven together by numerous scooters and threads of smoke.

It was good to be home, and we had a couple of days to get to know Kevin Burnand and his family before they left to return to the UK. The exchange had worked well, and we would be friends and colleagues for life (well, sort of pen pals, anyway). It was similar to that feeling you have for someone you had not met before but then share a particularly stressful or emotional event, like someone you don't know very well but with whom you climb to the top of a mountain. A bond is formed purely because of the shared experience.

Slotting back into Royal Perth as a senior registrar with a BTE was seamless, and I picked up working with my old mentor, Phil Goatcher. The difference was that I now had that little bit of mystique that a good storyteller has, like my cousin Howard, when the line between truth and hyperbole moves and shifts with the audience. However, there was no fooling Phil Goatcher. He knew that my double-barrel name and history of colonial military family in India betrayed bastardry in the family; he was versed in Shakespeare and wise. He had mentored me through my fellowship and was my finishing school to being a consultant. He knew my strengths and weaknesses.

I toyed with the idea of starting a practice of my own the following year but needed a public teaching hospital appointment. Such an appointment may not be necessary today, as I write, but then, before the emergence of the power of the private hospitals, it was essential if a surgeon was to practice to his limits. There were two factors that held me back and delayed my move to apply for a general surgery consultant post in a hospital. First, the move in Australia from a British type of socialised hospital health system to an American-type, private hospital system was nascent, and I wasn't sure whether to primarily pursue government public hospital practice as per the British system or concentrate on a private practice for the emerging American model. Second, vascular surgery was still officially a section of general surgery, and I was lured by vascular surgery. With a deficiency in that section, especially if it were to be my area of special interest, I needed further training.

I started covering vascular surgery in the hospital after hours and weekends to relieve the overworked incumbent vascular registrar to Marcel Goodman. Marcel became my mentor and lifelong colleague and friend. He offered me the opportunity to work the next year as the senior registrar to the vascular unit, and I was faced with a decision: Did I capitalise on my standing as a promising colorectal surgeon, with a reputation for being trained by Sir Hugh Lockhart-Mummery, or did I jump ship and join the vascular unit? If I jumped, would I be able to jump back again if I so wished in the future, or would the gap widen too much? I took the chance; for me, it was irresistible, and I signed up for another year as a noncommissioned surgical officer in Royal Perth Hospital and senior registrar to the vascular unit.

There are ambiguities that arise from the subjective meanings of words, and none more so than those words that label people. Varieties of people, religions, politics, nationalities, illnesses, and occupations are the seats of emotive subjective identification. Once somebody is labelled with an identity, they are stereotyped. It is like knowing how much money a person earns. Because money has a relative value, a judgement is instantly made, and the line of neutral thought is too sharp to sit on.

For example, if we think people are over-rewarded, it tempts us to envy; if too little, then it turns to pity. Since neither is a good or appreciated emotion, it is better not to know what your friends earn, and so it can be with labels that beg a judgement.

The label "vascular surgeon" was attractive and has been used to impart a degree of integrity in the theatre of the arts, as well as the operating theatre. Harrison Ford twice played a vascular surgeon, in *Frantic* and as Richard Kimble in the *The Fugitive*. The label invoked positive feelings. I liked that: an example of reaction to a favourable label. Conversely, in demarcation disputes, in any field of endeavour, a label can de-humanise and instantly engender strong negative emotions. Label someone a terrorist, and there is no room for any other human empathy. Why is that so? What does the term *vascular surgeon* mean to you? Does it mean anything at all? Maybe dropping the vascular component and just the label surgeon would make no difference, but I suspect the vascular is an intensifier because people are unclear as to what it really means. Is that mystique? Some automatically confuse vascular with cardiac and think it means a heart surgeon. Often, when the term *cardiovascular* is used, especially by health and finance departments, the vascular component is mentally blinded by the cardiac, and the funding flows to the cardiac, or heart of the matter, while the vascular component cries poor. This suggests judgements maybe driven more by emotion than reason, akin to the concept that perception can be more powerful than reality.

Cardiovascular disease for many simply means heart disease and the coronary arteries, and in a particular sense, that is absolutely correct. We refer to disease in the arteries to the kidneys as renovascular disease, and if in the arteries to the brain as cerebrovascular disease, and so it is for other parts and regions of the body. Yet each is a subset of the arterial tree. Arterial vascular disease can be regarded in a holistic way, with all the arteries possibly affected in the same way. Death from arterial disease anywhere is classified as cardiovascular disease, even if the heart and its arteries are healthy. No wonder there is confusion. For the vascular surgeon, if disease is seen in one artery, then it should be checked for it in all the body's arteries.

For many, *vascular surgeon* implies a restorer of beautiful legs and a remover of varicose veins. I was very clear what vascular meant to me; vascular carried the mystique of the highway through the body that is the aorta. The aorta is the river of life, and when it bleeds, it devastates, like a flood. I wanted to be an aortic surgeon.

The vascular unit at Royal Perth Hospital was an ideal training ground for the huge changes that loomed over the red horizon. From the start in the early 1970s, it was a pioneering and controversial unit. The founder was Bob Paton who, on returning from his further training in the UK, was appointed as a consultant general surgeon to Royal Perth and performed general and vascular surgery. He believed that vascular surgery would be better managed as a special unit, especially when dealing with the aorta. This was denied by RPH, and to do this, he left and set up a special vascular unit at the nearby Sir Charles Gairdner Hospital, which had been built originally as a chest hospital to deal with TB. With control of that disease, the hospital needed new direction, welcomed Bob Paton, and invited him to set up his special unit.

It was an opportunity he took, and he took vascular surgery with him. He started to repair aortas. The split and move left a deep rift in Royal Perth, and when vascular surgery for the aorta was required there, Bob was called in. When the leading neurosurgeon to RPH was found to have a large abdominal aortic aneurysm, Bob repaired it, and the general surgeons yielded to the formation of a special, dedicated, independent department of vascular surgery. The foetus of the specialty in its own right was conceived. The separation, like most divorces of the time, was bitter and unforgiving; surgeons appointed to the vascular unit were not permitted to perform general surgery, no matter how proficient and well trained they might be. It was from this beginning that Bob eventually took vascular surgery to become a specialty in its own right in Australia and New

Zealand, completely separate from general surgery. Much is made possible and can be achieved when driven by passion and determination. His achievement is an example of how passions and outcomes are paired. The power is in the energy generated when positive and negative passions clash.

The circumstances in which vascular and general surgery had been separated in the hospital were contained in a crucible that had another couple of important ingredients to enable vascular surgery to become a new force. "A courageous man will die on a lonely desert road and needs to have support to survive" and Bob was able to succeed in making vascular surgery independent because he had dedicated support from his peers and an ally in radiology. There are always opportunities that arise through independence, and RPH had a very strong interventional radiology department working with the vascular department.

The head of radiology, Dr Turab Chakera, was born in Tanganyika in Dar-es-salaam, and that added to our rapport. Another radiologist, Dr Anil Patel, had grown up in Uganda and was a pioneer in ultrasound in Australia. This all added up to a powerful mix at RPH. The prescribed separation of the two surgical disciplines made the special vascular unit strong and independent because it survived. On the other hand, Bob had been able to create his special unit at Sir Charles Gairdner Hospital and was forever thwarted by the refusal of the university department of surgery there to hand over their component of vascular surgery; those surgeons in the department who did vascular surgery had to wear two hats and serve two masters. There, vascular surgery was divided, and general surgery ruled.

Across the road at RPH, Marcel Goodman, who was working with the university department of surgery as a general surgeon and highly regarded, had also trained in vascular surgery during his time in the UK. He wanted to work with the fledging vascular department. Envied for his youthful success by the professor, who was embittered by the general and vascular split, Marcel was forced to make a choice. He chose vascular surgery at RPH and moved his general surgery off-site. The demarcation between vascular and general surgery at Royal Perth was complete. Varicose veins remained in the department of general surgery, and the role of the vascular unit at RPH was defined as an arterial unit with aortic surgery at its core.

I was to be a child of that unit and took the job of senior vascular registrar at RPH for 1981; I was mentored by Marcel. It was the days of the *MASH* TV series, and the operating theatre was a happy place; music played during the long operations, and there was a specialised united force of surgeons, anaesthetists, and nurses. Bob Paton had set up a service that covered the whole city of Perth for all vascular surgery, and the surgeons at RPH, Sir Charles Gairdner Hospital, and Veteran's Hospital combined to form a roster to cover all after-hours work for the whole state of Western Australia. Each had an appointment as a consultant to all the hospitals in the city and could either continue to manage any patient admitted under their care when on duty or hand over to a surgeon based in the hospital of admission. Only RPH maintained the ban on vascular surgeons performing general surgery; this became the key to RPH becoming the centre of the service.

The day I arrived in RPH in 1974, as a junior registrar, I had been shown around by the senior registrar, Frank Prendergast. Frank had further trained in vascular surgery at St Bartholomew's Hospital in London and at the Nuffield department of surgery at the Radcliffe Hospital in Oxford with the ex-patriot Australian surgeon Peter Morris, who became famous for his work in transplant surgery. Frank had been Bob Paton's protégé and on his return to Perth was appointed as surgeon on the vascular unit at RPH. Frank was probably the best trained of all and a pure vascular surgeon.

He and Marcel made a strong team, and backed by a united combined service under Bob, vascular surgery from all over the

State of Western Australia was covered. The state of Western Australia is a third of the whole of Australia: twenty-five hundred kilometres from north to south and fifteen hundred from east to west. In the 1970s and 1980s, the total population was less than two million. More than half the people lived in Perth, but wherever a vascular problem arose, including ruptured aortic aneurysms, the patients were transferred to a Perth vascular unit. Many from the country were transferred by the wonderful and famous Royal Flying Doctor Service over huge distances.

Western Australia was Australia's backwater and often ignored by the more populous eastern states. In fact, there was so much dissatisfaction with the federal government among West Australians that there was a genuine attempt to secede. This was a state that really had everything (except a lot of people), with huge wheat and sheep farms, forests, fish and rock lobsters, minerals, oil, natural gas, coal, and whaling (until 1978). The ghost towns that dot the eastern gold fields around Southern Cross and Kalgoorlie with its Golden Mile and their isolated graveyards tell a harsh history, and the size of the holes from the iron ore mining go some way to explain the growth of China and Japan.

Perth was the most isolated city by distance in the world. As a result, Perth had to be self-reliant, especially in medicine, and young doctors sought training at home and abroad with the attitude that they would be part of a community that would have to deal with all contingencies. It was a breeding ground for innovation and self-reliance. A mix of British and American medicine developed during the mining booms and the era of the great entrepreneurs. The entrepreneurs and mining magnates turned the state into rivers of ore that flowed across to Japan, filled the Swan River estuary with yachts and marinas, and won the America Cup. The America Cup was the ultimate sailing trophy, and taking it from the Yanks after they had held it against all challengers for eighty-one years was regarded as such a great sporting achievement that Prime Minister Bob

Hawke declared a national holiday. This was the state that could and would do anything. In cricket, it did just that, with Dennis Lillee tearing the heart (or the groin) out of every batsman in the world. Dennis even said, "G'day," to the Queen. In this heady atmosphere, I learnt everything I could about the aorta and how to repair it. I was ready and needed a consultant post.

To describe the Australian health care system and the huge changes that occurred under the federal governments of the 1970s and 1980s, in their attempts to wrest control of health care from the states, would probably only add to the confusion. Suffice to say, the states ran the major teaching hospitals, which were modelled on the great British teaching hospitals. Private hospitals were competing with the governments, state and federal, for the privilege of treating the rich and famous. The federal government exercised funding control of all doctors and picked up the pieces of health care outside the ambit of the state institutions and this included subsidising all general and specialist practices under Medicare. Despite the subsidies, the federally supported medical services continued to be known as private rather than the federal system, maybe because there already existed a federal government hospital system. It was for the veterans of World War I and II, Korea, and Vietnam with a chain of hospitals, one in each state of Australia, called Repatriation General Hospitals. The one in Perth was called RGH Hollywood. An opportunity arose for a new appointment as consultant surgeon to the RGH Perth.

For all intents and purposes, this was the hospital for returning soldiers. It was a backwater in a backwater, but it was special because it had a culture of its own and cared for old soldiers and their wives. It had all the pride and prejudices of the British Empire and all the honours and rorts of an army. The patients were loyal to the institution and the Returned Soldiers League (RSL). The doctors and nurses were either amongst the most caring or mostly asleep, according to whether they were visiting specialists or permanent doctors. There was a tendency to use long-term junior doctors; they were a mixture of those seeking shielding from the rigours of general practice or sheltering with a disability. Dedicated specialist doctors, who felt a debt to their country and those who had fought for it or were associated with the military, served the hospital with a sense of duty on a visiting basis. It was backed by the RSL and a fleet of federal government cars that would transfer old soldiers in comfort and style to the worst-equipped hospital in the state.

The Repatriation Hospitals were built the same in every state of Australia. Go into any one of them, and you could forget which state you were in, as you wandered through barrack-style wards and partly covered corridors shielding the weather side. The RGH in the Perth suburb of Hollywood was next to Sir Gairdner Hospital and sandwiched between that large overpowering state institution and the Karrakatta cemetery. One old digger called it the Transit Station and proceeded to tell me that Karrakatta was full of the indispensables. It was a humbling lesson from the old soldier and the ghosts of the indispensables: I should not consider myself important just because I was a doctor.

I had worked for six months in the RGH in my first year of training in Perth. At that time it was a sleepy place and I was working in orthopaedics between sessions on the snooker tables (there were at least twelve scattered around the hospital). The tables were shared among bored and sleepy old resident doctors and orderlies who were employed as returned soldiers needing repatriation into society. In the meantime the school of medicine in the University of Western Australia had discovered a mine of clinical material on which to teach its budding doctors in RGH Hollywood. The old diggers seemed to respond to the attention of the young, and the university repaid the hospital by establishing a dynamic and progressive department of surgery. Bill Castleden, a young surgeon from St Bartholomew's Hospital in London, was the surgeon to the unit. Bill was energetic, tall, blond (going egg-shell blond), handsome, and very personable; he had the poise of a long British medical lineage. Bill's unit was both general and vascular, and he was on the state vascular roster through Royal Perth. During his travels from Britain, he worked as a registrar in Royal Perth Hospital and acquired a master's of surgery in Perth. Bill and the university were transforming the RGH into a desirable teaching post for students and young surgeons alike.

Towards the end of my year in the vascular unit at RPH, Bill rang me up. I knew of him and had met him briefly over a vascular emergency, but our contacts had been cursory. He asked me to apply for a new post being created at the Veteran's Hospital: senior lecturer in surgery in the university department. I told him that I was flattered that he should ask me to apply and asked why me? Bill was always direct and said that he was asking a number of people to apply because the university and hospital had resisted setting up a post of senior lecturer on the grounds that no one would be interested in working at RGH, and he wanted to prove them wrong. He wanted to show that the unit was a sought-after post. I asked Bill who else was applying. He gave me a couple of names, and I thought both were better candidates than me; both had acquired their fellowships before me, and one had the higher degree of Master of Surgery. I was much less flattered and told Bill that I would not apply on the grounds that to apply for a job and not get it resulted in making people wonder why; that could be detrimental to future applications.

Bill rang me a few days later and again asked me to apply for the job. He said that I had a good chance because many of the old soldiers had vascular disease from the free or cheap army cigarettes, and he was looking for the vascular support that I could give him and the other applicants could not. I decided to apply and was thrilled when I got the job. Bill was democratic and treated me as an equal, despite his clinical superiority.

The job was everything I could have wished for at that stage of my career. General and vascular surgery in vast numbers provided a wealth of experience, and this was coupled with strong medical support in a teaching and learning environment. It wasn't much money, but I was used to that, and it was enough. The compensation in addition to the learning advantages was the university holidays that Bill and I shared. Selva Ratnam, the medical superintendent, was of Sri Lankan descent, and we clicked for a reason that was unclear to me for a while. Then one day at a social function, he pulled me aside and told me that he had really wanted a surgeon with a higher degree for the university post. He had agreed with the selection committee to appoint me only because of the strong recommendation of Don Fleming, my old nemesis and early mentor.

Now that was a surprise. I had always thought the Don considered me an incompetent. He had been the senior surgeon to the vets as well as RPH and was very well respected by all and especially Selva, who secretly wanted to be a surgeon. He had valued the Don's opinion and judgement above all other references. It was good feeling, and this show of faith bonded me as much as anything else to work and build the department of surgery with Bill.

Vascular surgery grew rapidly at the vets hospital because of the aging smoking patient pool; we established a good post-operative care unit for those having aortic surgery. My appointment as senior lecturer was only part-time, and in 1984, Marcel invited me to fill a visiting locum consultant vascular surgery position at Royal Perth; he nominated me for membership of the vascular section of the college at the annual meeting in Sydney. In retrospect, I think that nomination was more difficult to obtain than acceptance into the section, and as a result, I became a bona fide vascular surgeon. My appointment at RPH was confirmed to the status of full consultant. Enthused by the appointment and new interventions in vascular surgery, I took to introducing new techniques. I had the advantage of working in two major teaching hospitals and a large volume of work, with the opportunities to work beside a choice of like-minded colleagues.

The saphenous vein is a long vein that goes from ankle to groin. This is the vein that is involved with the formation of varicose veins. When not varicose, this vein has been used as a spare part and converted to an artery, particularly in the heart or legs, for renal dialysis and for repairing trauma. Arteries and veins are like one-way streets going in opposite directions. Until the introduction of a new operation, the saphenous vein had to be removed through an open wound and turned around because of the one-way valves in the vein. A procedure known as in-situ saphenous vein bypass was developed to reduce the extensive surgery involved in harvesting this vein to serve as an artery in the lower limb. This new method was said to be kinder to the patient while also having better haemodynamic blood flow.

The valves, instead of being turned around, were cut with a special knife on the end of a very long shaft or by an olive-shaped metal pull-through with blades imbedded. This new method had been presented in Sydney, and we thought it was very clever. It was the beginning of less invasive vascular surgery. On returning from the meeting, Marcel and I embarked on the procedure with some success, and this started a new era of exploring less invasive surgery.

The music continued in theatre, and academic discussions created the lyrics for research, while the joys of discovery played out to Woody Guthrie's patriotic songs.

CHAPTER 20

Research

"Eureka" is the expression of the pure joy of discovery. To discover a better way by evolving and improving survival is life. To believe in discoveries by someone else is faith. To attribute all to a superior being is religion. To research and discover defines what it really is to be human. And if there is no record, it was never done. Conversely, if there is a record, it must be true. Is that right? Research and recording is a pair. Research is a dangerous game of true and false; it is a hunt with a kill at the end for the hunter or the hunted. It is a gamble with elation and adrenalin at one end of the scale and the depths of failure and depressions at the other. It is a gathering of fair-weather friends and the drudge of a lonely wet day. It seeks out begging and territorial defence of acquisition. The highs and lows depend on the prize, and like any contest, it is at best a gamble. Research courts angels and monkeys. I am no angel.

I had pursued some research projects during my training and accumulated two years of pure research during that time, but it was a failure. Not because of failure to discover, but a failure to complete and record (which in research means publish). The reasons for failure to publish were complex; the answer was simple: ask the question, answer the question, record the answer, and inform your colleagues in recorded records. I had failed to publish and realised that presentations at medical meetings was insufficient without the permanent record.

During that first research job in Sydney, I had researched the efficacy of steroids on healing nerve injuries. The steroids did not help; the research was abandoned and never published. In Perth, I spent a year comparing the calcium levels in burns patients, where the extent of injury was visible and measurable, with the calcium levels in pancreatitis, where the extent of injury is not visible, to show that the fall in calcium levels in pancreatitis was an index of severity of the illness. The accepted theory at the time was that low levels of calcium in pancreatitis were a peculiarity of the disease. It was a brilliant success and applauded when presented at the World Congress of Surgery.

I was asked by the editor of the *British Journal of Surgery*, who was attending a World Congress of Surgery in Perth, to submit the work to the journal for publication. Instead I patriotically submitted it to the *Australian and New Zealand Journal of Surgery*, but the reviewers criticised the work. I felt discouraged, let it languish, and never resubmitted.

I spent another year researching the possibility of curing diabetes by transplanting insulin-making cells (islets of Langerhans) to the spleen. Harvested cells grew well in tissue culture in the laboratory and produced lots of insulin. The electron microscope pictures of cells making insulin in tissue culture was a eureka moment. Human foetal cells from abortions might be the answer to curing diabetes. We were touching on stem cell research, although we did not know it.

Two things happened, and the project was abandoned without any publication. The first was the ethical mine field of research with human foetal tissue, and the second was that the electron microscope suggested that the cells growing in tissue culture were developing cancerous tumours. It is not that I learnt nothing. To the contrary, I learnt a great deal, but I failed to recognise the value in a negative answer. I failed to persist when promise was evident. I failed to record and publish discoveries as they occurred because I was impatient for the ultimate answer, and I failed because of fear of the truth.

Most of all, I failed because I didn't work in a competent team. Leadership, planning, vision, persistence, and the ability to finish and complete the last mile is what I learned from the experience. Fortunately, I was eventually taught these qualities by Len Matz, who headed the pathology department in Royal Perth Hospital, where Robin Warren worked. Robin eventually won the Nobel Prize in Medicine for his work together with the persistent visionary and brave Barry Marshall, with whom I was a fellow registrar. Len taught me to publish.

Len noticed something unusual in a small group of gallbladders that had been removed for surgical reasons and asked me to look at the problem. Len was not called Tiger for nothing. He demanded everything that a good researcher should do and guided me to completion in a paper titled "Ischaemic Cholecystitis and Infarction of the Gall Bladder." What this means is irrelevant to the story, but what it led to was wonderful.

The findings in the paper with Len opened the way to studying the blood supply of the gall bladder and its relationship to the formation of gallstones. Now I started to feel the joys that come with good research. To find out what was already known, it was necessary to search the literature, and I was assisted by a Greek colleague who could read Russian. I learned the importance of colleagues with different skills. As a result, I discovered a wealth of information coming out from behind the Iron Curtain.

I sought and was given guidance and help by Turab Chakera, the head of radiology. He has remained a strength behind my endeavours. Turab teamed me up with David Hartley, who was the senior radiographer in the department; David made a special X-ray contrast medium for me to inject into the small artery that feeds the gall bladder after it had been removed surgically or post-mortem. I used the operating microscope in the animal research laboratory, courtesy of the staff there, who had befriended me in previous research.

The pictures were startling; I presented them at the College of Surgeons meeting in Hobart that year and published them in a paper, "The Angiographic Findings in Normal and Diseased Gall Bladders." The most important thing to emerge from this flurry of success was a seed of union between me and David. This seed was to lie dormant for a few years but then sprouted later.

This research was a factor in my appointment as senior lecturer to the Veteran's Hospital with Bill, as this was a University of Western Australia position. I was expected to do research as well as clinical work and teach. I now felt confident that research success was assured.

I was wrong. Isolated from my network of friends and colleagues at Royal Perth and without a suitable project, I searched for a question to answer. I can't remember the question I thought of, but I remember the dismissive response from the university to my request for some funds. The clinical load was heavy and growing; Bill was achieving success in his anti-smoking campaign, which meant that his time was shortening. I needed to pick up the load.

Bill eventually took a whole year off clinical work to fight smoking advertising in Western Australia; he spent much of this time sitting in parliament, in the gallery, exposing the complicity of state government and the tobacco lobby as a result of the dependence of the government on smoking dollars. I realised that Bill would save more lives with changes to public health than I would ever save operating on individuals. It was incumbent on me to provide the support for Bill and do the clinical work. I enjoyed the clinical work and gained from the experience; it was invaluable and made up for the lost operating time spent in research.

Then the head of the university department of surgery, who managed the units across all the teaching hospitals, called me in and pointed out that I had not been productive on the research side; if I wanted to continue in the position, I would need to show something in print. That is, I should publish or perish.

Bill asked me what else I had done in Royal Perth, and I informed him of the task I had been allocated as senior surgical registrar to set up some sort of quality assurance and outcome assessment program for the general surgical department. Bill said that was current and topical and even demanded by health care funders and providers. He went on to declare that QA could be substituted for research and, under the heading of audit and improvement, would be food for publication. It was at the time that personal computers were just starting to appear in everyday business management. We informed the Veteran's Hospital that we would like to set up an audit for quality assurance purposes, explaining that it would be great benefit to management because it would provide evidence and be a good management tool. Having struck the right management music chords, funds flowed, and computers and a programmer were provided.

We developed a program of linking a computer-generated hospital discharge letter with production of an audit of outcomes from data collection imbedded in the letter. The junior doctors merely entered data in a menu system, and that generated the prompt letter and stored the data in a format displayed as an audit. I learnt the value of strict routine development and analysis, as well as the Deming cycle of initiate, test, improve, and retest. It was so successful that other hospitals adopted the system; we commercialised the product with a company that developed and sold a surgical billing product called Rx. We chose the name of Qx and started to tie this on the back of the billing program for private practice, in addition to the discharge letter from the public hospital.

After a raft of publications, the College of Surgeons moved to disseminate Qx throughout all surgical departments in Australia and New Zealand; they offered it, at a price, to individual surgical practices to meet the growing call by government to audit outcomes. The College of Surgeons and the commercial company saw dollar signs and fell into dispute. The college decided to make their own program for sale, and the commercial company turned their efforts to the more lucrative billing program for surgeons.

The irony was that the quality improvement program ceased. Without nourishment, it survived for about ten years without updates and then died, as technology progressed and left it behind. It had served its purpose in securing my position, and I also moved on (or back) to more clinical work. I took with me many lessons in research and its partner, application. Not the least was the label FRED, which sat in large red letters over the computer screen in the junior doctors' office. I didn't know they liked the program so much that they should give it a pet name. Then they enlightened me that this was an acronym for "Fucking Ridiculous Electronic Device," and I learned how powerful and deflating derision can be.

The first really successful endeavour into clinical research was in the field of salvaging a patient's blood during an operation and returning it to the patient, instead of using the blood bank. The entry was by accident. As is usual for success, a number of fortuitous coincidences occurred, opening a door into a productive field.

In the eighties, AIDS scared the global community and radically altered medical practices. It was a major blow in shifting the right to test for a disease from the doctor to the patient. Until then, doctors ordered whatever they liked, whether the patient could pay or not. For example, I was never questioned about ordering a test, including for venereal diseases, until AIDS was identified and coupled with homosexuality. Then one day, in London, a man was admitted through casualty with serious injuries from a road accident. In preparation for the operating theatre, he had blood taken for testing, which included an AIDS screen. The test came back positive, and at that moment, his brother arrived; as next of kin, he declared that if we tested his brother for AIDS, we would be sued (he was a lawyer). This dilemma had never been included in a textbook.

AIDS was also associated with blood transfusions, and people were developing AIDS from untested and unknown infected donors. The concept of auto-transfusion, which is the returning of one's own blood, was therefore appealing. It was not a new concept, and its history fascinating. It was time to revisit the possibilities, and we asked the question as to why such a common-sense idea had been abandoned in surgery. Why did it have a bad reputation in surgery? Why was it associated with causing deaths? Why was stored blood from donors so successful, where salvaged blood and auto transfusion had essentially been rejected? Could it be because donated blood was reliable, easier to harvest, and readily available, with organised logistics, or were there some safety issues involved with harvesting salvaged blood at operations? Surgical suspicions are invariably founded in an observation, albeit sometimes just anecdotal.

In response to the developing AIDS epidemic, the Red Cross in Perth, which ran the blood bank, organised a seminar on reducing the use of bank blood and salvaging a patient's own blood during an operation. I was assigned the task of presenting the figures on how much blood the vascular unit transfused during aortic surgery. Vascular was selected as it was a regular user of blood transfusion, and the blood shed from the aorta should be sterile and clear of any contaminant from the bowel content or cancer cells. The blood bank proposed that we suck up the blood into a sterile bottle that contained a filter to take out all the debris and clots and then turn the bottle upside down and transfuse the collected blood straight back into the patient being operated on, accompanied of course by a gleam in the supply company's eye for the projected sales of the disposable collecting materials (the company was sponsoring the seminar).

Filtering was not a completely new idea; surgeons had tried it a hundred years before, using muslin cloth as the filter. Surgeons tend to take surgical myths (unproven beliefs) very seriously, and this practice had a bad reputation for inducing nasty reactions that could lead to rapid demise and death. We didn't know why, nor did the blood bank. It was a good opportunity to do some research into this question.

At that time, there was a young West Indian surgeon, Kishore Sieunarine, who had gone to the UK for further training and experience. He had met an Australian nurse, and they married and returned to the West Indies. Unhappy in the islands, Kishore's wife persuaded him to migrate to Australia. He ran into difficulties having all his medical qualifications recognised and had to go through hoops of examinations and further training in surgery, again with exams. Kishore was very smart, and the exams were not a problem, but securing the necessary training position in the College of Surgeons was. Recognising his abilities and sympathising with his dilemma, Marcel and I arranged for him to be attached to the vascular unit for research and surgical assisting. Fees raised from private practice for assistance were passed onto Kishore for sustenance.

IBM had come up with the first machine to salvage blood from the operating field, filter it, wash it clean with saline wash, and centrifuge out everything except the red blood cells, which were then given back to the patient. I can't remember why IBM should have such a machine; I think it came after taking over another company that handled plasma for blood banks. IBM had converted the plasma separator that extracted clotting factors for haemophiliacs into the blood washer. Anyway, the medical representative of the distributor of this IBM machine was at the above seminar held by the blood bank and suggested we try it. They let us use the machine free of charge for one year, allowing us to assess the products contained in the washings and the quality of the salvaged cells. This was at the beginning of what is now routine practice; it was an ideal time to be involved with the first cell salvage machine in Australia.

Kishore was diligent, intuitive, and thorough, and the results were startling and readily accepted for publication. They were instrumental in establishing the practice of blood salvage as routine in aortic surgery and proved the dangers of salvaged unwashed blood, so that myth became fact. We determined that the white cells in the salvaged blood were activated, like an angered swarm of African bees, and they released their enzymes into the plasma. When transfused straight back into the blood stream, they attacked everything they entered. This could lead to multiorgan failure, with the lungs particularly vulnerable, or uncontrollable bleeding, due to the release of plasminogen activator, which dissolved blood clots. Washing the salvaged blood before transfusing it back to the owner disarmed the white cells and removed the activator.

Eventually, the research progressed to a point where further funds were needed to buy a new machine. IBM sold their machine to the haematology department, which returned it to its original usage of separating plasma products. There were better dedicated machines appearing on the market, and the practice of blood salvage with washing was expanding. We applied to the National Health and Medical Research Council (NH&MRC) for a grant, which was short-listed for funding, but in the interview, we failed to answer rebuttals due to inexperience with the process. Eventually, we were unsuccessful. Maybe if we had persisted with NH&MRC or were more experienced in applying for grants, it would have been funded. Rather than try again, I took another tack and applied for the funds from Appealathon, a TV-based public fundraiser for medical research and health support. We were granted the money and bought a brand-new machine. After that, a problem developed, and I had another lesson to learn.

There had been a wonderful, encouraging culture in Royal Perth Hospital of absorbing costs of tests done for research. Research teams had often been networks of amateurs and professional academics. It spared the time-consuming and demeaning art of begging for money, while doing it for nothing. It was akin to an underlying volunteer organisation, and it spawned world-recognised medical achievers and Nobel Prize winners.

Then the introduction of computers and processing of large amounts of data brought good things, such as auditing and accounting, and bad things, such as removing the human side. It could not account for the value of volunteers. The absorption of research costs was exposed, and removal of this invaluable practice was acclaimed as a triumph for transparency and taxpayers. Money now ruled endeavours; volunteers were deleted. Investors in research advocated blue chip teams with track records. The evolutionary springs that allowed failures and gathering only for the sake of knowledge were assessed not for their intuition but by their bean count.

All this meant that to do further research, we needed substantial money. Departments were set on a course to charge one another for services, and accounting put a price on every favour. Cutting costs in the health sector, with progressive failure of pure socialist governments around the world, led to the cutting of throats in the purely socialist state hospital system. The first throat cut in this *Lord of the Flies* environment was research. To the accountants, research was a waste of money. The soul of the hospital might wither, but in the meantime, we had a problem. We had a machine but no one to help us use it. Until then, the anaesthetic assistant had run the machine during operations, becoming an expert. His services for this purpose were suddenly prohibited by the head of the anaesthetic department, on the basis that this was not part of the job description, and if it grew and became routine throughout the theatre, then technicians would demand a pay increase. The anaesthetic department could not afford that, and favours were no longer the ethic.

I learnt this lesson the hard way and suffered acute embarrassment. Channel Nine wanted some publicity they could use for Appealathon and thought the combination of AIDS, blood transfusions, Royal Perth Hospital, and machines was fertile ground for the TV audience. The hospital public relations officer was keen too. It was arranged that the machine would be filmed washing bovine blood from the abattoir (for demonstration purposes), and all was set up in a back corridor behind the operating theatres. It was arranged that at the appropriate moment, Colin, the anaesthetic technician, would pop out of theatre to run the machine for us.

All was ready, the bright lights were on, the machine was on, the ox blood suspended above the machine, and the cue was given for Colin. Nothing happened. Did Colin have stage fright? We tried again and again. Still no Colin appeared. The TV director started looking pointedly at his watch. Colin is coming, I was informed. We tried again; nothing. I went into the theatre and found Colin, who was standing still and not doing anything.

"What's the matter?" I asked.

"I can't come," he said. "The director of anaesthetics forbid it."

"Why?" I asked, almost dumbfounded.

"Because you didn't ask him permission for me to do it." replied Colin

"I asked you, Colin, and you've always run the machine."

"I know, but things have changed, and now I can't. I didn't know how to tell you in front of all the TV crew from Channel Nine"

I could hardly believe that one doctor could behave in such a fashion to another. I swallowed the humble pie, sought out the director, and asked, with my knees slightly bent, if he could possibly spare Colin for a few minutes for the TV run. The director graciously granted my request, and the episode was shown on the evening news, combined cleverly with previous operating room footage.

I was on TV. I showed the clip to all who visited our house. The tape resided proudly on top of the TV. One day, one of my sons wanted to record a movie. Yep, he used the one on top of the TV and recorded Arnie in *Conan the Destroyer*. He certainly picked the right movie. I have never been on TV again.

I have been blessed with good friends and colleagues. Without Kishore and the anaesthetist, this project would not have succeeded. Kishore gained a recognised college training post, and the quality of his research in the white cells of salvaged blood carried him across the remaining hurdles. It also meant that he had to leave the vascular department for a while and work elsewhere in general surgery to meet the training requirements; vascular was still part of general in the wider college surgical community, and the fellowship exams would be predominantly in general surgery.

The anaesthetist, Michael Hellings, and I have always seen eye to eye. We both started medicine late and had experienced another life. Michael had been a roofplumber and was very practical. He and I decided we would we run the machine ourselves because we thought it so important and because we perceived our patients did better. So when a ruptured aneurysm was admitted and taken straight to theatre, we would set up the machine between us. We grabbed moments between Michael setting up the anaesthetic and me preparing the abdomen for the operation. We worked well together like a left and a right hand. As a far as the machine was concerned, the anaesthetic technician could only stand and watch because he was still prohibited by the head of the anaesthetic department. It was still worth the time it took us, despite the urgency of the situation.

Then something happened that still brings a lump to my throat with an emotional feeling, a sort of admiration deep inside. This emotional feeling must be from a nerve at the core of what makes humans so good when they cooperate constructively. It is not relief. It is not the joy one might feel with the birth of a child or achieving a hard task like acing a final exam or reaching a mountain summit; it is even more powerful, and I am so pleased to have experienced this sense of admiration. The team of technicians in the operating theatres defied the head of the anaesthetic department and set up a roster to come in for any emergency and work for as long as it took; repairing a ruptured aneurysm could take hours, and they worked for nothing. They too believed it was the right thing to do. Other surgeons started to use the machine; sometimes it was the heart surgeons, and sometimes the trauma ones.

Sir Isaac Newton's third law of dynamics in physics is that every action has an equal and opposite reaction. And so it is with human dynamics. The anaesthetic department could not stop the technicians' pro bono work, but it could prove them wrong, and accounting was the tool. The blood bank was approached and secretly audited our bank blood usage in order to show that we used as much bank blood in elective aortic cases when using the cell saver as we did before the days of the cell saver. Since the cell saver cost the hospital money to run, with purchase of the consumables, and the blood bank blood was free to the hospital, the argument was going to be that cell salvage cost the hospital money, did not reduce blood bank transfusions, and should therefore be stopped. Anaesthetists were also paid a fee for transfusing bank blood if the patient was a paying customer, but there was no remuneration for transfusion with the cell saver. The incentives were against the use of the machine by all those who counted the money.

The anaesthetic technicians, despite no payment, kept a strict register on every emergency case where the machine was used, for how long, the amount of blood returned to the patient, and how much bank blood was used. The machine was not allowed to be used unless I granted permission, as the hospital did not regard it as their machine. That meant that my sleep was further disturbed by phone calls asking to use the machine with other surgeons' emergencies; the use was steadily growing.

I routinely gave permission. Out of interest, I would look at the register after a night's use. One day, I noticed a patient's name looked familiar. It was a common name and could be a coincidence. If it was my friend, then we had been to school together. We had played rugby next to each other on the same team, with me as scrum-half and him as fly-half (five-eight, in Australian vernacular). After Kenyan independence from Britain, his family moved to South Africa. When he migrated to Australia from South Africa, we played hockey together again.

The operation in the register had been done by the cardiac surgeons, for uncontrolled bleeding in the chest. The original operation was elective replacement of the aortic valve of the heart, in association with an aneurysm of the ascending aorta (the bit at the beginning of the aorta starting just beyond the valve out of the heart). It had been done the day before. The blood bank was running out of bank blood of that type; more than twenty-five units of blood had been transfused in intensive care. The surgeons had to take him back to theatre, and there was not enough blood to support the operation without the use of the salvage machine. The register showed that the machine salvaged and returned the equivalent of eighteen units of blood during the emergency operation. When I wandered into ICU, I found it was indeed my friend; he looked okay. All the efforts with the machine had been worthwhile in saving his life, if for nothing else.

The blood bank audit revealed that we had reduced our usage of banked blood by 90 percent, and whereas the average amount had been two units per patient, we had reduced that to only one patient in every ten needing supplementary bank blood transfusion. Blood salvage at operation became routine for appropriate surgery. The Sir Charles Gairdner Hospital across town purchased a machine and sent a team to America to train to use it. They went halfway around the world instead of halfway across town to learn, but that is the Australian and American way.

To be less cynical, it was a rival company's machine, and training in the United States was part of the deal. Those who were to run the machine would get a fringe benefit and a rare bonus of a trip to the States, at no direct cost to the taxpayer; it was built into the price. Indirect costs do not seem to matter in socialist systems that want to be seen as doing the right thing. However, who am I to be cynical when I've had my own share of sponsored travel to speak on research at international meetings?

Cell salvage became standard practice. Satisfied that the job was done, I moved on from the challenge of blood salvage in surgery.

PART 3

The Endovascular Revolution and Stent-Grafts

CHAPTER 21

The Endovascular Revolution

It was time to look again at what first stimulated my interest in vascular surgery. Rather than just be an observer, I wanted to engage as a player. Charles Dotter, the interventional radiologist at Oregon Health Services University Hospital, pioneered the concept of "surgery without a scalpel." He was the first to dilate an artery through the skin by putting a hollow rod over a wire that led into the artery of the leg and running the rod up and down the artery, like a chimney sweep. After he had pulled the rod and wire out, he stopped the bleeding from the substantial hole in the wall of the artery by merely pressing firmly down on the groin with his hands. The surgeons in his hospital could not believe it; they nicknamed him "Crazy Charlie."

Dotter made this statement in 1963: "It should be evident that the angiographic catheter can be more than a tool for passive means for diagnostic observations: used with imagination, it can become an important surgical instrument."

The procedure nowadays is most well known for being performed in the heart artery, using a balloon over the wire instead of a rod. There are many of us who have undergone angioplasty, with or without a stent, somewhere in the body. Most have heard of the procedure because it is so common. Nowadays, the number of procedures performed around the body with wires and catheters are so numerous that the list fills pages.

The innovation by Dotter, who started dilating arteries through the skin using a rod, galvanised Andreas Greuntzig to substitute an inflatable balloon on the end of a catheter for the rod, and then Julio Palmaz to add a metal support to the dilated artery when support was needed. Palmaz introduced the arterial stent, a latticework tube of stainless steel mounted on the balloon. It stayed behind after the artery wall was dilated. The stent acted as a tunnel prop. The balloon served to dilate the artery and expand the stent.

Dotter and Palmaz visited Royal Perth Hospital as speakers and left a lasting impression on me. I would like to have met Greuntzig, but he died too early in a plane crash, and I must remain content with having been a member of the Greuntzig Society and a picture of Dotter and Greuntzig standing together. I wanted to be involved and be able to operate with both surgical instruments and with wires and catheters. There was huge scope to make quantum leaps by combining the skills. It would fit with the rich history of adaptation surrounding the terminology. Charles Stent was a dentist who invented struts between teeth. Surgically placed structures that hold a position steady in the body are all known as stents. *Plasty* means "to form"; materials that can be shaped are called plastic, and operations that change the shape of things in the body are called plasties. Angioplasty therefore means to change the shape of a blood vessel (*angio*). The same applies for any other structure in the body, for example, blepharoplasty (eyelid), pyloroplasty (pylorus of the stomach), rhinoplasty (nose), and pyloplasty (pelvis of the kidney).

In the 1980s, all angioplasties in vascular surgery were referred to the radiology department for the procedure after an angiogram. The decision to treat with angioplasty resided with the surgeon, and that was policy. That was the rule. It was part of the demarcations that were being defined in the early computer age. Yet it seemed unnecessary and impractical to me to have this division. It limited my practice and the practice of my radiology colleague. We formed a team, Peter Kelsey and I, and we worked together in both the catheter lab (X-ray theatre) and the traditional surgery operating theatre.

We then combined the diagnostic X-ray angiograms with the decision-making process and could proceed from one to the other immediately, or work in the operating theatre and do surgery on one part of the artery and dilate another part with angioplasty, using whatever X-ray equipment was available. It worked well and led to us assessing new technologies and procedures together.

We knew one day it would not be necessary for us to work together all the time; we would split and join as the needs of workloads, innovations, assessments of new things, and complexity of a particular procedure might require. In the beginning, as a team, it served to keep the critics and union demarcations at bay. I taught Peter basic surgical skills, such as how to operate on the femoral artery, and Pete taught me catheter and wire skills. As time went on, we moved beyond the basics and learned new technologies together. It was indeed a wonderful relationship. Peter could admit patients under my name as the surgeon, as he had my standing permission, and treat them as he wished. In return, I could arrange for patients to have procedures on his list once a week. I called it Holy Tuesday, playing on the American political day; Tuesday was when I could operate through holes instead of cuts.

After a while, it dawned upon the naysayers that we had circumvented the system, and attempts were made to thwart us and restore the status quo. Peter, who had a radiation counter pinned to him whenever he used X-rays, was banned from doing procedures in the operating theatre with me because his radiation counter registered too much exposure from the equipment there. The X-ray machines in the OR had been designed for acquiring occasional still pictures to check surgical procedures, not for guiding operations with continuous images. I didn't have a counter because surgeons were not expected to be using X-rays to operate, and so what the administration did not see, the administration did not grieve, and I did not have to account.

Radiologists were not allowed to admit patients in their own right, known as having clinical privileges, because that freed them of any conflict of interest of doing diagnostic tests and proceeding to do a related procedure for a fee. How that differed from a surgeon or a cardiologist doing a test and moving directly to a procedure with their own decision escaped me for a while. Then I remembered that money is the root of all evil. These rules were the instruments of power and control. If the money distribution was controlled by administration, or government, then power and order could be maintained. Processes outside the control by money and independent thought processes severely threaten administrative organisations.

Of course, the factors of responsibility, accountability, and accreditation of skill sets play a part in policy making, but they are secondary instruments for power and control. I could understand that and realised that maintaining status quo was essential for maintaining administrative and funding systems. Administration and governing bodies have problems dealing with matters outside the box. Therefore, they resist change and are conservative by nature. The problem was that we had moved into a new era, with a quantum leap in thinking, and as a consequence, we were well and truly outside the box. We were ahead of the pack, in a sense, and there were no immediate tools to stop us. For this to happen, we had to be divided again.

Strategies are sometimes well planned, but this usually requires experience. In an entirely new field, acquiring experience and developing a strategy occur simultaneously. In retrospect, the strategy may appear clever and logical. In reality, it was most likely a murky atmosphere in which failures were obscured and disappeared, unless notorious for a disaster, and successes realised only in time and then given order. Fortunately, I was not in an important position nor considered the most senior surgeon. Marcel claimed the first of these as head of department and Marcel together with Frank the latter. This meant that I did not work under a spotlight. I did not have a strategy to end up where we eventually did; that goal was simply unknown and unexpected. There was the inner drive of a younger surgeon, and I felt that it was right to combine diagnostic and interventional image-guided radiology and surgery in the field of arterial disease. It seemed right to roll the problems into one team. The philosopher Bertram Russell said of partnerships that they work if the partners are equal, but when the share is unequal, it will lead to war. Peter and I formed a team under the partnership of the vascular surgery and radiology departments. In the beginning, it was an equal partnership. I gave him access to admit patients he wanted to treat, and he gave me access to facilities for patients I wanted to treat.

There are some basic tenets that one learns when hunting that I am sure are really part of universal animal behaviour. Some are instincts, and some, once learnt, become reflexes. In general, it is better to be out in the open and move slowly when you are not a threat, or threatened, and remain unseen when you know you are. It is an advantage to make good ground unnoticed and to do this from downwind (don't make bad smells). Where possible, gain the high ground, but stay off the skyline, and take opportunities to move unexpectedly and maintain an element of surprise. When committed, stand your ground. I don't think I consciously worked on this basis, as that might suggest that I was subversive or manipulative, but I guess it was inherent in my nature and possibly a result of my upbringing. Opportunity was ultimately the key factor. It was luck. I was fortunate that nobody else in Perth was interested in competing for the combined skills of surgery and interventional image-guided radiology at that time. Acquiring the combined skill sets was to define my future.

It was fortuitous that both Dotter and Palmaz should have visited Royal Perth at times when I was in research jobs, and I had the time and opportunity to go to their seminars and lectures, even though they were visiting the nonsurgical departments of radiology and cardiology. It was this that led me to become involved in angioplasty of vessels during surgery at both RPH and the Veteran's Hospital, by teaming with the radiologists, and to sewing on conduits to the femoral artery for the cardiologists, who wished to perform heart valve dilation with large balloons.

It was fortuitous that no other surgeons wanted to be involved and that Marcel and Turab smiled benignly on my activities, especially that Peter and I could work together so harmoniously and productively. In the beginning, this was no threat because the decisions for angioplasty were surgical and the procedure simple: balloon dilation over a wire in the femoral artery. This did not interest other surgeons, who were happy to delegate the procedure to their radiology colleagues. They did not see that I was developing a skill set with an advantage and a stepping stone into the future.

History tells the story that it was Dotter's work in the femoral artery that led to revolutionary changes to treating heart arteries with angioplasty and then angioplasty with additional stents. I could see that my involvement in angioplasty of the femoral artery was the doorway to a new field in arterial treatments, combining surgery and interventional radiology. There was no name for the combined skill set, and the term had yet to be coined. It is now called endovascular surgery.

My public practice at Royal Perth was only half-time, and some of this was for implementing and devising quality assurance measures into the hospital. The other half was split between the part-time university appointment at the Veteran's Hospital and developing something of a private practice in hospitals outside RPH. My part-time private secretary was frustrated by my priority for dealing with the public institutions. Medical secretaries are often proud of the practices they run, and they bask or shrink in the light or gloom of the practice volume and reputation. My reputation was good for complex patients who needed public admission but poor for looking after the more consumer-oriented and socially demanding patients seeking more personalised attention in private hospitals. My private secretary had little standing as far as working for me went in the private world of medicine.

I had long given up trying to justify my appointment with the university by doing research because without finance and facilities, I saw it as a waste of time. I had decided in my mind that if I did research it would be for interest and self-satisfaction, never to hold a position. I saw my role in the Veteran's Hospital as a working clinician and undergraduate medical teacher who would hold the unit together while Bill pursued the computer research and anti-smoking campaign. As a result, I was considered a good and experienced surgeon. I treasured that and thought of my dad, who said, "I don't care what you want to do: whatever it is, be the best at it."

It gave no grist to the mill of reputations in the private world, as I wasn't even considered an academic. In short, I was neither town nor gown. The reality hit me when I had to advertise for a new secretary. I was interviewed by the preferred applicant and told in no uncertain terms that I had nothing to offer a good, experienced medical secretary. Fortunately, another took on the challenge.

At Royal Perth, my commitment to the hospital suddenly expanded when the role of director of quality assurance was thrust upon me. Private practice was pushed further into the background. Although I had an interest in quality assurance because of the development of the computer audit program at Veteran's Hospital, it was not a role I sought or knew very much about. It was certainly not the immediate reward of money that spurred my involvement because that reward was small. It was a personal request from my old mentor, Professor Brian Vivian, who had taken on the task as part of rehabilitation after a stroke and wished for it not to die with his departure.

To make it a success was to show that the role that had been created for him was not a sop but a core function for the hospital. There was a rising national clamour for doctor accountability, and that was the assurance that this position would become important and influential. Sunday school lessons and student poverty had instilled a deep residing reassurance not to worry about money and that manna would appear from heaven when needed. There was an undercurrent of a sense of purpose that I could not define and that the threads of my involvements must tie together one day, even though they were in a tangle. Maybe it was secret ambitions for fame and recognition, which I denied and played down, that drove me to take on endeavours that widened the eyes of my friends and relations.

There was no doubt that I always thought about the names of famous surgeons who adorned various instruments and procedures, and I certainly wished that I would one day register a mark on surgical history. It was fascinating to learn the methods and tools of QA. I learned how to evaluate outcomes and service providers based on facts rather than reputations and anecdotes. I also learned the important lessons of the power of having the information prepared and working only with those who will work with you. To work with someone who is negative was to achieve nothing except wasted time and expense.

Then some exciting and challenging things began to happen quite rapidly. A new professor of surgery was appointed to the University of Western Australia. He called me in for a chat and bluntly told me that he was going to build a strong academic and progressive unit of full-time surgeons with postgraduate degrees such as master of surgery (MS) and doctor of medicine (MD). His point was not missed. I was not full-time, had no further degree or pathway to one, and owned a poor publication record. I was not an academic and did not fit in with his vision. Furthermore, Bill was moving to Fremantle Hospital as the professor of surgery; obviously, there was no longer any place for me. I had no option but to agree and arranged to take accrued sabbatical and the long service leave due to me after the seven years with the university. I was then informed that because I was only part-time, I was not due any sabbatical leave or pay in lieu.

I had covered many emergencies and nights and weekends after hours for no fee, on the basis that I was with the university and accrued leave in lieu. It appeared that I had been treated as full-time when it came to after-hours work. I considered it unfair that I was unable to claim the benefits due in lieu of payment. My response was that without the benefits of the university salary award, I had therefore not been required to do after-hours work as part of the university award and must be due a lot of money for many after-hours operations over seven years. Records of emergency rosters and the operating theatre registers were proof and basis for calculation.

The Veteran's Hospital owed me an enormous sum because they had used me without cost for up to five nights a week when Bill was away. The sum was never calculated or divulged to me. Instead, they offered me a round-the-world ticket and expenses to visit any institutions I wished for two months, plus three months' leave, in exchange for my claim. This was the manna from heaven because I could bolster my requests to visit famous institutions using the university as my flagship. Furthermore, the university could not sack me for another year because I was under contract, so I would travel under my current title of senior lecturer in surgery. All I had to do was give a report on where I had been, present my expenses, guarantee that I would continue to work at the Veteran's Hospital for at least six months on my return, and summarise how I benefited from the experience.

Selva Ratnam, the superintendent of the Veteran's Hospital, had valued my work as a surgeon and needed me to continue for a while to keep the unit going until a new replacement was found for Bill. Apart from his need to provide a continuing busy surgical service, Selva was a friend and vowed he was not going to abandon me. He offered me a consultant post outside the university when a new full-time university surgeon took over. I thanked him but declined. Instead, I took this as an opportunity to cease all general surgery and limit my practice to vascular surgery. My appointment as a consultant vascular surgeon in Royal Perth would be the anchor, and the rest of the time would be available for private practice. I was free to pursue my vision.

I planned a trip through London and then onto the United States. Larry Hollier, a surgeon with a great reputation for thoracic aortic aneurysm surgery, had been a recent guest speaker in Melbourne at the annual surgical meeting of Australian and New Zealand surgeons. He had worked at the Mayo Clinic and then moved back to his home state of Louisiana to take up a senior position at the famous Oschner Clinic in New Orleans. The combination of New Orleans, jazz, Cajun cooking, the Oschner Clinic, and a visit to Larry's unit made this a top priority. Larry had said in Melbourne that Australians would be welcome to visit if passing by that way. I contacted him, explained who I was, and was impressed by his warm welcoming invitation to visit. I also arranged to visit the huge Ely Lilley pharmaceutical works in Indiana; the representative in Perth encouraged me with some financial support in the way of accommodation and partly because I wanted to see the Indy 500 track.

A more important reason emerged for me to make the trip: to assess the status of laser technology and make a report on whether the Department of Health should fund a laser machine for angioplasty in Perth. I was selected because I was the only surgeon directly involved in angioplasty. Lasers were being introduced into surgery, particularly in the eye, and there was a strong eye research unit in Perth (sponsored by the Lions Club) working with the excimer laser machine. There was some promise of use for vascular surgery in association with angioplasty, and the government was conscious of a looming expense. One reason that lasers became so important was the Department of Health of Western Australia had funded a union worker who had flown to Sydney to have laser-assisted angioplasty on his leg.

With help from the union, he successfully claimed the fares from the Department of Health, using a scheme that existed to transport patients from areas where treatment was not available to where the treatment was provided. The spirit of this scheme was to provide free transport for people from remote areas in Western Australia who needed treatment in Perth. The union had used this as a loophole to justify the claim for expenses to send their member to Sydney because Perth did not have a laser machine. To pre-empt a flood of fare requests to see the Sydney Opera House, the state had applied to a special needs fund run by the federal government to purchase such a machine for the sum of two hundred and fifty thousand dollars, which was a lot of money in the 1980s.

Before making the purchase, the Department of Health wanted an assessment and recommendation on the type of machine. There was only one that was commercially available, the Trimodyne laser, made by an American company. It was a key billing attraction for an upcoming seminar and workshop in Los Angeles, and it all fitted together in my plans, which now had the blessings of the university, the Department of Health, the vascular surgeons, and Royal Perth Hospital.

A researcher in California was developing an excimer laser device to pass down an artery and cut away all the atheroma, narrowing the vessel. A young researcher in St Bartholomew's Hospital, London, had developed a glass lens on the end of a fibre-optic catheter that he had passed down to open blocked arteries with a pulsed dye laser. And Geoff White, a young Australian surgeon, was working in Los Angeles and writing about laser-assisted angioplasty and angioscopy, which was looking down the artery with a fibre-optic telescope. In the latter part of 1988, a seminar and workshop had been organised with Geoff through UCLA in Torrence.

I organised my trip around the world, starting in London to look at the pulsed dye laser, followed by a visit to Larry Hollier in New Orleans, viewing the Ely Lilly manufacturing facility in Indiana, assessing the laser machines in Los Angeles, and looking at blood salvage machines.

It was a wonderful trip to places I never dreamed I could ever visit; the report I wrote on the experience has gathered dust in the archives of the university department of surgery of WA ever since (or has long ago been shredded for want of space). I do, however, recall some aspects that were not included in the report. One evening, we shone a green pulsed dye laser light beam on the dome of St Paul's Cathedral from a research room in St Bartholomew's Hospital, and in Denver, I fell in love instantly with a girl showing me a cell saver machine in the Cobe factory, only to discover she was radiant because she was getting married the following weekend.

I took a train across the Rocky Mountains from Denver to Sacramento and saw the eucalyptus trees that were planted to stop erosion after the sluicing for gold (they now fuel Australian-type summer fires in California). I saw *Phantom of the Opera* in San Francisco, jested with panhandlers down on Fisherman's Wharf, and ended up at Geoff's seminar and workshop in LA.

Much has been said of first impressions. Mine of the United States were acquired in New Orleans in an office with walls adorned with multiple award plaques and a large plate glass window overlooking the Mississippi River, where the long river barges pushed by tugs were turning mistily into river steamers loaded with Huckleberry Finns. I realised how lucky I was to be in Larry Hollier's office, considering my character probably matched Huckleberry's more than that of an eminent American surgeon. There were a number of us in the room and an expressionless secretary in the adjoining one. The density of award plaques on the wall was awe-inspiring, and his nonchalant manner that Americans often beguile you with could only be responded to with a smile.

I presented myself to Dr Hollier's office at the appointed time and announced to the secretary that I was Michael Lawrence-Brown, a surgeon from Australia, and had come to spend the week at the clinic, as arranged. The secretary's eyes widened slightly with surprise, and she spoke on the intercom. Mutterings were all I could hear, and then I was directed to sit on a couch by a wall covered with more honour plaques.

After a few minutes, a gentleman walked in and announced that he was a surgeon from Sweden and had come to spend the week at the clinic, as arranged. There were more mutterings on the intercom, and the Swedish surgeon was directed to sit next to me on the couch.

After a few more minutes, three men who looked like grandfather, father, and son walked in; the youngest presented himself politely as the spokesman and announced that he was Dr Gucci; he indicated the grandfather and said this was the professor of surgery of the University of Milan; the other man was his colleague and senior surgeon, and he himself was the junior surgeon from Italy, and they had come to spend a week with Dr Hollier, as arranged.

There were longer mutterings on the intercom, and the space on the couch became fully occupied. Larry then emerged from his office with the warmest smile I had ever been greeted with, and we were all ushered into his office and welcomed. Larry outlined his week's schedule and then took us to the clinic, where he introduced his trainee fellow, his chief resident surgeon (senior registrar), and a young female anaesthesiologist.

It was a week of 5:00 a.m. starts, repeated ward rounds, multiple operations in simultaneous ORs, walks along the Mississippi levees, dinners in the French Quarter, and visits to Tulane University's Charity Hospital. It was a week that displayed the width of the cross section of American society. I watched the

Super Bowl (the final match of US gridiron football) on TV in an elegant Southern home with only white people and travelled on buses that only carried black people. At the zoo, I saw an Asian elephant that was best friends with an African elephant and wondered if the two species had ever been crossed (what would an elephant mule be like?).

The Italian professor insisted on a particular restaurant in the French Quarter that was an example of how Italian food should really be presented. He arranged a special room and then chastised the restaurateur volubly in Italian for imperfections in Italian etiquette. He insisted we all get up and leave, walk around the block, and come back when they had got it right. All seemed the same to me when we marched back in again. The problem was something trivial to do with mixing cheese and tomatoes, but I was very impressed with his power play.

I had always liked catching and eating catfish as a boy and enjoyed the blackened catfish in the food halls. I also took to the gumbo soup and jambalaya, a rice dish with alligator that Larry cooked with lots of tabasco at his house at the end of the week; he put on a barbecue for us, complete with three fiddlers from the bayou. It was a wonderful week. I asked why there were so many catfish in the Mississippi and revealed how naïve I really was (they were farmed).

I called into Hawaii on the way home and spent a few days with Peaches, who had been one of the women on the all-girls safari with Stan in the 1950s and then became a client and friend of his. Peaches had made lots of money with a seafood sauce she sold in a Waikiki Beach restaurant, where the Hilton Hotel now stands. Although she was eighty years old, she was very fit and great fun. We reminisced about Stan. Peaches knew lots of people on the island of Oahu; to the great envy of my sons, she drove me around the island to the surfing Meccas of the Banzai Pipeline and North Shore.

When I returned to Australia, I was at a crossroads. Clearly, my surgical partnership with Bill was over. My job with the university was at an end. What was more, the Commonwealth government, which owned the Veteran's Hospital, was selling all its Repatriation Hospitals around Australia. The Western Australian one was rejected by the state, which had first refusal and was being privatised. Should I take the offer of consultant and develop a private practice in Hollywood Hospital, as it would be called? It was a good offer. I guess it can be best described as the end of a partnership, and like great partnerships in cricket, when one partner is out, the other soon follows. My heart wanted out of Hollywood. I could not stay and watch what I had built in the hands of another.

Coincidently, there was another crossroads to be met. The end of the 1980s was the close of the era of extensive surgery and the beginning of a trend towards minimal invasion. Patients no longer wanted the pain associated with long scars and bulging incisional hernias. When Barry Jackson was the visiting surgical professor to RPH at the beginning of the eighties, he predicted the growing impact of minimally invasive laparoscopic general surgery, and this prediction came true with a rush. Gall bladder surgery with laparoscopic cholecystectomy was the leading example. Although early learners tried hard to form exclusive groups, the tide was too strong, and all general surgeons were being forced to make a choice to learn new skills to compete for practice or lose their work. This was especially so in private practice, where the patient demand and provision of equipment by private hospitals drove the demand.

In the end, it was a relatively easy decision for me. I had another skill set with vascular surgery, catheter, and wire skills. I focused on Royal Perth Hospital and my growing vascular practice, deciding to pour more energy into image-guided wire and catheter intervention. With the decision to cease general surgery, there was no need for me to learn the whole new set of skills developing with fibre-optic image-guided laparoscopic surgery.

Paradoxically, the more I specialised, the busier I became. A friend who had followed a similar path through general surgery into urology pointed out that surgeons greeting one another asked, "Are you busy?" rather than "Hello" or "G'day" or "How are you?" If you really want to tease your colleague, the answer was, "Too busy." I was getting too busy and upsetting my colleagues and family as I struggled to keep up with the time of day. I had too many different facets to my life, and in trying to please everybody, I was pleasing none.

It only took a little while for the general surgical referrals to dry up. What about the blood salvage project and starting a company to provide the service?

The trip to America opened my eyes in that field. Blood salvage was here to stay. The Oschner Clinic was one of many not-for-profit hospitals in the United States. That meant after paying all expenses and salaries, all the rest of the earnings went to growing the organisation and purchasing equipment. The Oschner Clinic had six brand-new cell savers. Our research had helped convince blood salvagers that washing was essential if blood was to be recycled, and the research was at an end. This meant that instead of researching the field, the effort should be in applying the technology. The Red Cross Blood Bank in Perth gently declined the suggestion that they service all operating theatres for a fee. Their business was based on blood donors, not blood salvage.

In Sacramento, I had met a former nurse who had set up a business of hiring out machines with an operator and making a living from this. I put the idea to a friend in a small medical distributor service in Perth, and he and his partner took it up with some success, until hospitals eventually purchased their own as standard equipment for operating theatres. Anyway, the blood salvage project had also ended for me. I was left with quality assurance and vascular surgery.

Younger surgeons tend to get dragged into committees and hospital advisory roles, partly because they are less busy in the beginning until they are well established, partly because they are still driven by an ethic to serve, and partly because they have not yet learned to say no. The quality assurance area was a good example and led me into another commitment of taking the chairmanship of the Western Australian Branch of the Royal College of Surgeons. In this capacity, I learned that if someone does not give you an answer to a request, the answer is no. I learned again to work with those who would work with me and not waste time with those who would not, and I met James Semmens. James was a public health researcher and later became a close friend who has taken me down the longest mile home on many occasions.

In 1995, the professor of the School of Public Health in the University of Western Australia, D'Arcy Holman, established the WA Data Linkage System to link data contained in the core health datasets of the Department of Health and more than thirty other population-based research datasets. The system was built on a foundation of nine core elements: birth, death, and marriage registrations; hospital separations; midwives' and cancer notifications; mental health service encounters; emergency presentations; and electoral roll registrations. Having established the linkage system, he wanted to increase its use because information is power, and it can be used as the basis for informed decision making. He requested and was granted an audience with the State Committee of the College of Surgeons.

D'Arcy convinced the committee that this was the ultimate quality assurance tool. He offered James to work with the college to examine the trends, utilisation of health care services, and outcomes for procedural care in WA. The outcome was that in 1996, we established the WA Safety and Quality of Surgical Care Project, a unique collaboration among the WA Branch of the College of Surgeons, the University of Western Australia, and the WA Department of Health. This was more manna from heaven, and research projects were started and kudos won in the world of medical quality assurance, patient safety, and clinical accountability. James was later awarded a medal from the Australasian College of Surgeons for his service to surgical care.

My quality assurance activities at Royal Perth Hospital, which started as an act to honour a mentor, had culminated in RPH being the first hospital in WA to gain the prestige of national accreditation, won an outstanding service award for me, and resulted in the Quality of Surgical Care program.

It was time to let the QA department sail on its own; my tenure as chairman to the local branch of the college was over. I freed myself of QA and left with time to concentrate on riding the flood of change flowing through vascular surgery.

Some years previously, vascular surgeons, led by Bob Paton, had persuaded St John of God Hospital in the Perth suburb of Subiaco to allow aortic surgery to be performed in private. It was a coup for vascular and the hospital because the main rival, Mount Hospital, had the prestige of open-heart surgery with a concentration of cardiologists, cardiothoracic surgeons, and intensive care specialists.

As the most junior vascular surgeon using St John's, I had difficulty competing for time in the operating theatre. After doing an emergency operation at the Mount, CEO Margaret Giles suggested I move my practice there. I said I would, in return for access to the cardiac catheter lab to perform vascular angioplasty procedures. Unlike St John's Hospital, there were no interventional radiologists to compete with, and the cardiologists were helpful and supportive.

The hospital granted my request and allowed me to modify the X-ray machine to cope with the differences between its design for the heart and my requirements for peripheral vascular work. Essentially, the cardiologists took cine pictures because the heart is always moving; I needed special still shots that I could overlay with digital manipulations to give me lasting images that I could use as a road map to negotiate long and twisted vessels in remote places using fluoroscopy to show the movements of the catheters and wires, like those machines that used to be in shoe shops where you could watch your toes wriggling inside the new shoe.

The power of competition launched me at the Mount into uncharted waters in Australia: a vascular surgeon with his own catheter laboratory for vascular angioplasty. My partnership with Pete continued, and he joined me at the Mount but became uncomfortable with the arrangement. He was meant to be full-time at RPH; he could not use the lab in his own right because there was already a radiology practice servicing the hospital, and he was not part of it. I suspect there was some pressure from his colleagues, who accepted that I worked with Pete in RPH in radiology but saw him working with me in my domain in the Mount as too much. We continued together at RPH, but the Mount was left to me.

CHAPTER 22

Path to an Aortic Endograft: Building a Bridge and Mr. Walker

Pete was a staunch fan of Dotter, and I had been converted too during his visit in the 1970s. One morning, we were studying X-rays of an elderly man. He had narrowing of the iliac arteries that go from the end of the aorta, at about the level of the navel, down to the groins on each side, where they are then called the femoral artery. By this stage, Pete and I were regularly treating the narrowings in the iliac arteries with balloons and stents introduced from the femoral artery, which passes just under the skin in the groin. This gentleman had smoked all his life, and as a consequence, his arteries were failing. Above the narrowings, he had the typical orange-shaped bulge of an aneurysm in the lower aorta. The narrowings we could treat easily from the groin, but the aneurysm needed the full opening of his belly in order to replace the aorta with a textile synthetic prosthesis.

The average normal diameter of this part of the aorta is twenty-two millimetres and is at considerable risk of bursting when sixty millimetres in diameter, which is about the size of a navel orange (surgeons often describe things in terms of fruit).

Pete said, "You know, one day, aneurysms will be treated by putting a device inside passed up from the groins. Dotter predicted it."

It was not an entirely new concept. The famous English surgeon John Hunter, who founded the Museum in the Royal College of Surgeons in London centuries ago, had tried to treat aneurysms by filling them with coils of wire to make them fill with clot and thrombose so that without blood flow, they would not rupture. He thought the body would cope by finding other pathways for the blood to detour around the thrombosed aneurysm and thus keep organs and limbs beyond the problem alive; it was a disaster, and the method was abandoned. In medical terminology, the natural detours for blocked arteries are called collaterals, and they were simply not big enough to cope with sudden occlusion of the aorta: the collateral damage, in military terms, was too great a price to pay.

For that reason, I was sceptical of Pete's prediction, but I did not dismiss it because so much was changing in the pursuit of less-invasive surgery. For the time being, the immediate problem in front of us demanded a large life-saving operation, and if I had to replace the aorta, I might as well replace the iliac arteries at the same time, using a trouser-shaped textile graft from the aorta above the aneurysm to the femoral arteries below. This operation was called an aorto-bifemoral bypass and was the standard procedure of the time.

"Pity we are not able to treat the aneurysm and the narrowings of the iliac arteries at the same time from the groin," said Pete.

Then in 1991, a circular came to my mailbox advertising the Royal Prince Alfred Hospital Week in Sydney, including a seminar by their vascular department on endoluminal treatment of abdominal aortic aneurysms. Juan Parodi, an Argentinean surgeon, had treated an aneurysm by inserting a folded textile tube up from the groin and then expanding it with a stent to have the tube span the aneurysm from inside. He would be the guest speaker and was to be part of a demonstration of the procedure to reline the aneurysm from the inside. The flyer said the operation would be performed on a patient for the audience to witness via closed-circuit TV (CCTV). Normally, such flyers were passed straight into the bin, but this one screamed out at me because of what Pete and I had discussed. We could almost hear Dotter clapping from the grave.

Pete agreed to come to Sydney with me, and I made the arrangements. The event was held in December and was fascinating, but there were problems, and the technology left much to be desired. The message was that there was a way, and it could work. I enjoyed going back to Sydney and to Darling Harbour, where all the old berths and warehouses were being replaced by attractive waterside tourist venues and restaurants. Sydney had changed so much; there was no way I could have driven a taxi again.

I basked in the ambience, and we had dinner looking over Circular Quay from the entrancingly restored Rocks area, while we planned what we would do the next year. I was reminded of how Jack Mundy, who headed the Builders' Workers Union, had stood with his members and refused to destroy the history of the area for the sake of modern development. An interesting world when the presumed uneducated stand up for preservation of the old and resist introduction of the new by the presumed educated, and it was an apt place to contemplate how we might progress against anticipated resistance should we pursue the new.

The answer was in the rocks. It would ultimately depend on the support of the common people: the patients.

Pete and I were convinced that we had the expertise and infrastructure to make an endoluminal graft to treat aneurysms. By this stage, we had experience with all the technology available, a great working relationship, research facilities, and the backing of premiere vascular and radiology interventional units. We also had the potential of getting David Hartley's help. I had been introduced to David by Turab in 1981 and started research with him. It was he who made it possible to examine the microcirculation of the gall bladder with a special dye he developed that allowed questions to be answered surrounding the link among gallstones, gall bladder disease, and the circulation of the gall bladder.

David had links with medical production, experience in making devices for interventional radiology, ingenuity, and intuitive engineering skills that had already made many things possible in Perth. For example, to enable cardiologists to visualise parts of the heart that were obscure because of the rotation limitations of the X-ray machines of the time, David invented and built a rotating X-ray table. If the X-ray machines could not be rotated around the patient, then the obvious answer to David was to rotate the patient under the machine— without the patient falling off the table. That was how David's mind worked; patients were secured with wide leather straps on David's rotating X-ray table. As a result, the cardiologists in Western Australia in the 1970s were recognised as leaders in the field of coronary artery angiography and angioplasty.

Interventional neuroradiology in Royal Perth was internationally recognised. In the 1980s, it had been in the forefront of the development of this specialty. David was central to this because he made it possible with his inventiveness and ability to create the tools needed for doctors to use. His designs and prototypes of tools for interventional radiology were of such quality and ingenuity that they were made available commercially through the company William Cook Australia; a link with practical commercial provisions was already formed.

David had done things for vascular surgery, as well. To enable X-ray images of the arteries of the body and legs with a single dose of X-ray contrast dye, he developed an integrated system of a moving X-ray table and timely acquisition of X-ray images. This involved injecting X-ray dye into the aorta in the abdomen and taking an X-ray immediately, then rapidly moving the top of the table so that another X-ray could be taken further down the body as the dye flowed past, and then again until all the arteries in the legs had been X-rayed, with just one dose of contrast. In the days before digital technology, this greatly facilitated diagnosis of aortic and peripheral arterial disease while much reducing the delivery of potentially toxic X-ray dyes.

Most important of all was that David was always good company, and that made it a pleasure to work with him. His other feats included the London-to-Sydney car rally, the Panama-to-Alaska rally, and many others. David raced cars, built boats, and fished for recreation. He had very skilled hands for working with all materials, from wood through plastics and metals. He once welded five VW Beatles together to make a vehicle for the charity-raising event of the WA Variety Club Bash in support of the Children's Hospital.

David had started as a radiographer in Royal Perth in the sixties and became the superintendent radiographer at RPH. Now with the changing trends in hospital management, from the networks of cooperative management to the accounting and business models, he was swamped with paperwork and entrusted with the task of making radiology business cases and budgets work.

He was one of four brothers and the son of a school headmaster with a strong socialist ethic. His father was a migrant from Britain who bestowed on his family principles of health, exercise, music, education, and forthrightness. David, if nothing else, was forthright. While his brothers had become very successful scientists, he had chosen radiography (for reasons I never understood). His brain was brilliant, his hands almost magical, and his hair red. There was a streak of defiance in David and the paperwork was frustrating him.

"How can you run a department in a socialist state system providing free health care for all at whatever cost in a capitalist country, where business models are based on growth and tax concessions?" he grumbled.

The state provided capped budgets, and there were no tax concessions because the state did not pay taxes. Additionally, there was a rule that equipment had to be bought and not leased because of the lack of tax minimisation incentive. David was in the typical Catch-22 situation all hospital managers found themselves in, where the incentive to have as few patients as possible was the most logical solution to be seen to be a good manager. The trick therefore was to make the department look busy and have just enough patients to justify its existence. The problem was that the radiology department had little or no control on the request for X-rays and was staffed by enthusiastic, diligent doctors who wanted to diagnose as many problems as they could. David's creativity was bursting out of its seams, but it was not directed towards accounting.

It was easy to interest David in helping us to turn our dreams into reality. He became an essential part of our little team, and we started exploring the possibility of developing an endoluminal program.

I learnt not to push David. The usual pattern was a suggestion by one of us, followed by a studious examination of the suggestion by David, a declaration that it would not work, and a presentation the next day of the answer, usually with a sample of the device. David's prototypes were invariably accompanied by a statement that "I think this will work, but there is a better way to do it." How to do it better was left in the air.

David's association with William Cook Australia was through his friend Geoff Reeves. Geoff was a West Australian who grew up in Northampton, a little town near the Coral Coast. This part of Western Australia is shored by coral islands, reefs, cliffs, and the wrecks of Dutch ships that had plied their trade to the East Indies in days gone by. There are famous stories about some of the infamous wrecks, as in the case of the Dutch ship the *Batavia*, which ran into the Abrolhos Islands; the survivors split into two groups and then had a war. Another was the *Gilt Dragon,* which crashed on the Zuytdorp cliffs near Shark Bay, scattering silver coins along the shore.

Geoff came from a wild, beautiful, and windswept landscape that he, like the Dutch, left behind for richer takings in more populated areas. He had worked for the American-based company Cook Inc. as a distributor of medical products out of an office in Melbourne. In the 1970s, the premier of the Queensland government, Joh Bjelke-Petersen, offered free land on the outskirts of Brisbane to people who would start up manufacturing businesses. Geoff discussed this with Bill Cook, the founder of Cook Inc. in Bloomington, Indiana, and took up the offer to move to Brisbane.

Geoff had a special relationship with Bill, who allowed him to set up William Cook Australia. Geoff then built an organisation manufacturing some Cook products in Australia; with his own initiative, he started manufacturing in vitro fertilisation (IVF) products for obstetrics. He also observed the burgeoning small animal vet market in Australia and made products for that. These were initiatives of his own and completely separate from the core business of the parent American company, which focused on the cardiovascular arena.

His success as an entrepreneur bought him some independence from the parent company, and he was able to explore the potential for medically related products. This was useful for David and RPH radiology, as they were able to have William Cook Australia make them special catheters, guide wires, and other useful implements for interventional radiology, especially for neuro-intervention, which was Turab's special interest.

Geoff was to be a key link in what followed in the next few years. It was fostered by Geoff's west coast origins, but to say he was wary of the wrecking reefs of the west coast would be an understatement. Geoff was all too aware of the dangers of new worlds, new ventures, and human reactions to disasters, as symbolised by the wreck of the *Batavia*, and he took much on his shoulders. There was no other company in Australia that we could have turned to, and again it was fortune and not intention that powered the endeavour.

From the inception of the disciplines, Bill Cook had been a pioneer catheter and wire maker for the fields of interventional radiology and interventional cardiology. He is purported to have started his large international company from his home garage and built it up to be worth billions of dollars. Bill must have remained sympathetic to home inventors, and between Geoff and Bill, they got to know many inventors, including David.

Important to us were Dotter, Gianturco, Lawrence, and Hal Coons. Bill Cook set up the Dotter Institute in the Oregon Health Services Department at the University of Portland. Cesare Gianturco had made a spring out of a stainless steel wire that he folded into a number of Zs and turned this into a circle by fusing the first and last strut of the Zs. He made, in effect, a self-expanding stent—a spring—that he thought would be useful in keeping large veins open. It was not initially intended for arteries, but in 1986, David Lawrence and Cesare Gianturco combined a Gianturco stent with a Dacron vascular graft, making a stent-graft, and tested it in the aorta of animals. It had the potential to be an arterial stent-graft, just what we needed, and to our great good fortune, it was a Cook product.

The original experiments by David Lawrence and Gianturco had been presented at the Radiological Society of North America (RSNA) meeting in Chicago in 1986. The RSNA was, and still is, the largest meeting of the health care industry in the world. This means that much was presented there, but much was missed too, as it was too large an event for anyone to hear it all. Pete had not missed the implications of Lawrence's experiments and Dotter's vision. We now had an opportunity to take it further and make the dream a reality.

The device that Juan Parodi had used was based on a very large Palmaz stent sewn onto a Dacron graft; the combination was mounted on a balloon to expand the stent. It was very strong but had no spring in it. We knew that we would not have access to an experimental large Palmaz stent made by Johnson & Johnson; that privilege was already taken. We would have access to Gianturco Z stents through Cook and any amount of vascular Dacron graft material from the discarded off-cuts from the operating theatre. Geoff would back us with making prototypes without charging us for materials or products that we wanted from his facility in Brisbane.

In December 1992, armed with plans and ideas, Pete and I again attended the annual RPA hospital seminar; this time, we were accompanied by David. This seminar focused our attention on access problems and stemming the bleeding from the large holes that needed to be made in the artery to enter the tunnels. We decided to proceed along the lines that had been started by Gianturco and Lawrence and make some devices that we could test in the animal laboratory. The answer to controlling the bleeding from large holes in the arteries was to come, believe or not, from Geoff's devices for egg harvesting in IVF: large tubes with self-sealing, airtight silicon disc valves.

There existed a belief that everything that was used to treat people should be tried and tested first in animals, but animal rights groups criticised this practice. While use of animal laboratory facilities was restricted and controlled, I could gain access because of past projects and a good relationship with the research facility. The problem was not the logistics of research or animal rights issues or Michele's abhorrence of such use of animals. The real issue was that no animal was suitable for what we wanted to do.

We knew that one of the problems we had to address was finding a secure way of attaching the stent-graft to the inside of the artery wall to prevent it being washed away. Until then, all technology had been directed towards what is called occlusive disease, where the problem was to treat a narrowing or blockage of the blood vessel. This could be likened, in an engineering sense, to tunnelling. Sometimes, it was sufficient to just make the passage, but other times, the wall had to be supported. The balloon may suffice sometimes, and sometimes the passage made by the dilating balloon needed to be supported by a stent.

With aneurysm disease, the physics was completely different. This was not tunnelling; this was bridge building. A bridge head needed to be established at each end of the gap, and the bridge had to be strong enough to withstand all forces that would be exerted on it. Bridges are usually built to withstand forces many times stronger than the worst-case scenario. Aircraft are built to withstand about three or four times worst-case scenarios because the engineers have to factor in excess weight. In building an endoluminal stent-graft, our problem was to reduce the size so that it could be passed up the artery from the groin when introducing the device and retain sufficient structural strength to resist disruption over the remainder of a lifetime. The stent-graft would have to maintain a strong new channel inside the weak-walled aneurysm. We had to minimise size and maximise strength and make something small enough to fit into seven millimetres, large enough to replace a tube of thirty millimetres, and strong enough to withstand the fatiguing motion and pressures in the aorta for at least ten years. And we could not afford to fail.

We decided to commit a surgical transgression and knew that to do so was going to precipitate strong criticism, if not censure. We chose to make an anchor for our Stent-Graft and have it hang by hooks, like a tapeworm. The part that was to precipitate a storm of reaction was that we intended to straddle the anchor across the origins of the renal arteries to the kidneys. The reasoning was that this is the strongest part of the aorta and the best place to lodge the anchor. The criticism would be that the wires crossing the entries to the renal arteries would affect blood flow or damage the integrity of the opening of these precious branches.

The main biological question we had to answer was whether the presence of the wires across the openings would form a latticework, upon which the lining cells of the aorta would grow across the orifice and seal the entrance. If blood flow to a kidney is restricted, the kidney releases renin, a substance that makes the body increase blood pressure to force more blood to the kidney. The added risk, therefore, was that we might cause an eventual blood starvation of the kidneys, increasing the blood pressure to dangerous levels. Our expectation from mathematical calculations was that a wire across the opening would have no more effect than a wide grid in the drain hole of the kitchen sink, about 6 percent reduction in cross-section area. We concluded that this would not compromise the flow to a kidney with a good artery. The biological response was the unknown here; we needed some proof that the insert would be safe.

Z stents were implanted in growing animals and positioned across the openings of major arteries using X-ray guidance, just as is done in people when stents are needed. The stents were passed up from the groin in a compressed state, inside a sheath, and then released by withdrawing the sheath and holding the stent in the desired position at the same time. Growing animals were chosen on the basis that the response with new growth that might seal the openings to the branches would be most vigorous. After six months, we found that the branches remained open and virtually unaffected by the presence of a wire across the orifice. We judged that the risks of not securing the anchor were much greater than any risk of blocking an artery.

In the beginning, we deemed it necessary to have stents only at the sites of each bridgehead, or landing zone, where the attached textile would need to sit tightly against the artery wall to keep the blood inside the new channel and not leak around the outside of the device. A rigid metal device can easily be held in position while withdrawing a compressing sheath by supporting it with a rod positioned inside the sheath behind the device. Not so with a textile that has no longitudinal support. How were we going to hold a floppy long Dacron tube in precise position during deployment?

David devised a rod with a shepherd's hook on the end that would hold the device by the leading end and another tag to hold the bottom end. These holds could be released when the graft was in position. We progressively added other stents along the textile to counter crumpling of the textile and resisting twists during insertion.

I then had a puzzling experience. Thinking that these new ideas of relining the inside of aneurysms were essentially sound and only needed further work on ensuring reliable delivery and secure attachment, I decided to treat a popliteal artery aneurysm this way at surgery. The artery behind the knee is the popliteal artery and can sometimes grow aneurysms; complications may cause loss of the leg. The operation to fix them incurs quite extensive surgery around or behind the knee joint, using a vascular graft to substitute for the artery. Vascular surgeons either use a synthetic textile or take a large vein that the body can do without and use it as an artery substitute. Instead of tying off the artery and sewing in a bypass graft, which is conventional, I passed a harvested vein down through the aneurysm behind the knee and then sewed the vein graft to the inside of the artery above and below. That is, I went through the aneurysm and relined it, instead of detouring around it.

The first time I did this, it was rewarding and surgically elegant. The second time, the vein graft kept collapsing inside the aneurysm, and I could not understand why. Surely, I thought, the blood pressure would keep the vein graft open when blood flow was restored. It should not collapse. Quite the opposite was happening. It should be held wide open by the blood pressure, but it was not. It was a bad feeling to have something not work and not to understand why, when everything tells you it should.

I redid the procedure. No change. The same thing happened again, and I could not understand why. I had to accept the failure that day and redo the operation in the conventional way. Then I visited John Anderson in Adelaide to watch how he treated a dissected aortic aneurysm. A dissected aorta is when the blood flow forces its way through the inner wall lining of the aorta—usually through a crack on a bend—and then the blood flows between the inner linings, called the intima, and the outer wall of the artery, called the adventitia. In this false passage, there is little or no outlet for the blood forcing its way in to escape. The pressure in this false lumen is maintained at or close to systolic pressure (the highest the blood pressure reached when the heart beats). When the blood runs away into the organs and limbs, the blood pressure will fall, and the heart valve closes on the main chamber of the heart, while the heart fills again from the filling chambers, getting ready to beat again. This is the diastolic phase.

Because there is little or no outlet for the blood being pumped into the false lumen, it means the pressure in the false lumen of the aorta is always as high as (or higher than) that in the true lumen of the aorta. The true lumen is compressed as a result, and flow is reduced or maybe even blocked. Inadequate blood flow in the true lumen or its branches carries the consequence of death or loss of limb or organ, including the arteries to the heart itself. The body below the problem responds by demanding more blood and sends messages to the control centre, the brain. The brain causes the blood pressure to rise higher and higher and makes the problem of compression of the true lumen by the false lumen worse and worse.

This was occasionally treated by making another opening at the end of the false passage to allow the flow back into the true lumen and relieve the compressing pressure. The theory sounded good, but the procedure did not always work and could be difficult, which is why I wanted to see how John did it. The most important thing I gained from the visit was that measurement of the pressures in the true and false lumens clearly confirmed the persistent dominant false lumen pressure. It was then that I realised that simply relining the inside of an aneurysm might fail if there was any flow and pressure around the inlaid tube. The inlay tube must be given extra support. That explained why my popliteal artery graft failed. David and I went back to our endoluminal stent-graft design and made sure that the whole thing was lined with spring-type stents that would create sufficient radial force and strength to resist contained pressure around the stent-graft, especially during diastole, when the pressure would be lowest.

Finding it impossible to make any headway trying our delivery systems in animals in the research laboratory, I asked David if it were possible to make an artificial model of an aneurysm on which we could try out various devices and methods. Our problems in the animal centre were that the X-ray equipment was an obsolete gift; we had not developed blood loss control strategies properly, the animal could only have one experiment performed by law, and if there were any problems (and there were always problems), then a week's research time was lost. Some animals died from too much anaesthetic or loss of blood before the end of the procedure, the operating table collapsed on one occasion, causing unspeakable havoc and mess, the delivery systems failed, people who were meant to help forgot or simply didn't turn up, and it was costing money we didn't have. In addition to all these problems, the animal anatomy was simply different from humans. What is the point, I wondered, in developing something for a pig that was no use for a human? It was like developing a small boat for a nice little river and then expecting the boat to sail the seven seas.

David made a model that was a work of art. He made a gelatine mould of a real aortic aneurysm and the arteries below it, as far as the groin. He laid this in a dish, which he progressively filled with polyurethane resin over days until the mould was covered. When the final layer of resin was cured, he melted out the gelatine. Then control valves were constructed by modifying those used for laparoscopic IVF egg harvesting supplied by Cook from air flow-valves to fluid-flow valves and fitted to each groin. Fluid to simulate blood was pumped in by a servo pump through the top of the model and out through a branch vessel. The whole thing was neat and clean, and it could be used multiple times in one session. Most importantly, since there was no animal contamination, it could be used under X-ray equipment in the radiology department. It was a wonderful toy; we called it Mr. Walker after the *Phantom* comic strip character (objects used under X-ray machines for testing and calibration are called phantoms). Mr. Walker also served the purpose of giving me space from distraction when people asked where I was. The honest reply was, "Oh, he is operating on Mr. Walker." This deterred any disturbance, whereas a reply that I was doing some research would be an invitation to interrupt.

Two things lasted long after Mr. Walker had served his purpose. The first was that the blood control valves became standard. The second was one of the most important decisions we ever made. It was also contrary to surgical practice and hence most controversial. We decided that with endoluminal grafting, good X-ray imaging was paramount and more important than theatre-standard sterility. We could take measures to compensate for the non-theatre sterility standard, but there was no way to compensate for the inability to see clearly what we were doing. In the 1990s, theatre-type mobile X-ray equipment was greatly inferior (if not positively dangerous from emitted radiation). To cap it all, the X-ray equipment would overheat and shut down because such X-ray equipment had never been used for this purpose before. Even in radiology, the more sophisticated machine would overheat on occasion. In operating theatres, it was the norm.

How much radiation the pioneers in operating theatres accumulated, we will never know because they didn't wear radiation counters. To have a radiation counter was routine for radiologists and cardiologists but not for surgeons. Pete was already banned from using the X-ray machine in main theatre by the radiation safety board because of the levels recorded on his counter in days before we even started on the endoluminal program. It was sometime before I acquired my radiation counter, and by then, I was using more modern equipment. I lost all the hair on my legs from the radiation and my hands never sweat.

This was a monumental decision that went against every other unit in the world attempting to develop endoluminal grafting of aneurysms. The problem was not just sterility; it was the administration of anaesthetic and the ability to convert immediately from the minimally invasive procedure to full open surgery. It was a measure of the importance we attributed to good imaging that it should be a priority. It could not have been done without my long-suffering anaesthetic colleague, Michael Hellings. Michael, who had supported me through the blood salvage years, was now called on to anaesthetise for periods in the semi-dark so we could see the X-ray screen more clearly; he was deprived of space and had to be prepared for blood loss and sudden emergency open surgery.

If we had a disaster, it could be the end of both our careers. When a death occurs on an operating table, the coroner and police attend immediately; nothing can be touched until they arrive. I could not bring myself to imagine such a scene. That it never happened in those developing years may have been fortuitous. There is no doubt that careful planning and good imaging enabled us to see any problems together with over-engineered safety features, which contributed to keep us safe. The type of confidence that I imagine Formula One racing drivers must have—that death will not be their lot—combined with reliable team strength were components that also served us well, but what made it possible to start was the courage and skill of Michael Hellings.

CHAPTER 23

The First Year of Endoluminal Stent-Grafting

1993 was the first year we tried endoluminal grafting in people, and it was almost a disaster. The project was probably lucky to survive. We have to thank the good standing of the departments, the faith placed in us, and the quality of the backup surgery that salvaged these failed attempts.

The first person we tried to treat was an elderly man whose aneurysm had leaked, which means it had bled a little into the surrounding tissue without torrential haemorrhage. He was in pain and not fit for an operation because of weak lungs and heart. We succeeded in placing a Stent-Graft and believed we had achieved what we set out to do; the patient survived the operation and went home. Being a new operation of a very special type, the hospital was keen to publish this in the press, but I declined on the grounds that we were not sure he was safe and were wary of making sensational claims. A few weeks later, I learned that the man had been readmitted to hospital with further leaking of his aneurysm. He was made comfortable and passed away.

We attempted to treat two other people who were deemed unfit for major surgery and needed aneurysm repair. We did not understand the mechanics involved and failed to deliver the stent-grafts satisfactorily. Despite having been pronounced unfit for surgery, we had crossed the Rubicon, and the die was cast. We had committed to treat and could not retreat in either of these cases. Surgery has been compared with a plane taking off; there is a point after which you cannot abort the take-off procedure. We were married to completing our commitment and did so: both these patients survived and were fixed by the transfer to the conventional operating theatre and conversion to open-wound surgery, despite the initial predictions of unfitness for such an operation.

At this stage, we decided that we should not continue with the program and it was halted, amidst profound disappointment.

A little while later, a colleague operated on a patient to revise an old vascular Dacron graft of the aorta. A few days after the operation, the patient had a heavy internal bleed from a tear in the suture line holding the graft to the artery. This created what is known as a false aneurysm. A false aneurysm is a bulge on an artery resulting from an injury; it has no true strong arterial wall and is contained only by the compressed tissue around it, like a big blood blister. It was too dangerous to operate on again, with the certainty that any attempt would precipitate uncontrollable haemorrhage. For him, we placed an endoluminal stent-graft across the rift in the suture line. The procedure was easy and cured the problem. We had been forced out of retirement, and the program was fortuitously redeemed. That year, we went again to the Sydney meeting in December with some experience and a lot of determination.

Up to this point, the only stent-grafts that had been used were simple, single straight tube structures. Mother Nature, or God the Father, did not make us with only a single tube; somehow, we had to devise an endoluminal stent-graft with branches. The end of the aorta divides into two branches called the iliac arteries, one for each lower limb. The iliac arteries in turn branch into the internal iliac artery for the organs in the pelvis and the external to go on to the limbs through the groin, where it becomes the femoral artery. The femoral artery is the most accessible large artery, as it is close to the surface; this is why the groin is the site of access to the arterial network. That is where the manhole is for the underskin network.

Aneurysms of the aorta most commonly occur in the segment between the branches to the kidneys and the end where it divides, called the infrarenal aorta. There is usually a short segment of aorta just below the renal arteries that is normal and serves to land the bridgehead for a stent-graft. Not so at the bottom end, and to attain this bridgehead, it is necessary to go on down into the iliac arteries. The problem, of course, with a straight tube is that you can only choose one of the iliac arteries. The initial answer to this problem was to indeed choose one iliac artery and block off the other, to make sure that blood did not flow back up into the aneurysm. Then a detour, or bypass, was made to give blood supply to the leg on the side that had been blocked off. The detour involved open-wound surgery and stitching a vascular graft from one groin to the other with a tunnel beneath the skin just above the pubes (in surgical terms, a femoro-femoral bypass).

One of the cardinal principles of surgery, however, is "Do not destroy normal anatomy." After all, the body evolved or was created that way and is the best there is. We wanted to secure a sound second bridgehead in the iliac arteries and maintain the shape of normal anatomy. This meant we needed an endoluminal graft like an inverted Y. We wanted to make a bifurcated endoluminal graft. Surgical vascular grafts came readymade, thanks to the pioneering work of Dr Michael DeBakey in Houston; they looked like a pair of trousers. There had to be a way, and we would find it.

We went to Sydney at the end of 1993, and so did Tim Chuter. I liked Tim and admired him for his ingenuity. He was an American from San Francisco and had cleverly used a trouser graft by folding one leg up inside a long waist of the trousers and then ingeniously devised a mechanism to go up the other side and pull the tucked-up trouser leg down into that side, thereby creating a new pair of trousers inside the aorta and both iliac arteries. Tim's accent was not purely American; he told me that he spent about ten years of his boyhood in Tanzania and that he was originally British. He had moved to New York after acquiring his basic medical degree in the UK. It was nice that we had something in common. He stimulated us and spurred our efforts to make a branched graft.

We tried to emulate Tim and made many pairs of trousers for Mr. Walker. While it worked sometimes, it often twisted. We did not find the system reliable; the pulled-down limb still needed support to avoid the potential to collapse, as described before. We reluctantly abandoned the idea, but not before we realised that going from a simple tube to a branched configuration entailed going from two dimensions into three dimensions, and the problems would be cubed rather than squared. We've been most mindful of that worthwhile lesson ever since. Whereas orientation of a simple tube was immaterial, orientation of a branched graft was critical.

One day, while pacing the corridor outside the X-ray theatre, waiting for a case to start that involved stenting a long segment of narrowed iliac artery, for which we would have to chain a number of stents together (one alone was of insufficient length to span across the whole length of the narrowed segment), I was struck by the thought that we could build branches into an endograft by chaining segments together. We frequently did it with stents for occlusive (narrowing) disease and knew it was very commonly done in heart arteries. If a pair of trousers was inserted into the aorta, with one long leg for the side from which the graft was inserted and one short leg to hang free in the aortic aneurysm, then we could come up the other side and insert a stent-graft into the short trouser leg and thereby down into the iliac artery on the opposite side from the long leg. We could make the trouser graft that way.

"No," said David. "It won't work. We won't know which side the short leg is when we deploy the device, and it will be too hard to get a wire into the short leg from the other side, especially if it pops out in an awkward position."

He was right; if it could not be done reliably, then it would be dangerous, and we'd be in no better position to trust it than we would be with Tim's idea. I felt deflated.

The next day, David came back and said, "There is probably a better way, but I have worked on the idea of one long leg and one short leg to be completed from the other side. I have something that I think will work. Here is a sample that we could try on Mr. Walker."

By this stage, we were using a great number of Gianturco stents. We had started by buying them from Cook Europe at six hundred dollars each. These, apart from being expensive, had hooks on them. This made them good as an anchor in the aorta, but we had to remove the barbs, which were not needed when we sewed them along the inside of the graft for the required radial force and support. David therefore started making our own Z-stents for about a dollar a pop by simply bending dental wire into Zs between two nails in a block of wood and then joining the ends to complete the circle by making a little sleeve that went over the end struts. This he strengthened with solder or a weld.

The result was that one strut in each constructed Z stent was more visible on X-ray. David, in making the stented trouser graft with one short and one long leg, had lined up all the visible struts down the side of the short leg. We would know exactly the position of the short leg and where it would deploy. We tried it on Mr. Walker, and he was fine.

Because Mr. Walker was made of resin, the aneurysm and iliac vessels could be seen clearly through the resin when a light was shone from behind him. At night and on weekends, I took Mr. Walker home with me, placed him on a glass coffee table in our living room, shone a light up from the floor, and used the new trouser graft to practise getting a guide wire into the short leg in every position on the clock. It was reliable. We had a branched, or bifurcated, stent-graft that would work. It was more bulky than a straight tube and would need a delivery system that provided the ability to turn the graft to the desired orientation. The iliac arteries take a spiral through the pelvis, and when the aorta dilates, it also lengthens, like blowing up a long party balloon. That could really put a twist into the iliac arteries; the orientation of the graft could be very different from the predicted position after passage through one of these tortuous vessels.

Placing a device inside the body from a remote access site demands control of the device until a desired step is executed. In some ways, it was like controlling a spacecraft from Earth. We were worried about losing control and precipitating an emergency surgery operation in a patient who was having an endoluminal stent-graft for the very reason that they weren't good candidates for surgery. Emergency surgery is generally more risky than a planned elective procedure, and converting from a minimally invasive approach to an invasive operation was akin to changing horses in midtorrent.

At this stage, we had failed and had to convert on the two occasions mentioned above, but we had not killed anybody, and we had saved some from certain death. I was most conscious that if someone died because the procedure went wrong, the idea would be sent to the Library for Failed Ideas. The whole concept of endoluminal grafting was at stake, and there were many vascular surgeons who had already condemned the concept as a failed experiment. We felt we could not afford to fail, and yet the only people to whom we could offer the treatment were those perceived as unable to withstand conventional surgery. This type of procedure was more stressful on the operator than for the patient. To insure against mishap, we had multiple safety steps. If we faced a major criticism, it was that the delivery system was over-engineered and there were too many safety triggers to prevent premature deployment. That criticism, we were happy to shoulder.

To ensure we had control, David devised a system whereby the anchor stent with the hooks would be contained in a cap until we were satisfied with orientation and successful entry and positioning of the wire that would carry the extension into the short leg from the other side. The cap could only be released by removing a safety catch. The bottom of the long leg was also held by another safety catch so that we would always have control at both ends. The delivery system and mounting of the grafts in the delivery system was a work in evolution and improved all the time. Mr. Walker withstood the operation many times and instilled in us a feeling of confidence, and we remain grateful to him for that. There came a time when we were ready to show the world.

Up until then, Geoff Reeves, who was the managing director of William Cook Australia, had supported us from a distance in Brisbane, on the other side of the continent. He was a personal friend of David's, but I had not met him. David invited Geoff over to the west, and we had a meeting over a barbecue in David's backyard. Geoff threw his hat in the ring and said that from here on, it was a joint project. He would supply all the products we needed and pay expenses. We would make prototypes, and he would supply Stent-Grafts sterilised in proper facilities in Brisbane. Geoff had always wanted to tap deeper into David's talents, and David resigned his position as superintendent of radiology (he was employed part-time by Cook Australia and part-time by the cardiovascular division in the hospital). David was going to devote himself full time to this project. Being part of Cook had procurement advantages for the project and tax advantages for Cook. The Australian government had a scheme to stimulate research and development. The rules were that if a research and development arm of a company was seen to be separate from the manufacturing arm, then all expenses in research would be 150 percent deductible.

It clearly suited Geoff Reeves to have the research and development in Perth and the manufacturing in Brisbane. It was agreed that the hospital would have Stent-Grafts made free of charge, as long as it was involved in the development and test arena. Being partly employed by the vascular department meant that David still had access to all areas and facilities in the hospital. David provided the yoke between company and hospital.

CHAPTER 24

The H&LB Endograft

In August 1994, Mr. P was the first person to receive a bifurcated endograft. The operation went just as we had hoped, and we felt that we really had something to offer this new era of vascular surgical-radiological intervention. I invited Geoff White, now a leader in this field in Sydney University and Royal Prince Alfred Hospital, to be our guest speaker at our state conference later that year. After the conference, he joined us in Royal Perth for a day devoted to aortic aneurysm disease and endoluminal grafting. At a dinner that evening by the water on the banks of the Swan River, Geoff congratulated us on our achievement, welcomed us to the world of endovascular surgery, and invited us to run a workshop and present our stent-graft experience in December at the Sydney meeting.

The little in-hospital meeting had outgrown its parent venue of Royal Prince Alfred Hospital and become an international attraction. Geoff White had a large network of American colleagues from the time he had spent in the United States. Many of them joined with Europeans, Australians, New Zealanders, and our colleagues from South East Asian nations in what was to become the premiere meeting for aortic endoluminal grafting. The venue that year was the All Nippon Airlines Hotel, across from the Sydney Opera House.

By December, we had treated six people with the Perth Bifurcated Endoluminal Graft and attended the meeting with our manuscript, ready to announce to the new vascular world what we had achieved. Geoff and Ted Dietrich from Phoenix were forming a group called the International Society of Endovascular Surgeons. I could join, and if I presented at the meeting in Sydney, the manuscript would be eligible for publication in a brand-new publication: the *Journal of Endovascular Surgery*.

The workshop was for people attending the conference to look at the new ideas in this exciting field of endeavour. It was held the day before, and we shared our room with Dr Michael Dake of Stanford University in California, who had teamed with the Dotter Institute in Oregon to make grafts to treat the thoracic aorta in the chest. His device was a tube constructed similarly to ours; his was also based on a combination of Gianturco stents and Dacron vascular graft material. I had not realised that Cook was involved in this new venture to develop a commercially available stent-graft, but I was not surprised, since they made the Gianturco stents and sponsored the Dotter Institute. It was an exhilarating experience, and I could hardly wait to present our work to the audience the next day.

You cannot imagine how I felt when walking through the trade exhibition towards the auditorium to see an endograft very much like ours on display in a small booth. Claude Mialhe, a French surgeon, had come up with the same ideas and implanted a number that year. There were, of course, differences in design, materials, and delivery systems, but the basic concept of the trousers with one short leg and one long was the same. Claude had even started a company, MinTec, to market his invention. Claude had a different delivery system and was using the memory metal nitinol instead of stainless steel; he also used a different textile. The modular concept with introduction from both groins was the same. I was stunned.

A Scottish company called Vascutek had been formed a few years before to make Dacron vascular grafts in the UK to compete with those made in the United States. There were two rival companies in America. Meadox produced the grafts originally designed by Dr Michael DeBakey, and a company called USCI made similar Dacron grafts based on the design by Dr Denton Cooley. DeBakey and Cooley both worked in Houston but were rivals.

The competition in the Dacron market had been quite fierce, and the Scottish company had made inroads. They wanted to supply grafts to RPH, and I agreed to have a meeting with their research and development representative, Stuart Rodger, while in Sydney. Stuart was interested in our Stent-Graft device and encouraging. He said he would look into helping us to make the stent-graft and could certainly supply the Dacron, but he was concerned about patent issues and his ability to use the Gianturco stent technology.

A new era was dawning in an old world of business and patent laws, and this was my first experience with them. I was unofficially supported by William Cook Australia, a subsidiary of Cook Inc., an American firm. Our foundations for the project were therefore a gentleman's agreement based on a historical friendship, an unfunded development program in a state hospital based on good network cooperation, and an interested but wary Scottish company.

The prospect of future cooperation with Vascutek was enhanced by another coincidence: the manager of the manufacturing was of East African Asian decent and went to the same school in Nairobi as I had.

Amid the energy waves of this conference, driven by a storm of intense interest in what was recognised as a quantum leap in vascular therapy, a very encouraging thing happened. After my presentation, Dr Frank Veith, who ran the largest international vascular conference in New York, introduced himself and complimented me on the presentation. I knew of Frank because of the reputation of his annual symposium. Marcel had attended some of these over the years, and I often wished I could go to one, and I would have, if they weren't so expensive.

Frank Veith had made his own special graft that he used for treating aneurysms and was interested in the valves we had developed to introduce sheaths to control bleeding. David and I arranged to send him some samples to New York, and in return, he read our manuscript for the journal, returning a favourable opinion.

John Anderson also spoke at the Sydney conference; it was good to see him making his mark nationally as a leader in the endovascular field. John was a consummate technician as an open-wound surgeon and an endovascular surgeon. His wire and catheter skills were clearly far beyond the expectations of his colleagues. He had emerged as a champion for viewing vascular surgeons as endovascular specialists beyond the confines of conventional open-wound surgery. John was provocative, with a background of military training in Duntroon, which is Australia's Defence Force Officer Training Institution. He had qualities of strength of purpose, conviction that what he was doing was right, and a tough Glasgow background with a jutting jaw to match.

While I had progressed with my own catheter lab in private practice and had reasonable catheter and wire skills, they did not compare with John's. I did not have his confidence or the recognition he had achieved. Instead, I had a team behind me and David's friendship and ingenuity to give strength, achieve visions, and fulfil promises for the future. The Sydney meeting made me realise that I needed a champion in the cauldron of competition; this was going to be a race in the Hippodrome of medicine, with chariots from the countries of vascular surgery, cardiology, interventional radiology, interventional neuroradiology, interventional angiology, and government regulators. As John and I were already friends through our involvement with other interventions for arterial occluding disease, and we were nonradiologists performing angiography, with interventions using catheters, guide wires, balloons, and stents, it was natural that we would get together at meetings. This time in Sydney, I asked him if we could include him in our team as a test pilot for the next year; he was not one to avoid a challenge.

Then came a blow. Pete Kelsey was made a tempting offer to join a private radiology company in Perth and work in their magnetic resonance imaging section. Pete, with his eye always on the future, had made MRI another interest. The offer was too good to refuse, and the hospital would not contemplate him changing from full-time to part-time just to work with me and David. Ever considerate, Pete organised for another radiologist called Jay Ives, who had trained in North America and had excellent skills, to take his place on the team. Jay had a desire to change over from working with the neuro-intervention team to working with me on our project. Jay's experience and training for the highly specialised neuro-intervention meant that he had great skills, and it was considered that his knowledge and expertise in basic vascular radiological intervention would fit with our new treatments for the aorta. He settled in very quickly. Jay and I have remained friends ever since.

Despite at least six years work with Pete, I was not allowed to work in my own right in the X-ray theatre. I needed Jay in order to continue working with the imaging facilities in radiology, but he also had MRI knowledge and had been in charge of the MRI service at RPH from its inception; after a relatively short period, he was made a tempting offer too good to refuse by the rival X-ray company in Perth. Like Pete, Jay was not permitted to stay and work with me part-time. The instability in partnerships unsettled me and made me realise how dependent I was on other disciplines and how vulnerable to denial of access to imaging, which was essential. If the endovascular program was to endure, I needed access to imaging for operations in my own right, as I had in the private hospital. I also needed a stable, skilful clinical partner in the endovascular field with his own facilities; my relationship with John Anderson strengthened as a result.

Marcel and Frank, my surgical colleagues, could not have been more supportive and joined in the endoluminal session with the radiology department; this was welcomed and essential for the project, but it posed a logistical problem because it changed the pattern of behaviour and how one group perceived the other. If I were to be given rights to use a theatre in the X-ray department, then it was feared by the radiology administration that Marcel and Frank would also seek such rights, and radiology would be swamped with surgeons. It was agreed that vascular would build its own X-ray theatre in time, and in the meantime, the endoluminal grafting sessions and my other endovascular work would continue under a joint arrangement with a radiologist.

When Jay was going to leave, he offered to come back part-time just to keep the project going. He was told, just as Pete had been, it had to be all or nothing. This was the first hint that things in the future were not going to be as closely knit as when Pete and I started. It was hoped that a young talented radiologist called Andrew Holden might take over. Andrew taught me that "the enemy of good is better" and then went to better pastures in Auckland. Instead of Jay, a very good training radiologist, Greg Van Schie, also originally from New Zealand, was promoted to vascular radiologist. We were all elevated because Greg was nearly seven feet tall. Little David McClure, the vascular trainee, was only slightly more than five feet tall and literally had to stand on a box when working with Greg. Before Greg, we might have occasionally gazed upwards seeking guidance from above; we now started to develop permanent cricks in our necks.

With this degree of turnover of the team members from radiology, I was glad of the backup from John Anderson; I took out specialist registration in South Australia in order to work with him legally whenever I wanted. Even though surgeons in different states had the same training and were fellows of the same college, who took the same examinations, it was necessary to register separately in every state if we wanted to work together; my list of registrations was starting to match my growing publication record. For the time being, I knew that all would be well while Turab was still in charge of radiology, but my childhood instincts prepared the back door for any danger ahead.

Spurred on by our experience, we laid plans. I was aware that because we could make something work in our team in Perth, it did not mean that it could work in a less supportive environment. Perth had the advantage of seclusion. We were the most isolated city in the world by distance, and it almost needed a life-savings to afford travel out of the state. The compensations were encased in cooperative expertise and relative freedom from undermining professional jealousies. This was our plan: If we developed something, we would test it in Perth until satisfied and then get John to test it in Adelaide, with David and me there to support him. Then we could return to Perth with his suggestions and modify accordingly, retest, and when satisfied, get John's opinion again; a Deming quality improvement cycle, in effect.

For example, driven by attention to keep the device sterile for implantation, the initial method was to load the sterilised device into the delivery system on the operating table in the X-ray theatre at the beginning of the procedure. The anchor stent had to be loaded very carefully because of its sharp exposed hooks. The first time John did this, he pricked at least three of his fingers, shedding his own blood on the graft during loading. He nursed his magic fingers, declined to try again with another Stent-Graft and delivery system, and washed his hands, literally and metaphorically, of any further attempts to load grafts. Fortunately, we had brought backup Stent-Grafts and loaded one for him, or he would have abandoned the operation and the plan to work together while it was still in the gestation period.

David developed a cartridge in which was loaded the premade Stent-Graft, with the anchor stent and its hooks all safely sheathed. The cartridge was sterilised and ready to fit into the delivery sheath, and then the Stent-Graft was railroaded from the cartridge into the sheath and into the aorta on a stiff wire. All from the groin. The cartridge came complete with its own valve and fitted perfectly into the valve of the sheath. It worked well, and John was still our champion.

John's pathway to his own catheter lab was similar to mine. He started in the Queen Elizabeth Hospital in Adelaide, another state hospital with a Royal reference to the British Empire. He teamed with a radiology colleague because he wanted to acquire the skills for angioplasty in the peripheral arterial system and needed access to the facilities. He had also been stimulated by the experience of witnessing angioplasty during a period of training at Stanford University in the States and saw the benefits of adding these skills to his armamentarium. The Ashford Private Hospital had allowed him to use their cardiology catheter lab in return for vascular services to the Ashford Hospital. The cardiologists were supportive because a vascular surgeon could back them should they ever have a complication.

There was one important difference between John's experience and mine. John was ostracised by some of his own vascular colleagues. His colleagues perceived that he was performing angiography and angioplasty by self-referral and offering a service they could not. They decided he was breaking Medicare laws and had him investigated by the government Medicare Department for over-servicing. He was exonerated by Medicare investigators but withdrew into his private practice with a bitter taste in his mouth and a determination to develop skills beyond any other, and he did. A few years later, a colleague in Britain, where vascular surgeons did not have the opportunities that we did, once described him as "the vascular surgeon who became an interventional radiologist." That may be true, but not by examination, and he continued to be a skilled operator through an open wound, and his patients loved him. Nor was John backward in coming forward in recounting stories of his skills. He became an international champion. At a conference in Shanghai many years later, it brought tears to my eyes to witness hundreds of Chinese delegates give him a rousing ovation as his name was announced and he headed for the podium to speak. I've attended meetings on every continent and never seen such a thing at a medical conference. Applause was common after a good informative talk, but unheard of before. John became a veritable vascular pop star.

The immediate consequence of John's isolation in Adelaide was that he was hungry for peer contact. Whenever I went to Adelaide to support a case or learn a skill, he would have me stay at his home. Adelaide is two and a half hours ahead on the clock in summer time and three and a half hours in flight time from Perth. John immediately extended the invitation to David when we joined forces to develop Stent-Grafts for aortic aneurysms.

We would stay up discussing skills, surgery, and devices until two o'clock in the morning and then work through his list the next day in the X-ray theatre. The work would extend until almost midnight on occasions. We never seemed to tire, driven as we were by enthusiasm, success, and wonder at what could be achieved with wires, catheters, stents, balloons, stent-grafts, and numerous ancillary devices, such as snares, cutting balloons with little razor blades attached, coils, and suction apparatus. Fuelled by coffee and Chinese takeaway, we were almost reluctant to go home at the end of sixteen hours. Shifts of nurses, anaesthetists, and radiographers changed seamlessly through the day and night. By simulator standards, we could not have done it and should have fallen asleep or become incompetent, but simulators do not pump adrenalin, nor do they give such elation that thrills with real-time achievement.

We could do in one day what would take a week with open-wound surgery. We were as tireless as Halstead was purported to be on cocaine, but we had only the elixir of endless rewards.

We did not lose sight of the ultimate reward: the relief of symptoms in the patients or the protection of their lives. To say there were no disappointments or failures would be blindness to the truth, but the overall tally was much in favour of the benefits, and without the pain and problems that go with open wounds.

For John, the impaired cognitive effects of Alzheimer's disease became tragically apparent in his mid-sixties. He exhibited the first major loss of memory in front of more than a thousand delegates during a presentation at his last Veith meeting in New York. Amongst all those doctors, not one perceived the problem. I was not present at this meeting and heard on the grapevine that people had noticed subtle changes at work, despite his ability to still repair arteries superbly. It is the recent memory loss that disappears first because the cerebral step to file the data is lost, leaving previously learned things intact, at least for a while.

I wished it away, but no willing would change the inevitable. He came across to Perth and was reinvestigated because I could not believe the diagnosis and because he had successful treatment in Perth a few years before by Turab's team for an arterio-venous malformation in his head. I wondered if that might be related.

It was not, and the scans of his brain showed that it was shrinking. It was like his racing brain, fuelled by caffeine and starved of sleep, was burning up. His drifting away and the tyranny of distance between us meant that I could not even provide the daily companionship I wanted to share with him in his hour of need. I also could not help Marie, who was steadfast in her support of him. This was another of the silent unhappy moments in my life. It was also a poignant realisation of my own vulnerability, being only one year younger, and how friends and colleagues can seemingly abandon the troubled because they don't know how to deal with the tragedy themselves.

The pioneers of the endovascular revolution will remember him as one of the greatest and for the training and skills he passed on, and it's best that way. A sad feature that paralleled John's movement along the Alzheimer's pathway was the atmosphere created by the competitive nature of the evolving technology and the skill sets that went with it. I am reminded of the quotation from the French Revolution by Duc de la Rochefoucauld: "We are not always displeased by the misfortunes of our best friends." In Australia, it's called the tall poppy syndrome; the nature of its history is to push them up in order to tear them down. We do it to cricket captains repeatedly. For me, he will always be the most skilful surgeon for complex endovascular aortic repair; he lived more than a hundred work-years of any other surgeon.

The manuscript we submitted to the Sydney meeting was rejected by the journal's peer review team. That was a disappointment. The comments and opinions expressed by the reviewers must be taken seriously by the editor; otherwise, the process of peer review amounts to nothing. I accepted the rejection without rebuttal. To say I did not have dark feelings about the reviewers would be too kind, and I suspected one surgeon I met later in the UK of being the reviewer who had been the most scathing. He was way ahead of his time in bringing the skills of catheters and wires to vascular surgeons and had built the first endovascular theatre in the world. It had the latest X-ray equipment and lots of space and an operating table for open surgery, as well. It was a special-purpose built theatre and honoured by the Duke of Edinburgh, who ceremoniously opened it.

I went to Scotland especially to see it because of the intent to build one in Perth and also to visit Vascutek, the graft manufacturers whose headquarters and factory were in Glasgow. The surgeon in the Glasgow Infirmary was extremely helpful and gave me a copy of the plans to use as an example for one to be built in Royal Perth. He was an excellent surgeon and worked well with an interventional radiologist in the endovascular theatre.

It was with the deepest regret that I witnessed open-wound surgery for an aneurysm for a patient with a colostomy that had been made as part of cancer surgery. He was going to close the colostomy, restore the function of the bowel, and repair the aneurysm during the same operation. It was an ideal case for an endoluminal graft. I realised that he did not support the one thing that was going to be the catalyst for vascular surgeons to get aboard the train in the dawn of the new era. He had the train in the station in his new theatre, opened by the Duke of Edinburgh, but he had missed it. The rejection of our paper was a minor misfortune by comparison. It took two years to get our paper published after the first rejection, and it was not in the *Journal of Endovascular Surgery*. I took it as an omen to keep working out of the limelight.

Strange, that the influence of the grapevine was stronger than the printed word. I was taught that if the work was not published, it hadn't been done, but here I was, receiving requests by young surgeons to train with us and learn endovascular surgery. The young sustain us, and never has it been more true than in those early days of developing Stent-Grafts. There is more than one young surgeon who burnt his career chances in surgery by becoming so interested in developing stent-grafts that they neglected to complete their conventional surgery training and qualify to sit the fellowship exams. And there is more than one senior surgeon who failed to guide their protégé into the right path and selfishly (or unthinkingly) used him or her for their own dedicated support. This was going to be a tough field, and there were clearly going to be career casualties. The fortitude from all the past battles to establish vascular surgery as an independent specialty in Royal Perth Hospital and the strength of the alliance with radiology and hospital administration were going to be sorely tested to meet the challenges already present and those looming darker on the horizon.

A young surgeon, Shane MacSweeney, came to work with us from the UK, and we learned of the work of Brian Hopkinson, who was also developing an endovascular graft. Hopkinson's graft was along a slightly different pathway; he was at the forefront of developing the method of taking a straight tube to one side and blocking off one iliac artery. His graft was again a combination of Gianturco stents and Dacron. Shane was to take up a consultant post with Brian as soon as he finished with us in Perth. He was very keen and helped us resubmit an updated version of our original paper. Shane was big and strong but a little in awe of his New Zealand counterpart, Malcolm Gordon, who was also with us for the year and whose hobby in New Zealand was hunting wild boars with pig dogs and a knife. There are very few surgeons that can dissect with a knife, and Malcolm was one of them. Most surgeons use scissors and forceps. Malcolm used a scalpel like a wand.

Brian was supported by Waquar Yusuf, a very talented training surgeon. Waquar is the only trainee I know who was invited as a guest speaker to Australia while still a trainee. He had already written a textbook on stent-grafting for aneurysms and was an example of the budding surgeon way ahead of his time in a field yet to be accepted and in danger of never qualifying.

Then a young Irishman, Tom Browne, came to work with us. His ideas on how to accommodate major branches into the stent-grafts, by making holes in the graft and then proving the concept, was the first step in the fenestrated graft. During that year, together, we explored ways of guiding the positioning of the hole over the opening into the vessel to be preserved by using a catheter or angioplasty balloon, threaded out through the hole and into the branch artery. We called the holes windows and then added finesse by changing this to fenestrations.

These four were among the many young who inspired us. The names of countless soldiers are inscribed on the forgotten memorials beneath the statues of the generals who fought wars for God and country, yet we respect the tomb of the Unknown Soldier most of all. Many of the young surgeons and radiologists of this era are the unknown soldiers of the vascular revolution, for which this maybe the only tome.

There were young radiologists, cardiologists, and cardiothoracic surgeons who also became involved. We developed a close relationship with a radiologist called Richard McWilliams, who worked with Peter Harris in Liverpool hospital in the UK. Richard came to Perth with another idea: to make branches into stent-grafts in the arch of the aorta. His idea was to enter the artery that goes to the arm, the brachial artery, and use a sharp pointed wire in a protective plastic catheter taken back up the arm artery until it rested on the stent-graft in the aorta, and then pierce the fabric, boring a hole through which was inserted a cutting balloon. The branch was completed by deploying a small stent-graft from the hole to the arm artery. This we called a retrograde fenestration. After the experimental work in Perth, he treated a patient in Liverpool, successfully restoring blood flow to the left arm; he presented his work at the following Veith meeting in New York.

Another was Kishore Sieunarine, who was by then an advanced trainee in vascular surgery in the ANZSVS. He had gone to Sydney for the year to work in Royal Prince Alfred Hospital, and that was why Shane was able to join us. The professor in Sydney was John Harris; he headed the unit in which Jim May and Geoff White worked. He agreed to take Kishore for the year so that he could complete the requirement for trainees to get experience outside their mother hospital.

Until Kishore went across to Sydney for his term in further training, David, Kishore, and I worked in a little room in the X-ray department to sew Dacron graft material on to the stents that David made. The workload was piling up, and with Kishore away, it was decided we needed more infrastructure help. A sewer is what we needed. The sewer would need to have some understanding of what we were doing; David was very particular about delegating critical tasks. Dacron graft material came in a crimped form that held it open like a ringed tube. This made it difficult to cut to the exact required length because it would stretch by three times when pressurised or pulled out to length, and then it would spring back when released. We learned to iron out the crimps and cut our cloth to length. Sewing the stents that were really springs could be fun too because they had to have a diameter greater than the textile to ensure the radial force. Holding a spring in a compressed form while trying to sew it to a cloth tube carried the risk of it jumping out of the hand and across the room. In the beginning, until we learnt the techniques, it was like working in a room full of frogs.

The Stent-Graft, expanded to full size, would be up around thirty millimetres in diameter, and the loaded device measured only six or seven millimetres in diameter. We constantly worked on reducing the size` of the delivery systems but refused to compromise on strength, knowing that these devices would need to last for at least ten years, as was the case with the conventional surgery of the time; that had to be our yardstick. The sewer would also have to understand about the loading. A decision was made that we needed a dedicated sewer as a priority, but we knew it needed to be a special person.

David wondered whether a Vietnamese migrant seamstress would be most suitable because of their reputation for fine work. I was still worried about the potential for criticism of our sterility measures in the stent-graft construction. Sue Morriss was the head vascular theatre nurse; she always supported our program and never complained when she had to arrange nursing teams and instruments to work in X-ray theatre. I knew she had a hobby of sewing from hearing her talk about it with other people. If Sue was interested, she would be above criticism for surgical sterile technique. She turned out to be keen to give up her job in theatre to sew for the program full-time. It was arranged, and that freed up David and the rest of us for other things. The hospital gave us space in another building, and Sue was set up in a clean room with an air pressure cabinet, paper hats, gloves, and masks, as in an operating room, with special measures to guard against infection.

Our progress was steady, and our reputation was growing (although it hardly matched that of Sydney and the unit in Royal Prince Alfred). The Sydney meeting in December that year, 1995, attracted so many from so many different countries that it was truly an international meeting. Tim Chuter came, and we got to know him better. It was held in the new convention centre in the redeveloped Sydney Darling Harbour complex. We were again invited to show the Perth Graft, by this stage called the H and LB Endograft, at a workshop and present a paper in the auditorium. We had problems that year because the time in the workshop was taken up by an entrepreneur with a company called World Medical, presenting a new form of tube graft.

Then our sample device, its delivery system, and assembly manuals that had been meticulously prepared by David were stolen. We had arranged to pass them on to John Anderson after the workshop so he could take them home to examine and give us feedback. John placed them all on a table while he spoke with someone asking questions, and when he turned to pick them up, they were gone. He reported to the police for the record. We never found out who stole them and returned to Perth somewhat sadder and wiser.

However, our progress had been noted, and we received invitations to speak at conferences in Europe and the United States. The first of these was Ted Dietrich's meeting in Phoenix, Arizona, in February. I had never been to America and was most excited. To make sure that we were recovered from the jet lag and allow time for Geoff Reeves to introduce us to the executives of the parent Cook Inc., we arrived a couple of days early. We were not yet that important, but Geoff arranged to pay our expenses.

We stayed at a tidy small hotel, and at breakfast, a young man introduced himself as a surgeon from Sweden and asked if he could join David and me for company. His name was Martin Malina. It was a Sunday, and we wondered what we could do for the day in the way of sightseeing. We asked a friendly waitress, and she suggested we hire a car and drive up to the Grand Canyon. At the car hire venue, we inquired about the cheapest car for rent. It turned out to be only slightly less than a Cadillac, so we hired a limo and started out in style, with room to spare.

"My boss is staying in another hotel," Martin said. "May I ask him if he'd like to come along? He talks a lot, but he's a nice guy."

"Sure," we replied. "The more the merrier."

Krassi was the boss's name, and he was obviously more important than we were, judging by the size of his hotel.

Krassi didn't look Swedish; he was short, dark-haired, and square like a Mediterranean weightlifter. As we got to know him and could ask the odd question (when he stopped for breath), we learned that he indeed was originally Bulgarian. Krassi was from a privileged background; his father had been a government official in the Communist Party, but he had fled the Bulgarian communist system and ended up a refugee in Sweden. His full name was Krasnodar Ivancev, so named Krasnodar because of his father's admiration for Russia. Life was certainly getting interesting, and the trip to the Grand Canyon was a memorable long day. I remember still being a little jet lagged, dozing off on the way back to the dulcet tones of Krasnodar in the comfortable Cadillac.

The next morning, we were ready for our big day. The conference was starting at the Phoenician Resort, a mid-morning meeting was arranged with Cook, and I was speaking after lunch. I was nervous at breakfast and barely paid attention to the others, until the friendly waitress asked us what we thought of the Grand Canyon.

"Oh, it was nothing," said Martin. "We have hundreds of them in Sweden."

Geoff had not told us that the Cook parent company may not want us involved with Stent-Graft projects under their flag. I guess he didn't want to deflate us before the meeting. Their position soon became apparent. David and I were seated at one end of a long table with our device to show and demonstrate deployment of the loaded prosthesis, and the executives were at the other end. The bowl of flowers that should have been in the middle was missing. We were waiting for Tim Chuter, and I learned that Cook already had stables with Tim in San Francisco, Krassi in Sweden in Malmo, and Brian Hopkinson in Nottingham. Brian, as the professor in Nottingham, had supervised Tim when he wrote his doctorate at Nottingham University. Tim had graduated from medical school there. He had also done some training in Malmo, and there were therefore links between the other three stables. While the other stables were linked, we, like Perth, were isolated. The outcome of the meeting was surprisingly positive, and of the devices shown, the Perth device, thanks to David's engineering skills, was clearly the most professional, that is to say, it looked the least homemade.

My talk included a short segment on the potential dangers and failure modes of stent-grafts. I showed the microscopic appearance of a fatigue fracture on the stump of a hook we found sheared off in a graft that we retrieved at post-mortem for an unrelated death. Then I showed X-rays of sheared-off hooks in the living. My intent was to demonstrate the power and fatigue factors associated with the placing of stent-grafts in the aortic environment. I thought it was a good talk.

Geoff White was chairing the session and asked if anybody else on the panel of speakers had any experience with broken hooks and elicited a solemn choreographed shake of heads.

The fact that the grafts they were using did not have any hooks was by the way and completely lost on the audience. I should have pointed out that if they had no hooks, they would not see any fractures, but I was still inexperienced in the art of being on a panel.

I have a hiking friend who snores loudly and from whom we seek as much distance as possible when the campsite is small. He justifies his snoring on the grounds that it keeps the lions away.

"Did you see any lions last night?" he asks when anyone mentions the snore word.

"No," we say with solemn shakes of our weary heads.

"You see? You should be grateful that I snore" (there are no lions in Australia).

Now here was a dilemma. As an independent doctor who considered it his duty to report the findings of research honestly, was I clashing with commercial interests? There was already a view in Britain and Australia that doctors should not receive support from companies for research and development because it would compromise the integrity of the researcher and corrupt the results. Here was another dilemma that idealists fail to recognise: If the people in commercial companies didn't support development initiatives, who would? It was a minefield. While we had received material support for the project and accepted the expenses paid for the presentation of development work, I had never received any personal payment. Clearly, we were starting to be leaders in the field, and if I didn't pay attention to problems and look down the track to warn others by imparting information, it was not just our project that would be scrapped; the whole concept of endoluminal grafting for aneurysms was at risk.

Geoff Reeves said he was going on to Bloomington to stay with Bill Cook for a few days and assured us that there were no problems. Geoff advised that we go back to Australia and get on with it quietly in Perth. I was beginning to learn how small Australia was and how big America was.

Well, no directive to shut down came. Instead, there were invitations to travel and speak at other venues. Roger Greenhalgh wanted to visit us; we had a pleasant few days together when he stayed in my home and spent time in the theatre. He invited me to present at his meeting in Charing Cross Hospital in London, another in-hospital meeting, like the Royal Prince Alfred Hospital, that grew into an international meeting and the premiere vascular conference for the UK. Here was a chance to visit Brian Hopkinson in Nottingham. The invitation came with a price tag and a reward. The price was that I would have to write a chapter for the book Roger had started to put out at each meeting; the reward was that expenses would be covered, and we would be introduced to Europe.

David and I travelled to Nottingham via Marseilles, where we attended another meeting, and this time, Geoff Reeves came with us. In Marseilles, we stayed in the most expensive hotel I had ever experienced, where the price of one beer would have a bought me a whole meal with wine in the venues I was more used to. The tip was almost a wage. Geoff was joined by his counterpart from the UK, who drank like a fish and left Geoff with the bill and a grin, saying, "That's one up for the Poms."

Stanley visited me while I was in Marseilles. He had been travelling as a young Aussie through Europe and had a job on the ski fields in Austria. It was so good to see him. He turned up late at night, tanned, fit, and happy with the news that he had met the girl he was going to marry. Marseilles was now special for me, and we had evenings by the beaches and meals in restaurants up little coves, with white cliffs bathed in the moonlight around us and a view over the shimmering water. There were stresses and strains in this new era of vascular surgery, but there were also moments of pure delight.

We received a good welcome in Nottingham and joined Brian Hopkinson in theatre with his radiology colleague, Simon Whittaker, and Waquar feeding them with the bits and pieces for their Stent-Graft. Then, as planned, they inserted a Perth bifurcated graft. Their skills were evident as they weaved their way through problems, and I gained first-hand knowledge of how fortunate I had been to have access to high-quality imaging. I could hardly make out markers and positioning of the graft during its delivery and deployment in the images on the theatre's overheated mobile X-ray machine. I was amazed at how much the almost blind could do; it was beyond my scope and confidence.

Working with them and sharing views in discussions afterwards was a lesson in the benefits of cross-fertilisation of ideas. It was also a warning to avoid stubbornness born of competition. I wondered how much this would play a role in the development years of endoluminal grafting and endovascular surgery. There were going to be winners and winners, as sometimes different ideas would be different strings to the same bow, and there would be some losers. In surgery, there is a view that if there are many different procedures for a problem, then probably none of them are that good. Eventually, only the best will last the test of time. The crossroad, at that stage, was whether the long and short trouser leg graft with a modular structure was going to prevail, or would it be the more simple straight-tube grafts, combined with some surgery.

"Keep it simple, stupid" the saying goes. There was no question that the single straight-tube stent-grafts wore the "simple" label for the stent-graft options. The real question was, how simple is the surgery that goes with it?' How simple the surgery relates to the prowess of the surgeon; some surgeons make all operations appear straightforward. In my view, it was not always that simple or easy to perform, although it may be dismissed that way. I suspected that the open-wound surgery component to any endovascular procedure was going to be a blind spot. I was even more convinced that we should continue to pursue modular endovascular grafts and work to eliminate any open-wound components. However, I also wished for cooperative research and development. With John Anderson, I had a soulmate; our ideas seldom clashed. Brian, on the other hand, could provide the real and hypothetical challenges that needed to be faced before the verdict of failure or success was brought down.

The first Charing Cross meeting of Roger Greenhalgh's that I attended was very similar to the first Royal Prince Alfred meeting, but with more annuals to its name. The chapter we contributed to his book was "Should an Anchor Stent Cross the Renal Artery Orifices When Placing an Endoluminal Graft for Abdominal Aortic Aneurysm?"

Roger had a knack for asking the challenging questions, and that proved to be very important in providing a forum in this new era. I enjoyed the meeting very much and felt I had a good colleague in Roger. Shane MacSweeney had been one of his trainees and part of the reason for the invitation for me to speak at the meeting.

In fact, that meeting stimulated so much interest that, like the Sydney meeting, it had to move venues, and thereafter, although it was still called the "Charing Cross meeting," it moved to Westminster and the Imperial Sciences University. Roger continued to invite me for the next few years, and I continued to work on chapters for his books. In reality, it is a poor way to publish because the books, unlike the journals, are not catalogued for reference in the same way, and writings can be buried in the Library for Lost Books.

There was, however, an important benefit in that I could write freely, without censor. Writing chapters for Roger served to exercise my mind and channel my thought processes, but I am not sure the writings had the same impact as the articles in peer-reviewed journals. They were certainly not referenced often, if ever. Undoubtedly, the combination of chapters in the books and the opportunities to speak and present to a wide international audience was invaluable and fuelled a grapevine with a stalk that rivalled the one that Jack built.

The international meetings that grew out of the endovascular revolution had become a circus, but not at all in a derogatory sense. If you had a good act and put on a good performance, you were invited to the next year's meeting and also to other meetings around the world. Medical meetings were big business and had to make money to grow and survive. Well-known names were used on flyers as drawcards. The vascular meetings were growing like mushrooms, and in joining the circuit, I was whorled around the world.

CHAPTER 25

The Global Affair: Discovering What We Did Not Know at E2B

The flurry of activity around the world was starting to condense, with more structure and support by industry, while regulators were chasing hard to catch the tail of the monster that endoluminal grafting was becoming. You may well ask why such a situation could have developed at all without regulation. Surgeons should have the freedom to use whatever is available to them to fix a problem, as long as the materials are approved for biological use and within the boundaries of the field. Surgeons have always had freedom to make and use tools for their trade; instrument trays are covered with instruments affectionately or historically bearing their inventor's names or the names given to them by the inventors. We had a popular instrument called George, named after the autopilot in an aircraft because it always went in the desired direction for the surgeon. It was not called George in any other hospital. In other hospitals, it was a Lahey or Lortat-Jacob or something else.

Homemade stent-grafts were initially made by surgeons on the operating table, where they combined graft material with available wires, sutures, and stents. There must always be a reasonable balance between freedom to tailor to a situation and restriction to experiment. Should any harm be inflicted as a consequence, the law is the arbiter. When commercial interests become involved, then so must regulators. Homemade devices become unacceptable when commercialised and made available to others. For medical acceptance of a therapy, evidence is needed. Anecdotes are not sufficient evidence to advocate a treatment for general use, nor is expert opinion, although both may be influential. In the order of strength of evidence in medicine, anecdote and expert opinion are the lowest (some advocate they be discounted completely). Appealing to expert opinion in the field of logic is a false argument. Precedent may be a fundamental in law, but not in medicine. A higher level of evidence is needed because in high-risk areas of medicine, death is always lurking, particularly so for the aging, where it may be a coincidental natural cause. Did Mother Nature do something, or did we? Therein lies the question, and the answer resides in higher levels of evidence.

If documented evidence and standards were not forthcoming, procedures would be condemned and sent to the Library for Lost Ideas. To avoid dismissing or concealing deaths caused by doctors as a result of a surgical and anaesthetic mishap by simply labelling them natural events, such as an unforeseen heart attack or stroke, all deaths within thirty days of a procedure are automatically labelled an operative death by international convention, even if it was an accident and the person run over by a truck. Since the advent of regular quality assurance measures and auditing of outcomes with computers, which tends to clear doctors of any misdoing or misreporting rather than implicate them, new procedures have been heavily scrutinised, especially those associated with conditions where death lurks. There may be doubt about whether a doctor did the right thing in the absence of definite evidence, such as an X-ray showing a forgotten instrument left inside the body, but there are no doubts if the device fails. In the case of endoluminal stent-grafting, the whole operation was done with image guidance and recording. It was CCTV evidence.

Manufacture requires specifications and in-built quality control; that is what commercial companies do, subject to regulation. Manufacturers were quite rightly wary of taking on faulty homemade devices that might land them in lawsuits or compensation claims that could destroy their companies. Dow Corning's problem with silicone breast implants was a good example. Some companies avoid the risks by not getting involved with medical devices. The Department of Fluid Dynamics of the Commonwealth Scientific and Industrial Research Organisation (CSIRO) in Australia prohibited involvement of its organisation in medical research until sometime in the mid-1990s; when I wanted to try Kevlar as a material instead of Dacron, this material was simply unavailable for our purposes.

The Korean War is said to have been the birthplace of modern arterial surgery with prosthetics. War is an epidemic of trauma, and surgeons from time immemorial have been tidying up after wars. Surgery in the field had advanced so much that surgeons wanted to save limbs with arterial injuries, rather than simply amputate to save the life, so they tried replacing injured arteries by transplanting similar ones from soldiers who could not be saved. The transplanted arteries disintegrated when rejection set in, and patients sometimes bled fatally; surgeons learnt to use Dacron shirt material instead. In the 1950s, it was common for surgeons (or their co-opted wives) to make their own vascular grafts from Dacron, until Meadox and USCI had the confidence to make them for the market. The commercial product, with all its safeguards and controls, was much better and completely accepted, to the extent that no one thought there was a time without it, and that took a period of only ten years. It appeared that this would also be the case for homemade Stent-Grafts.

We were given a boost, again through the support of Turab, when an international radiology seminar was held in Perth.

We were asked to perform a live case demonstration for the delegates at the conference; the images were beamed into their auditorium by closed-circuit TV. It was a trend that gained popularity at the time because image-controlled procedures were ideal for closed-circuit TV. The custom of demonstrating procedures to an audience goes back in history, which is why in Europe, and especially Britain, operating rooms are still called theatres. There are historical pictures of surgeons demonstrating operations in ORs exactly like theatres, with tiered seating.

Hal Coons, a radiologist from San Diego, was a guest speaker and friend of Turab. Hal was famous for his work on the kidneys and removal of kidney stones through the skin. To do this, he developed sharp plastic rods called dilators with sheaths that would run on a wire, previously positioned via a hollow needle, down to a stone inside the kidney. He was then able to pull out the rod and thereby leave the plastic sheath as a tunnel down to the kidney. His tool was known as the Coons dilator and was incidentally and conveniently marketed by the Cook company. David had modified Hal's dilator, and we were using it as part of the delivery system of the device for the Perth Bifurcated Stent-Graft. Hal was keen to meet us, and we of course wanted to meet him. He turned out to have a very engaging personality, was terribly pleased that we had incorporated his tool, and wanted to watch us. The problem was that he could no longer enter X-ray theatres because he had overexposed his hands to radiation during his working years. We agreed to let Hal watch from behind the radiation-proof glass window in the control annex. All was fine for a while, but then it was too much for Hal: He had to move in closer to see. The result was that he ended up standing behind me with a protection lead apron over his body and his hands behind his back. What a great compliment.

By this stage, there were frequent requests to use the Perth bifurcated system, and to cover costs, we sold some, as a way of repaying Cook Australia for its support. We placed the money in an account, and a substantial sum accumulated; I used it for research and then, in innocence, wrote a cheque out to the company for the balance to repay them for the supplies they had provided, as I had no commercial basis to make money.

Cook declined the money on the grounds that they had not manufactured the devices we made and were in no commercial position to sell the product without government regulatory approval. I gave the funds to the hospital as payment for use of its facilities and equipment for our research. This started a fund that has given extra meaning to Paul Kelly's lyric, "from little things big things grow." It was then that Geoff Reeves decided to commercialise the operation, and following Therapeutic Goods Authority (TGA) approval, the graft was launched in 1998 as the H&LB graft during an endovascular workshop and seminar John Anderson ran in Adelaide.

Claude Mialhe's Min Tec device was purchased by Boston Scientific and given the name Vanguard. Tim Chuter's idea was marketed by Endovascular Technologies as the EVT Stent-Graft. Medtronic brought out the Aneurex Stent-Graft that Tom Fogarty and Stanford University had been developing and then purchased the World Medical Stent-Graft and rebadged it as the Talent Stent-Graft. Meanwhile, Cook was associated with developments in four different sites—the United States, the UK, Sweden, and Australia—all based on the Z stent technology. The only commercial one was the H&LB graft.

We addressed a number of problems and setbacks along the way. The revelation of the broken hooks served to persuade Cook to allow David to design and make our own anchor stent; this was stronger and more reliable. When Boston Scientific bought out Mialhe and started to market the graft as the Vanguard, I anticipated they were going to block our use of the Meadox graft material, which they already owned. We were, of course, their major competitor, and if they could block us on the rationale that we were adulterating the textile, by ironing and fashioning it, then they would. At the next Ted Dietrich meeting in Phoenix, I introduced Stuart Rodger of Vascutek to Geoff Reeves. I asked Geoff to make a deal with Vascutek to have them supply noncrimped Dacron to William Cook Australia for the purpose of making Stent-Grafts. Geoff grumbled about not wanting to deal with other companies based on past nonproductive experiences, but he appreciated the dilemma. In the context of Geoff's obvious lack of enthusiasm and the small size of the market for Vascutek, I thought Stuart was very good to me to bear up and continue the negotiations to the conclusion that Vascutek was named the textile supplier.

No sooner had the deal been struck than the anticipated happened: Boston Scientific withdrew supplies of the graft material, declaring that it was being used improperly. I suppose it might have been possible to acquire the material by an indirect avenue, but this would pose real problems for the ability to market a nonapproved product. Boston Scientific would have effectively stalled or fatally injured our project if I had not had the foresight to see this problem coming. It served to caution us further on how treacherous the path we were on was; we were reminded of the theft of our samples and material at the Sydney meeting, and the need to anticipate and prevent problems was re-enforced. In other words, we had to stay one step ahead.

We developed another special friendship from the annual Phoenix meeting with Wolf Stelter, a larger-than-life German surgeon from Frankfurt. While preparing my talk in the slide preparation room, Wolf leaned over from the adjacent machine, where he was checking his own presentation, watched a video in my screen, and murmured, "This is better than playing golf." He then invited me to visit him on my way back to Australia. After the meeting, I stayed in his house, ate German green sauce that he proudly made (it looked disgusting but tasted wonderful), and attended his theatre the next day.

Wolf was the leading German pioneer in Stent-Graft work at the time and a friend of Claude Mialhe, whose device he used. Mialhe had developed the first commercially available modular bifurcated Stent-Graft, based on an idea claimed by Wolf, which was manufactured by George Goicoechea's company MinTec under the name Stentor and was first implanted in 1994 by Mialhe and Wolf in Frankfurt. When I walked into his theatre, he introduced me and announced to his theatre team, "Today, we will all speak English." And they did, until something became complex and there was a temporary lapse. I tried to imagine the expressions that would appear on my team's faces if I had told them all to speak German.

Wolf was a disciple of Professor DeBakey in Houston and had trained there for aneurysm surgery. He recounted how elated he was to win a place on DeBakey's team and the profound disappointment to be fired during the first operating session, for a problem during the surgery that DeBakey blamed Wolf for.

While sadly changing his clothes, another senior surgeon, Dr Stanley Crawford, smiled at him and said, "Don't worry. Dr DeBakey fires everybody on their first day. Just turn up tomorrow as if nothing happened."

Wolf did, and after a while, Dr DeBakey asked, "Didn't I fire you yesterday?"

"Sorry," said Wolf. "I have trouble still with my English."

Of course, Dr DeBakey did not always sack people on their first day, but he admired Wolf's fortitude and agreed to train him. As a result, Wolf had the best teacher in the world and DeBakey the most loyal of followers, who wore cowboy boots drove a Cadillac in Germany wearing a Stetson hat, and visited Dr DeBakey in the States whenever he could. Wolf relates that some years later, when they talked about this while DeBakey visited Germany, the transplant pioneer smiled at him and said, "I know that was not your fault. We have a saying from my home in Louisiana: 'If you can't stand the heat should stay out of the kitchen,'" and they both laughed.

Wolf became very important to our development team, and between us, we started building Stent-Grafts in modules that we called the Composite Stent-Graft. This was a major step forward towards building inside the aorta and developing branches and complex structures. It also opened the door to an immense outpouring of German energy and ingenuity. The fax machine in Perth spewed drawings and ideas at all hours of the day and night. Wolf visited us regularly and once, on his way to a Sydney meeting, he left his glasses at the bottom of the Swan River after a wine-fuelled swim, during a twilight sail on Mike Hellings's boat.

Knowing he could not read properly, I enjoyed watching him chairing a session in Sydney, using the program like a conductor's wand. Only Wolf could have pulled it off. Another time, when preparing his talk for a Sydney meeting, his helpful son did something to the slide program, and when Wolf arrived in Sydney, his talk had been converted into an unusable, alien format. Undaunted, Wolf announced to the audience that everybody must be weary of visual effects, and he was just going to talk to them. He started a trend.

The vulnerability of endoluminal stent-grafting in the commercial world started to become more apparent. I likened it to driving through the bush, where one had to constantly be on the lookout for an elephant or rhino that might suddenly block the road. I once saw the Mombasa train derailed after hitting an elephant and a VW completely reshaped by a rhino. Both vehicles had been stopped in their tracks by the contact with the animals.

The endovascular revolution was in danger of being derailed in an equally spectacular fashion. MinTec, the start-up company with Claude Mialhe's stent-graft, sold their graft just in time to Boston Scientific. Being in the vanguard of development, it was aptly named the Vanguard Stent-Graft by Boston Scientific and marketed prominently in Europe. It was set to be the dominant device for the foreseeable future, but then disturbing reports of failure emerged, mainly through the Eurostar Register, set up by Professor Peter Harris in the UK.

The metal skeleton of the Stent-Grafts were made of nitinol (nickel-titanium alloy); they were corroding and the grafts collapsing, like bridges falling in a tsunami. The corroded struts formed stakes that pierced holes in the heart of the textile fabric. The naysayers seized upon the findings to condemn the endoluminal grafts in general. In response and damage control, Boston Scientific appointed a respected surgeon, Jock Beebe, from the University in Michigan, to investigate. Jock was a former naval office. He was tall with a shock of wiry hair and a military bearing. He had a deep bass voice one could imagine penetrating the fog at sea with reverberant chimes. He was perfect for penetrating the fog that was enveloping the stent-graft concept. There is no doubt that if Jock had set out to bring the endeavour to an end, he would have succeeded in persuading companies and regulators. It certainly brought the Vanguard to an end.

However, Jock realised that not all Stent-Grafts had failed. Although he cautioned that maybe this was merely a function of time, he stopped short of condemning all Stent-Grafts or recommending halting further development. He invited all the pioneers to meet in America at Sea Island, Georgia. He persuaded the commercial companies to participate and fund this on the basis that it was in their best interest to have a forthright discussion on the future of the technology; he called it the E2B. This was a play on "Endovascular to Be (or Not to Be)." Jock insisted that we were there to discuss what we did not know and repeated this often enough to ensure that confusion reigned supreme in the certain knowledge that we didn't know what we didn't know, and we didn't know where to go.

It is difficult to describe the dynamic of this meeting. It had the air of indulgence in a congenial setting, belying the undercurrents of suppressed competition, distrust, and naïve exposure. We were exposed and vulnerable, like the strange horseshoe crabs exposed on the beach by Sea Island's receding tide. Lawsuits between some companies for breach of patent and use of each other's technology were in progress, and the rivalry between inventors and scientists seethed. I realised Jock was smart because if we discussed what we did not know, then it could not be patented afterwards because revelation at the meeting would render it prior art. We could not discuss ideas or things we did know, and had not patented, for the same reason or because someone would steal the idea and file a patent first. We learnt that the ability to patent was the lifeblood of commercial survival.

It was interesting that the smallest letter in the alphabet, i, has so much power to change an ethic: *patents* and *patients* were marrying in the worlds of commercialism and medicine, for better or worse.

So what did we talk about? Some of us were altruistic, some sought fame and new office, some sought only knowledge and answers, and some sought commercial gain. We discussed the problems and spared the solutions. We did not discuss prostheses or commercial products and concentrated on how to sustain the concept of endoluminal grafting. It was the opportunity to identify those parameters that were different from open surgery and how we needed to think differently if we were going to succeed. This meeting of pioneers was historic because it identified the key players. There were some notable absentees. Whether that was because they declined or were not invited or not recognised as pioneers at the time, I did not know. Those who should have been there and were absent include the unknown soldiers of the revolution.

It was an important meeting because Jock emerged as a statesman and a spokesperson for the endeavour. In effect, he stayed the execution of the concept, which could have gone the way of the laser technology not so long before and into the Library for Failed Experiments. There was fierce opposition to the concept. One prominent opponent, the editor of the *Journal of Vascular Surgery*, accosted me in the men's room at the Charing Cross annual meeting and told me I should not be doing what I was. Another had thumped the table at the conference dinner that night to emphasise that I was "wrong, wrong, and wrong."

Jock gave me encouragement and tacit support throughout those early years. We formed a lasting network in an era when feelings ran high. He's the only one I know to have quoted one of the chapters I wrote for Roger Greenhalgh's books. It made me wonder if the unknown readers were as essential as the unknown soldiers in this endovascular revolution.

Chapter 26

The H&LB becomes the Zenith

Terminology was also evolving in the new field. Endoluminal grafts were also called endostents, endografts, stent-grafts, and endovascular grafts. In America, Cook had started to notice the impact of the Perth bifurcated system (which later became the H&LB Stent-Graft in Australia). The parent company sent a team of assessors to Perth.

Unfortunately, an acute retinal detachment occurred in the eye of one of the assessors, Joe Roberts, and he needed urgent attention to save his sight. The head of ophthalmology, Ian McAllister, was a colleague and provided prompt attention. Whether this helped endear them to us would be speculation, but after his eye had been fixed, we teased Joe that his eyes had come out on stalks when he saw the H&LB Stent-Graft. The successful emergency eye surgery helped convince Joe of the high standard of medicine in Perth. He was a great guy, and I liked him very much, whether he was going to support us or not. Joe was big and strong and oozed humanity. He endeared himself to Michele with stories of how he had opposed the Vietnam War.

Later, we received notification that John DeFord, Cook's new vice president, had decided to amalgamate all the global effort and commercialise our graft. John requested we prepare a demonstration of the H&LB Stent-Graft and present the outcomes and experience.

I was completely confident that we could do this. By this time, teaching the techniques of implantation and demonstrating the use of the system was routine. Kishore had started a system of a histogram for each case, with colour codes for each outcome and complication. The system had lapsed while he was in Sydney, so we employed a computer programmer to set up a spreadsheet program to update the records and keep them current. As backup, we had case notes and X-ray records with medical ethics approval and written guidelines for the selection of each case. When we combined those under the labels of Perth Bifurcated System and H&LB Stent-Graft, we had performed over one hundred and fifty grafts in Western Australia alone. An equal number of our Stent-Grafts had been distributed through the eastern states and a smattering overseas.

After a little while, we asked for a printout to see how we were tracking; the computer programmer said that he had been unwell and that he would give us the data in a few days. This went on for some time, and I eventually lost patience.

One weekend, I arranged for my research colleague James Semmens, who was now a professor, to help me hack into the program. We looked through the database and were devastated to see only indecipherable hieroglyphics. There was not a single case record that could be used in the program. This meant that we had no collated records for more than eighteen months of operations. There are few times that I have felt worse in my life; I was at a complete loss as to what to do. There was no way I could see how we could rectify the situation before the Americans arrived. Apart from the embarrassment we would face, there was the issue of loss of opportunity. I perceived my options were to either resign or disappear.

After a while, James said, "What about that team of nurses you had when you were researching the value of population screening for aneurysms? Could they be brought in to look at all the notes so we can make a new database from scratch?"

"What about the images and X-ray analysis?" I asked.

"We can employ a radiographer to give us measurements, and then we could group outcomes and do an analysis. That would also give us the secondary scientific advantage of having only one dedicated observer and thereby remove the common criticism of variable observer error. There is a benefit in looking at all the cases again because they can be examined in the light of what you've learned in the past two years. You *have* learnt something, haven't you?"

I liked the "we" because it meant that he was on board to help me, but I wasn't sure about the rest of his argument. Considering what I had just discovered, I did not appreciate his sense of humour at that moment.

James added, "I have other resources and chart reviewers in the university." He went on, "How about you get a dedicated radiographer to handle all the images, while I will deal with the chart review?"

I asked Graham, one of the radiographers who had shown an interest in the stent-graft procedures and often ran the X-ray machines during the operations, if he'd like a full-time job for a limited period, looking at X-rays. He said yes and added that his wife was a trained radiographer and would help too if we wished. We did wish it.

Turab again helped by seconding Graham to our department. James organised a veritable powerhouse team of chart reviewers, and we acquired a dedicated room to use for the project. We grouped types of cases and outcomes. Graham organised displays of sample problems and solutions. We analysed and stratified all the cases performed, from the very beginning up to the date the review started, and added others as they were done. Graham had a special eye for observation and an insight into the variables and degrees of difference. I cannot justly describe how good a job he and his wife, Cathy, did; the display he arranged for the arrival of the Americans was a true work of art.

Cook finally set the date of their visit for April of 1998, and we were ready for them. John DeFord arrived with his assessment team and a daunting array of pioneers. How he had persuaded the others to give up their development plans and throw their weight behind the Perth team, I'll never know. He did it, and I was humbled to think that they should agree. I'm not sure that I would have done the same if in their shoes, and I felt for them. I expected a degree of severe criticism, if not resentment.

John DeFord very skilfully brought the various parties together, set the agenda in the discussions, and chaired the meetings. We presented all the data from the review and explained the examples in the display. David left no doubt in anybody's mind that he was the person who could make the ideas work and build products to professional and commercial standards. We explained the reasons we decided on the materials we used. In particular, we had to justify our choice of stainless steel over the more touted nickel titanium alloy, nitinol. Our corrosion testing revealed that the nitinol wire available at the time would corrode and stress and fracture. Noncrimped woven Dacron was the easiest to handle and packed smallest of all the commercial graft materials. We explained that we were using materials that had already passed the tests of compatibility and that durability and biocompatibility took priority over the desire to achieve smaller profile devices, even though that was still an aim.

Tim Chuter came on his own; it was an unusual situation for Tim, and I suspect he was not very comfortable in the beginning. Brian Hopkinson had been appointed professor of surgery in Nottingham for his pioneer work in endoluminal grafting, and he brought Simon Whittaker, his radiology colleague, with him. These two took to the event like true Brits, with understatements and politeness. Since the British still considered Australians to be really a class of rival Brits, it was not so hard for them.

Krassi Ivancev brought Roy Greenberg, who was training with him in Malmo, as his partner and companion. Destiny was written all over Roy, a young American vascular trainee from New York who was clearly ambitious. He had worked as an intern with Tim, who was the resident surgeon in New York during their junior doctor days. Tim had also worked with Krassi in Malmo before, and this was the connection. They all knew each other well. Roy's boss, Ken Auriel, had the foresight to encourage Roy to acquire catheter and wire skills with some radiology training. Ken had just been appointed to the Cleveland Clinic as chief vascular surgeon, and it was planned for Roy to join him as his off-sider as soon as his training was complete in Malmo; the clinic was building a special image guidance-equipped OR for that purpose. That was foresight at its best in this new era.

We arranged to implant six Stent-Grafts that week and involved the teams above in two cases each, to familiarise them with the H&LB Stent-Graft. The second case for each team invariably went through more smoothly, with little further instruction. The direct theatre involvement was backed up by bench demonstrations and reverse engineering to reveal all the mechanics and rationales.

These were already experienced operators and teachers, and in the beginning, it was almost a question as who was instructing whom. A debriefing was held after every case. David and I insisted that the protocols we had made, born of hard lessons, were to be adhered to while we were instructing.

I'm glad we had the foresight and workload to have two cases for each team. It is said that getting doctors to follow instructions was like herding cats, and I admit to having been daunted by the task. In the end, the week went without a hitch. Evenings were filled with congenial gatherings; West Australian wines and seafood combined to complete the welcome and hospitality. A reading of Henry Lawson's "The Loaded Dog" replaced the after-dinner speech and befitted the occasion, with its description of the pursuit of perfection in the making of the device.

John explained that it was no longer the H&LB Stent-Graft; it was now the Zenith endovascular graft, which incorporated all the designs and attributes of the four stables. It was the coming together of a global effort. The ethic he wished to instil was that henceforth, it would be a joint venture between all of us to continue to develop, test, and teach others. We became good friends, and our friendships have stood the test of many challenges and a long time.

CHAPTER 27

Quo Vadis: Hardships and Setbacks

The coming of the Americans coincided with the opening of a new facility in the Medical Research Foundation Building attached to Royal Perth Hospital, and the opportunity to formally open the facility was not lost. A section on the top floor was leased and funded by Cook Australia, and David was appointed the head of Cook R&D, Western Australia. I was able to retain him as a part-time service member of the cardiovascular division in the hospital, and this afforded him rights to work in the hospital and use its facilities, which were paid for if necessary.

It was a good working relationship. The pace and demand was already stretching us in Australia and New Zealand. Now thinking of providing for the rest of the world was a sobering thought. Geoff Reeves had said before, "This is played like a game, but the stakes are real," and I thought back to how Monopoly had been played in the Snowy Mountains work camps for real money.

Geoff issued the challenge: "Are you guys prepared to hold on to this tiger's tail? It's going to take off."

The federal government's tax incentives continued for companies performing bone fide research. This suited Cook, and it suited us very well to have all manufacturing of Zenith grafts located in the head office in Brisbane or Europe, and for us to continue in isolation. Divorced from commercial incentive, we were able to concentrate on research and development. There was an added component of teaching and training that we were pleased to be responsible for: the built-in feedback associated with this activity. Our communication with vascular units in Australia and New Zealand was already extensive and was now to be multiplied manyfold with an extending global market, particularly Europe and increasingly South East Asia. The future promised to be exciting and rewarding, albeit demanding.

We were left with enormous tasks after our colleagues returned to their own homes in the global spirit of cooperation and the Americans had flown off into the Western sunset. These tasks could not have been tackled without the support of my ever-loyal colleagues in the departments of vascular surgery and radiology, operating theatres, and administration, who wanted the project to succeed and were proud of their efforts. The spirit was one of inclusive cooperation. In addition to our working, teaching, and development load, we now had larger tasks to handle. The two most pressing obligations were provision of backup services to surgeons and radiologists in Australia and New Zealand and continuing to acquire data for Cook in America. The Americans needed data to commence the process of US Food and Drug Administration (FDA) approval for the product to go to market. The FDA was not in the habit of accepting non-US data, but the company believed the quality of our initial findings would assist in expediting the approval process. That aside, we now had the enormous task of teaching globally. This would be done by publishing in journals, presenting at medical conferences, presenting our experience to individual units around the world, and most of all running teaching workshops in Perth. "Endoluminaries" was the name given to a particular form of workshop for users set up by Geoff, and it became a popular part of this effort. The format spread to South East Asia, Europe, and the United States.

As if we did not have enough problems, I was then confronted by a "rush to the head" by the head of hospital administration, who decided to restructure all the clinical departments in the hospital under the guidance of the King's Fund from the UK. Facilitators and advisors from the King's Fund were employed at great cost to implement their newly derived hospital change management scheme. Forty leading clinicians were closeted in a hotel for three days and nights in a think-tank. As far as I know, I was the only one to break ranks and leave the hotel during that time, as it was a condition of involvement to stay put.

I had to visit a sick patient on whom I had operated in a nearby private hospital, and I saw that as my professional priority. It broke the spell for me, and I foresaw grave problems looming ahead for our department. The plan was to amalgamate individual departments into groups that aligned either on an area of clinical expertise or a system of the body. For example, all types of cancer would be under the cancer division and all cardiovascular disease under the cardiovascular division. Although it seemed sensible at first sight (or from within the closeted think-tank), what it failed to recognise was that on a Venn diagram, each department had multiple intersections with other departments. Whether they liked it or not, departments of different sizes and political influence that were traditionally partners in therapy, or competitors, would be forced together or apart, bringing about an inevitable change in balance, affecting resource distribution. Conflicts of interest were bound to arise. As vascular was a small department faced with change, anyway, and already a veteran of the war of independence from general surgery, with intersects across the clinical spectrum, I perceived a recipe for disaster and voted against the new structure proposal. It was a secret ballot that was won 39 to 1 (I considered it unwise to own up to being the only dissenter).

At first, the amalgamation with the powerful and influential cardiology department and the much-respected cardiothoracic surgery department worked to our benefit, and all three of us engaged enthusiastically to synergise and maximise our potentials in the newly formed cardiovascular division. Although we were small, we brought the endovascular graft to the table and used this to gain much-needed access to facilities. Then the inevitable conflict of interest happened. It was unexpected and accompanied by consuming passions in all parties. It came from left field: it was the carotid artery issue. I was reminded of the quote "If you think everything is going well, then you don't know what is going wrong."

For nearly fifty years, cleaning out the carotid artery of atheroma to prevent strokes had been controversial; only recently had it been universally accepted as a good surgical option. We were proud of our involvement in the trials run in the UK and the United States, which proved this; the association of one our neurologists with the steering committee that ran the European Carotid Surgery Trial (ECST) out of Edinburgh was influential. We considered ourselves among the leaders in this field in Australia. Because of my involvement in the endovascular field, we started exploring carotid cases that might be better served by an endovascular approach with angioplasty and a stent, instead of open-wound surgery. Work with the carotid artery had always been done by vascular surgery or neurosurgery, with help and advice from radiology and neurology.

Then cardiology entered the field in America, led by Gary Ruben, an ex-pat Australian cardiologist who teamed up with a Czech interventional neurologist in Alabama, Gerry Vitek. Gerry had left Czechoslovakia after the Russian invasion. Cardiology entered this field with vigour, courage, and the conviction born of coronary artery angioplasty and stenting and had the skill set and facilities to do it well. Neuroradiology was an arm of radiology with strong links to neurology in the neurosciences division but not in the cardiovascular division.

Neurosciences did not approve of the cardiovascular division entering the carotid field for this purpose. They reasoned that the end organ was the brain, which was clearly within the endovascular domain of neuroradiology.

The administration sought to resolve this conflict through a mechanism set up by the change management scheme, whereby the directors of each division had a forum for problem resolution and policy making. The divisional directors forum smilingly set up a team of two cardiologists and two neuroradiologists to work together; the vascular surgeons would be observers until the system was working well and would then be included. Until then, vascular surgeons would continue with the open operations on the carotid artery and salvage any arterial problems that might occur from the endovascular procedures.

A training trip to visit Gary and Gerry in Alabama was organised and funded by the hospital. The administration of the hospital saw this as an eminently suitable solution, and off the group of four went to visit Gary for training. They returned and started working together. The lessons of the eternal triangle were overlooked for what suited the major parties.

In chemistry, if a drop of strong acid is put into a glass of water, the water turns a little acidic, but nothing else happens. If, however, a drop of water is placed into a glass of strong pure acid, then all hell breaks loose, as the acid molecules compete for the water. A more graphic picture is imagining leopards and lambs instead of acid and water. So it was when the one little operation for the carotid artery was dropped into the glass of radiologists and cardiologists. The administration failed to remember that coronary artery angiography and angioplasty had been sheared off from radiology by cardiology years before in controversial circumstances, and the ways the two disciplines solved problems were quite different. The operators in each discipline would not be the champions they were without great self-belief. They could not find a way to compromise with their core techniques and work together. The intended cooperative venture dissolved into acrimony. This was recognised as a potentially dangerous situation for any patient to be literally on the end of the wire in the midst of a dispute. The interventional cardiologists and neuroradiologists agreed to split with each other and do it their own way.

Radiology approached vascular and invited us to join them in their neuro-intervention theatre. It was natural for me to agree, as I was still working with radiology on aortas and because the mainstay of intervention for carotid disease was still open-wound surgery, where the imaging for diagnosis and management resided mainly with radiology. Furthermore, we already had an interest in angioplasty and stenting in the carotid artery.

I did as I would have done if we were an individual department. I never considered that cardiology would feel they needed us or that we had betrayed them. I was very wrong. Cardiology felt bitterly betrayed, and the leader felt so strongly that he was close to tears as he vowed to withdraw all vascular support from within the division. Although I had not considered the dilemma before, it suddenly dawned on me that the situation was dire. If I was seen by radiology to be siding with cardiology, I would threaten the aortic program. And if that collapsed, then we ourselves would be destroyed from outside by loss of support from Cook, at the same time losing all credibility for Perth. Our demise would be global and irreversible.

I had to accept that if I were to be seen to be siding with radiology, the department would be destroyed from within the cardiovascular division. I could not extract us from the conflict, partly because most of the patients presented for carotid artery intervention came through the vascular department, and partly because it was too late. The first song I tried to learn on the guitar was "Tom Dooley," and the words about the eternal triangle rang in my head.

Another die had been cast, and the only way to have the conflicts of interest resolved was to resort to the wisdom of the divisional directors. The result was that vascular popped out like a melon seed between the powerful fingers of radiology and cardiology, almost propelling it to oblivion. We were mortally wounded as a department. For a while, we did continue to work with radiology on both aortic and carotid fronts and duly published our results in both fields of endeavour. It did not last. After leading radiology for nearly twenty-five years, Turab handed it over to another colleague, and the relationship with radiology started to sour. The dispute damaged all three departments. Both cardiology and vascular surgery were excluded from endovascular intervention for the carotid artery, and radiology was diminished in the process. The endovascular program for the aorta eventually had to be taken off-site, but for the time being, the endovascular aortic program had been quarantined from the surrounding disputes. Machiavelli was right; it was best that the aortic program was not exposed.

I did not realise that the hospital had decided to sacrifice vascular for the greater good of the entire hospital, which was served primarily by radiology. This was a bitter lesson in the centre of such sweet success for the aortic project. I had always believed that there should be a special operating theatre with best available imaging machines for intervention, such as were found in X-ray or cardiology, and that this proposed theatre should be able to accommodate the full range of open-wound surgery. The plans, following the visit and help to the Glasgow Infirmary in Scotland, were on the table, and we were in the queue for capital works.

The crunch came when we reached the head of the queue. Radiology, which had been so supportive in the days of Pete and Turab, vehemently opposed the building of such a theatre with X-ray machines in the main theatre block, which would be out of their control. The hospital made the excuse that there was no money for capital works that year. It was not unusual for hospitals to run out of budgeted funds, and I accepted that after having waited so long, we could afford to wait a little longer.

A slap in the face came when my working colleagues in radiology informed me enthusiastically that they were having a new X-ray theatre built, including a new machine for image-guided intervention. On asking whether we could use it, I was informed that it would not be suitable for us. I returned to the administration, where I was met by the CEO and the director of the clinical divisions. Upon asking about the redirection of expenditures, they informed me that building for us would be new capital works but to build for radiology was replacement. They didn't look me in the eye, and between the lines, it was patently clear that they were saying they could afford to deny vascular, but they couldn't afford to deny radiology. I understood the practicality of what they were saying, from a management perspective, but I could not overcome the feeling that their explanation was essentially dishonest, and told them so. I informed them that I could no longer work in the institution under the circumstances and would have to retire. I used the word *retire* because that meant a possible return, as a player who's retired hurt in cricket: less final than resigning, but the immediate effect was the same.

In retrospect, I might have succeeded if I had continued to be persistent and patient, but a problem of a direct personal nature had appeared: angina. This was a distraction, and distractions are associated with errors. A cardiologist investigated me with a nuclear scan of the heart and an exercise test with an ECG. Neither was positive, and I was declared fit. This was reassuring, so I withdrew to take stock of the situation. On the one hand, things were very good. The Zenith graft and Cook R&D WA were doing well. David was busy and in control of his own facility. Sue was ensconced in her new sewing room, while David engaged a radiographer called Andrew Bartlett, who used to work in radiology and was now freelancing in the catheter labs in the private system. Andrew was assigned to work with David as a planner for sizing and measuring grafts to fit aneurysms. Adding a planning service was a good step forward and indicative of health in that sector. On the other was the nagging worry about my own health.

Planning for a graft was like a tailor measuring for a suit. David and I believed that optimising successful endovascular grafting was associated with good planning. We therefore urged Cook to provide this service on the basis that optimum results were required for acceptance of concept and procedure. This was especially true after an article appeared in the *British Journal of Surgery* titled "A Failed Experiment," decrying endovascular grafting for aneurysms.

In order to achieve optimum results for patients receiving the Stent-Graft, regular training workshops were instituted where surgeons, radiologists, and cardiologists attended in groups of six every month. These were successful three-day sessions. The routine was for the attendees to fly into Perth on a Monday, spend time practising with the device in models and on the bench on Tuesday morning, witness a case on Tuesday afternoon with me, spend Wednesday morning learning how to fit a Stent-Graft to a particular aneurysm using CT-X ray pictures at the research centre with David, and see another case with Frank in the afternoon. An enjoyable evening together would always follow in a Perth restaurant. Finally, they would attend an X-ray session early on Thursday, where they could join us in discussing and assessing potential cases. We reviewed outcomes and problems. After this, the attendees usually witnessed another case with Marcel before flying out from Perth that afternoon. These workshops proved very successful by the fact that they were oversubscribed. Clearly, our relationship with the outside world was still healthy.

The outside world coming to us was a message that they were the key to survival of the project in Perth. Remembering that Perth is the most isolated city in the world, it was some feat to draw so many attendees. The learning process was reciprocal, with David and I paying attention to feedback and suggestions from the visitors. I started to get fat as a result of too many good dinners. I was also on the world stage, attending regular meetings in America, the UK, and Europe. Between all this, there was travel to South East Asia, India, and South Africa to instruct and lecture on grafting and what we had learned. I particularly enjoyed working with colleagues in Singapore, Malaysia, and Hong Kong. I grew up in East Africa with its large Indian population and have always liked spicy food; these trips held these culinary attractions as well. Work in India was also enjoyable.

These were heady times for me, and my overseas hosts received me with impeccable hospitality. I must have sat in a veritable who's who of restaurants around the world, but the pleasures of my professional travels were shadowed by a gnawing doubt about the state of my health. I felt I needed to look after myself now.

Endovascular work is associated with much less post-operative care and worry than major open-wound surgery, and despite the workload, I was happy with my life outside medicine. My boys were finding their own way. I was happy to travel, teach, or guide a procedure without payment, except for expenses and the concession that I could take Michele with me whenever I wished to do so. It was a good arrangement that absolved me from claims that I was being mercenary. I could thus maintain the ethic of teaching my colleagues with interchange, free, and without favour. I could also spend time with Michele, albeit mostly on long-haul plane flights, and not be tempted to stray for company.

Geoff Reeves had readily agreed to this arrangement, being a seasoned traveller himself. There was health and harmony, therefore, in the family sector. On the other hand, the strains in the hospital were beginning to take their toll. They seemed so unnecessary, and I realised that forces were manipulating budgets and decisions behind closed doors. I withdrew steadily to my refuge in my private practice and the increasingly supportive environment of the private system. The days in the private catheter lab were enjoyable, and I used them more and more for teaching and learning with colleagues. Frank worked with me regularly, and Marcel and I continued to operate together on complex cases. John Anderson would come over to help me from time to time, and in return, I visited him in his private catheter lab in Adelaide. It was as if I needed his consolation as much as he had needed mine before.

There was health to consider, but I feared interruption to the momentum. There was too much at stake.

CHAPTER 28

The Break: A Surgeon Becomes a Patient

Everything came to a head in April of 1999. Michele and I travelled to London so that I could make a presentation at Roger Greenhalgh's Charing Cross meeting at the Imperial Sciences University and then vacation in Scotland. Preparation for such presentations also involved writing another chapter for Roger's annual book, and this, on top of everything else, left my mind somewhat exhausted and numbed. I needed the respite of country air and some physical effort to clear my system. Walking was the chosen remedy.

We walked the West Highland way. This is a classic walk along the eastern side of Loch Lomond and across the moors between the mountains. We walked all the way from Glasgow to Fort William, and on the last day, we walked past Mount Ben Nevis in brilliant sunshine. Being April, the mountain was topped with snow; it looked so tempting to climb. We sat on a bench eating a packed lunch and looking at the mountain through a gap in a pine forest, deciding then and there we would try to climb it the next day, if the weather was favourable.

After lunch, we climbed a hill, and I experienced the chest pain again. It did not recur after that, and we climbed Ben Nevis the next day. However, I decided to get my heart checked out again on my return to Perth.

I was reticent about going back to the same cardiologist in the private hospital. I felt that rejecting his previous reassurance that all was well would be contradicting him; going back and questioning his judgement would be rude, and I'd be perceived as an interfering doctor. There should be no difference between doctors and other people when it comes to seeking medical help. In reality, this is not so because doctors tend to have their own opinions and can be more critical when they encounter an examining doctor. Knowing of their own inadequacies and defence mechanisms, they may be dubious of their colleague's façade of assurance and competence.

I also felt I could not consult my cardiology colleagues in Royal Perth Hospital because of the bitter dispute that had preceded my symptoms and could not see a way of developing a rapport. That thought was most unreasonable and unprofessional on my part, but I felt vulnerable. I asked the catheter lab staff in the private hospital, since I was using a cardiology catheter lab, whom they respected the most. Without hesitation, they recommended Randall Hendriks, a younger up-and-coming interventional cardiologist. So I went to see Randall, whose public hospital appointment was in Fremantle.

Fremantle is not Perth, according to Fremantle citizens, but it is part of Perth, according to Perthites. Perth and Fremantle are a conurbation, with Fremantle the port at the mouth of the Swan River, and the Swan River Settlement (which later became Perth) upriver. Captain Charles Fremantle had been a lieutenant under Lord Nelson; following gallant completion of worthy naval assignments, he was tasked with creating a presence in Western Australia to thwart the French. At the behest of Admiral James Stirling, who was designated governor of the colony-to-be, he did this at the mouth of the Swan River, which he disliked because it was not navigable through its mouth but otherwise suitable.

After completing his duty, the port was named after him, and he sailed away, leaving isolated Western Australia for more populated and exciting places. The main Swan River settlement was established upriver the same year in better surrounds and later named Perth by the British minister for the colonies, George Murray, after Perthshire, his own constituency in Scotland. George Murray, James Stirling, and Charles Fremantle were all pillars of British might and power. There was no further argument on the ownership of Western Australia. The historic rivalry is manifest in two separate Australian Rules football teams, the Fremantle Dockers and the Perth West Coast Eagles, with two fierce contests each year.

Randall's working at Mount Hospital was convenient, being situated on the river between the two and sufficiently distant from the public hospital system; I would have respite from all conflict. After listening to my symptoms, Randall proposed that he do a coronary angiogram as the definitive test, and I agreed.

I was now on the receiving end. Randall was good, and the puncture into the femoral artery in my right groin was almost painless. He let me watch the monitor as he injected dye into the left and then the right coronary artery. I could feel the discomfort in my chest each time the heart beat after the injection of X-ray dye as it flowed through the arteries of the heart.

From my angle, they looked fine to me, and expecting his reassurance, I was taken by surprise when he pointed out that at the origin of the left main coronary artery, there was a tight stenosis, greater than 70 percent. Because the narrowing was at the origin of the vessel, where the catheter was positioned, I had missed it from my angle on the operating table, but I knew with a sinking heart that this was a very nasty place to have a significant problem, and I had one.

"If this blocks at the origin," Randall said, "and you have a coronary thrombosis, it will be instantly lethal. This lesion is called the widow maker. There is no other supply to the left side of your heart and left ventricle. You should have an operation quickly. I suggest that you stay in hospital and have coronary artery by-pass surgery."

"What about a stent," I asked, "like we do for the kidney artery?"

"It's never done in the left main coronary artery, Michael, and especially at its origin. It's too risky. Any problems at all, and we have no salvage option. You would be dead in minutes. You must have a bypass."

I always knew I was in trouble when my mother called me "Michael" instead of "Mike." I thanked Randall for his advice but explained I needed some time to tie up loose ends, and then I would take the time off for the operation. Randall was clearly anxious and asked if I would see a cardiac surgeon in the recovery room and make arrangements before I went home. I was definitely on the receiving end and found myself unable to think clearly. I found myself relinquishing control of my life and submitting to advice and plans that were mixed with fatalistic submission and false reasoning. I was all too aware of the medical side, and it seemed unreal. I was concerned for my family. I had a will, my affairs were in order, my family trusted the doctors and the system, and I knew of no alternative. I would have the operation at the Mount, in the hospital where I worked.

After sorting out the loose ends in my practice and leaving the communications in the good hands of Maike, still my secretary, and the patients to be triaged by Barbara, the practice nurse, I went to see the surgeon for a formal consultation and operation plan. It was decided that I would not have a blood transfusion, unless absolutely necessary, as I had haemochromatosis, a condition with too much iron in my system. It was rather like me rusting from the inside, necessitating a unit of blood to be removed every three months. Some loss of blood during the operation would even have some benefit for my condition.

Just at that time, cardiac surgeons had developed a technique for coronary artery surgery that did not involve bypass on a heart-lung machine. It was called "off-pump heart surgery" and had been developed because of the AIDS scare; it also had the appeal of reducing the risk of perfusion syndrome and memory loss caused by small bits of debris from the machine travelling up to the brain as microemboli. The surgeon suggested this, and wanting to keep my brain in as good condition as possible, I agreed. This technique is now criticised for its high failure rates caused by the difficulty of sewing to the beating heart; that segment is meant to be held still during the sewing. We did not know that then, and it seemed a good idea at the time. I was only fifty-five.

The heart operation was not the first time I had submitted to the knife. It was the magnitude of the surgery, the interruption to my life, the first real threat to my mortal existence, and the concern on the faces of Michele, Stanley, Trevor, and Gareth that tore at my heart. All of a sudden, those things that had seemed so important at work paled in the face of the possibility that they might disappear from me forever. These were feelings on the inside, while externally, I tried to show a brave face and entered into the preoperation discussions with what I thought was sensible composure. The magnitude of the operation was diminished by the frequency with which it was performed and the expectation not just of normality, but even of a better life afterwards. It was an offer too good to refuse, with more than a hint of "too dangerous to refuse." Doctors are said to make dreadful patients and have a reputation for things going wrong. Surgeons know too many of the complications and are reputed to be the most ambivalent and difficult patients. I could see in my mind's eye the ripping apart of my chest by the mechanical ratchet spreaders. Images of the London torture dungeon refused to fade out, despite the constant murmurings of reassurance. Sir Hugh had taught me that errors did occur more than they should when doctors are patients because staff omitted embarrassing examinations on colleagues, did something different with good intent or bypassed protocols with misguided kindness to sensitivity. For example, when I offered to sew up one of his abdominal wounds with a cosmetic stitch I learned in plastic surgery because we were operating on a VIP, he responded with the comment "If I believed it were better I would do it for all my patients". I determined to be a model patient and follow each and every instruction. I reassured myself that I was in the care of friends and professionals. They could do with me as they wished.

That was all I remember from before the operation. I was transported to the operating theatre in a surreal mist of well-wishing familiar faces, but I woke in horror in the Intensive Care Unit. The gentle preoperative reassurances had evaporated, my left leg burned with electric shock, and the anaesthetist's endotracheal tube that was still stuck in my throat felt the size of a telegraph pole. I empathised with terrified mutes. Michele was there somewhere in the sea of faces, trying to calm me down, and I spotted a cardiothoracic surgeon colleague in the crowd. With all the gestures and strength I could muster, I silently implored him to remove the tube in my throat. He was not my doctor. He was visiting one of his patients in ICU.

The struggles started inside me too. I had, after all, determined to be the model patient. I settled down, probably with the help of a narcotic, and the tube was duly removed and comfort restored. My left leg still burned; my own training told me that this was occurring because the long saphenous nerve had been cut when the vein was harvested for one of the bypasses. I did not like it but knew it would be okay with time. Being a model patient, I was not going to complain—very much. It was enough that I was alive.

Florence Nightingale sent me an angel that night, and by morning, I felt comforted, and having always liked the first light of day, my spirit lifted. I submitted like a baby as I was cleaned and clothed. All I needed was a nappy, but instead, I had a catheter to supplement the two huge drains in my chest. By the evening, the catheter in my bladder and drains in my chest were gone. I could rest peacefully, as long as I didn't cough or breathe too deeply. I settled down to sleep that evening and waited for the angel to reappear. She didn't. She had left for London and had nursed me on her last night of duty.

Instead, I fought with a conscientious captain of ICU-vistan. The oxygen mask had been ordered, and by God, I was to use it. I couldn't stand it and felt I was being asphyxiated. The angel had allowed it to rest close to my mouth and let the oxygen flow across my air intake. A demon forced it on my nose and mouth, tightening the strap. I pulled it off; she put it on tighter. I pulled it off, and she put it on tighter. I felt defeated, and by morning, I disliked her intensely (the feeling was either mutual or unnoticed). She said she knew I was a surgeon and that it was good for me to have a taste of my own medicine. Death by a thousand cuts was my inner thought.

Later, in a more contemplative frame of mind, I examined the experience from a different perspective. Maybe the second night nurse did a better job than the first in doing what was best for me. Should surgeons have to undergo a simulated experience, with all the tests and ancillary treatments they might order a patient? Where are the lines between functioning with common sense and robotically following dictum? Where does compassion that might risk life or limb end and cruelty in preventing loss of life and limb start? Is there a wider perspective involving class discrimination in all this? If surgeons should undergo such simulations, should nurses have to do the same?

I harked back to the days I worked with prisoners, who were also in a situation of complete dependence on authority. Is a prisoner similar to a patient and vulnerable to harm while under state care? If so, should prosecuting lawyers and judges do the same and experience some form of prison life before they prescribe punishments for others? And what of politicians who enable or disable, as the case might be; what should they have to experience? That may be where the answer lies, since ministers who make decisions change and lose elections so often, it would be impractical. Surgical training is borrowed from the training of airline pilots and using simulators. So while reality maybe impractical, virtual reality and hypothetical workshops are feasible. It is always a good exercise to turn the coin over when considering a decision and consider how others might feel.

The ICU had problems with other patients on the second morning, and I was moved out, feeling unwashed and unloved. Soon I was in a nice room in the ward, sat out of bed, and left to contemplate. The trip to the bathroom a few feet away left me feeling as weak as a kitten. I had just climbed Ben Nevis, and now I had trouble covering a few feet on a horizontal plane. I had refused blood transfusion and hence was severely anaemic; that was why I lacked energy, I mused. The reflection in the mirror supported this.

Over the next few days, well-wishers and family came and went through a haze of nauseating narcotics. Maike came over from the office and sat with me when I was alone. My family meant more to me than ever. I wanted them to stay, but I tired easily. The nurses were kind but changed often, and the one therapist who provided me with steady support was Sue, the physiotherapist. I looked forward to her daily visit. It was she who walked me, made me breathe, hurt me when she made me laugh, and chided me to be better and stronger on the stairs. I know she was only doing her job, but she made it feel like she was really doing it for me, and that she liked me, and that is what made it special.

There were expectations of me to meet certain benchmarks. I recognised myself at the end of the bed with similar expectations of my own patients. I knew that achieving benchmarks reassured the staff that everything was in order. I had not anticipated or expected the amount of effort I would have to put in to meet them, but they thought they should have been achieved more easily. I went home on time, with no complications.

I felt so beaten down by the surgery; I had never had a heart attack or suffered heart failure, and I had been reasonably fit for all my life. So it was a lesson for me about the disadvantages of preventative procedures, a reminder to me that aneurysm surgery should be as minimally invasive and with as little stress physically and mentally as possible. Most people having elective aneurysm surgery were in a similar position to me. They were usually well and essentially without symptoms when they were diagnosed. The surgery was not going to make them feel better because they were without debilitating symptoms in the first place. After discharge from hospital, I struggled upstairs that I had taken two at a time before. I couldn't ride my bike around the park circuit without stopping, and I developed a cough that hurt my chest and made me so angry that I wouldn't have been surprised if Michele had left me for respite.

I walked around the little lakes in our nearby park and fed the ducks and the long-neck turtles with little bits of bread. The animals gave me consolation; the turtles would move towards me when they saw me coming. It was reassuring at a time when I looked at the world through eyes that might not see it for much longer, and it was so beautiful. I mixed emotions of sadness with frustration and anger. Was I depressed? If so, was I psychotic, neurotic, or just normal?

Michele was working in the Adult Migrant Education Centre, teaching English as a second language, and I took note that other people had more problems than I had. When home, I caught up with the backlog of data processing and analysis for the aneurysm project. James visited regularly and sustained me and my interest in producing papers for the journals. The occupation helped, and then I tutored Brendan, the advanced vascular trainee; he visited me and studied for his upcoming examinations between glasses of red wine. It was good to see him pass.

The time finally came for me to go back to work. It was three months after the surgery, but I still didn't feel fit enough to take calls after-hours. I asked the surgeon if I could have more time off or at least be excused from the emergency roster.

The response made me feel ashamed when he told me that all his patients went back to work after three months (another benchmark). Why didn't any of them look to see if anything was wrong? It was not really my nature to ask for favours or shirk my duties.

I returned to work but could not cope with the load. The hospital atmosphere was no better, and radiology still denied our access to facilities while they continued to block the building of a dedicated vascular theatre. I no longer had the strength or the will. I took a long service leave, worked only in my private practice, and retired from the public hospital. It was not an easy break after twenty-five years.

Chapter 29

The World of Private Practice: Taking the
Zenith to Its Zenith, and Medical Theatre

I had a part-time private practice for many years, but now I was moving completely into the private sector. To cope with the loss of the public hospital commitment and the hole this left in my life, I leaned on the advice I once received from a Canadian surgeon (he was a visiting lecturer for the Australian College of Surgeons). This was when I was charged with implementing quality assurance measures in the hospitals and trying to encourage other surgeons to audit their own results.

In response to my question as to how to persuade people to be involved, he had said, "Don't worry about those who won't join you or who oppose you. That's a waste of time and energy, and the effort is futile. Work with those who want to work with you."

The other bit of advice I received at the time was from a colleague who repeatedly ignored my request to be involved in quality assurance. When I confronted him, he was obviously irritated and responded, "Michael, when are you going to understand that no answer means no?"

In private practice, I could choose the people I wanted to work with. That luxury was not always available in the public system, as colleagues were more likely to be prescribed than chosen. In the private system, if I made a request and received no answer, I could choose another option or ask someone else. So taking the example of John Anderson, who had worked only in private practice for some time and prospered, I entered one of the most productive periods of my life in private practice.

I had more lessons to learn if I was to do well in pure private practice, without the financial safety net and the protection of a public hospital appointment. The ethic that I had been taught as a medical student, and held dear as a public hospital consultant with a salary, was that medical decisions should not be influenced by money. This was going to be tested. It is said that doctors should not play Robin Hood in the application of their trade by charging some patients more than others, which effectively means taking from one to pay for another. I had to think about such things. In public practice, there was a guaranteed income that could sustain even if it did not make one wealthy. In private practice, it was quite common to find oneself in a Catch-22 situation, and what to charge a patient for a particular service was an example. For the same procedure I could charge (in ascending order, nothing, the Medicare rebate, the Medical Benefit scheduled fee, the AMA rate, the insurance or workers' compensation rate, or whatever I liked, if I could get it. I concluded that this was a mixture of socialism, as Enid would have it, and capitalism, as I expect Bill Cook would advise it. In thinking about this, it became clear to me that Australia was very much a mixture of socialism and capitalism. There was a wide avenue in which to play Robin Hood.

The division of practice into public or private was too simplistic. There are, in fact, three systems in Australia. The first is the purely socialist system of the state government, where medical services are free through state hospitals and some community facilities. This system is funded directly by the states and indirectly by a Medicare payment, according to a formula, from the federal government. Money is limited; the promises are not. The job of the managers, looking at it cynically, is to provide as little as possible to the least number that can safely satisfy the baying public before elections. This may concur or conflict with the motives of the providers, who work for reasons of their own. These may be to acquire education, experience, status, reputation, power, or simply job security and satisfaction. Like all pure socialist systems, they are susceptible to corruption and failure. They continue in varying forms of success or failure, depending on the impurity of the socialism within the institution.

The second is known as the private system, but in reality, it's the federal system. It is a subsidised capitalistic system. Here, the doctors and many other health care workers are heavily subsidised by Medicare, and the patient pays a varying co-payment. The hospitals are paid by the insurance companies, and the premiums are subsidised by the federal government. General practice, radiology, pathology, and other diagnostic and health care services are also subsidised by the federal government through a Medicare payment on a fee-for-service basis. It is based on the fact that the provider makes a profit and pays some back to the federal government as tax (unless they're religious organisations that historically redirect services to the needy). If they make a persistent loss, they fail and withdraw the service. This system's survival is dependent on success. The weakness is that it is subject to manipulation and some control through the subsidy arrangements and the taxation office.

The third system is truly private. There is no government funding. Interestingly, this is probably the most successful. The fees are often exorbitant by comparison; nobody complains in public, and they sue if unhappy. It deals with consumer-driven surgery and diagnostic intervention; it's largely cosmetic surgery, expatriate, and overseas patients. It is entrepreneurial, competitive, and growing.

The nature of my practice would determine which character in Robin Hood's band I played; there were a number to choose from. I had only two rules: First, never send a debt collector; second, view nonpayment primarily as an expression of dissatisfaction with my work and pursue any enquiry into nonpayment from that angle. I had always enjoyed medicine and the personal connections that go with good practice. I would treat money as I always had: as manna from heaven. It would be there in the mornings. My public contribution would be the supply of free education for my colleagues, unpaid research, and pro bono service to the Australian and New Zealand Society of Vascular Surgery. I could diagnose and advise public patients through my private practice via the federal Medicare scheme and refer them on if they needed hospital admission for treatment.

Barbara, or Barb, as she was affectionately known, came with me. She was a very special nurse who had similar views. She had started nursing in the early days of cancer care, looking after patients having chemotherapy. The constant emotional drain took its toll, and she moved into the vascular field, testing people for claudication, that is, their limited walking distance, or when they started to limp from muscle pain resulting from lack of blood supply, which is angina of the leg. It is named *claudication* after the emperor of Rome, Claudius, who limped.

Barb's clinical skills led her to look after the leg ulcers and nonhealing wounds in the vascular clinic, and she became an expert in this field that historically was a surgical orphan surgical orphans are those areas poorly treated within the realms of surgeons, as they need constant and dedicated care, which is what nurses do so well, and so they have taken over; I will spare you the list of surgical orphans.

Barb kept a session at Royal Perth, where she continued to run the Leg Ulcer Clinic. Barb was my partner in practice. She was always there to watch over the patients and handled the practice when I was away. She supervised the patients in the ward with leg ulcers. Barb was so good that people never questioned whether she had an official right to do this; they just rang her for advice. I am sure more patients came to the practice to see Barb than they did to see me; the Silver Chain Home Nursing Service would refer recalcitrant nonhealing leg ulcers to us as a last resort. Nurses were not allowed to charge patients, but I charged for her services and welcomed the changed legislation to recognise nurse practitioners in their own right.

Without Barb, I could not have sustained my global involvement in research and development for the Zenith endograft. I knew that if a patient had a problem while I was away, she would deal with it or either get Marcel or another colleague to take over if we couldn't resolve it over the phone. Surgeons have their colleagues cover for them when they're away, but colleagues have their own practices as priorities, and hence the great value of Barb for triage, advice, and continuity of care.

The teaching workshops and clinical component of the Zenith courses moved with me to my private practice. Every Friday morning, my office was packed with doctors, planners, and visitors when we looked at the X-rays on the viewing screen on the wall of my consulting room. There was standing room only, but the view across Perth and up the Swan River made up for any inconvenience. These meetings were key to the planning decisions for the medical management and the tailoring of special stent-grafts.

Kylie, also a nurse by training, having worked in a cardiac catheter lab as a catheter and wire feeder was appointed as a full-time planner; her engaging personality and background melded with David's training in the art of planning to make her the backbone of the planning department. This was finally the acknowledgement we had been seeking from Cook on the importance of good planning. Andrew had never been entirely comfortable with Cook because of his independent character, still planned on a subcontracting basis.

After the meeting, David, Kylie and I would hold a teleconference with Barry Thomas and his troops in Brisbane about the Zenith graft. Barry had taken the job as product manager for the Stent-Graft in Australia. It had been a difficult position because of its growing complexity and rapid expansion. Barry was ideal and brought something special and strong to the venture. He was based in Brisbane. After he was appointed, he took a six-hour flight across the country to meet us. Barry was a nurse by initial training and had evolved from a Nimbin flower-power child to a right-wing business executive with a noticeable list to the left. He had a soft heart that endeared him to Michele and a thick skin that protected him from David. He had learned the commercial trade with Johnson & Johnson. After circling each other for a while, Barry merged well with David and me. I presume he liked us, but you wouldn't know from the heat in some discussions. The ultimate commercial success of the Zenith owes much to Barry.

My office was clearly a temporary solution. Combining this with an expiring lease in the Medical Research Building prompted the fitting out of the Cook R&D Centre in West Perth. The new facility would eventually house nine planners, machines to receive CT images from around the world, an X-ray machine for teaching and research, an engineer, a sewing room, a conference room, David's invention-strewn office, and a visitors' book that was virtually a register of endovascular enthusiasts from around the world.

There was a time in Australia when complex and high-tech surgery could only be performed and researched in a teaching hospital, but Medicare had changed that, and the technical advances thrived in the private system. Not that Medicare was detrimental for the Australian public. Quite the reverse, it ensured quality care for all and set up the competition between public and private systems. More than a public-versus-private rivalry, this was also a state-versus-federal intergovernmental competition, and it had teeth. Every action spawns a reaction, and what happened after the introduction of Medicare was that private hospitals, which were previously small exclusive concerns that catered to mainly bread-and-butter surgery for the better-off or religiously committed, had to suddenly compete for business.

If there were to be substantial costs for treatment in a private hospital, against no cost at all in the public hospitals, then private institutions would have to provide better service to justify the payments. The private hospitals were not restricted by legislation. They were free to compete, and compete they did, very effectively. Where government skimped for cost saving or forced egalitarianism, the private sector indulged. The rooms were more comfortable, and there were better radios, TVs, tempting meals, and little services that make a self-concerned person feel better. They endeavoured to radiate competence and went out of their way to attract competent, respected professionals to work in their institutions. In particular, they catered to surgeons. As many patients as one could handle found beds at convenient times. Operating times were available without having to fight, plead, or coerce, and extended operating hours were provided. Congenial gathering places that had been eroded away in public institutions were beckoning in the private hospitals; in particular, there was good food and drink to be had in the theatre complexes between cases. Operating theatre lounges, rather than being seen as privileges for the elite, were appreciated as meeting places for communicating and consulting with colleagues. Private hospitals extended hospitality to surgeons and doctors, and they in turn responded with custom and requests. Ultimately, surgeons want a quick, effective, comfortable course of treatment and outcome for their patients because it makes their job easier and more rewarding.

The private hospitals responded strongly, with hospitality and technology and an atmosphere of mutual appreciation. Whereas previously, surgeons provided their own instruments and sutures, these were now provided. Old familiar instruments rested like antiques in surgeons' private instrument cases. The size of the case and the nature of the adornment of the owner's name or initials had traditionally symbolised a surgeon's age and standing. The row of cases on racks at the theatre door slowly disappeared to homes or Third World countries as surgeons retired, moved on, or passed away.

Younger surgeons were provided for and drove the era of minimal invasion with fibre optics and digital images. New technology invariably appeared in private hospitals before public ones. They catered to the younger, highly trained surgeons. It was not a disadvantage for me to leave the major teaching institutions of the British traditional mode and work solely in the high-tech Mount Hospital in the high-tech American style. At the time, it was actually being run by an American company. I settled in full-time at Mount Hospital, with full access to the cardiology catheter lab. I had been helped by the hospital in previous years to have the manufacturer modify cardiology machines to suit my vascular requirements. Now I was invited to be involved in the choice of the replacement.

There were other advantages and reassurances. The intensive care unit was run by the same doctors who established intensive care in Royal Perth. The Mount had targeted high-tech requirements and was the only private hospital in Perth involved with open-heart surgery. This meant a full range of every specialty that mattered to me was immediately available. Above all, there was no rancour and no empires. I had flexibility to travel when I needed and could choose those to assist me or whom I wanted to teach. One institution regarded me as someone who should be grateful for the privilege of working there, as I was in the beginning, and should not be a nuisance, like Oliver Twist asking for more. The other institution adopted the opposite approach.

My social conscience was tired, frustrated, and pitted against a greater imperative to be practical to meet the passion for R&D

and educating others about endoluminal grafting of aneurysms. I rationalised the leaving of my alma mater by convincing myself that it was better for all concerned. The future of the graft and the freedom for vascular surgeons to have access to catheter labs in their own right were paramount. I saw access to facilities and acquisition of the skill set as the most important factors in the world for vascular surgeons. Whatever the odds, the oppositions, and the hurdles, it had to be achieved. Endoluminal stent-grafting of the aorta was the battleship, and Australia was aboard it. My positioning as a co-inventor of the Zenith and being one of a very small number of surgeons in the world with access to a catheter lab in their own right meant that I had a much greater purpose than self-indulgence.

I felt the double weight of the need to further prove the concept of endovascular surgery for aneurysms and establish the future of vascular surgeons with a catheter and wire skill set for aneurysms and occlusive disease. For vascular surgeons to convince their colleagues in the related disciplines of interventional radiology and cardiology that we had much to offer, it would not be enough to be as good as they were because we were coming from behind. We had to offer more, and we could because we diagnosed and operated. To be complete and unbiased in our recommendations for treatment, we needed to be complete in our skill sets of open and endovascular surgery. I had been given this chance to lead and felt the heavy weight of responsibility.

I expected to suffer after losing junior hospital doctor support that underlies the running of the public institutions and spares the senior doctor of many routine ward duties and day-to-day decisions. The junior doctor and teaching hospital infrastructure backs up the boss and addresses unexpected problems. No longer would I be able to refer complex cases or those who were uninsured from my outside private practice to the vascular unit to engage their support. No longer could I treat uninsured patients as in-patients without incurring hospital fees for them. Although I could see them as outpatients or for consultation, I knew I was to lose the privilege of being their doctor and surgeon through operations and illness needing hospital care.

Steeped in my mind was how important I had been to my bosses. I had the illusion that I had been essential to them. Now I would have to face working alone without what I had thought was essential support. My private practice had existed part-time for many years, and the question could be asked as to why I had such qualms. The reason was that to that point, for all my consultant life, my private practice had either been subsidiary to the teaching hospital commitment or worked in tandem. Now, I was solely self-reliant and unable to fall back on the public bastion, except to hand over a case completely and relinquish any right to input and management. I was surprised that instead of missing the support, I relished the security of doing it myself and being directly responsible. Brian Vivian had taught me to value the senior nurses, and that was one of the most important lessons I ever learnt. The clinical acumen of the senior ward nurses is sure and sound and trustworthy. If such a nurse tells you a patient is sick, then that patient needs to be seen immediately. If a nurse you know and trust tells you a patient is all right, then sleep well. The consistency and slow turnover of senior nurses in the ward, ICU, theatre, or catheter angiosuite more than substituted for junior doctor support, with its high turnover.

The skills of the operating theatre nurses are unique and an excellent source of surgical assistance. I knew them all, and their help and support were invaluable. With permission and generosity of the Mount Hospital, I employed Sue Girvan, one of their theatre nurses, as my constant surgical assistant. Sue was very experienced and had previously worked in the vascular theatre in Royal Perth as the senior vascular OR theatre nurse. Nurses are a truly unsung group of special people. Doctors may be valuable brains and carriers of responsibility, but I came to realise that it was nurses rather than doctors who were the backbone of hospitals. They never let me down, and I was guilty of taking their support for granted on some occasions.

To be fair to junior doctors, this was a hospital providing for planned and elective workloads. Where the junior hospital doctor value comes to the fore is in the acute, casualty, and emergency arenas. Having been immersed for so much of my surgical career in acute and emergency surgery, with its organised chaos, it was the contrast with order and the ability to plan and prepare that appealed so much at this time of my career. It was the ideal setting to give me the opportunity to maximise my commitment to the endovascular aneurysm revolution.

My exit from the teaching hospital coincided with the other events and movements I have described; no single factor is responsible. It seemed almost natural that I should leave. My heart surgery was more a catalyst than a reason. If anything, it allowed me to pass on the role of head of department and exit side stage. It excused me, my colleagues, and the hospital for the demise of the unit and enabled me to continue my involvement with the Zenith and continue to work with David and Cook outside the hospital. The evaporation of the spirit of cooperation, the squeeze of resources, and the loss of senior wisdom had meant an end in the land of the Lord of the Flies; the pig was dead.

It was by necessity rather than design that the research and development followed me into private practice at a crucial time in endoluminal grafting of aortic aneurysms. Whether it was real or just perceived, with the view of the global endovascular forum through our prism, it made no difference to what we did because we believed that the weight of proof-of-concept was as much on our shoulders as anywhere in the world. With the other grafts failing and there being nothing better than the Zenith, we had to prove, for the sake of concept, that endoluminal stent-grafting of aneurysms was preferable to open-wound surgery.

Endoluminal grafts were being used around the world in a patchy fashion and were a mixture of those that were homemade and those available commercially. The long-term reliance on endoluminal grafting was dependent on efficacy and global acceptance of concept. It was only the commercial products that would satisfy regulators, who were accelerating their efforts to safeguard the public and oversee a new and uncharted area. It was vitally important that commercial products did not fail. They were subject to close scrutiny and the prey of the many detractors who would lose from the success of the inventions and gain from their demise.

The FDA had the strongest infrastructure to regulate introduction of new technology, simply because the United States led the world in the supply of medical products, especially in cardiovascular technology. What the Americans had not conceived or invented, they had acquired or enticed into their country for further development, through the strength of their economy and freedom of thought. Although Cook Australia was US owned and the graft would be eventually theirs, doctors in America were impatient and complained bitterly about their lack of access to products that were available in Australia, Europe, South East Asia, South America, and South Africa.

For the moment, Australia found itself a leader. From what had started in Argentina, the introduction of endoluminal grafting for aneurysms to Australia was through Royal Prince Alfred Hospital, attached to Sydney University. They had led the way and showed the world new developments through the annual Sydney meeting. The unexpected success of the H&LB Stent-Graft, that went global as the Zenith graft, catapulted Perth onto the world stage, with me as the spokesperson. The invitation in Sydney had opened the door to stages around the world.

The contribution of the H&LB graft to the ultimate success and acceptance of the concept as being superior to open-wound surgery has been largely ignored. It became the backbone that sustained the concept amidst the fall of other devices. When the original Claude Mialhe graft sold out to Boston Scientific and the large American company relabelled it as the Vanguard graft and then crashed, it could have taken the rest of us with it. Images of tearing, corroding, collapsing, and failing Vanguard grafts were on the internet and displayed at every meeting. Its failure almost brought down Boston Scientific. The concomitant failure of the EVT graft left the Zenith shouldering a huge responsibility as the longest survivor of the era.

The World Medical Co., which sounds like a large firm but was actually quite small, produced a durable graft that had many of the features of the H&LB graft, but it did not compete well in Australia (which was loyal to the local product), although it became increasingly popular in Asia and Europe. After World Medical was purchased by the Medtronic Co., it was rebadged and sold commercially as the Talent graft. The Zenith and Talent withstood the ravages of time, fatigue, pressure pulses of circulation, twists and turns of the body, and the commercial world. We developed repair modules for Stent-Grafts that had moved, which could also be used for other graft types, and this helped sustain the concept.

Regulators have to neither suggest nor drive innovation. Their role is a gatekeeper, and the gates start to close with detection of a problem or objection by a peer who identifies a threat to human safety. In the United States, endoluminal grafts were being tried by individual institutions according to their system of IDEs (investigation and device evaluations), with strict rules of engagement. The strict process to follow for US approval takes years. There is absolutely no doubt that approval for sale by the FDA strongly influences approval in other countries; the reverse is certainly not true, and trials of devices outside America carry little weight in the States. Medtronic's Aneurex graft was first to market in America. It had the advantage of being US-designed and -manufactured, with a smoother path to approval without trying to use foreign data.

However, early failures threatened to repeat the history of failed grafts and added to the cries of "a failed experiment." Taking on commercialisation of an endovascular graft was causing headaches and sleepless nights for corporate executives and damaged more than one company. Medtronic had the foresight to purchase the Talent graft and as a result had two horses in the stable: Aneurex, which became popular because it was the only one available in America without a special investigator's licence, and the Talent, which was favoured in Europe and Asia.

During this time, some Zenith grafts were inserted in the States under IDE licence, especially at the Cleveland Clinic; significantly, Roy Greenberg chose a Zenith for presidential candidate Bob Dole. The Zenith may not have had FDA approval, but it certainly had a reputation and peer approval.

There were a number of differences between the Talent graft and the Zenith graft, essentially in the materials used and the delivery system. In design, they were very similar, and these qualities bestowed the most important factors of reliability and durability. This did not surprise us, as we always believed that it had been created following that meeting in Sydney, when our samples and specification documents were stolen. We could not prove that, nor did we want to because it was in our interest that it succeeded for proof of concept. If it was a copy, then we were flattered and pleased to have helped. Watching the approval process from outside the United States and being drawn into the process through endeavours to have the Zenith graft approved for market taught me many valuable lessons, and one in particular.

When a company believes it is ready to market a product, it makes a number of claims relating to what the product can do. The company then needs to back this with a trial of use in humans. To do this in the United States, the company applies to the FDA, which obviously carries a huge responsibility. Like all responsible organisations, it probably receives little thanks and can be quite severe in its judgement. So the lesson is, do not promise too much.

Imagine two similar products vying for approval. There is competition and a temptation to claim that your product is better than the other. To claim one is better may be good publicity but poor strategy. Like the wise doctor of the Pilbara, who always prepared his patients for the worst outcome so they thought he did a good job in difficult circumstances, it is wise to avoid extravagant claims. The primary tool of regulators is examination of whether a product meets the claims made of it. Whether the claims are sufficient to satisfy the medical community is a different question and has to be presented in a different forum for approval and acceptance, namely a peer medical one.

For example, product A claims that it can do something right 97 percent of the time, and product B claims to get it right 94 percent of the time. The results show that product A got it right 96 percent and product B 94 percent. The regulator can approve product B, which is medically inferior, because it met the claim it made, but it cannot approve product A because it did not, even though product A performed better than product B. Product B may satisfy the regulator but not the docs, and there is the potential scenario of neither succeeding because A failed the regulator test and B the peer review test. Concepts may go down in the process.

The Talent and Aneurex story is a good example. The Talent graft failed to meet unreasonable claims made for it and get FDA approval, and the Aneurex started to fail the medical peer review. The need to have both regulator and peer acceptance of concept and product was the mountain facing us. The focus of endeavours was clearly to gain approval of the Zenith by the FDA for market in America. It already had peer medical approval as a result of the evidence collected in the UK trials and use over many years in many places outside the United States.

The British have their own way of assessing technology and are past masters of the clinical medical trial. The organised infrastructure of the British National Health scheme makes these trials feasible and more reliable for complete evidence collection. The British, led by Professors Roger Greenhalgh and Janet Powell, started a trial through Imperial Sciences University in London to compare endoluminal grafting of aneurysms with open-wound surgery. This was the trial that would launch the endoluminal method into the future or condemn it to the past as, indeed, a failed experiment.

I could sense my colonial and military ancestors rising from their graves to battle with, or for, the imperial cause. Never was Machiavelli's statement that "the initiator has the enmity of all who would profit by the preservation of the old institutions and merely lukewarm defenders in those that would gain from the new ones" been more true. The regulator test was therefore US-based and the medical peer review UK-based.

To add pressure on us, it was clear that the endoluminal grafts that would be used in the UK trial would be mainly Zenith and then the Talent. This was going to be a de facto trial of the Zenith. The scene was set by a debate held at the Phoenix meeting on whether the endoluminal method compared with open-wound surgery. The debate was led by Professor Peter Harris from the UK, who spoke for open-wound surgery and opposed another good friend, Wolf Stelter from Germany, who spoke for the endoluminal method. The British excel in the art of debating, and Peter was a master artist. He weaved a web of sarcasm, pun, innuendo, distracting false analogies, and veiled insults in a way that only masters of English and debating can do. Wolf, on the other hand, despite great conviction and passion, had to debate in his second language and lost. He was ensnared in Peter's web, and I could see it happening.

Afterwards, I said to Peter, a committed endovascular supporter and architect of the Eurostar Registry to collect data on endografts, "You've put us back ten years."

Although there was an understanding that these debates were meant to be intervals of fun in what can otherwise be wearying events with a deluge of facts and figures, many true words are spoken in jest, and his win carried weight.

However much I believed that we were right and should be vindicated, I was wary of the conclusions that would come out of the UK trial. The results of clinical medical trials are a bit like legal court case trials. They depend on the questions asked, and there is always lingering disagreement on the judgement and distrust of the reasons given. They are usually followed by an appeal. Trials are followed by trials. This was not going to be any different for us, and the weight of responsibility for a product in this dangerous and emotionally charged field was heavy. It was made heavier by the relative cost of the products on the market. New products are always expensive, having to recoup the costs of research, development, insurance, and legal fees. Not only were preservers of the old institutions vociferous, but so were the purchasers of the new technology for the public. There were many who were very keen for the concept of endoluminal stent-grafting of aneurysms to be condemned.

Research is a hard taskmaster and a jealous dictator. Like all dictators, it can be corrupted, needs good press, and is fraught with risks of manipulation and blindness when mixed with commercialism. An adverse finding or revelation of a weakness could mortally wound a development project. When mixed with risk to human life, pain, horror events, and financial ruin, the burden of responsibility is enormous.

Players in the field of exciting new ventures want to star and have the skills and prowess to take pride of place on the stage. The stage for endovascular grafting of aneurysms was the live case medical conference. Should the players fail, their careers could be curtailed. If the failure can be sheeted home to device fault or supply error, the player maybe spared at the expense of the product; it becomes a battleground for survival. Blame is the spear and instrument of attack with any adverse event, and defences are mounted to counter the attackers. Blame can be pointed at obvious targets in the chain, from the basic research stage to the finest wire or the last step in production.

Whenever there is a failure, especially a failure causing injury or death, then the regulators are hauled before the public judge. Regulators are the ultimate vulnerable target for blame when all else fails. As a consequence, they are wary. They become inured to accusations of obstruction because they know the risk to themselves. For regulators and authorities, one yes may be worse than a thousand nos. For us, with a product built on available approved materials with surgical and engineering intuition, based on anecdotal experience, and negotiating a veritable minefield of unknown patents, this was an adventure that would fit well beside those of Jules Verne.

Champion operators and performers on the medical stage are like sporting champions. This was an era in cardiovascular medicine when live case demonstrations were key attractions at conferences, and scenes from operating rooms were beamed into auditoriums for all to see. Skilled operators who were also good entertainers made the arena exciting and attractive. That was important for the organisers because medical conferences were big business. The stars, like sports stars, rose rapidly to prominence. Any problem, and the product moved into the firing line. The stars survived by changing teams or equipment. The product that fell short was short-lived, bought, or sold-out. The analogy could be extended to all aspects of premiere league sports, but this was like Formula One racing: a crash would likely cause serious injury to driver and machine.

Was I a driver? Yes, sometimes at conferences and always at the teaching workshops.

Did I enjoy it? Yes, most of the time, because I only used the devices we designed and made, and I was in control of patient selection and expected outcome. In other words, when I maintained control and was able to ensure that the patient understood what was happening with public display of the procedure, I felt confident. I liked to teach surgery, and this was teaching. Yet there are great dangers in public displays of skill and innovations. The medical field is often compared with aviation; this extends to air shows, which are renowned for occasional and spectacular disasters. That's what brings the crowd. The secret thrill that it might happen. It is an underlying malignant attraction to a blood-sport.

The reality was that I couldn't change teams because as co-inventor, I was inextricably committed solely to the Zenith Stent-Graft. I was coach and playing captain. I was a gladiator in the colosseums of modern medical theatre, and the accompanying lavish conference dinners echoed with the silent cry of "Eat, drink, and be merry, for tomorrow we may die."

Was I a champion? No, I was insufficiently extroverted to be really entertaining; my skill set was not flamboyant, and I disliked being the centre of any drama. I hate things that go wrong. I knew that my insecurities and any consternation would be immediately apparent to the wolves at the ringside. I've witnessed disasters unfold in live medical theatre at conferences with a sense of growing horror and wished fervently to avoid such a scene. Some players thrived on difficulties and unexpected challenges; they drew the audiences into the drama. They seemed able to deflect criticism and conjure a happy ending, even in the face of a tragedy in theatre. These were the stars of Medical Broadway.

When unexpected or entirely new problems arose during a case, we labelled them "Italian jobs." This came from *The Italian Job,* the classic movie with Michael Caine that described a successful gold bullion heist that went wrong during the escape when the bus crashed on a mountain escarpment. The bus was perched with the back half hanging over the edge of a cliff; the bullion was at the back and the crooks in the front, keeping the balance so the bus didn't tip over into the valley below. Any attempts by the thieves to move to recover the bullion or leave the bus threatened to tip the bus over the cliff, and they all had differing ideas of how to fix the problem. My worst nightmare was to be faced with an unexpected problem during a demonstration and be overcome by cries of "I have an idea." It was losing control to an audience of experts, outnumbered only by their own ideas.

Soon after John DeFord turned the H&LB graft into the Zenith, he arranged for us all to attend a meeting in Venice. At that meeting was Barry Katzen, an eminent American radiologist from Miami. Barry ran a popular meeting every year, and in this new era of the endovascular revolution, he wanted to include us in his program, with a live demonstration of a case with the Zenith graft. He asked me if I would do it and proposed that it be beamed to the States via satellite, as this would be both novel and circumvent the legal and registration hurdles for me to operate in America.

The invitation was most flattering. It was an opportunity to showcase the world. The proposed date was January 26, which happens to be Australia Day. After meeting with Barry and John DeFord, I walked around the square in Venice and pondered how best to do it. There would have to be someone in Miami to describe the device and its delivery system and present the information on its performance. This was my job, but I could not be in two places at once. The obvious answer was to have a colleague do the operation in Australia while I acted as the mediator in Miami. The most accomplished operator and performer was John Anderson; his theatre in Adelaide was modern, with a newer machine and better ambience to showcase Australia to the Americans.

It was agreed that the Perth team, all of us, would go to the Miami meeting, and John would do a live case in Adelaide that would be transmitted by satellite to the conference hotel. The scheduled time in Miami was 10:30 a.m., which meant that it was midnight in Adelaide. Adelaide being the City of Churches emphasised its uniqueness by having its time zone on the half-hour. John would start the operation at midnight to satisfy the TV audience, and again the sporting analogy sprung to mind. At the appointed hour, the satellite images appeared on the giant conference screen. John and his team were standing at the ready with the patient asleep and hidden under the usual green drapes, but the X-ray machine poised over the patient was draped in a very large sterilised Australian flag (after all, it was Australia Day). The graft was expertly shown to the American medical fraternity on a most appropriate day.

Disasters during operations televised on closed-circuit TV are often obvious to all, and sometimes, only a few of us really know what's wrong. Sometimes, an adverse outcome is leaked later. Not all deaths and injury from an operation occur in the theatre; probably most happen in the post-operation period. Despite the mishaps and cringe-worthy episodes, live case demonstrations persisted for their teaching value in some forms, but measures to eliminate the blood-sport component and negative aspects have reduced real-time exposure. They are much less of a draw than they were at the turn of the century, when they were so much in vogue in the cardiovascular field.

The revolution in the technology brought with it new techniques and skill sets for the minimal invasion operation, which needed to be taught very quickly, and real-time demonstrations served this purpose. After the novelty wore off, the negatives took over. Boredom with yet another demonstration of a technique that had become routine and a growing antipathy to seeing any adverse event displayed on the giant screen turned people away. Whether the legal profession played any part in this because the evidence was on display, I don't know. Prepared videos of real procedures and delayed telecasts began to replace real-time demonstrations.

As a co-inventor and pioneer, I was expected to demonstrate and teach, but I was determined to advise and operate only on those for whom there was a clear benefit and every expectation of a good outcome. If I was to operate, then I would select a suitable patient and perform in my own theatre. There was a view that real-time operations were the best way to teach observers how to deal with problems. I did do some public operations that were transmitted to audiences within Australia and internationally, avoiding any tragedies. The flirt with publicity and risks of displaying difficulties, or worse still an adverse event, reinforced Professor DeBakey's advice that it was much better to educate practicalities in one's own environment and classroom. The monthly workshops in Perth served that purpose comfortably.

I wondered during that era why patients participated in the medical theatre. Some may not have wished it and felt it was their duty to be an instrument for teaching. Others may have accepted on trust that the doctors would do the best they could in their interest, and some, I suspect, agreed for reasons of financial advantage (expensive procedures or prostheses would often be supplied free in exchange for their participation). Undoubtedly, some enjoyed the theatrical experience and actively participated. Many procedures were performed under local anaesthetic, with the operator interacting with the patient as well as the audience; this was quite apparent on the screen. Most surprising to me was that some patients want to be proud of their doctor.

This last motive was revealed to me when I was apologising to a patient for leaving the country fairly soon after his operation. In doing so, I expressed that it was a somewhat unwanted chore rather than a pleasure and certainly not a holiday. I was admonished, quite rightly, and made to realise that it is a very great honour to be asked by one's peers to speak to them. Some patients probably felt that they had teamed up with their doctor, and it certainly looked that way on occasion. I do understand that possibility because it relates to the special bond that can develop between surgeon and patient. I may not have always fulfilled the conference and workshop conveners' wishes and expectations, but since being admonished by my patient for alluding to the task as a chore rather than a privilege, I have always tried my best. I spent many hours between 2:00 a.m. and dawn preparing slides and videos of operations and hope that I have not let down those who believed in me.

Chapter 30

The Aortic Advance

The endovascular stent-graft, being delivered from a remote site, was constructed in modules that were delivered like building blocks. It was an endoluminal construction. It was like building a space station; any loss of control would spell disaster. When success was regularly achieved in the segments of the aorta that did not have major branches, the challenges of the adjacent and more complex segments taunted us. Every time a solution was achieved, it served to open the gate to another field. Solutions were like steps to the pot of gold at the end of the rainbow, forever moving away. We developed windows in the walls of the stent-graft through which we could project branches and in this way handle segments of the aorta with important branches that had to be preserved. The main arteries to the kidneys, the gut, and the liver are examples.

When we became proficient, we moved to teach others and often from another state or country. The aim was to get to the end of the endovascular rainbow and treat every segment and every branch of the aorta with a minimally invasive approach. While the aorta continued to be the focus for us, the valves of the heart were being tackled by cardiologists, cardiothoracic surgeons, and vascular surgeons who were colleagues collaborating in the endovascular field. Some even started doing this by a direct puncture through the chest wall with a sheath into the apex of the heart, when the path from the groin through a twisted diseased aorta posed too many hazards, but the groin approach remained the preferred entry site to the cardiovascular system.

Years before, in another field of surgery, I had seen eminent surgeons visiting Australia perform operations to teach or demonstrate new techniques. I observed a tendency for very difficult problems to be served up to the visitors. A number of visitors left problems behind, and one advised me to resist the invitations to operate away from home to avoid this. With the more complex operations, I made this a firm policy, and to its credit, the company understood. Would-be operators with the new modules would therefore visit Perth to learn about the new modules, study their delivery systems, plan for them with David on the bench, and then join me in the theatre for a demonstration. When they were confident and had a suitable case of their own, we would vet the planning and selection and then travel to their theatre and guide them while they did the operation. In that way, the patient's doctor was still his or her doctor. This ensured the best chance that the operation would go smoothly, and the doctor who operated retained responsibility and continued with the post-operation care.

Doctors in this situation tended to be more choosy with the cases they selected. This policy made me less attractive as a guest performer, but in the longer term, it was the key to durable new modules and methods. The number of skilled endovascular operators multiplied quickly. The visitors' book for attendees was graced by the names of most Australian and New Zealand vascular surgeons of the era, together with a great number of international vascular surgeons who were well known leaders in the field or would become so later. A steady sprinkling of interventional radiologists, cardiologists, and cardiothoracic surgeons' names filled out the multidisciplinary record.

If I had accepted more invitations to operate on the world stage at live case conferences and lead the operating teams, I might have become a more famous (or infamous) operator. I sometimes wonder if I should have accepted these invitations, like many of my colleagues did, and starred along with the champions like John Anderson, Jim May, and Roy Greenberg. Instead, I was happy to guide other surgeons in their operating rooms and comment on a panel. For better or worse, I increasingly declined invitations to operate outside my own theatre and only accepted invitations to present papers at conferences or to teach in a workshop.

In the beginning, it was easy for me to be new and different on the podiums of the world, because we were innovating new and different things. Traditionally, it was taught that once a scientific paper was presented, it should not be repeated. It did not work that way on the world stage, and a good act was recruited for another meeting. Speakers for many premier meetings were by invitation only. A speaker was only invited when his presentation was brought to the attention of convenors who wanted the same or similar for their next meeting. The rationale for inviting a speaker to repeat the performance was that there were a series of meetings around the world, and it was acceptable to repeat a presentation to a different audience. Partly true, but many of the audience would travel to attend the different venues, in which case it was substantially the same audience. Then it was justified that hearing a good talk for a second time was like reading a good book a second time. There was always appreciation for points missed, forgotten, or repeated.

In reality, medical meetings had become big business. They evolved from forums for discussion to educational circuses. Repeating material was justified on that basis, especially when invited. Daring feats of novelty, skill, and expertise made for a serious circus, and failures were as lethal as falls from any high wire without a net. I tried to make each presentation different in its own way and enjoyed using the surprise factor. This was feasible during the development and progressive stage, with

David's ingenuity and engineering skills keeping us ahead. I had to be increasingly ingenious as the endovascular field gained other speakers and achieved a critical mass of data for concept acceptance with users and regulators.

The talks and workshops concentrated on education, and the journal publications served for scientific revelation, as they were subject to peer review. I kept in my mind Justice Michael Kirby's quote: "It is not the greatest sin to cause occasional offence: to be boring, unkind or self-righteous competes for that award," and I tried hard not to be boring.

Speaking at such prestigious conferences and seminars is not without its stresses, and for each of us, the stresses are unique. In the beginning, I had to compete for the sake of the concept and for those I represented. This was accompanied by a passionate belief that what I was doing was right. After the concept was proven and the graft commercialised, the passion subsided and was replaced by the imperative to educate. Competition was driving the revolution; competitors thrive or do not survive on their reactions to stress. The causes of the stresses vary with each individual, and the outlet for the stress can be expressed in many different forms, from a rash to some other reaction.

A simple example that stressed me was travel. Since Perth is exactly on the other side of the earth from New York, for me to speak there, I could travel for thirty hours in an easterly direction or thirty-plus hours in a westerly direction, depending on the jet stream. It eventually became too taxing to arrive, exhausted, to speak for a few minutes, with biorhythms polarised. The compensation of meeting overseas colleagues and making new friends, networking, and listening to these friends and colleagues started to fall behind the fatigue factors.

Furthermore, each meeting led to other invitations. I could have travelled to speak in North America, the UK, Europe, Africa, or Asia every week. It is difficult to say no to earnest colleagues and good friends who are being generous and extending both a hand of support and a compliment, with invitations that others would cherish. Yet if you try to please everyone, you end up pleasing no one. More and more, I wanted to stay home. I could not present if I did not work, and I still had to run my practice and workshops in Perth, research, and teach. The worst imaginable scenario for me would be that I was on the other side of the world when a patient I had operated on developed an emergency complication. I made it a rule to only operate on the simplest cases the week before going overseas. Consequently, the weeks prior to that and the two weeks on return were exhausting.

The medical students' feedback was negative in the extreme because of my repeated absences; they resented being delegated to another tutor. I had obviously dropped them further down the priority list, and they felt it. The criticism stung. I reacted by dropping undergraduates and persuading myself that postgraduate endovascular instruction was a better role for me. My ego seduced me to believe that my global role was more important than the local, and I forgot that teaching starts at home. When away presenting at a conference or teaching, there was little or no time for family, and the phone calls were invariably at difficult times. The time differences also made practice management awkward. I could not afford to be out of communication with the practice, and if people didn't know I was in a different time zone, then the phone could ring in the early hours of the morning. On the family side, I would text or leave messages like "Say hello to the children for me" because it was always an awkward time to speak to them.

At least I had some peace on the aeroplanes during long flights and time to reflect and contemplate. I became conscious of how I was pampered in business class; the more I flew, the more points I accumulated, and the more I was feted. Of course, I benefited by the rest and maybe performed better on arrival, but I questioned whether it was fair on my colleagues travelling to conferences in economy class because they were paying for themselves. I did not give it a thought in the beginning and was grateful for the relief. Then in an idle moment, I pondered on the actual costs. The company or conference organisers were paying with pretax dollars and claimed my fare back as a tax deduction: taxpayers were subsidising my fare. The family and recreational travelling taxpayers in economy class were paying with post-tax dollars. They were subsidising my seat while uncomfortable in their own. Should I write to the politicians or publish a paper suggesting that businesses and companies only be able to claim the equivalent of a standard seat fare as a tax deduction? I answered myself in the negative because the company may then send me on a standard seat fare. I decided it would be better to keep quiet, as I had nothing to do with how the system worked. That was a lesson in how commercialisation insidiously corrupts. It need only seek silence.

Finally, believe it or not, it was the five-star hotels that laid the last straw on my loaded wagon of discontent. I grew to dislike them. I was still a student at heart and retained a student's value for money. As I was whirled around the world in a distorted value system, I clung desperately to the past, like holding onto the sand when diving below a wave in heavy surf. Something that had been a treat and should have continued to be a pleasure was unfortunately turned into emptiness when I realised the veneer of friendliness and eagerness of hotel staff wore through to expose the reality that this was all about commercialism and not the true love that family and friendship gives.

Once exposed, the survival imperative in the rough infrastructure of capitalism glared out from the torn fabric and held restrictions that projected hotels as prisons or boarding schools. Asian hotels were more appealing, with better value for money, despite using a Western franchise, and I perceived a difference in value between Asia and America that was wedged wider by the frequency of travel to both. I started to ponder the reasons why so much of the Western world was being outsourced to China. I grew up with an item stamped "Made in Britain" or

"Sheffield," if it were of steel. Now, wherever I went, the items were stamped "Made in China."

No one made excuses for outsourcing, and national pride gave way to global exploitation above and beyond the colonial era. For me, there was no longer any incentive to shop overseas. As the famous comedians of the sixties, Peter Cook and Dudley Moore, said in *Beyond the Fringe*, "I can get all that at home." I started to feel a sadness when reading a label "Designed in Australia: Made in China" and realised that eventually anything that we invented would likely go offshore.

Most of all I resisted the urge to think of Americans as different. These were my colleagues and friends. They were easy and comfortable with their systems, and I should do in New York as the New Yorkers do and tip the waiter generously.

"Don't let it get to you," a sympathetic American friend and colleague said. "Have a drink, charge it to someone else, and relax."

The more we have, the more we expect. I noticed, paradoxically, that often those with the most paid the least and were the least likely to shout the round of drinks. Often, when I tried to shout a round, I was told it had already been taken care of, as I had already been generous in travelling so far. I learned to be more gracious in accepting hospitality when away and responding in kind when at home. I turned my conscience away from what was fair and looked more towards optimising my time and efforts. I resorted to travelling with my own multivolt-tolerant kettle, a cup, and a packet of tea that I would supplement from any local store with proper milk and some fruit. I would then camp happily in my room, content that I could make my tea while I worked in the early hours of the morning without ringing for cold silver service.

Then I started to appreciate that travelling to teach was an opportunity to see the world, and rather than worrying about life in hotels and conference centres, I made sure that Michele and I could supplement the work with exploration to see the wonders extending in front of us. We climbed the Twin Towers the year before they fell, walked across Scotland, and visited real places in Asia, Europe, the Americas, South Africa, and even Antarctica: Rome, Venice, Athens, Copenhagen, Stockholm, Paris, Berlin, the Forbidden City (where the guide solemnly informed us that the emperor had a thousand "cucumbines"), the Temple of Heaven, the Great Wall, and many more wondrous places that had existed only as myths and stories of heroes when we were at school. That I should see where Caesar spoke had to be special, and how remiss I would have been not to take a few minutes to see the real magic of human endeavour that was all around us.

I began tipping in Australia and enjoyed the smiles of gratitude on the faces of the backpacker waiters and immigrant taxi drivers. Eventually, this helped me realise that the importance of being important was not important. When I could step back enough to observe my colleagues vying for the pecking order and struggling on the world ladder, I realised I was coming to the end of my dash. It was time to hand over my baton to a younger spokesperson from an iconic institution that was more suitable to America and the global stage. I could start taking the advice to have a drink and relax. The unimportant irritations that burned me up were merely signs that I was looking to blame something else for my weaknesses, difficulties, and dilemmas.

It is strange how a solution presents itself to a dilemma if the problem is recognised and pondered. After all the daily distractions fade into the background and sleep takes over, the brain works on finding the answer, like leaving the brain to work out how to throw a ball and land it on a target. Of course, it takes practice to build up the reflexes, but that's what productive worry is all about. In the end, the most important elements of all are timing, training, and luck. The main dilemma for me was how and when to jump off a moving train. I did not want a push from behind or a nasty fall when going too fast.

A way was presented to me. Roy Greenberg's appointment to the Cleveland Clinic provided the perfect time, the right person, and institutional backing. This would suit Cook better. Timing was the key, and the final push for FDA approval to market the Zenith in America was the opportunity. Roy was ready. He had run the trial of use for the USA from the Cleveland Clinic. If approval was given, he would have the baton.

CHAPTER 31

The FDA Panel: April 10, 2003

The Aneurex graft, being first to market in the United States with approval by the FDA in June 1999, was enjoying booming sales in the largest market in the world. This placed Cook behind the Aneurex and made them very keen to gain American approval. Cook knew that the big market was the States. The success of the Zenith graft around the world paled against the potential benefits of approval by the FDA for the American market.

It was not only a sales issue in the United States; it was also a matter of gaining complete control of the product they owned and wresting it from the disproportionate influence of the Australian subsidiary. Cook needed a body of American doctors to be the experts with the Zenith, and logically, this was not going to happen until the product was available to them. The more success and experience the Australian, European, and Asian users acquired, the more frustrated the potential American users became, and this translated into some anger against the company.

A common statement heard at US conferences was, "Why keep showing us the product and having it dominate talks at medical conferences if we can't use it?"

To start in the States required a limited number of selected doctors to have approval from the FDA to be an investigator for device evaluation (IDE), and then there was a lengthy process for permission to run a multicentre use trial. The Australian data, although valuable in its own way and sufficient outside America, did not really expedite the process in the States. Eventually, the green light was given for the Zenith to go for trial, and Roy Greenberg ran the pivotal trial from the Cleveland Clinic. The data looked good, and the FDA panel date was set for April 10, 2003. David and I flew to Washington to share in the final week of preparation for presentation to the experts assembled by the FDA. If the presentation failed to pass the panel, it could take years before it could be presented again, during which time the question of why it was not approved in America would hang like a pall in every other country.

I came to understand why Cook had been somewhat hesitant to develop in Australia, as it would have been better to develop, investigate, and evaluate in the States, as that would lead directly to a trial, as happened with the Aneurex. If the stable for the horse was in the United States, it could run elsewhere in the world, but if the stable was outside America, it could not run in the States. It took a long time for David and me to really see that; in retrospect, it was a great compliment to us that Cook continued to support our work in Australia in the development and introduction of Stent-Grafts. American companies were appropriately restricted in the introduction and use of new devices in humans, but their laws did not apply to us. As a result, American companies would often try their new devices in other countries to see if they worked, while keeping US stable ready to run trials if the devices proved to be good. Other countries could benefit by this policy because they had access to new technology much earlier, but they paid the price if the device failed.

David and I were there as observers and, where necessary, as advisers and commentators. We knew this was an American matter. It was for the home team to make the plays. Roy was central to the presentation of the data. Tim Chuter was to present and demonstrate the device and its deployment, and Dr Richard Green, from the University of Rochester, presented the comparative advantages of the endovascular approach to that of open-wound surgery. Ted and Matt collated the whole presentation, and Neal Fearnot analysed the data. Neal worked for a Cook subsidiary called Med Institute at Purdue University and had managed the whole introduction into the United States, optimising the use of the Australian data. We were housed in a hotel in Washington near the FDA offices. A function room was rented for the week and converted to a work area, as I imagined a war office would be like.

American freedom of speech and democracy were clearly evident in the room that week. There was no rank pulling. By the end of the week, there were no omissions, no unanswerable questions, and an impressive analysis of the data. In particular, nothing was hidden, and when panel day arrived, the team approached the venue with a confident air of pride in the honesty of their work.

The lead-up to the panel meeting and the years of absorbing rumours of the ferocity of the FDA and its ability to frustrate combined to create a heavy atmosphere in the large hall, which now had standing room only. Fortunately, someone had reserved a seat for me, and then Frank Veith sat next to me and conveyed his wish for the Zenith to succeed.

First, the chairman welcomed all and invited any person in the public to come forward and speak if they wished (a bit like a marriage celebrant calling for anyone who objects to come forward or forever hold their peace). A tall, impressive man stepped up to the podium. It was Bob Dole, the former US senator who had been treated in 2001 for aneurysm by Roy with a Zenith Stent-Graft in the Cleveland Clinic.

"I am not here today to endorse a specific product," Dole said. "I'm just here to tell my story, and I'm happy to be here today."

He then said something about having to go to Ground Zero in New York to give a speech to the firemen. He apologised for not being able to stay but wanted to hear the result later. Then he left. The mood that he had created percolated through the room.

The presentations went without a hitch, just like the rehearsals. Then the panel started to ask questions. There were some curly, incisive thrusts. There were hypothetical scenarios, future projections, and trick questions from all around. These were parried and genteelly negotiated and at the same time answered with a forthrightness that also pre-empted the obvious question to follow as well, thereby moving the initiative a little further away from the array of experts, ranging from psychiatrist through bioengineer and statistician to pathologist. I could not fault the performance on either side, and then the statistician on the panel started to raise questions. Benjamin Disraeli, while prime minister of Great Britain, is purported to have said, "First there are lies, then there are damned lies, and then there are statistics." I wondered where this was going to lead.

It was now Neal Fearnot's turn. I had known Neal for a number of years and did as much as I could to help with the Australian data. He had carried the responsibility for the strategies, and there had been more than a little flack about how long the process had taken. The salesmen were restless. The statistician on the panel, a woman, was well versed in all the weaknesses of clinical trials in surgery, a male-dominated area, because of the multiple parameters beyond anyone's control. Her attack was like a cavalry charge from the side when the outcome of the battle was in the balance.

Neal met the challenge head-on, and I realised his worth when I lost any grasp on the arguments of offence and defence when the level of mathematics escalated so quickly, and to such a high level, that the eyes of the others on panel and all of the audience glazed over. I had no way of knowing if the statistician was satisfied or not. The heat generated by the arguments evaporated the content completely. I have held Neal in great respect ever since: one who could sing in the beautiful language of mathematics.

By a vote of eight to zero, the panel approved the Zenith Stent-Graft device and its H&L-B one-shot delivery system. I could rest assured that my work was essentially over. Roy had the baton firmly in his grasp.

There was one very important task left to take care of that day. Terumo, a Japanese company, had just purchased the Vascutek Vascular Graft Co., which supplied the textile material for the Zenith Stent-Graft. If this company had a stent-graft waiting in the wings, it could kill the Zenith graft on its honeymoon. It could do what Boston Scientific had done almost ten years before and forbidden their material to be used in the Stent-Graft. I wished I could be less sceptical and suspicious of success, but I felt compelled, even in this hour of relief and celebration, to gain the attention of the company product managers and seek assurance that they were aware of this and would seal a deal with Terumo for a supply of graft textile material into the future.

This they did, and David and I flew back to Australia to do what we did best in Perth. We concentrated on developing the Stent-Graft further. David worked away on new designs, trialling new materials and different ways of sewing. He extended his network of special users through Roy and Tim in the States, and we expanded the cohort of special users through Europe, Australia, New Zealand, and Asia by collaborating with them to create tailor-made grafts for special problems beyond the standard devices.

CHAPTER 32

America Sails and American Sales

When Cook was granted approval to sell the Zenith Endovascular Stent-Graft in America, it was a game-changer. In the lead-up to approval, the company had prepared to meet the coming demand and swung manufacturing in Bloomington, Indiana, into full-scale production. Clearly and absolutely, the centre of further research and development was intended for the United States, and the company slipped into the pattern of doing R&D in America and trialling innovative products within an IDE licence to Roy or Tim in the States and selected users overseas.

Outsourcing of manufacturing might occur in the future, as happens with globalisation, but for the time being, it was to be firmly entrenched in Bloomington; the facility had been built primarily for that purpose. Measures to appease any users affected by the shift of focus from Australia to the States would be done by funding conference sponsorships and support for continuing medical education. Education would be the key to compensate for any concerns. There would now be a release of funds in the cycle of production, sale, and return. The funds to support conferences and education would come from profits rather than the company reserves. Complete control was vested in Bloomington, and Perth was set to wind down.

David and I had essentially served our purpose and were summoned to Bloomington. We flew there to spend a day with the president of the company and his management team. It took more than a day to get there, but it was imperative that we be there in person. There was much to discuss, and I cannot recall any meeting that was ever more poignant. The hardest part for me to believe was that we went to Midwest America from Perth for the day.

It would have been foolhardy not to accept that control and management should rightly be in the company's headquarters. It would have been even more foolish to think we were in any strong position to negotiate. This was a private company in Bloomington, where Bill Cook lived and the company thrived. He had built it from his garage to be worth billions, as judged by Guidant's offer to buy it in 2003; its value and sphere of influence has soared since. He built it on the railroad of guide wires that he made from modified guitar strings; the carriages that travelled on these rails were the catheters and balloons that he made for angiography and angioplasty. He had ventured into the new field of technology for cardiovascular disease with the pioneers of diagnostic and interventional radiology and cardiology.

Angioplasty of the coronary and peripheral arteries had changed the world, and Bill had ridden shotgun beside the innovators such as Dotter and Judkins. He had funded institutions like the Oregon Health Services University, where he built the Dotter Institute for research, and he had made catheters for the Cleveland Clinic. Bill was no stranger to innovation and risk. It was he who had strategically intervened to support David and me after my Phoenix presentation; he trusted Geoff Reeves and gave him free rein to innovate in Australia. The venture into the Stent-Graft market had been a major change for the company, and the Australian involvement was based on the trust that Bill had for Geoff's judgement.

This time, he had taken a great risk to back a radiographer and a surgeon in another country. It was a change for the company to back a surgeon; I know more than one company representative who thought I was a radiologist. One, in the UK, even ventured to inform me confidentially that the company did not support vascular surgeons doing wire and catheter work. At least I knew where I stood and how little they knew of me. It spoke volumes for Bloomington that I never felt such sentiment there. As far as I could tell, their decisions were practical and not sentimental.

In the dying decade of the twentieth century, Cook's core business in cardiovascular disease had been eroded by successful competitors that were producing more popular guide wires, catheters, and balloons, using improved materials for cardiology work in the coronary arteries. Competitors' products that were more nimble in the hands of their users were taking their toll on Cook sales. A sojourn into the coronary stent market had not worked, with the stent having a fatal flaw, and that had made Cook wary of the prosthesis market. They had never been involved in textile prostheses and were understandably worried about another damaging venture and their declining cardiovascular profile.

This was exacerbated by the demise of the other stent-grafts and the troubles for the companies that had taken them to market. They did have a history of success on their side with Bill Cook and the Gianturco Z stent. The self-expanding Z stent was their trump for the aortic prosthesis. The stent-grafts were based on Z stents, our designs, and David's modifications. The textile was proven safe and had been central to vascular grafts for decades. The high regard that the medical profession held globally for the Zenith Stent-Graft underwrote the company's commitment to manufacture.

A change occurred because of internal company reasons known only to those behind the Green Door. Changing honchos can be a bloody affair. John DeFord was replaced by

Kem Hawkins, and we felt this on the other side of the world. At that stage of development, it was disturbing to be asked to work with someone new, someone I had not developed any rapport with and only knew vaguely from a meeting in Phoenix, where I had upset the company over the presentation of the fatigue-fractured hooks on the Cook Gianturco stent. I was unsure of how the change of leaders would affect us. I need not have worried; the momentum of the Zenith Endovascular Graft carried us over the hurdle of the potential dilemma of divided loyalties. John wished us well, and we developed a very good rapport with Kem.

Change disrupts because it mixes risk with success and failure and creates an atmosphere of anxiety, tension, and competition. Personality clashes become inevitable as parameters change to expose underlying strengths and weaknesses. Different qualities and personality traits are required for different phases of development. This means different CEOs or presidents or vice presidents fit better into different phases. Although John DeFord had not led the company's first exploration into aneurysm stent-grafting, nor did he have the opportunity to take it to the final stage, his contribution was enormous, and to lose him as a leader was a shock for all the innovators of the Zenith. John's contribution was too great to be forgotten, and the friendship with him has lasted beyond the internal halls of business.

I had a lot of respect for John; we had a good working relationship, bordering on friendship beyond the confines of the workplace, and spent a lot of time with him, including a Thanksgiving with his family in Indiana. When he came to Perth to rebrand the H&LB as the Zenith, John told me he knew what to give the others in the team, but money didn't seem to count for me. I declined to assure him that he was wrong, instead related the story of how an old Sikh trader in northern Tanganyika had rescued Stan with a fan belt for a Dodge

Powerwagon. He could have charged the earth but instead had told Stan, "It's yours; I'm hungry for friendship, not money."

Friendship has a different set of values to business, and the friendships of the development phase had given way to the harshness of pure business.

Now with the promise of leading the potentially huge aortic stent-graft market, the company tails were up. Kem was in charge, and personal feelings were irrelevant for the sake of the team. The secondary benefits would be the need for ancillary products and more sales. The use of one product bearing a parent name gives confidence to use the same name for the next offering. Success in translating research into a useful product encourages investment in further research.

Our meeting on that day trip to the States was to determine a new course. We started with a tour of the new facility. It was a large multistorey building with an impressive portico. On the first floor was the largest clean room I've ever seen. Wearing gowns and paper hats, we entered the factory of the Zenith Endovascular Stent-Graft. There were rows of technicians sewing textile grafts to anchor stents and Gianturco Z stents, the same way we did in Perth. The assembly lines for the delivery systems were followed by loaders of the stent-grafts into the delivery system, as David had devised. The quality control and movement into the steriliser was seamless. The whole area was the size of an Australian Rules football field, which is twice as large as that for any other type of football. I could not believe that this magnificent facility had grown out of a homemade stent-graft in a small backroom in Perth, the most isolated city in the world.

Time and tribulations had taken their toll on the road to Bloomington. David and I were on our own and not in a very strong position. I wished that Geoff Reeves and John DeFord could have been with us at that meeting. I had moved on from Royal Perth and had a weak hand. While I was running the teaching workshops in Perth out of my private practice in the

Mount Hospital and had presented regularly at international meetings, the lack of institutional backing meant that I had little to offer to a company like Cook, which could choose any number of famous institutions in the United States. They could also choose from an array of prominent doctors to work in the R&D field and be the future spokesperson. Roy was to be that person at the Cleveland Clinic, and Tim would do his share from San Francisco. I had, after all, already handed my baton over to Roy.

To make my position even weaker, the Royal Perth Hospital vascular unit had been wooed by a rival company and was no longer using the Zenith Stent-Graft for their patients, a fact used gleefully by the competitor. It was an unspoken embarrassment that the hospital that sired the team that made the Zenith no longer used it as their preferred prostheses. That's business, and the loss of Royal Perth as a test and education centre affected the royalty deal that had been negotiated because ongoing trialling and teaching were part of that deal. Why would a foreign company support a unit at odds with its colleagues and promoting a competitor, while receiving royalties for the device partly developed in the institution? They didn't.

Cook did not seem to count it against me personally and were familiar with interdisciplinary rivalries and hospital politics. They knew of the work David and I had done separate from the hospital, and the setup in Perth satisfied them for the research, development, and teaching that we had done. Without friends to give advice, I needed something to draw on to give me fortitude for the meeting with the company's executive. I drew on the following experience.

Fred Keller, a prominent radiologist from Oregon Health Services University Hospital and former president of the Radiological Society of North America (RSNA), took over where Dotter had left off. He had been in Perth when we transmitted the first live case to their conference and visited us with Hal Coons when he came up to watch the case. Fred and I had hit it off, and he invited me to visit. It was another unusual bonding between radiology and vascular surgery, like a cat loving a dog.

The visit was arranged with a stopover in Portland on the way home after one of Frank Veith' s New York meetings. I looked forward to the visit and was relaxed after the tensions of New York. Fred was most welcoming and hospitable. I agreed to share an informal session with surgery and radiology trainees the night before I was due to speak formally.

After talking about stent-grafts for a while, one of the trainee surgeons asked if I had read the latest editorial by John Porter for the *Journal of Vascular Surgery* (Dr Porter was editor-in-chief of the journal and senior surgeon in the OHS hospital). I said I had not yet received the journal in Australia. He gave me a copy and suggested I read it before the morning; Dr Porter was known to bang his stick on the wood floor to interrupt and ask questions during a presentation. Apparently, he could destroy a speaker he disapproved of, and he disapproved strongly of endovascular stent-grafting.

I stayed up late that night reading his editorial and rearranged my presentation. Each slide that brought up an issue was followed by one that answered the question so that I could answer without stalling or, worse, shooting the answer from the hip.

Sure enough, the next morning, three slides into the presentation, Dr Porter started noisily banging his stick on the floor. I survived the confrontation sufficiently well to be assigned a book review for the journal of vascular surgery. It was the best lesson I ever learnt about the idea that forewarned is forearmed.

I knew the company's agenda and was therefore forewarned. I had discussed with David that our best outcome would come from seeking amicable concessions from the company without trying to change their determination to centre any further research, development, and governance in the States. They had the whip-hand now with a licence from the FDA. We did have some credit that we could cash in; they recognised David and me for our work and efforts to bring the Zenith to this point, but as far as negotiations went for the future, we were our own advocates.

It was a very courteous and forthright meeting, and democracy and free speech were again evident. Notwithstanding, it was ruthless, and I knew that decisions had been made before we got there; documents had already been drawn up for us to sign. We were not there to negotiate or argue on decisions already made and deemed irreversible. That would have been fruitless, but we were able to negotiate some concessions for further development and have input into future cooperative research. It was better to be dignified and grateful for what the Americans had made possible, pick up the chips, and keep the friends we had.

After a pleasant dinner, we were tired, with a long journey home still ahead of us the next day. Kem comforted me by saying he was due for some sleepless nights if the venture hit the rocks, with so many doctors having access to the device. He pointed out that he would be lifting a weight from my shoulders. He had once been a teacher, and we both knew how hard it is to teach old dogs new tricks and change patterns of behaviour, like trying to change someone's handwriting. American doctors had already learnt with the Aneurex, which had a different deployment sequence and system. They would undoubtedly run the gauntlet of mishearing instructions for use and entering false patterns of recognition. Kem realistically expected problems and mistakes; he reminded me that in taking the Zenith into the global market, he had taken on my sleepless nights as well, and with that, he wished me good night.

Cook could do without me. I might be useful for the occasional idea or opinion, but I was no longer essential. Roy had the baton. I was not employed by Cook, and our agreements had been gentlemanly. I was assured that support would be available whenever I travelled to teach or speak at a conference. I was made a consultant for Cook, in the same way that American doctors were, and would be paid a fee for the days I worked at any requested teaching, training, or think-tank services organised by the company; that was American law and had to be transparent. I was always welcome at their research and manufacturing facilities, and in return, I would give my opinion when asked and would assign to them any patents for future designs. They in turn would assume liability and legal costs. Our relationship had always been based on trust, and it had not been sullied.

While I was dispensable, they could not do without David. It is impossible to replace a one-of-a-kind, but I'm not sure they realised it at that stage. Anyway, David was employed by Cook, so his relationship with the company was inherently different from mine. He was in, and I was out, in more ways than one.

Cook suggested that David relocate to America and continue his work at the Dotter Institute. He agreed to try. Cook was extremely busy across America. Roy swung into teaching users at the Cleveland Clinic, and changes occurred quickly after that. Barry Thomas moved to Bloomington and ran the global implementation of the Zenith from there. His experience in the years when Australia was the engine was invaluable, and he proved a great success.

CHAPTER 33

Out with the Tide

The rules of the FDA now applied across the world because they applied directly to Cook's marketing in the States. No trial or investigation could be organised by Cook without prior FDA approval. I could no longer steer policy for use of device or look at outcomes the way I had before. That had entirely shifted to America. I changed tack and concentrated on trying to better understand the physics, mechanics, and flow dynamics involved with endovascular stent-grafting of the aorta, seeing that as a productive way of staying involved. With this in mind, with David away and my outcomes research stymied, I turned to the relationship that had grown steadily with the scientists Kurt Liffman and Ilija Sutalo in the CSIRO Fluid Dynamics branch in Melbourne.

I still had opportunities to show and discuss our inventions and travelled to instruct colleagues in Singapore, Kuala Lumpur, Hong Kong, Taiwan, and to some extent India, China, and Japan. The rules had changed—probably for the better—but it was now necessary to declare all financial interests and commercial support at the beginning of any presentation. This carried the obvious benefit of transparency, but it also had a downside in that everything that was said afterwards was discounted by some as pure sales talk; it tainted presentations with motives of vested financial interest as distinct from the desire to offer something more to vascular surgery and cardiovascular disease.

Losing control of outcomes research meant that I could no longer use data and evidence to convince medical audiences that it was a reasonable and sensible thing to do. Not being able to back images of clever devices and anecdotal cases with outcome measurement and analysis curtailed credibility. To maintain trust with an audience, I could only speak on the history of the device, technical changes, future possibilities, and the physics of haemodynamics as it affected the aorta.

Talking to Americans about devices they were not yet allowed to use frustrated them, but free of sales implications and vested interest. The Zenith, driven by US and global sales, was clearly a commercial product and had lost the innocence of pioneering innovation. Fortunately, a vestige of the former image persisted in Asia, where I travelled to inform and instruct users on advances they could use without FDA limitations. Legally, special and complex grafts could be made in Australia for individuals as custom-made devices, but it was illegal for me to document the outcomes because that would be viewed by the FDA as a nonapproved trial for Cook; it was also contrary to Australian Therapeutic Goods Authority (TGA) requirements that each device be unique. Good medicine gave way to goods administration.

I was not required to instruct on the standard device, as this was well covered by company representatives. My mentoring and instruction was restricted to the more complex cases that used the fenestrated system to place branches in important arteries. The workshops in Perth served as part of this and continued to attract doctors from around the world. South Korea and India were added to the list for training, but again, the writing was on the wall, and as expertise grew in other parts of Australia, New Zealand, Europe, North America, and Asia, I became redundant. It was easier to run workshops closer to people's homes and in less isolated cities, like Hong Kong.

I made the best of it and enjoyed the teaching trips and conferences. In idle moments, I thought of the places I had been and how events are like a wheel that only touches the ground for an instant; it is pure chance that one should be there at that moment. I had stayed at the Taj Hotel in Mumbai; what if the wheel of time had touched there when the Pakistani terrorists attacked? The instant for an event may be brief, but the thought lingers much longer.

The influence of Perth survived longer than intended and would not have lasted as long as it did if the attempt to relocate David to America had worked. He was not happy so far from home and worked more productively in his own facility in West Perth, where he could run things his own way, with a staff he had selected and would do anything they could for him. David's R&D star did not diminish, as mine was doing. He developed a planning and technical consultation service for everyone who would avail themselves through the electronic transmission of X-rays from around Australia, New Zealand, Asia, Europe, North America, and Brazil. He made prototypes of customised complex grafts that were sent to Brisbane for remaking, sterilising, and shipping. In so doing, David developed a liaison with some of the most innovative and skilful doctors around the world with the newer and complex versions of the Zenith. He travelled to advise doctors on the technical workings of the complex delivery systems.

As part of the consultation and advisory team, I continued to play a role in the invention of advanced devices. Whereas David would advise technically, I would advise clinically when needed, and we continued to be a team. David being one-of-a-kind meant that Perth survived for as long as it did and continued to provide a global service from West Perth. We had been partners in innovation and teaching since the beginning, and David kept it that way. It naturally fell to David to spend most of his time in consultation, planning, and working with doctors who did not need my input for complex cases in Australia and Western countries.

I spent more time with colleagues in Asia, where my clinically expertise was put to better use. We remained under the radar and kept our innovative contributions free of publicity. Only the inner circle knew, and the patents kept rolling out. The absence of the media spotlight could be taken as a measure of our unimportance or of our success in not drawing attention to ourselves with adverse events, in one of the most complex areas of medicine, where adverse events occur with or without intervention. While the international scrutiny continued unabated, we were allowed to work without that distraction.

I came to appreciate the dilemma that innovative companies and individual initiatives face in a country like Australia. When the companies are not owned by Australians, any success will be judged by the success of the product in the global market, and if owned offshore, it will be taken offshore simply because the market in Australia is too small by comparison. When something becomes global, the Australian market size can be dispensed with altogether if troublesome or noncompetitive.

If the product is Australian owned and succeeds, it will probably be taken over. That is the reality. Beware that you are not overcome by your own success. In the commercial world, sentiment and fair play only go so far; they have a limited life span of one or maybe two management generations. Then if demands become in anyway difficult, it is easier for the company to just walk away. What we did was possible because an Australian subsidiary manufactured it, giving us some semblance of autonomy. Australia continues supplying the most complex stent-grafts. Manufacture of the other models are shared between USA and Europe. What happened in the end is as I have described.

Very few ideas actually translate into useful products, and the potential for wastage is immense. Success seems to require a recipe of talent, freedom of thought, opportunity, timing, and a spark. Who knows where the spark may come from, but something of that nature is there when success occurs. For us, it was a fortuitous association and goodwill. Adoption of an idea or technique can spread like a bushfire. The spark is undoubtedly associated with timely conditions. The minimal-invasive takeover of surgical practice, in which all endoscopic and image-guided surgeons were consumed, was an example of fuel ready to burn. Be it fire, flood, or tsunami, they all contribute to the tidal effect that sweeps all before it. The Zenith had been swept along by the tide of minimally invasive surgery.

CHAPTER 34

Where Were the Scientists?

In the mid-1990s, CSIRO, whose research was primarily for industry, industrial manufacturing, and mining, entered the medical field. Before that, medical research was specifically excluded in that organisation. When this restriction was lifted, Kurt Liffman approached me and wanted to know if CSIRO could offer us something; he ran the Fluid Dynamics Laboratory in Melbourne for industry and mining. His job was to construct working experimental models to identify the cause of real problems that theoretical modelling had failed to predict. It is not always possible to account for all variables and parameters, and that's why science requires experiments as well as theories. I thought he could really explain the reasons for the failure of some Stent-Grafts.

It became a very special privilege for me to work with Kurt, his colleague Ilija Sutalo, and their team of CSIRO scientists. It is always productive to work as part of a team of different disciplines. The learning curve may be as steep as the summit of Kilimanjaro, but the view from the top when the clinging clouds clear can be rewarding.

At first, working with the scientists was stimulating and novel, but then it was frustrating because we were on different pages, and then the revelation came: we needed to synergise the science of physiology with the science of physics. We had to move into bionics, where life fuses with mechanics. In the living, adjustment occurs automatically (and sometimes instantly) through feedback systems, and that is physiology. Adjustment to a machine for an identified problem requires human mechanical input or programming; it's only possible automatically with a constructed feedback-driven system, possible now with computers.

When combining the living with the mechanical, adjustments to the mechanical might be obsolete before it is completed because the living had already changed the original problem, and mechanical changes can create new problems instead of addressing the original one. Once this was identified, we could predictably adjust the models in the experimental rig in a way that reflected the normal physiological response using a computer program. We had a good time and were productive. Following publications and some presentations on the pounding disruptive forces in the endovascular environment of the aorta, Kurt and I were invited to Washington to participate in an FDA workshop on how research and development should proceed in this new field of endovascular prostheses.

My experience with the FDA had been either through the jaundiced eyes of industry and frustrated users or in discussions at medical conferences with FDA prostheses assessors. The room held about one hundred people the FDA had invited from their own ranks and the device industry. There were engineers, research personnel, and about six medical doctors. I felt most honoured sitting in the front row with five of the most respected aortic stent-grafting doctors in the States. It resembled an orchestra, with a conductor from the FDA facing the medicos in the front row, scientists and engineers in the rows behind us, and company managers at the back.

In the first session, the front row was very vocal, dominant, opinionated, and high-pitched, like the violins. In the second session, the chair orchestrated silence in the front row and brought on the more sober strings in the second row, and in the third session, the big brass at the back joined in for the crescendo. Finally, the convenor, Dorothy Abel, conducted all the sections, playing in harmony. It was a magnificent performance that I thoroughly enjoyed. Kurt's presentation was fluent, and I was most impressed with his mathematics vocabulary. It precipitated discussion from many in the second and back sections, who were also conversant with the language, and added to the pressure on the front row to keep silent (except for one colleague who had studied engineering before medicine).

In addition to the physics and mathematics, we had discussions on materials and testing methods. Amongst many of the revelations, I came to understand why the nitinol had corroded so badly in our early experiments but lasted so much better in newer generation devices due to alloy adjustments and electropolishing. The discussion on testing methods was crucial because it involved making a decision on whether all devices had to be tested in animals before use in humans. There was a strong body of opinion from the government pathologists that no device should ever be used in humans unless so tested. The opposite view was that animal testing was entirely irrelevant because animal anatomy was different and the altered anatomy in the pathology of aneurysm disease was nothing like any animal part. The compromise reached was brilliant and earned the FDA much respect for its pragmatism. Animal testing would be mandatory for biocompatibility of any material. Real-life simulators and bench testing would be appropriate for device delivery and deployment. This was what we had done, and I was relieved as much as anything.

Kurt was good value in Washington. He arranged a visit to NASA and introduced me to an old colleague of his. Kurt had done his PhD in astrophysics at Rice University in Texas and then worked for NASA. He had a special interest in the composition of meteorites. I usually threw conference name badges away, but I kept my visitors badge to NASA as a special memento. I was a little disappointed in what I saw in NASA. Instead of gleaming spacemobiles, spacesuits, and the Starship *Enterprise*, I saw single-storey buildings with tired or discarded appliances stored in overloaded rooms mostly devoid of people. I felt as I imagine Dick Wittington must have in London. Maybe I missed the good part.

Kurt's colleague in NASA dispelled any doubts about brain power and after the affectionate greeting I soon lost track of their conversation.

Then Kurt took me to the Carnegie Institution for Science Research, where another colleague was researching meteorite composition. Where NASA was government funded, the Carnegie Institution depended on private philanthropy. The difference in quality of the buildings and equipment were like chalk and cheese. Why is it always like that? Maybe because governments give chances to all, but private institutions only give chances to the best. Both produced wonderful science. NASA was famous for space exploration and Carnegie for research into astrotelescopes. Carnegie gave complete freedom of thought without ties of necessarily finding an application.

I liked the scientist in the Carnegie Institution; he was wiry and sinuous like a rock climber and spoke with an English accent, but what endeared him to me most was that his filing system was similar to mine and my accountant's: There were piles of papers spaced all over the floor in full view. Nothing was hidden. It was a little hard to cross the room to politely shake hands. Then he and Kurt conversed rapidly in my weak second language of mathematics, and I was ignored.

Washington was more like everything that Dick Wittington expected of London. I was enthralled with the history displayed, from the top of Arlington Cemetery to Capitol Hill; time was too short to see all the venues and tourist attractions. Abraham Lincoln had a fascination for me that went beyond his stand for human rights because he had Marfan's syndrome (sometimes known as "Spiderman syndrome"). In Marfan's, the limbs and fingers are long and the body short, like a spider. Lincoln was the same height as his colleagues when sitting but much taller when standing, and his fingers exhibited arachnodactyly. Marfan's is associated with aortic aneurysms, and Lincoln was found to have a large thoracic aneurysm that would probably have killed him sooner rather than later if the bullet had missed.

Two experiences taught me something to take away with me. The first was in the Smithsonian Museum in the migrant section; there was a display on how Asian migrants, especially the Chinese, were detained and treated when they arrived in America. Australia was doing almost exactly the same, one hundred years later. The other surprise was that Kurt was not interested in the display of the lunar landing and the lunar module. I thought he would have been bubbling over with enthusiasm to expound on his first love of astrophysics. Instead, he was bored and irritated and merely said that he knew all about the stuff on display and would much prefer to get to the airport so we wouldn't miss the plane home (the flight wasn't scheduled until the evening, but he had a horror of a Washington traffic jams). I irritated him almost beyond words when I mentioned that I had read that the landing was all a hoax staged in the Arizona desert, perpetrated for political gain. We went straight to the airport after that, and harmony was restored in the comfort and security of the departure lounge once Kurt was reassured we would not miss the plane home.

After working with Kurt and Ilija, I started to present physics and flow dynamics at medical conferences. The first talk carried the element of surprise. It was so different from anything presented before. It was novel. I then committed the sin of boring the audiences to tears. My talks were reduced by Frank Veith to six minutes. I resorted to writing a chapter on haemodynamics with Kurt and Ilija for the Australian vascular textbook, *Mechanisms of Vascular Disease,* and then another in *The Oxford Textbook of Surgery.* I started looking to the future and worked with CSIRO to design a totally plastic aortic stent-graft with no metal and no textile fabric. Light, curable polymers were wrapped around a balloon that would carry the stent-graft to a desired site, where it would be cured there by light carried inside the balloon via an optic fibre, like curing poured concrete in form work on a building site.

Plastic means "to form; able to be moulded." That is what I believed would be the future. Dentists do it, so why couldn't we? Remember that Charles Stent was a dentist. It started to work; the device exhibited natural memory for shape, and we could change the flexibility by varying the chemical proportions. I was very pleased and excited.

It failed to gain any enthusiasm for commercial support, and offers of support for the project from CSIRO were rejected by the company I had assigned the patent to. Quite rightly, the company asked why they should change to plastics when they already had difficulties keeping up with the recent innovations that were working well, and there were still more modifications in the pipeline. There was no need, or desire, to research further quantum leaps in technology. CSIRO had been restricted to a fee-for-service role, and there was no incentive for them to proceed on a pro bono basis; led by their business managers, they factored in future development potential to their fee for service charges, which were consequently disproportionately high for what was being produced, and that irritated the company. The idea died on the vine (or went to sleep for forty years, like Rip Van Winkle; I was told I must be dreaming).

Exploring the possibilities of researching ideas and developing innovations with CSIRO was stimulating; the scientists were enthusiastic and inquisitive. The reality was that the organisation was going through change itself and exploring the potential for self-funding. To do anything required negotiating through business managers, accountants, and lawyers: good people who dealt with reality and hard cash. To do their job, they needed answers about predicted results, time in hours, applications, potential earnings, and how much money was on offer for research. They seemed to have no understanding of the uncertainty in a new field of exploration, which surprised me for a scientific organisation, and I came to appreciate that assessing the potential benefit in return for providing resources within financial constraints and risk minimisation was their job; they needed estimates and real figures.

A brief period of allowing scientists to have a stake in commercial development was thought-provoking, but it was nipped in the bud by purists who believed that anything that relied on taxpayer-funded employees remained taxpayer property. What they achieved was suppression of incentive in the scientists we worked with. It is probably fair to say that Cook was regarded as a cash cow with funds available. The money was swallowed by a machine that produced mountains of printed logo-adorned paper and hastily produced, unimpressive prototypes.

Whereas the research looking into the physics and mechanics of failure modes for aortic stent-grafts had been rewarding and useful, exploring new technology in plastics and ultrasound sensors was exploring the unknown, and there were problems of ownership of intellectual property between CSIRO and Cook, and demands for up-front payments. Cook saw dollar signs in the eyes of the CSIRO management and was wary of being milked.

All I wanted was a low-cost pilot feasibility study, but it was not to be. As a consequence of the different motives of Cook and CSIRO, more time and money was spent on formulating plans and proposals with hypothetical milestones than on doing scientific experiments. Although the scientists were excellent, and progress was made quickly with experiments when they were done, the costs were high on a fee-for-service basis instead of a royalty or joint venture agreement.

After a very limited time experimenting in Melbourne, the endeavour came to a sudden stop, like the lights going out with time expired on a coin machine. This was to be a long-term project, but after the company was presented with an embarrassingly large bill for the short time spent with the scientists, it pulled the plug.

The company held the patents, was averse to shared development projects because of past experiences, and did not need a new product like this at the time. CSIRO were not going to donate in kind without promise of future reward. My experimenting and liaison with CSIRO was essentially over. It was the wrong time and the wrong place.

There is no way to counter purists who believe there should be no commercial attachment for researchers. Even though the FDA, national health research organisations, centres for research, CSIRO, and patent law firms all understood the necessity for the liaisons, the professors would cry foul and retreat into the Bastilles of universities that never funded such endeavours, but they were always keen to administer research grants for an infrastructure fee and claim any success as their own. I grew to resent such aloof dismissals.

I tried to introduce a laparoscopic element to supplement the endovascular approach. A bright young trainee surgeon in Manchester won a scholarship to travel and work in two innovative centres in the world. Her name was Shirley Fearn, and she chose Yves Marie-Dion's unit in Quebec to look at laparoscopic vascular surgery and our centre in Perth to look at endovascular surgery. She developed instruments and devices with David. We showed that it was possible to use laparoscopic surgery to insert an aorto-bifemoral bypass with our access devices, and we could also introduce stent-grafts that way. We proved the concept at a workshop by teaching twelve surgeons in two days in Perth, and I presented the concept at the Charing Cross meeting in London.

After publishing the work, that idea was also put to sleep beside Rip Van Winkle and the plastic graft. The story of Rip Van Winkle had disturbed me as a boy. To me, at that young age, forty years was a lifetime. It worried me with a terrible feeling of sadness for the loss of time and opportunity, but now, older and wiser, I understand the meaning of "before its time."

My influence was gone, and whereas in the past, I had could exert pressure for certain actions and have access to funds, I no longer had the authority to do this. I was, in fact, in danger of being thought of as a crank. One day, someone determined that I had overstepped the mark, and I was informed that I had no managerial role at Cook; we were not joined at the hip. I had taken liberties. It is natural for surgeons to expect others to do what they were asked, and anyway, I was doing what had been natural before.

I murmured apologies but added that while we were not joined at the hip, we were grafted together. It was a cheap shot that served nothing except a lift to my sense of self-righteousness, and that, in the words of Justice Michael Kirby, "competes as a sin." I had become boring and self-righteous.

Invitations to speak continued to pour in; some had become routine annual events, where the invitation was almost taken for granted. Apart from the logistics, I struggled with my conscience in order to continue without good new material and avoid causing disappointment and overexposure of older material. I declined most of the invitations. Eventually, spurred on by Frank Veith, who was fighting a losing battle in America on the move to make vascular surgery a specialty independent of general surgery, I spoke at his meeting on our shared passion for vascular surgery to stand on its own.

Frank arranged a special keynote presentation and gave me much more than six minutes. This ended with me in New York, informing UK and US vascular surgeons that they were all still classified as general surgeons without their own specialty. I rudely pointed out that this was in contrast to Australia, New Zealand, and some European countries, who had de jure vascular surgeons with their own specialty. I railed that until they were wholly in charge of their own training and destiny, they would not be in charge of the facilities they desired and the training they wished to impart to their younger colleagues.

Until that happened, vascular surgeons would continue to struggle to compete directly with radiology and cardiology for facilities and privileges to practice in the endovascular field, and lay and professional people alike would continue to hear the word *cardiovascular* as pertaining only to the coronary artery. I went on to say they were also holding up progress for the rest of us because of their influence.

Vascular surgery grew out of the work by US and UK pioneers, and now I had gone beyond causing an occasional offence; I had been unkind. In so doing, I had committed all three of Justice Michael Kirby's greater sins: I had been boring, self-righteous, and unkind. To make it worse, my presentation, which was scheduled for just before lunch, was moved to the afternoon because the morning session ran over. The afternoon session was inappropriate for my presentation, and a number of other factors limited any impact I might have had on the delegates.

The chairman of the session, Dr Robert Rutherford, had written the definitive textbook for American vascular surgery; it was used by trainees everywhere in the world, and he was certainly stung by being labelled a de facto vascular surgeon. The intention was to get the message out to those who were still tied to general surgery, to let go of the rope, pick up the paddles, and go with the current sweeping vascular surgery. I tried to stress the importance of the right equipment and training for minimally invasive vascular surgeons to compete in the future.

Timing and luck were absent that day, although the surprise factor was certainly present. When I looked around the audience, I felt I had cast my seeds on stony ground, but I am sure some will grow to help my like-minded colleagues acquire the privileges and facilities that go with a super-specialty.

Vascular surgery did become a specialty in its own right in the UK following a strong push by the younger surgeons and trainees, many of whom had sought training in Australia for endovascular experience. In March of 2012, I received this email:

> Dear Michael,
>
> I am delighted to share this news with you. This was a momentous day for British Vascular surgery.
> Best wishes
>
> Waquar

The mail had an attached memo from the president of the UK Vascular Society, with this sentence:

> Today, I am pleased to announce that, as of the 16th March 2012, statutory approval has been given by Parliament to recognise Vascular Surgery as a Specialty independent from General Surgery in the UK.

When I was president of the ANZ Vascular Society, I had been awarded honorary membership of the UK Vascular Society after a talk I gave at their annual meeting in Harrogate, in recognition for the influence of the ANZ society on practices and attitudes in the UK. It was very gratifying to see this happen. Vascular surgery is likely to achieve the same status eventually in the United States. I hope that I persuaded at least one surgeon there to move from one pole to the other.

CHAPTER 35

A Time to Go or a Time to Stay

During my years of involvement in quality assurance and surgical auditing, I learnt that worry is good as long as it is productive. In this new millennium, it was time to take stock to preserve the best, recognise what was productive, and reorganise. Realistically, David and I completed our quantum leap in the treatment of aortic aneurysms when we, together with Roy, Krassi, and Tim, developed a device to treat the arch of the aorta. Roy died in December 2013 at the age of forty-eight, after a long battle with cancer. David and I had retired, John was ill, and Wolf had become paralysed after a spinal operation.

The baton was lost. The race was over. The further advances with complex aortic stent-grafts had brought younger minds and skilful hands to the working technology that was available to people across the world. There would be refinements of the Zenith and extensions of its application. The concept of endovascular treatment of aneurysms was assured. The Zenith would have to pass other tests, as determined by commerce and better technology. For me, the experience of exploring another leap into plastics served to show that it is hard to spark twice in the short term, and as far as development goes, to leap again was too soon. Although a discriminatory argument, it was realistic to admit we were getting older. Although Krassi tried, it was too much to expect of him on the edge of retirement. The psychological energy stores needed to strive against all odds deplete with time, and life's experiences alter priorities. With age, the rewards become more short term, and the drive to persist for achievement fades, together with the stubbornness to resist a push from an unwanted direction. You can see the desire to take over in the eyes of the young. A look conveying tolerance replaces one of respect for reputation and past achievement or position. To not move aside is to court disaster.

A surgeon can stay hidden in the operating theatre, which becomes his cubby hole as long as no harm is done. This means that the repertoire of procedures contracts as skills fade and prowess diminishes. To an older surgeon, the operating room may become his refuge and the staff his attentive family that welcomes him, serves him, laughs at his jokes; he relaxes with decisions in default mode. He is, in a word, secure against the challenges of the future. Inside the operating room, he feels he is still a Type A personality. There are usually no windows in an operating room; he does not see out and chooses to ignore the sounds of the downgrading of his rating outside. How long can he stay cocooned in this phase before the young wolves and legal eagles tear apart the carcass? It is sad to see older surgeons face disgrace in a court of law at the end of their careers or be the subject of tearoom gossip about how much slower they are and how good they used to be. And the echo of the quote from the time of the French Revolution by Duc de la Rochefoucauld: "We are not always displeased by the misfortunes of our best friend" rings out the essence of gossip. Any activity that relies on talent is vulnerable in this way. Is it worse for a surgeon than for a sportsman or leader of any kind? The answer is probably no, but for all of them, there is a time to go.

Alternatively, the surgeon vacates the operating room to fill another role, such as a legal or insurance adviser, a medical politician, or an educator. Some fulfil their lives with pro bono work that can be combined with travel for missions or charity organisations in poorer countries. Some assume a "wise old man" role in a functioning unit or administration. The challenge is to accept diminution and not suffer with relevance deprivation. To retire suddenly and overwhelm the wife in the kitchen is rarely a mutually rewarding experience. Wives seldom rush to a surgeon's bidding, as OR nurses do, and never laugh at their silly jokes. So retiring a surgeon is a problem, and retiring is a problem for a surgeon.

Planning retirement is often neglected, but I have seen it done well by some. For example, I took my friend Bob Lusby to see the Shipwrecks Museum for something nonmedical to do when he stayed over for the weekend, after visiting for a workshop during the heydays in the nineties. I saw Bob studiously looking at various things and obviously quite enthusiastic. Like the Shipwreck Coast of South West Africa, many a ship has wrecked itself on the Western Australian coast, as the Shipwrecks Museum in Fremantle can testify, with stories such as the wreck of the *Batavia*. Cyclonic winds blow from different directions as storms circle over and intensify when they cross over treacherous, often uncharted, reefs and accounted for ships on the way from sea to safe anchorage, especially the square-riggers battling the prevailing south-westers and associated winter storms.

Much can be learnt about human behaviour in the face of adversity; life is full of surprises and veiled lessons. Later, over a seafood lunch and a glass of Margaret River wine, looking out to sea across the old fishing harbour, where battles for the America's Cup had depended on reading the wind, and where the waves hid those who had failed such tests in years gone by, I asked him what had interested him most and was surprised by his answer:

"Well, you see, Mike, I'm not very interested in the sea at all, but I am very interested in wine, and I bought some land for a winery in the Hunter Valley in New South Wales. It'll be a family business when I retire and some fun in the meantime. I was very

interested in the construction of the museum building; I think
I can use the same system to build the cellars for the winery we
are building."

Bob now runs Tintilla, a winery in the Hunter Valley, with his
wife and children. Two of his sons run the winery as winemaker
and viticulturist, one son does promotions, and their daughter,
who studied economics, does the marketing. His buildings are
as fine as his wine, and his retirement is a fine example of how
to change careers.

PART 4

The Seventh Age

CHAPTER 36

My Family and Other Matters

I entered the new millennium with a split chest and resignation from my alma mater, in retreat from an acrimonious situation in the hospital that had threatened to engulf endovascular surgery in a turf war across Australia. Persistent angina added to the challenge to keep the momentum going for the future of the Zenith graft until the Americans had FDA approval. A cyclone had crossed the coast, and I was forced to assess the damage and chart a new course. Maybe there would be as much value in the things around me as there was in the absorbing work with the stent-grafts. My castle was my family; where was that at the time?

I looked back at how good a father I had been and was appalled. I had neglected my sons to the fortunes of the winds and the waves, to Michele's care, and to Mother Nature. They had all grown up on the beaches of Western Australia and loved the surf and the outdoors. There was hardly a surf break between Augusta in the south and Indonesia to the far north that had not been cut through with the fins of their boards between first light and dusk. Night surfing at City Beach had been a favourite pastime when they were younger, and they rode the breaks off the coasts of Europe and North America when they travelled as young men. Needless to say, their academic achievements were all similar to mine when I had been that age: not brilliant and barely enough for tertiary entry. I should have spent more time helping them with their schoolwork and communicating with their teachers. I was no good at either. I had been impatient, distracted, and when I did try, I had expressed irritation or fallen asleep. Their teachers had no trouble sizing up my attitude, and that had not helped.

At least the boys had the saving graces of their mother's good nature, her social ethic, and a love of life. I guess the family holidays in the south-west by the beaches, camping holidays with a metal detector in the goldfields, family-friendly Chinese restaurant meals together, and trips to sporting events served to make bonds between us. My greatest joy is to watch them go off surfing together and know that they are comfortable friends. To see them with their wives and children speaks volumes for the power of love over reason and gives meaning to the belief that there is life after death.

Michele had worked hard at her career as a teacher of English as a second language, and her recounts of migrants' problems and their ordeals had imparted a depth of understanding for other people that gave the boys great people skills, even if academic support at home could have been better.

I reflected on how the children of many of my colleagues had suffered with having to take a back seat to the careers of their fathers, as my children had. Especially those of first-generation migrants, where the focus and success of the family depended so much on the father's ability to make a life for them all in the new country. Without extended family support or financial help, the children are vulnerable to peer-pressure during the physical and emotional absence of the parents. My observation was that the family home provided the anchor. Changing homes, which implies peers and friends too, as migrants do when they arrive and again as their fortunes improve, or changing partners (which migrants are also prone to do due to changing family dynamics in a new environment), had a silent damaging effect on the children. Fortunately, Michele had held the home and our marriage together. She had been our anchor, and the boys had been given a chance. Without the physical public hospital commitment and relieved of the emotionally exhausting demarcation disputes, I was given a second chance to pay more attention to my family.

I looked around to see where they were. Since seeing Stanley in Marseille in 1996, when he came down from working in the ski-pistes in Austria, he had finally come back to Perth with Maike and taken a postgraduate diploma in town and regional planning, which he added to his degree in geography. He was preparing to take Maike back to her village in Germany and get married.

Trevor was still working in a pub in London and preparing to travel around Europe. He did not want to ski like his brothers because he had ruptured the anterior cruciate and medial ligaments of his knee in hockey, necessitating two knee reconstructions. This caution did not extend to his love of surfing, and Trevor, like his brothers, carried his surfboard under his arm and surfed along the European coast.

Gareth, after a stint of mustering sheep on a motorbike guided from a spotter plane above on a pastoral station in the north-west of Western Australia, was working with a German company teaching snowboarding and skiing to Austrian tourists during the winters and instructing surfing on the beaches of southern France, Spain, and Portugal in the summers. In August that year, they would all be in Germany for the wedding. Here was a family matter with an opportunity for me to really re-engage. And, it was not about me.

Private practice gave me the freedom to structure my surgical life alongside the research, development, and education commitment I had to the Zenith and set time aside for the family. The work in the public hospital involved mainly emergency work, and in the private hospital practice, it was almost entirely elective surgery. I moved from reactive surgery to proactive surgery. Also, for the first time in my life, I was entirely my own boss. I could freely decide when to work and when to do other things.

A pattern had emerged of stringing a number of things together when travelling abroad. It was duly arranged that I would go to India to deliver a couple of lectures and instruct for a few cases of stent-grafts in Mumbai on the way to the wedding in Germany. Michele went on ahead to make sure her surf-sculptured children were suitably attired. In the business lounge at Perth Airport, I spent the time before boarding polishing my talk on the computer and became so engrossed that I nearly missed the plane. In my haste to pack up the laptop, I dropped my wallet. During transit in Singapore, I discovered the loss and rang the lounge in Perth, described where I had been sitting, and asked if it had been found. The answer was no, and the card loss was reported. It was cancelled and another would be sent later. A Cook travelling companion loaned me some cash in the interim.

My family knew me better than I realised. Michele was buying suits for the wedding for the two younger men, and when she presented her card, it would not work, and she was told it was cancelled. She tried to use it in the bank for cash, and it was confiscated in a foreign language. Michele told me later that penetrating through her hysterics were the words of her sons: "It must be Dad."

The wedding could not have been better for my rehabilitation. It was not merely a family matter; it was an international village affair. I had had no idea how many Australians worked the ski fields in Europe. Surfers on snowboards descended from the mountains to celebrate and join what must have been the whole village. There were Australians wearing tee shirts that said "There are no kangaroos in Austria," speaking German with Austrian accents, which apparently grate on those around Hanover, who speak Hoch Deutsch, Germans speaking no

English at all, Australians and Germans confusing each other with the word "nine," and it didn't seem to matter. Everyone was in love, and it was as far removed from a medical conference as I could possibly get. What's more, they got married twice, first in the Rathaus, meaning the Town Hall, which is apparently a government requirement to be married, and then two days later in the village church, in a traditional German way with the "two-person sawing of the log."

They travelled to the reception in a hay cart; it was in the adjacent village, near the buildings that Hitler built during World War II with earth roofs growing grass and trees, so they wouldn't be seen from the air. I wondered if they had been the inspiration for Hundertwasser to grow grass and trees on his buildings. They served to remind me how much the world, and not just Africa, had changed in my lifetime.

Maike's half-brother, Hansi, translated Stanley's speech into German as he spoke, and Stanley repaid the compliment for Hansi. Gareth just spoke in German with his Austrian accent and translated my speech. Trevor, like his mother, never stopped talking. The reception went on until seven the next morning, as the custom was that the married couple could not leave until after the last guest had gone.

Schnapps is not just one drink; it has many different flavours and suited the variety of guests. It served as a great mixer. Around midnight, I engaged in a conversation with Greg Shannon, a school and surfing friend of Stanley's. Greg was very handsome and athletic. He was so good at snowboarding that he had turned professional and starred in competitions. It disturbed me that he was taking Gareth off-piste to snowboard down mountains. I had not known how good Gareth was at snowboarding. I guess he never told me for fear that I would worry or, worse still, lecture him on the dangers of avalanches and falls. Greg went on to give me a most gentle and thoughtful lecture.

I should not take life so seriously, he said, and should take time to look again at the wonders of the world and feel the air, the earth, and the water in all its various forms. Greg, whose father was also a doctor (a psychiatrist), was teaching me from his heart, as if he wished the same for his dad. He was telling me that although it may be too late for me to teach the young, it was not too late for me to learn from them. It was not about me spending more time to help my sons; it was that they were caring after me. It was a sobering note.

Greg and I discussed the possibility of me retiring and what wonderful things I could do; he had just passed thirty and announced that he was retiring from professional snowboarding because his knees and reflexes were not quite so good. He was starting an adventure company with an Austrian colleague; they were going to guide trips down canyons in the Alps. He described how indescribable the sensations could be and was excited about this new adventure that would feed his zest for life.

It was nice that my son got married in Germany. There was richness in the mixing of the ultra-new Australian surf culture and the traditional German country rituals, the merging of the southern and northern hemispheres and the fusing of snows and sands. But the highs are only matched by the lows.

Early one morning, after returning home, I received a tearful call from Stanley. Greg and his partner, Hansi, had been swept over a waterfall when exploring a new canyon and were found in the pool below. Greg's encouragement to "appreciate the life we have and live it to its fullness" was now immortal.

Gareth came back to Perth in 2003. I wondered what he would do, considering his adventures and lifestyle in Europe. He announced that he was going to be a high school teacher, and that took the wind out my sails, considering my attitude towards teachers. I tried to dissuade him on the grounds that it was no longer a highly regarded profession; teachers' colleges had been easier to get entry to on that basis. A measure of the value put on the profession was expressed in how poorly they were paid, I commented, and if he dedicated himself to teaching, it would be a thankless job.

He disagreed and said that those were precisely the reasons why he was going to become a teacher and work to return it to the status and high regard it once enjoyed in the community. He pointed out that many countries in Africa and Asia held education as a core value, and that teachers were very well respected. China was a good example. His point was that the value the general community put on education was reflected in the faces of attentive, or inattentive, children and that universities were only as good as the students they received. At the time, they seemed keener on getting students from overseas than they were from Australia.

Gareth went back to school, gained a better university entrance score, completed his degree, and fell in love with Kristin, a Canadian backpacker, with whom he worked restocking supermarket shelves at night. At the end of the final year of his degree, she returned to Canada, leaving him with an aching heart. He still had a year to do to acquire the diploma of education to qualify him to teach. He had done well, and the university offered him the opportunity to do a master's. He declined and announced that he was going to Canada to marry Kristin.

"Don't be ridiculous," I said. "What will you do when you get there? It won't be the same. You'll be seen differently in the different environment. You're just setting yourself up to look foolish and get hurt. What about finishing your diploma first?"

My fatherly problem-solving concern had made me forget my own romance.

He went to Canada; he wooed her father, Bernie, on the golf course, and enrolled her mother, Maggie, and her brother Mike in his mission to marry Kristin. He enticed Kristin out of the family home in Vancouver, and they moved in together in Ucluelet, a fishing village on the west coast of Vancouver Island. Gareth surfed along the grey shores between the logs in the sea and the rocks on the shore. He used his biology degree to get work inspecting the catch on the fish wharf. They arranged for us to visit and rented and paid for a log cabin by the sea. Kristin showed us her outdoor kitchen, which was a picnic table looking out over the sea beside a forest footpath, along which wandered deer and the occasional black bear. It was a truly romantic place that enriched heart and soul.

The wedding was at Big Bar Lake, at the holiday home four hours up the Fraser River. It was magical. Kristin appeared from around the corner from a neighbour's house on a small motorised barge that Bernie had built. The barge sported the Canadian and Australian flags, and the band played "Waltzing Matilda" as the barge pulled into the shore. They were married by the smallest woman I've ever seen. She was Canadian First Nation and stood between them on a large rock on the grassy bank of the lake, between squalls of wind and rain. I remembered the African quote at our wedding: "Rain on your wedding day is a blessing for fertility." They had three children in four years.

We left them in the Canadian wilds to honeymoon in a canoe around the lakes while we went to Vancouver, where I met Canadian colleagues and discussed endovascular surgery and vascular training. Thereby was born a very fruitful professional Canadian connection, as well as acquiring another daughter-in-law.

The Canadians had taken endovascular grafting of aneurysms to new heights. During the next Veith meeting, they took me to Madison Square Garden to see a hockey match between the Vancouver Canucks and the New York Rangers. The Garden had always born attraction for me since the coming of Cassias Clay, alias Mohammed Ali, and they introduced me to a whole new world. The Canadians don't seem to feel the cold.

Gareth and Kristin returned to Perth; he finished his Dip. Ed. and took a job teaching maths in the Margaret River region, near his beloved surfing breaks.

What of Trevor? Trev taught me lessons so poignant that they hurt. His greatest asset was his spontaneous flare for the moment and his ability to seize it. It was this that made him a sportsman. Our family's traditional sport was field hockey because of our connection with the Indian Army. Hockey is strong in Western Australia, and the National Institute for Sport made Western Australia the centre for hockey in 1984. Australia had made its mark at the Olympic Games in hockey in 1968, and much of the credit must be given to the role played by the WA players who fired the team up. The state attracted the best national players and some internationals into the local competition because of the Institute of Sport.

Trevor was first selected to play for the state at the age of fourteen and continued in the state teams to eventually captain the under-eighteen team. He was selected to play in the classic league alongside friends from his club, which boasted a number of Australian internationals. One of them, Paul Gaudoin, went on to captain Australia at the Olympic Games.

Parents are naturally proud of their children's achievements, and we followed his matches and competitions across the country. It was an opportunity to gain insight into high-level sport. Sport of one brand or another is an activity that most of us observe, some more passionately than others. The joys of winning are clearly visible and infectious, and we indulge at a great financial cost that we never seem to begrudge. In Australia, the cricket captain is paid more than the prime minister of Australia and the president of the United States combined. Yet everybody complains about politicians' salaries but never murmurs about the salaries of elite sportsmen. As observers, we imbibe the joys of winning without the pain and effort of playing; we walk away from the downsides with little remorse as we give the thumbs down to the losing gladiators in the Colosseums of the modern sport.

That's sport, and it's only a game, but is it? When it becomes personal, the games can be deadly for a player. Inevitably, the immediate family is drawn into the trials and tribulations of elite sportsmen, and because the rewards are so evident, little is said about the downside. The negative effects are almost inevitable for the players. The demise of most boxers is evident in the numbers who end up punch drunk on skid row. Few elite sportsmen continue to thrive unless they have some other particular skill set, and many are often left with physical and psychological damage. Winning and adrenalin are drugs, and the addiction leads to withdrawal symptoms, similar to all drugs.

Becoming involved as a parent was eye-opening. The highs of selection, the hype, the travel, the camaraderie, winning, and celebrations were joyous, and the ooze of self-esteem was infectious. The lows were in the undercurrents of rivalry that often ran dangerously close to jealousy. Perceptions of favouritism and influence weaved threads through motives of seeking perfection. The mixed motives of coaches, players, relatives, and entrepreneurs became increasing complex. All were at the mercy of the devils in the media, who choreographed the merry dance in the court of publicity. Information is said to be power, and publicity means money. The two go hand-in-hand.

As a parent, I only had eyes to see my son on the field; I watched his every step and projected my emotions on to him. Trevor had emulated and then surpassed my levels of achievement in sport, and I experienced a virtual reality. There is no replacement for the instant joy of winning and the indulgence of pride in achieving an admirable record such as scoring a goal or winning a national championship. The inevitable feelings of sadness, regret, and shame that serve to balance the pinnacle are more insidious and linger longer. The area under the curve, however, is probably the same for winning and losing in the end.

For me, the moment of loss of that sporting innocence was as vivid as the unexpected loss of a patient after an operation. As parents, we were called to a team meeting a few weeks before the boys, who were in their late teens, were sent inter-state to play in the national championships. After the briefing and pep talk, the team manager gave each member of the team a jar of pills that were described as vitamins; the pills were to be taken daily. As parents, we were called upon to make sure that the players followed these instructions for the sake of the team. But as a doctor, I was curious as to what was in the pills (at this time, the scandals of drug usage in sport were emerging in the press).

My conscience demanded I question the practice of administering any unknown medication and particularly in the context of sport and scandal. I held my tongue for fear of making a scene or being seen as an ugly parent; most importantly, I didn't want to affect Trevor's rapport with the coach and team. I could have taken a pill and had it analysed, but I did not. My silence was shameful for a doctor, and the defence that I was not alone was not justified. The only thing that came out of the experience is a little more understanding for the impossible dilemma that must have confronted many, if not all, elite sportspersons at the pinnacle of their careers; innocent players get caught up in drugs and are fraudulently dosed. The pills, I assured myself and my conscience, were indeed harmless multivitamins with mainly vitamin C to ward off common colds. After all, hockey was amateur sport for the players at the time.

The anterior cruciate ligaments in Trev's knee were ruptured in a nasty fall. Knee reconstructive surgery was new (I learned of it at a medical conference), and Trev underwent reconstruction that failed. It was done again, and after a couple of years, he worked his way back to Classic League Hockey. It was a concerted effort. In the first big match, apprehensive about stressing the knee, he did not dodge a contact, and his clavicle was fractured. After returning, he was a star for a brief moment, but then the reconstructed cruciate ligament snapped again.

The effort to achieve was replaced by a precipitous withdrawal from the addiction that all athletes have to endorphins, adrenalin, and elation. The sport that had been so important and all-consuming now left him feeling empty and in pain. In hockey, there was no financial reward or fallback job to build on, and the years seemed wasted. The future loomed dark with pain and loss of physical freedom, time, and opportunity.

In my work as a vascular surgeon, I've had to amputate limbs that could not be saved from crushing trauma or the ravages of arterial disease. I learned that there is a strange phenomenon whereby young amputees are known to be attractive to some people, and they are reputed to make excellent partners. One of the reported attributes is that amputees are often unselfish and resourceful, radiating an admirable inner strength. The suggestion is that those who survive adversity and pain gain strength and other qualities.

He eventually accepted giving up competitive sport but refused to accept any limitation to his love of surfing; he travelled Europe and South East Asia with his surfboard and eventually returned to Perth. Trevor did gain something from his ordeal that was far more valuable than money and career: he carried a depth of human understanding and a resilience that proved to be invaluable after he became a physiotherapist, with a special interest in treating injured athletes.

His inner drive directed him to become the physiotherapist for a number of high-profile sporting teams, starting with the Fever, a netball team. I had no idea what a fast and furious game this was, but I could clearly see why there were so many knee injuries. Trevor gained a reputation, and when he moved onto other sports, his experience went with him. If money had been the motivation, he would not have accumulated the skills and expertise. The lessons he learnt inspired him to further training, and the rewards followed. The choice of how much of our time in life is exchanged for money and how much is exchanged for other values is one of great importance. Some things like friendship, education, and experience are invaluable.

Trevor and Jasmine met as part of a bridal party in a Margaret River winery, and that flare of spontaneity was reciprocated. It was interesting to observe the difference of romance in the thirty-year-old age group from that of the twenties or late teens. There was no innocence; this was replaced with a wariness to commit again, born of more experience in life.

One morning at breakfast, when Trev and I were having another energised discussion on something upon which we actually agreed, Jasmine challenged my son with, "Oh Trev, don't be so defiant."

By the time the laughter settled and Trev had got the wind back in his sail, a good basis on which to get married had been established. Trev was going to learn to be compliant.

Seeing Trev and Jazz so happy together was like having my cup filled to the brim. They married in the gardens of Caves House, above the famous surfing beach of Yallingup in his beloved south-west of Western Australia. It was a truly modern, traditional Australian wedding, complete with babe in tum, which Trev proudly pointed out to all those gathered in true Trev style. Jasmine smiled in her knowing way. This was an Aussie wedding to fit beside the German and Canadian ones. Each was different in setting and style but all the same in feelings and sentiments. I had never seen Trev so happy until their little girl, Ruby, was born, and then the cup overflowed.

CHAPTER 37

Life beyond Surgery

I developed a friendship with Andrew Bartlett, a Zenith planner, born of his role and also because we were both working closely with David. Andrew and I were drawn to each other because we were intimately involved with the Zenith graft. Our relationships with Cook were unusual and hard to define, more of necessity than design. We had been essential to the product's success, but I suspect neither of us were people the company would have chosen. Andrew was born in Yorkshire, and Englishmen see Yorkshiremen as different (it probably goes back to the War of the Roses). Yorkshiremen are fiercely independent and a race apart.

True to his roots, Andrew had two passions. The first was a love of the outdoors and walking, and the second was a mission to not spend a penny more than was absolutely necessary to acquire the object of his desire. Andrew did not go to church on Sundays; he went to garage sales. In 1990, he joined a colleague at Royal Perth Hospital and organised a two week walk in the Kimberley region. The trek in the Kimberley became an annual spiritual pilgrimage for Andrew.

In 2002, he invited Michele and me to join him and his walking group for the annual July trek. He was well aware of my heart bypass surgery in 1999, its outcome, and the subsequent stent in the origin of the left main coronary artery a year later. He planned for Zenith grafts on a contract basis and to supplement his income was a radiographer in a cardiac and vascular catheter theatre. He knew the risk of inviting me to trek in some of the roughest terrain in Australia but gave me the gift of confidence, for which I continue to be grateful. At the time, I didn't realise how valuable that gift would be.

The Kimberley sits in the lower southern tropics and is coolest in July and August; it's very wet in December and January during the southern summer and extremely hot at Christmas time. That is when the cyclones form in the northern parts of Australia; Darwin was flattened by Cyclone Tracey on Christmas Day in 1974. In July, the southern winter, when the Inter-Tropical Convergence Zone and the monsoons disappear up to India and the northern hemisphere, the Kimberley is dry and cooler and most suitable for a walkabout. The geology is sandstone, and sandstone is like a sponge, so that much of the immense amount of water dumped on northern Australia in the wet is held and released steadily into streams and rivers that run all through the dry season. Sandstone is also very beautiful as it weathers, with rock falls, cracks, and fissures that colour with minerals and lava flows. The light at dawn and dusk flows across the sandstone outcrops and plays in the rivers, making reflections in the pools of the pandannus palms and paperbark trees. Boab trees, like benign old women with tubby, naked children, sit watching the scene or group together to whisper in the wind about the secrets of the rock art that shelters in the overhangs and recesses of the gorges.

The Kimberley is a beautiful place where apart from the rough dirt roads, there are very few tracks, and the paths of humans have long since gone. Only the meandering paths of feral cattle and animals that move silently at night mark the land. The silence of the animals is signified by the resident freshwater Johnson River crocodiles that inhabit the many rivers; at night, their red eyes gleam back along the torch beam from the little islands in the pools and streams. Sometimes, the night's silence is broken by the howls of the dingoes. In the daytime, the blue of the waterlilies is gilded by the golden, silky grevillea trees that stand and wave from above. In the evening, the cliffs glow like fire as the light in the sky moves back down the spectrum from blue to deep red. At the moment the sun slips below the horizon, it leaves a glow like molten iron replenishing the ore of this oldest continent that yields so much.

I let go of the yearning for the land where I was born to indulge in the words of Dorothea Mackellar, when she thought of her birthplace in Australia:

> I love a sunburnt country,
> a land of sweeping plains,
> of ragged mountain ranges,
> of droughts and flooding rains.
> I love her far horizons,
> I love her jewel-sea,
> her beauty and her terror –
> the wide brown land for me!

For that instant, the lands I feel for are joined again in Gondwanaland through the cousins, baobab and boab, forged by the fire sinking into the earth.

In a cloudless cool air, the stars shine like luminous paint, and one can almost see Jupiter's moons in the night sky. Again, I wonder at the stars as I did as a boy, lying in the open bush with Stan, and I remember him. The Milky Way dominates as it moves across from east to west; sleeping under the stars means that no watch is needed to tell the time. The dark form in the mass of stars is known as the Giant Emu in the Big Sky country; it stretches like the hands of a clock in the Milky Way. In Brazil, it is called the Jaguar. I cannot remember what it was called in East Africa (or if I ever knew its name in that sky). With the identity of the land shielded by darkness, the view of the stars in the Kimberley is the same as that in Tanzania and is the only thing that has never changed in my life. It is comforting that the Southern Cross is in the Australian flag; it sews all the threads together for me. It is the one thing that cannot be taken away or changed by the fourth dimension. While the annual trek in the Kimberley is a pilgrimage to my roots, it also serves to remind me that ethnically, I belong to neither Australia nor Africa. The stars take me beyond all that.

The ordinance maps of the Kimberley that we use for walking are very detailed, with accurate contour lines and markings for rivers, pools, and waterfalls, but there are few names because seldom has a person been credited with a discovery, and the Aboriginal names have been lost or ignored with the removal of the people. The maps were made by aerial survey. It is ironic, considering the way the Aboriginal people were treated by the colonials in the Kimberley, that the range of hills dividing the Kimberley should be called the King Leopold Ranges, after the most brutal and worst colonial ruler of Africa. Early walkers, such as Grey, were looking for cattle pasture, and one group used this activity as a blind for smuggling. Prospectors and naturalists made tracks that cannot be seen on the rocks or have disappeared in the sand. Rock art and dinosaur footprints are the lasting markings. Only the rock art documents human visits, for up to maybe thirty thousand years.

Walking groups are often diverse, and Andrew's is no exception. Many who walk with him are exceptional people, such as Bruce, who joined the group when he retired from being a commercial pilot. He had flown a plane that carried the cartographer and navigator who mapped the Kimberley. He had literally flown over every inch of the Kimberley and now wanted to touch and feel it. On these walks, men outnumber women by about five or six to one. The women on one walk voted Bruce as the man with the most developed feminine side. They wanted to recruit him to boost their numbers. Bruce was immediately teased by the men, but he was unfazed and returned more than he copped.

Speaking of cops, in 1975, Bruce had to fly the Pilbara police from Port Hedland to a mining site at Karratha, where the workers were demonstrating against the dismissal of the Australian Prime Minister Gough Whitlam by Sir John Kerr, the British representative of the Queen. When the six burly policemen confronted the demonstration, they noticed Bruce standing in the front row with the demonstrators. Bruce certainly knew how to make a statement, and the demonstration was without police violence. Apparently, the trip back in the plane was in silence.

Andrew gave me the gift of a new life. He played down the physical demands of these treks and extolled the attractions of the beauty, spirituality, uniqueness, and pure joy of getting to know oneself through minimal subsistence, self-reliance, and group harmonics. However, these were not walks in the park. Food and everything one needed had to be carried and last for twelve walking days. There were no prescribed trails, no food drop-offs, and no footprints to follow. The only paths were those of the feral animals, useful only if they happened to be going in the direction of the compass bearing. The only communication or sign of the outside world was by satellite phone for emergency and the twinkling of the high jets, on their way to and from Asia, passing through the still stars and moving satellites.

Andrew shared everything, and he shared the leadership with Tony Gavranich. Tony was of Croatian heritage, extremely strong in mind and body, and generous to a fault. Tony had moved to Derby years ago, and after working as a court clerk, where he got to know nearly everyone in the town, he took a job with a friend who owned the Derby Bus Company, and then he met the rest of the people of the Kimberley and all those in the Aboriginal communities. Tony would walk the Kimberley on his own for days and weeks and was to Andrew as Kit Carson— the army scout—was to a Yankee army captain. Tony was the eyes and ears and bank of local knowledge, and together, they explored and followed the river courses while helping others find the secrets of the Kimberley.

I learnt and came to understand a lot more about leadership. Surgeons are expected to be decisive and lead by example. A surgical leader is a dictator in the operating room because the surgeon carries a responsibility that cannot be delegated. A surgical leader must be seen to lead by example.

When driving in the African bush, Stan's vehicle always led from the front, and when walking, Stan was usually second in line, behind the tracker or pathfinder, because he had the rifle and needed eyes for danger ahead rather than to follow the ground. His prime role when tracking dangerous game was as protector. Only when the dangerous quarry was in sight or there was a known danger in the bush ahead did he move up to the front. When all was ready for the client to shoot, with camera or rifle, Stan would stand to the left, so that the quarry and client were in his vision and his rifle free to move and protect. The shooter moved up the line from number three, and the tracker moved back to safety. This sequence is clearly shown in the opening elephant scene in *King Solomon's Mines* starring Stewart Granger (Stan stood in for him in the real-life photo shoot).

Andrew, as leader of a walk, led from the back like a shepherd. He saved his energy from the competition for pecking order and pathfinding to ensure that the weakest in the group survived and made it through to the end. Interestingly, Andrew's leadership role is again as protector; it's just the danger that's different. It's not an animal (except maybe a saltwater crocodile, if closer to the sea); it's the danger of being left behind, getting lost, or breaking down and being unable to walk any farther. Andrew and Tony needed to keep the whole group in their sight; one of them would only move to the front at critical times for decisions such as which way to go because of terrain or obstacle or pathfinders' disagreement.

It was fascinating to see how the best was drawn out of the members in the group and watch how the group dynamics were guided, rather than being led or forced. Harmony invariably developed or returned to members from previous walks. The harmonics played out to lift individual performances beyond expectations. Survival is a great leveller, and good walkers made it as much with their minds as they did with the strength of their legs.

Although many struggle to complete these walks, all those guided by Andrew and Tony have made it, every year, for the past twenty-one years. As the number of walkers increased and time schedules dictated availability, it's become necessary to split the group and have some walk with a different leader. Whether by chance or sheer bad luck, there have been four helicopter evacuations from the groups that were not led by Andrew. One evacuation was for a crocodile attack, one for a ruptured heart valve after marching through a rainstorm, one for a severe fall down a waterfall, and most recently for food poisoning. From what we've done on these walks, any one of these events could have happened, but they didn't; that reminded me of the lucky surgeons who never seemed to get into irredeemable situations.

Andrew's gift to me was the confidence that I could walk the Kimberley with a twenty-kilogram pack and survive for two weeks, despite the failed heart surgery and stent in the left main coronary artery. If I had collapsed and died, he could have been called irresponsible for taking me to such a remote place with difficult terrain. Michele, who is little with the stamina of a donkey, challenged me that if she could do it, then so could I, and we embarked on the first walk with much trepidation. It was agreed that if a helicopter was needed to evacuate me, we would bear the cost.

My previous experience working in the Kimberley reminded me of the similarity of the countryside with Tanganyika; the similarity of the boab to the baobab was surreal and drew me spiritually. There is no doubt in my mind that walking the

Kimberley each year has been a life-changing experience. Since that first walk, my health of mind and body has been geared to this annual spiritual gathering of friends. It was my physical rehabilitation and mental positioning to accept that the aneurysm project was no longer mine, that my role in the vascular world was coming to an end, and that it would soon be time to move on.

My eyes were opened to the choice of being like an old lion sitting alone on a carcass, unable to eat and thrive, because all the time was taken up keeping the other creatures at bay or, having had my fill of the choicest morsels, walk away from the pride and leave the rest to those who would handle it better. These walks reminded me that there are lots of things to do in life.

To move on from surgery was not a sudden decision. It was more like a gentle drift from the main current. In 2003, FDA approved the Zenith for sale in America, which was followed by a number of unexpected rewards in Australia. The College of Surgeons of Australia and New Zealand gave me a special reward for excellence in surgery and presented this to me alongside Graham Clark, who invented the bionic ear and started Cochlear. To say I was embarrassed to be acknowledged in that way and alongside such prestigious company would be an understatement. What followed surprised me even more, and it's still hard for me to fully accept the honour of being named Officer of the Order of Australia (AO).

Looking around at Australians who have been so honoured, it is clear that it is also often the gesture of farewell; Australians do not appreciate those who rest on their laurels in public places. I knew I could never again emulate what had been achieved. It was time to go before the memories were soiled, but there were three tasks left unfinished. They were to have a female vascular consultant surgeon in Western Australia, to hand over my private practice for the benefit of my patients, and to fulfil my goal of providing equal access to image-guiding machinery (X-ray angiogram machines) for vascular surgeons in public service.

In 2005, I took a job with the WA Department of Health to restructure vascular services and provide access and equipment in the teaching public hospitals. Royalties paid to Royal Perth Hospital for the Zenith graft funded the X-ray equipment needed for the facilities in the teaching hospitals. In 2006, Shirley Fearn, who married an Australian and changed her name to Jansen, was appointed as a consultant vascular surgeon to the Metropolitan Health Authority and based at Sir Charles Gairdner Hospital.

I gave Brendan Stanley my practice. He was from Adelaide and had been rotated through RPH when training, just before his fellowship examinations at the time of my heart surgery. We became friends during my recovery period and maintained contact after he returned to Adelaide to take up a consultant position in the Veteran's Hospital there. He came back to Perth, took over my private practice in a seamless transfer, and boosted the consultant surgeon numbers to Fremantle Hospital as part of the restructure.

All this was achieved by August 2008, with a bonus of two extra training posts for vascular surgeons in WA and two extra hybrid theatres for surgery needing high-quality imaging, planned for the New Fiona Stanley Hospital. I am happy that they are there for the benefit of the people of Western Australia and for the next generation. It could not have been done without the rewards that came from the development of the Zenith Endovascular graft.

It was time to go.

Whatever happens to me now, I know that there is life after death. My genes live on in my sons and their children, to be dispersed wherever the wind will blow them. My grandchildren are a very special delight because they are so clearly wondrous about the world around them and open with their motives and feelings. I hope that I can give them time and watch what they do and see how they use the lessons and genes that have been passed down to them. They say that life goes full cycle. Life is not a circle; it is a helix. While someone may end up in the same place on earth within the first three dimensions, they will be in a different place in the fourth dimension. In that space of time, there will be different elements in the surroundings. There is much to prepare them for in what will be their world.

I claimed that I wrote this book for my family, for the inventiveness and ingenuity of Australia and its migrants making new lives, for those who wish to become doctors, for the ephemeral band of colonials of East Africa that will soon be lost to history in the fall of the British Empire, and for that lofty gift of friendship that emerged as a universal value. That would be true. But now that I have finished, I realise I also wrote this down for myself because of the emotional catharsis experienced during the writing and realisation of how very fortunate I have been.

In writing, I was taken down game trails that weaved and crossed. There are many people I loved who were not on the trail followed in this book or on the paths when they crossed; they are another story. To see all the game trails on the Serengeti in its entirety, from Ngorongoro to the Masai Mara and the southern shores of Lake Victoria, one needs to be high in the air with the eyes of a vulture, but to immerse the senses in the Serengeti, one must be in touch with the soil and can only walk one trail at a time. If you have read this far, I hope there was something in it for you.

A question flirted with me as I wrote. Should I return to East Africa in my second childhood to relive the feelings of belonging, the vibrations of African humour, the animal calls in the night, the sounds of the languages, the rhythms of the music, the scent of the earth in the rain, and the haze of the sun over the Great Rift Valley? Would the pull to see my roots again be irresistible?

CHAPTER 38

The Wheel of Time

Eventually, the pull was too strong, I could no longer resist and made a return to East Africa. The feelings on return were too complex and confused to describe properly. Rip Van Winkle had woken up after forty years; the language had changed, and people smiled at my out-of-date Swahili that percolated back into conversations. English dominated, and it was hardly ever necessary to speak Swahili, other than to enhance the humour and for the rapport that only language can bring.

The population had swelled to fifty-five million in Tanzania and forty-five million in Kenya. The economic growth rate in Kenya was 6 percent, but the refugee influx from war zones to the north and west was enormous. The divide between rich and poor was starkly visible, with direct public payment evident for civil servants, and as the truck drivers and road users paid their dues at the many roadblocks, I wondered why this was accepted as part of daily life.

I suppose it was just a fee, or toll, without the red tape. There was clearly an unwritten working economy. Undoubtedly, there was crime born of necessity and mostly based on opportunism, but there was also an honesty, again based on unwritten rules, and it was all stirred by diverse ethnic groups and religious affiliations. The written laws were based on British law, which was as far away from the street law as the rich were from the poor.

I felt no aggression towards myself for the sins of my fathers, rather a welcome because of my birthplace and my Swahili, but then, I was interacting with people and not bureaucracy. I never thought of Swahili as being accented, and this was a revelation. In the manner that the Queen's English and Hoch Deutsch are regarded as the benchmark for spoken English and German, so also was Zanzibarian Swahili regarded. Since my Swahili was essentially Tanzanian based and more than fifty years out of date, I must have sounded quite different, like listening to English from a newsreel or Australian accents from the 1950s.

We did go to Zanzibar, and one morning, while waiting for Michele outside a clothing and material store, I was approached by a middle-aged hawker selling packets of the famous Zanzibar spices. I didn't want any and explained in Swahili that I now lived in Australia and could not take them back because of the seed content.

He plonked himself beside me on the steps, and we engaged in conversation; he wanted to know how I came to speak Swahili. He was tired, hungry, and dispirited, but it was not a ruse for sympathy. After resting for a while, he rose to leave and, in the Swahili people's way, bid me a courteous goodbye. At that moment, I gave him a little money to buy breakfast. He hesitated before accepting because I had not bought anything, and then, I saw the same look in his eyes I had seen with some grateful patients. He said nothing, but the next day at a chance meeting, he greeted me with a smile without trying to sell me anything, and that said it all.

I felt at home, but was I?

Michele and I stayed with my cousin Howard and his wife Sue, and we visited Sue's daughter Jenny in Voi, a hundred and fifty kilometres up the road from Mombasa to Nairobi. Jenny and her husband, Kevin Carr-Hartley, managed the largest sisal plantation in the world, employing five thousand workers. Kevin's grandfather was Carr Hartley, a famous game trapper, and the family adopted the double name that was so well known. Consistent with the family wildlife history, part of the estate was converted to a game park; the elephants were everywhere.

Similarly, large numbers of elephant were in Tsavo National Park across the road, where the David Sheldrick elephant orphanage is situated. It was started to deal with the little orphans from misguided elephant culls during overpopulation, during droughts, that went hand-in-hand with poaching stimulated by the ivory trade. Migration occurred across the road, as Pete and I noticed when riding our bikes from Nairobi to Mombasa. It is very important to preserve migration routes wherever possible because a blocked route can wipe out entire generations of animals, as Mark and Delia Owens point out in their book *Cry the Kalahari*.

The Chinese were building a new railway and a new road from Mombasa to Nairobi, and they were built high up on an embankment, which I guess was a clever way to remove all the changing land contours. Tunnels had been constructed at regular intervals to allow wild animal to migrate. This new infrastructure flagged the huge Chinese investment and involvement in Africa but also underlined that this was still Africa.

Howard commented that like pedestrians stepping off an overcrowded pavement to avoid a clash, trucks were going to fall off these embankments; sure enough, we saw two on their sides at the bottom of the embankment on the bit of road that had been completed. The thought that struck me most was the enormous difference in traffic volume from when Pete and I cycled on it. Only segments of the new road were open, and Howard drove mainly on the old one. The traffic was almost entirely trucks because Mombasa Port served almost all of East Africa and also the eastern Congo via Uganda.

Jenny sponsored a baby elephant in the orphanage. This allowed Michele to visit and delight in feeding the little elephant with two huge bottles of milk. Tsavo and its elephants are best described in Daphne Sheldrick' s book, *An African Love Story*. The fondness for the little animals shone through the wardens. The knowledge and depth of understanding of animals displayed by the park rangers and safari tour guides bodes optimism for wildlife survival in Africa. The guides in Tanzania's Selous Game Reserve and Ruaha National Park could name every animal and plant, using common and scientific terminology. I could not fault them despite my previous experience as a guide; they knew far more than I ever did. Whereas I had learned on the job, they had formally studied. This was a measure of modern Africa.

The experience of driving to Nairobi from Mombasa convinced me that I should never complain about roads or traffic again. The dichotomy of British road rules of driving on the left and the semblance of "Every driver for themselves" masked the extreme tolerance and skill of the drivers. It was like walking on a busy, overcrowded pavement, with the crowd going in both directions at the same time across the whole width of the pavement and nobody colliding with another, weaving and subtly changing speed, as we do. Sometimes the vehicles were so close that hardly the width of a piece of paper separated them, yet they seldom touched. The historic cacophony of horns was absent, and lights signalled warnings and intents. Any faulty lights were fined at the roadblocks.

In Nairobi, the thorn tree that my sister had planted on Stan's grave was fully grown, and the base occupied the whole of the grave site, tilting a plaque Adrian had made for him. It brought tears to Howard's eyes as he cleaned the grave stone, and that started burning nostalgia in my mind's eye.

My high school was in immaculate condition, with newly painted old buildings bearing the same motto— "To the Uttermost"—and students in long grey flannels with blazers bearing the Prince of Wales crest on the impala's head, prominent over the motto on the top pocket. The only difference was that the students were hurrying between classes instead of dawdling, and they were all black.

Richard Leakey was still alive, and his eyes twinkled brightly over a glass of red wine as we chatted. He had been appointed chairman of the Kenya Wildlife Service and was back in control of the anti-poaching campaign. He still worked hard at palaeontology; the Nairobi Museum was full of the wonderful discoveries of hominids from all over East Africa, the land where humans were born.

Richard literally embodied the human spirit to survive. He had lost both legs in a plane crash and walked stiffly on his prostheses, bearing a little more weight, like the rest of us. His first renal transplant lasted twenty-one years, and his second was functioning well, together with his transplanted liver, despite the wine. When advised by the medicos in New York University, where he was appointed professor in palaeontology, that he needed a new liver but was unlikely to find a donor in New York, he had returned to Kenya, the place where he wanted to die, where fifteen of his students offered to help him. One of them travelled with him back to New York, and both returned well. How better to describe the spirit of commitment and generosity that will drive Africa in this century? I had indeed cycled in the helix of time to be back in the place where I too was born.

The most striking change was the level of protective security in Kenya. This was partly for the threat of political activism and partly for crime. The tourist industry had almost collapsed, weighed down by traffic congestion and security restrictions. Once-thriving fishing charters, which were based on catch-and-release of game fish, had dried up through the fears of tourists for terrorists and longline overfishing by Asian fleets. Tanzania was noticeably less affected. On a positive note, the movement away from each other, because Tanzania had followed the socialist route and Kenya the capitalist, had changed back towards a regional union, with ease of travel being restored.

Fifty years seemed so long—a lifetime—and yet in evolutionary terms, it was no time at all. But the evolution was stark. Aside from the humanity change, there was a clear change of startling evolution in southern Tanzania. This was the area of the great tuskers, and poaching for ivory had been organised to a military campaign level. Those elephant that survived to multiply at the end of the intense poaching era were either tuskless or had very small tusks. The survival advantage of large tusks had been replaced by the survival advantage of having smaller tusks and removing the poaching incentive.

In Kenya, there was an enlightening and energetic dynamic that promised much for the future, but it was clouded by fatalistic submission to forces of overwhelming human mass, hemmed in by threats to survival from disproportionate distribution of resources and outside attack. Beyond these observations, I would say no more, for lack of information and any authority to comment, except that I had ambivalent feelings of belonging and being a stranger.

I returned to Australia and luxuriated in that sense of freedom from constant threat to survival (or at least the constant reminder by the presence of security guards, electric fences, and guard dogs). It was like the way we feel when we get away from an international airport security checkpoint. I am glad that I visited, but I brought back another question: should I take up the offer to claim Kenyan citizenship again?

I think the answer is in the music made by the sounds of the wind and a banjo:

And the wind can be heard
As it blows across the billabongs,
You'll come a-waltzing the Kimberley with me.

That sense of yearning to belong was felt one evening when
there was a function at the University of Western Australia to
thank all those who had worked to establish the David Hartley
Chair in Radiology and the Lawrence-Brown Chair in Vascular
Surgery. It was wonderful to see the delight in Turab Chakera's
eyes as he peered out from his wheelchair over the gathering
of colleagues and friends from the university, the government
of Western Australia, and the Cook Company representative.
He was content that a life's ambition to establish an education
base for radiology had been fulfilled, and I heard David's words
echoing in my mind: "This will probably work, but there is a
better way."

Just after a professor for vascular surgery was selected,
I was invited to attend a meeting in Stanford University for
pioneers to celebrate twenty-five years of stent-grafting for aortic
aneurysms, with the reminder that many of us were already
gone, and we could not wait for the fifty-year mark. Balancing
this sobering thought was information from another school
friend that Pete, who cycled with me to Mombasa from Nairobi,
had not died, as I had previously been led to believe, and was
alive and living in the wilds off Vancouver Island, so after the
meeting, I visited him.

He had left the Canadian paratroopers to study and became
a schoolteacher in northern Manitoba, coordinating remote
schools in the Arctic. He refused to look at views from clifftops
overlooking the Sooke River, on the grounds he had a fear of
heights. I don't know if he was teasing or had genuine post-
traumatic jump syndrome because he was a veteran of more
than thirty jumps. He was living a frugal life amidst books,
art, and vintage bicycles from the Tour de France races of
1950s. I laughed at his ambivalent feeling towards the black

bear that broke his glass house to eat the tomatoes; using the North American pronounciation. We shared a pure joy of being together again. He had not seen another Kenyan boy or spoken Swahili for more than fifty years, and we contemplated on how far and wide we had been dispersed by that wind.

Now I sit on the patio looking over Geographe Bay in the south-west of Australia and watch the mob of thirty western grey kangaroos gardening on my Kikuyu grass lawn. The various parrots share the birdbath in turn with yellow-winged New Holland honey-eaters, robins, firetail finches, splendid fairy wrens, a pair of kookaburras, a family of magpies, and a willy wagtail. Occasionally I see Joe Blake—the snake—king skinks, and a monitor lizard, representing the reptile brigade. All these Australian animals try to make up for the African animal space represented only by the grass that has a symbiotic relationship with the roos. Much to the disapproval of my neighbours, even the little rabbits feel welcome and maybe a little protected in the garden from the hawks and eagles above, the dogs next door, and an elusive fox. I contemplate what Australia would be like if we farmed kangaroos instead of sheep.

That dream is for another life and another story.

Printed in Australia
AUHW011554150519
312240AU00001B/1

9 781984 502445